IRAQ AND THE
LESSONS OF VIETNAM

Also edited by Lloyd C. Gardner and Marilyn B. Young
from The New Press

*The New American Empire: A 21st Century
Teach-in on U.S. Foreign Policy*

IRAQ AND THE LESSONS OF VIETNAM

Or, How Not to Learn from the Past

Edited by LLOYD C. GARDNER
and MARILYN B. YOUNG

THE NEW PRESS

NEW YORK
LONDON

Published in the United States by The New Press, New York, 2008
Distributed by W. W. Norton & Company, Inc., New York

LIBRARY OF CONGRESS CATALOGING-IN-PUBLICATION DATA
Iraq and the lessons of Vietnam, or, How not to learn from the past / edited by Lloyd C.
Gardner and Marilyn B. Young.
    p. cm.
  Includes bibliographical references and index.
  ISBN 978-1-59558-149-5 (hc.)
  ISBN 978-1-59558-345-1 (pbk.)
  1. Iraq War, 2003–.   2. Vietnam War, 1961–1975—United States.   I. Gardner,
Lloyd C., 1934–   II. Young, Marilyn Blatt.   III. Title: Iraq and the lessons of
Vietnam.   IV. Title: How not to learn from the past.
  DS79.76.I7253 2007
  956.7044'3—dc22
                       2006031274

The New Press was established in 1990 as a not-for-profit alternative to the large, commercial publishing houses currently dominating the book publishing industry. The New
Press operates in the public interest rather than for private gain, and is committed to
publishing, in innovative ways, works of educational, cultural, and community value that
are often deemed insufficiently profitable.

www.thenewpress.com

Composition by NK Graphics, A Black Dot Group Company
This book was set in Warnock Pro

Printed in the United States of America

10 9 8 7 6 5 4 3 2 1

This book is dedicated to the idea
that we can learn from history.

Contents

Acknowledgments

The editors would like to acknowledge André Schiffrin and Andrew Hsiao of The New Press for their persuasive powers in launching this project, and their conviction that history does matter. We thank them for providing the arena—and thank our authors for providing the agenda—for debate.

IRAQ AND THE
LESSONS OF VIETNAM

Introduction

LLOYD C. GARDNER AND MARILYN B. YOUNG

The specter of Vietnam has been buried forever
in the desert sands of the Arabian Peninsula.
—George H.W. Bush, 1991

In the first week of August 2006, Defense Secretary Donald Rumsfeld came to Capitol Hill to testify in open session before the Senate Armed Services Committee. The war in Iraq, now in its third year, had become a desperate struggle against myriad forces unleashed by the American invasion. It was not supposed to be this way, of course. Once Saddam Hussein had been eliminated, Iraqis were supposed to lead the way to a new Middle East. That had not happened. Instead, Iraq verged on complete chaos and civil war. Rumsfeld faced a hostile committee, with both Democrats and Republicans challenging the way the war had been conducted. Once the administration's media superstar in the days of "mission accomplished," the defense secretary, with his clever witticisms and sarcastic put-downs, no longer charmed his audiences.

"We need to be realistic about the consequences," Rumsfeld said in his opening statement. "If we left Iraq prematurely, as the terrorists demand, the enemy would tell us to leave Afghanistan and then withdraw from the Middle East. And if we left the Middle East, they'd order us and all those who don't share their militant ideology to leave what they call the occupied Muslim lands from Spain to the Philippines." Then he reached back in American folklore for some note that would resonate with angry legislators and turn the war into a new chapter in the national epic. "Americans didn't cross oceans and settle a wilderness and build history's greatest democracy only to run away from a bunch of murderers and extremists who try to kill everyone that they cannot convert and to tear down what they could never build."

Editorialists suddenly awoke to what they heard in Rumsfeld's statement. It was the domino thesis from the beginning of the Vietnam War! And now here it was again, only this time coming after the Iraq War (also sometimes known as Gulf War II) had already claimed 2,500 American lives and perhaps more than 80,000 Iraqis in a conflict that now appeared endless. The *New York Times* declared that Rumsfeld was "stuck in a time warp."

"You could practically hear the dominoes falling as he told the Senate Armed Services Committee yesterday that it was dangerous for Americans to even talk about how to end the war in Iraq."[1]

The increasingly skeptical *Times* editorialists, who had originally supported the war—as they had Vietnam in its early and middle years—were not the only ones to voice criticism of Rumsfeld. As might be expected, the neoconservative phalanx that had pushed for war felt they had been deceived, too, but not, of course, by the objective. As conservative critics had hammered McNamara in Vietnam, the current generation of neoconservatives is already ready for the history battles that will inevitably accompany the Iraq "syndrome." "Successful counterinsurgencies," argues one prominent neocon, Reuel Marc Gerecht, "are always ugly and morally challenging. What is so sad in Iraq is that the civilian losses caused by the U.S. are not compensated by a larger American military effort to secure the country from holy warriors, insurgents and sectarian militiamen who live to slaughter innocent civilians and Iraq's chance for a more humane, democratic future."[2]

Treating the Iraq War as a mismanaged effort with tragic consequences is stunningly like the conservative revisionist argument about Vietnam, only this time it is associated not only with neoconservatives but with liberals as well. Thomas Friedman, for example, who writes that his heart is with the "Democratic mainstream," not the dovish elements of the party too ready to abandon the mission, sets out the main postulate for a historical critique that will preserve dangerous illusions about both Vietnam and Iraq. Accusing the Bush administration of massive errors of judgment, he asks, "Why did you 'tough guys' fight the Iraq war with the Rumsfeld Doctrine—just enough troops to lose—and not the Powell Doctrine of overwhelming force to create the necessary foundations of any democracy-building project, which is security?"[3] While neither liberals nor neoconservatives can find anything good these days to say about the way the war was managed, the truly significant lessons of Vietnam for Iraq—and for the future—remain largely obscured in current political debates in Congress and among the punditry.

What can't be obscured is that thirty years and more after the fall of Saigon, the United States finds itself bogged down once again in a war against an enemy whose low-grade weapons defy the technological superiority of the world's greatest military power. Why did this happen? The lessons of Vietnam had supposedly been learned. "Shock and awe" had replaced the graduated escalation that failed in Vietnam. Never again, the nation was told, would American soldiers be called upon to fight a war political leaders in Washington lacked the will to win. And yet here we are, seemingly back where we left off (or rather where we began, with the domino thesis) in Southeast Asia. The specter of Vietnam looms darkly over Baghdad and the

Green Zone, and its shadow spreads far to the east across Iran to the resurgent Taliban in Afghanistan.

What should have been learned instead? If nothing else, Vietnam taught that advanced technology and military force cannot solve political problems that arose during and before the old colonial era when Europe ruled the world. The ambitions that produced the colonial empires and the opposing forces that broke them down are little changed today. Indeed, if anything, the search for energy resources and global outlets is more pressing in the twenty-first century than it was at any time during the original Age of Imperialism, when the quest took explorers and exploiters into faraway lands. Today, the stakes are higher, the rivalries greater, the faraway lands uncomfortably "closer"—and the future more clouded than at any time in the past. Vietnam was often called the last of the colonial wars, but Iraq is most certainly the greatest so far of the neocolonial wars as the great powers seek out spheres of influence and special advantages in the oil-rich areas bordering the Persian Gulf.

The essays presented here offer serious commentary on the question of why the real lessons of Vietnam have been ignored, and why—as in the last days of the Vietnam War—the Bush administration seeks to blame war critics and leakers for this new tragedy. "They want us to be divided," Rumsfeld admonished the Senate committee, "because they know that when we are united they lose. They want us pointing fingers at each other, rather than pointing fingers at them." It is time indeed for finger-pointing, Mr. Rumsfeld, time for an accounting of the lessons of Vietnam.

The United States emerged from World War II as the world's only true superpower, despite Cold War rhetoric that from time to time pictured the Soviet Union as equal, if not superior, in military strength. Washington's reconstruction of the world order was actually facilitated in some ways by the Cold War. Its economy thrived on the perceived challenge of an "evil empire" to be overcome by dint of successive technological breakthroughs from Hiroshima to outer space. Anywhere one looked around the globe the watchword was American know-how. It is hardly surprising, therefore, that Americans developed a sense of their history as the story of an inevitable rise to global preeminence based on such achievements as atomic energy and computers. With the collapse of the Soviet Union, moreover, the last "evil empire" disappeared, prompting simplistic assertions about the "end of history"—understood best, it was explained, as an end of resistance to the spread of liberal capitalism and political democracy around the world. Now the United States could really get down to the business of extending the benign influence of free markets to all the world.

It became increasingly fashionable in Washington think tanks and political journals to talk about the United States in a semi-ironic way as the new Rome—but with a crucial difference that set America apart from earlier empires. America's cultural influence, writes a friendly European observer, Josef Joffe, editor and publisher of *Die Zeit*, makes this new Rome unique. "John Locke wrote that 'in the beginning all the world was America,'" Joffe comments. "Today, he might muse, 'All the world is *becoming* America.'" But there is a catch. "If so, all the world does not necessarily like it."[4]

Joffe might worry about the perils of overreaching, but others fear a resurgent isolationist mood cutting short the mission just before what Secretary of State Condoleezza Rice calls the birth pangs of a new Middle East bring forth the new age. In the aftermath of the defeat in Vietnam, isolationism supposedly undid plans for the permanent American Century. "Whereas in the 1920s," wrote the master memoirist and would-be redeemer of Vietnam mistakes, Henry Kissinger, "we had withdrawn from the world because we thought we were too good for it, the insidious theme of the late 1960s was that we should withdraw from the world because we were too evil for it."[5]

As Kissinger argued, Vietnam had indeed given pause to the U.S. self-perception as founders of an "Empire of Liberty" and the notion of a world eager to receive American ideas. Thomas Jefferson had first used this term as a rationale for the Louisiana Purchase. American imperialists following Jefferson, writes historian Paul Johnson, have carried on the tradition in the Iraq War. Most important, they have always been "good" imperialists. "America's search for security against terrorism and rogue states goes hand in hand with liberating their oppressed peoples. From the Evil Empire to an Empire for Liberty is a giant step. . . . The empire for liberty is the dynamic of change."[6]

Thus the Iraq War was destined to end, in both military and political ways, with happy Iraqis pulling down the statue of Saddam Hussein. In an early revelation about a war sold on false premises, from missing WMDs to spreading democracy, it turned out the statue scene had also been staged. Nothing went right afterward, beginning with the looting of Baghdad museums. By midsummer 2006 Johnson's perceived dynamic of change was moving in a very different direction. Only 32 percent of the respondents in a *New York Times*/CBS poll believed the president had handled the Iraq War in a successful way, while 69 percent believed the war had made dealing with Middle Eastern issues more difficult. More than 60 percent believed the war had not been worth the costs in loss of life and military expenditure. Finally, the poll marked a dramatic change from 2002, with nearly 60 percent now saying the United States should not take the lead in general in attempting to solve international conflicts, a negative swing of more than fifteen points.[7]

The *Times* headlined these results as denoting the dangerous growth of isolationism, as if talking about a resurgent plague. Instead, as in the Vietnam War, the swelling discontent reflected an unwillingness to continue following leaders who misrepresented and manipulated intelligence around policy decisions to obtain public consent to forcing change with bombs and bullets. Citing Woodrow Wilson's struggle, as Kissinger did, is a common way of cautioning Americans against abandoning the Empire of Liberty theme. But there is an ironic side to Wilson's thought that better explains why the lessons of Vietnam were not learned. Woodrow Wilson never wanted to join the Allies in World War I, except as an associated power with its own set of war aims superior to those of all the others engaged in the fighting. His most important objective was preserving American freedom of action. Walter Lippmann, America's premier pundit of the first half of the twentieth century, once remarked that Woodrow Wilson perfected isolationism as his foreign policy. When it proved impossible to stay out of Europe's wars, as the Monroe Doctrine had urged, Wilson "reversed it and instead of saying we'll stay at home and be moral, he said we'll go abroad and make them all moral. And then we'll feel just as much at home as if we hadn't gone abroad."[8]

The British prime minister, Tony Blair, has proved to be George W. Bush's most loyal ally through thick and thin as they pursue a Wilsonian quest to create a Middle East safe for democracy. Blair's motives are the subject of Professor Alex Danchev's essay. Only by becoming Bush's accomplice, he writes, could the prime minister feel sure he had done his best to preserve the supposed "special relationship." "Iraq . . . was sold as a good war," writes Danchev, "but it was precisely the selling, or the misselling, that gave it a bad name. It was in fact a war of the worst kind, a war of false pretenses; manufactured, as one might say, and of doubtful legality."

Indeed, Great Britain has been deeply involved in Iraq from the moment the new country was created out of provinces of the old Ottoman Empire at the end of World War I. Tony Blair's concern for British interests in the area where troops were sent in Gulf War II was no less than that of his famous predecessor David Lloyd George, who in 1920 put the British mission delicately to the House of Commons in describing the new country's frontiers, which encompassed Mosul, Baghdad, and Basra. "It is not proposed that we should govern this country as if it were an essential part of the British empire, making its laws. That is not our point of view. Our point of view is that they should govern themselves and that we should be responsible as the mandatory for advising, for counseling, for assisting, but that the government must be Arab."[9]

As Lloyd George once spoke to the House of Commons of the tasks of the League of Nations mandate in the oil-producing area now called Iraq, Blair spoke to Congress in full-blown Wilsonian rhetoric. "I know it's hard on America," he admonished the legislators, "and in some small corner of this vast country, out in Nevada or Idaho or these places I've never been to, but always wanted to go. I know out there there's a guy getting on with his life, perfectly happily, minding his own business, saying to you, the political leaders of this country, 'Why me? And why us? And why America?' And the only answer is, 'Because destiny put you in this place in history, in this moment in time, and the task is yours to do.'"

In 1954 President Dwight D. Eisenhower had described a perilous situation in Southeast Asia, where, unless the United States stepped in, free countries would fall over like a row of dominoes. Tens of millions were threatened with Communist tyranny—and the West would be deprived of the area's vital resources. If Vietnam "fell" to Communism, he said, the tragic consequences would be just incalculable:

> You have a row of dominoes set up, you knock over the first one, and what will happen to the last one is the certainty that it will go over very quickly. So you could have a beginning of a disintegration that would have the most profound influences.
>
> Two of the items from this particular area that the world uses are tin and tungsten. They are very important. There are others, of course, the rubber plantations and so on.
>
> Asia, after all, has already lost some 450 million of its peoples to the Communist dictatorship, and we simply can't afford greater losses.

Kennedy told interviewers that he believed in the domino thesis and sent 15,000 "advisers" to Vietnam. Lyndon Johnson then set the example for fixing intelligence around policy by launching a war in August 1964, seizing on supposed unprovoked attacks on American warships in the Gulf of Tonkin. As John Prados writes in his chapter, "President Johnson already had an interagency group actively preparing additional elements for his escalation, including target lists for attacks on North Vietnam and drafts of the text for a congressional resolution that would authorize the use of force in Vietnam. That text was ready when the Tonkin Gulf incident took place." The Johnson administration sent half a million soldiers, and the Air Force dropped more bombs than ever before in the history of warfare in an effort to prop up a military junta in Saigon.

When the war literally went south, the original rationale for involvement in Vietnam, the domino thesis, lost its power to convince anyone. The Central Intelligence Agency sent Lyndon Johnson a memorandum in 1967 that questioned, however timidly, if it had ever been valid. "If the analysis here advances the discussion at all, it is in the direction of suggesting that the risks [of an unfavorable outcome] are probably more limited and controllable than most previous argument has indicated."[10] It was too late, for Vietnam had congealed for Lyndon Johnson and his successor, Richard Nixon, into a hard mass around the single issue of credibility. Pentagon officials in the Johnson administration reflected among themselves about how much the military intervention had been determined by a supposed Wilsonian desire to see Vietnam a successfully self-determined country free of Communist domination, and the answer they gave one another was only about

10 percent. U.S. aims, wrote one of Robert McNamara's assistants at the Pentagon, John McNaughton, could be quantified: "70%—To avoid a humiliating US defeat (to our reputation as a guarantor). 20%—To keep SVN (and then adjacent) territory from Chinese hands. 10%—To permit the people of SVN to enjoy a better, freer way of life."[11]

Nothing changed when Nixon came into office. It was too late for any other argument to be offered for continuing the war, and impossible for his administration to admit the obvious—that Vietnam had not been a question of the wrong military strategy—for fear of undermining public support for other extended positions. The sole reason for "staying the course," Nixon said, was that the United States not appear a "pitiful, helpless giant," unable to keep its promises in any part of the world. But the war itself had lost credibility with both opinion makers and the public at large even as Nixon was swept away by the tides of Watergate. At the end in Vietnam, after all the advisers, after all the defoliants, after half a million troops, and after all the bombs dropped, American forces had to come home.

A timid Congress that had cowered before Johnson's dare that they repeal the 1964 Gulf of Tonkin Resolution finally summoned the courage— ten years too late—to attempt to rescue the Constitution from the "imperial presidency." A high-level official had said the Gulf of Tonkin Resolution was the functional equivalent of a declaration of war. The 1975 War Powers Resolution, known as the War Powers Act, was supposed to prevent future Vietnams by requiring the president to obtain congressional approval before sending American forces into hostilities, and to continue with periodic reports until the end of the conflict. The Senate Foreign Relations Committee addressed the question of what the resolution required:

> The purpose of this provision is to prevent secret, unauthorized military support activities and to prevent a repetition of many of the most controversial and regrettable actions in Indochina. The ever deepening ground combat involvement of the United States in South Vietnam began with the assignment of U.S. "advisers" to accompany South Vietnamese units on combat patrols; and in Laos, secretly and without congressional authorization.

Andrew Bacevich writes in his chapter of another lesson that went unheeded: "Belatedly settling accounts with Richard Nixon (and perhaps Lyndon Baines Johnson), the Congress attempted through this measure to reassert a legislative voice in decisions to undertake or sustain military intervention abroad. When it came to reducing the prerogatives of the commander in chief, however, the practical impact of the legislation proved to be essentially nil." It was another lesson not learned as Congress handed over authority to the Bush administration with a series of votes to authorize the use of force in more blatantly fraudulent circumstances than Vietnam.

Before he left office under threat of impeachment, moreover, Nixon attempted to apply a lesson from Vietnam to the Middle East. The so-called Nixon Doctrine, announced in 1969, looked to regional stabilizers to carry the burden of American interests. There would be no repeat of sending 500,000 troops into the swamps of Southeast Asia, he promised. Instead, the United States would supply the shah of Iran, for example, with all the weapons he could afford—and, unfortunately, more than he ultimately could afford and still keep his throne. The 1979 Iranian Revolution undid the Nixon Doctrine, and the American response began the sequence of events that led to America's present predicament in the Iraq imbroglio. In the next decade, the Reagan administration was not at all displeased with Saddam Hussein's actions in the Iran-Iraq War, sending a special envoy, Donald Rumsfeld, to assure the dictator that the United States understood his concerns and was not unsympathetic.

Unhappy former Nixon officials, meanwhile, complained that the War Powers Resolution dangerously weakened the presidency, and faulted his successor, Jimmy Carter, for abandoning the shah to his enemies. It was symptomatic of a national illness they called the "Vietnam syndrome." For some, the term simply meant reluctance to go to war again under similar circumstances; for others, however, it was about wrong strategic decisions and a lack of will. The end of the Cold War intensified concerns for American Century enthusiasts that the lesson of Vietnam transcended the Soviet-American rivalry: American arms must always be seen as the ultimate solution to political questions, not the ultimate question mark. President Jimmy Carter committed the gravest sin in this view, calling the war the result of an exaggerated fear of Communism. Carter's inept attempt to free hostages taken by Iranian militants only added to the campaign to "rebuild" the nation's defenses and "stiffen" national will.

As the world entered the post–Cold War era it was imperative Vietnam not be seen as a "defeat." Vietnam existed in memory outside the Cold War. It was a marker in terms of self-confidence in constructing the New American Century. Overcoming the Vietnam syndrome was essential for another reason. As Christian Appy writes in this volume, "Another, perhaps less noticed connection between the wars in Iraq and Vietnam is that in both cases the United States sent a disproportionately working-class military to kill and die while asking or demanding virtually no sacrifices from more privileged Americans at home. Despite the differences between the Vietnam-era draft and the current all-volunteer force, both systems put most of the dirty work of warfare in the hands of people with significantly fewer choices and opportunities."

Later Republican efforts with the Christian right were directed at solidifying the argument used with such groups that the war had been lost by comfortable elites, whose thinking lacked moral fiber. "It was, after all, however imperfectly pursued," intoned Reagan in dedicating the Vietnam Veterans Memorial, "the cause of freedom; and [American soldiers] showed uncommon courage in its service. Perhaps at this late date we can all agree that we've learned one lesson: that young Americans must never again be sent to fight and die unless we are prepared to let them win." Though he claimed not to be speaking "provocatively" at the dedication of the memorial, his words suggested the war was lost in Washington by a less than dedicated political leadership unworthy of the dead whose names were inscribed on the wall.

For a time it worked well. The opposition was cowed. And that was the lesson Reagan and his successor, George H.W. Bush, wished to impress on the nation during the run-up to the first Gulf War in 1991 to drive Iraq out of Kuwait and away from the Saudi Arabian oil fields. Bush went beyond Reagan's statement to assert that the quick American victory in the Middle East revealed the Vietnam syndrome as nothing but a specter, something that might scare liberals but not men in the mold of the rugged Reaganauts who had won the Cold War. While he had succeeded in gaining a congressional resolution empowering him to go to war against Saddam Hussein in Gulf War I, Bush vowed privately that he would take action regardless of the outcome of the vote. Gulf War I effectively nullified the War Powers Resolution, the last frail restraint on presidential freewheeling in foreign policy. "The specter of Vietnam has been buried forever in the desert sands of the Arabian peninsula," he exulted after the quick victory. "It's a proud day for America—and, by God, we've kicked the Vietnam syndrome once and for all."

Bush thus completed what Reagan had started in reimagining Vietnam as a sanctified noble crusade. Vietnam was now a lost battle in the Cold War, which, for all its mismanagement, did not provide a cautionary lesson against future involvement elsewhere in the postcolonial world, only a warning against allowing American policy to be determined by political leaders not sufficiently dedicated to victory. Yet George H.W. Bush still seemed inadequate to some officials in his own administration, someone not really dedicated enough to the permanent American Century thinking that had arisen when the Berlin Wall came tumbling down. Saddam Hussein still ruled in Baghdad, and it was argued that Iraq had quickly reconstituted its weapons of mass destruction (WMD) programs—at least according to Iraqi exiles and American neoconservatives who envisioned a reverse domino theory that would begin with the toppling of Saddam Hussein and lead to a democratic revolution across the Middle East.

As Gabriel Kolko writes in this volume, in both Vietnam and Iraq policy preceded intelligence and determined the outcome. The case for war was made in the latter instance on the basis of reports such as those the CIA had discredited about Hussein importing uranium from Africa. "A year before the invasion, most of the intelligence community agreed that reports that Hussein was attempting to import uranium were false, but Bush ignored them and often cited such fictions to justify invading Iraq."

The endeavor to remake the Middle East was championed by Defense Secretary Donald Rumsfeld, whose immediate response to the horrifyingly brutal attacks on the World Trade Center and the Pentagon on 9/11 was to use the disaster as a reason for attacking Iraq, though there was no evidence of the Iraqi leader's connection to or complicity in the terrible events of that tragic day. Only a few hours after the attack, Lloyd Gardner writes in his chapter, Rumsfeld was ready to take on the task of removing Saddam Hussein. "Go massive," he urged his aides. "Sweep it all up. Things related and not."

The objective was not simply to take down Saddam Hussein but to reestablish credibility in the post–Cold War era, to finally correct the errors of Vietnam and what came after in the Carter and Clinton years. While there are no Pentagon Papers revelations as such in the Iraq War, bits and pieces of information are emerging not only about how the war on Saddam Hussein was planned long before 9/11 but also why. Late in 2001, *Newsweek* commentator Michael Hirsh tells us, one of the magazine's reporters asked a member of Rumsfeld's powerful Defense Policy Board why the administration should take on Saddam Hussein, who was unconnected to 9/11. He responded: "How do you send the message of strength as Ronald Reagan sent it, that we don't allow these things—you inflict damage. . . . There's a feeling we've got to do something that counts—and bombing some caves is not something that counts." In back of this statement, adds Hirsh, is the view that "Arabs respond to force." It was the sort of statement made to justify continuing the failed bombing campaign Rolling Thunder in Vietnam, and in particular Richard Nixon's 1972 Christmas bombing of Hanoi.[12]

Rumsfeld insisted that ridding the world of Saddam Hussein had nothing to do with protecting American access to Middle Eastern oil in the increasing competition with China and post–Cold War Russia. Where Eisenhower in 1954 had been open enough to talk about tin, tungsten, rubber, and markets for Japan, with respect to Vietnam, and George H.W. Bush in 1991 had said that "our jobs, our way of life, our own freedom . . . would all suffer if control of the world's great oil reserves fell into the hands of Saddam Hussein," George W. Bush's administration and its closest ally, British prime minister Tony Blair, dismissed all such talk as conspiracy thinking. Insisting that the war was not about oil, Defense Secretary Donald Rumsfeld declared in November 2002 that "it has nothing to do with oil, literally nothing to do with oil."

In fact, a much stronger case can be made that oil was more crucial to American thinking in Iraq than were the raw materials of Vietnam. As Bush critic Kevin Phillips writes, the UN sanctions imposed on Iraq after Gulf War I specified that Hussein not sign agreements to turn over oil fields to foreign companies. The key beneficiaries of the sanction regime, therefore, were the British and American companies that already dominated the Iraq oil fields. Continuation of the sanction regime depended upon there *being*

WMDs and, as it became clear, fitting the intelligence around that assertion. "In short, the weapons of mass destruction drumbeat was substantially tied to oil and had already done its essential job by the time the invasion took place. Accept this logic and it makes mincemeat out of the Bush-Rumsfeld-Blair pretense."[13]

Put another way, the post–Gulf War I sanctions were a holding action useful until a casus belli inevitably removed the threat of Saddam Hussein changing the oil regime. Walter LaFeber in his contribution points to the long-term ambiguity in Chinese-American relations that, as the struggle for oil and natural gas became more intense, took on new urgency in the aftermath of 9/11 and the American forward movement into areas close to China's strategic interests, raising tensions as in the days of the Vietnam War. "The growing U.S.-China confrontation evolved because of Bush's determination to move into areas close to China, and the Chinese challenged the United States directly in places peculiarly sensitive and important to Americans."

The disappearance of the weapons of mass destruction from the rationale for war was planned for from the beginning. Already in 2002, Vice President Richard Cheney had tried out the second line of Bush administration rationalization. Cheney is beyond question the most powerful vice president ever and certainly a more important figure from the beginning than the usual top figures on foreign policy, the secretary of state (then Colin Powell) and the national security adviser (then Condoleezza Rice). By ridding the world of Saddam Hussein, he argued in the fall of 2002, and installing a democratic government in Baghdad, the United States would start a ripple effect across the entire Middle East. "Extremists in the region would have to rethink their strategy of jihad. Moderates throughout the region would take heart, and our ability to advance the Israeli-Palestine peace process would be enhanced."

President Bush liked that approach. In his 2002 State of the Union message Bush seized on a World War II analogy for a phrase, describing an "axis of evil"—Iran, Iraq, and North Korea. While the phrase "axis of evil" reminded fellow conservatives of Ronald Reagan's description of the Soviet Union and Cold War days as well as the glory days of World War II, Bush's main concern was to link Iraq with 9/11 and fasten on weapons of mass destruction to justify preemption—in a way, however, that would still move Congress to support him if no WMDs were found. America went into Iraq in March 2003 promising to change the history of the Middle East and to overcome years of "realist" compromises with tyranny. President Bush spoke of the mission as a sacred duty that had fallen to him, in traditional American mythology, as an unwanted course of action forced on the nation to prevent the proof of Saddam Hussein's ambitions appearing first in a mushroom cloud. From the outset in Iraq, George W. Bush talked about his mission to free the country from tyranny—indicating for his Christian conservative base that he felt he had been destined to undertake the task of spreading freedom to the Middle East. At a meeting with Palestinian religious figures, the president said, "I'm driven with a mission from God. God would tell me, 'George, go and fight those terrorists in Afghanistan.' And I did, and then God would tell me, 'George, go and end the tyranny in Iraq.'"

Superficially, and especially after the quick "victory" in Afghanistan and the toppling of Saddam Hussein's statue in Baghdad, Gulf War II did seem to be totally different than Vietnam. Fears that Iraq would require house-to-house fighting against guerrillas that might look something like the search-and-destroy missions of the earlier era appeared ridiculous in the days just after Bush declared "mission accomplished." And even as the Iraq project came apart at the seams, Bush seized upon the Israeli-Hezbollah war in the summer of 2006 to justify his war using the same terminology. Addressing a Coast Guard audience in Miami, Florida, he asserted that it was all of a piece with policies that promoted terrorism. "For decades, the status quo in the Middle East permitted tyranny and terror to thrive. And as we saw on Sept. 11, the status quo in the Middle East led to death and destruction in the United States, *and it had to change.*"[14]

By the third year of the war the administration was increasingly desperate to find a new credibility issue to rally public support. Rumsfeld, who also thought that Gulf War II would be another quick victory, now found himself and the nation in Robert McNamara's shoes, entangled in a drawn-out war that seemed endless. Words and phrases from Vietnam reappeared—especially, as Marilyn Young observes, the term *counterinsurgency*, even though the American military fears it connotes a failed strategy. In fact, counterinsurgency was never absent at all, as the American actions in El Salvador and Nicaragua in the Reagan years demonstrated. There was also a feeling that, somehow, the enemy insurgents did not fight fair, with their improvised explosive devices (IEDs) and suicide bombers. As Young writes, policy makers blame the insurgents for the way the war is fought, as if there were a choice, but "surely insurgents fight the United States as insurgents because they have no other choice, not because they decide to leave behind their aircraft carriers, precision bombers, drones, B-52s, attack helicopters, and all the rest."

In her essay, Elizabeth L. Hillman points out that the role of women, especially African American women, has increased—in fact, it has saved the volunteer army but has not wrought major changes. "Despite their willingness to serve, women have not been able to rescue the U.S. military from the fundamental threat posed by the end of conscription, nor have they changed its fundamental nature."

One need not dwell on counterinsurgency or the new volunteer army that has replaced the draftees of World War II and Vietnam, however, to see that Iraq was not the antithesis of Vietnam its sponsors claimed.[15] In 1965, Robert McNamara and his generals assured President Lyndon Johnson that if the Vietcong came out of the jungles and fought in large units, American forces would "clobber" them and the war would be over sooner. This assurance was given as part of the campaign to convince the president to send the first 100,000 troops to Vietnam, an escalation that led to half a million troops being involved there and nearly 60,000 American dead. Acknowledging that resurgent Taliban attacks were up in supposedly pacified Afghanistan in July 2006, Defense Secretary Rumsfeld declared, "Every time they come together they get hit and they get hurt . . . the more that are in one place, the easier they are to attack."[16]

In Vietnam, the enemy was able to emerge out of the shadows of the jungles and even, in the 1968 Tet offensive, to attack the American embassy grounds themselves. While Tet did not signal an inevitable military defeat, it did foretell the continuing inability to protect America's Vietnamese friends. Many Iraqis believed, said a Rumsfeld questioner, that a civil war had begun, but the secretary of defense would only comment, "They're going to have to engage in a reconciliation process." More than 1,600 people had been killed in the six weeks after President Bush's visit on July 31, 2006, praising the progress made. After an attack on a market in a tense town south of Baghdad that killed forty people and wounded another forty, frantic relatives of the dead and wounded scuffled with Iraqi guards. "You are strong men," jeered one man, "only when you face us, but you let them do what they did to us."[17]

The idea of reconciliation and strength in Iraq brought another unlearned lesson of Vietnam to the forefront. In a chilling concluding essay, Alfred McCoy explains the way power assumptions (not reality) lead to torture. "Once torture begins, its perpetrators—reaching into that remote terrain where pain and pleasure, procreation and destruction all converge—are often swept away by frenzies of power and potency, mastery and control."

On July 12, 2006, General George W. Casey Jr. asserted that he would need more troops in Baghdad to "take care of the terrorists and death squads" attacking civilians. Pentagon consultant and former West Point instructor Andrew Krepinevich commented wryly about the situation in the rubble-marred capital and the American stronghold, "It's now the yellow zone, not the Green Zone." Rumsfeld announced he was sending 4,500 additional troops to Baghdad to keep order between the religious factions and to attempt to quell the continuing violence. These troops were not new forces from the United States as such, but soldiers whose tours of duty were extended involuntarily. Yet Rumsfeld continued to wonder if Iraq was in a civil war, one that the United States—in the end—could not do anything about no matter how many additional troops went to Baghdad. On July 25, 2006, he seemed bemused by the prospect. "Oh, I don't know," he began an answer. "You know, I thought about that last night, and just musing over the words, the phrase, and what constitutes it. If you think of our Civil War, this is really very different. If you think of civil wars in other countries, this is really quite different. There is—there is a good deal of violence in Baghdad and two or three other provinces, and yet in 14 other provinces there's very little violence or numbers of incidents. So it's a—it's a highly concentrated thing. It clearly is being stimulated by people who would like to have what could be characterized as a civil war and win it, but I'm not going to be the one to decide if, when or at all."[18]

More citizens were killed in Iraq—at least 3,438—in July 2006 than in any other month in the war until then. "I think the time has come for these leaders to take responsibility with regards to sectarian violence, for the security of Baghdad at the present time." So said the American ambassador to that country, Zalmay Khalilzad. But under a new security plan "aimed at overhauling [Prime Minister] Maliki's failed efforts, some of the city's most violent southern and western areas are now virtually occupied block-to-block by American and Iraqi forces, with entire neighborhoods transformed into miniature police states after being sealed off by blast walls and concertina wire."[19]

When Rumsfeld reluctantly appeared before a Senate committee in public session, Senator John McCain scoffed at the notion that shifting forces to Baghdad was the solution. It was, he said during the hearings, the mole-hole game. "What I worry about is we're playing a game of whack-a-mole here," with insurgent activity popping up in places that troops have vacated. "Now we're going to have to move troops into Baghdad from someplace else. It's very disturbing." At a mid-July 2006 meeting of G8 leaders in St. Petersburg, nevertheless, President George W. Bush still sounded an expansive Wilsonian note in talking about how Iraq also tied in with American expectations for Russia. "I talked about my desire to promote institutional change in parts of the world," Bush said of his one-on-one discussions with Russian president Vladimir Putin, "like Iraq where there's a free press and free religion, and I told him that a lot of people in our country would hope that Russia would do the same." The gibe did not impress Putin, who replied, "We certainly would not want to have the same kind of democracy that they have in Iraq, quite honestly." But the remark was never really directed at the Russian leader; rather, it was meant for those who might be souring on the Iraq War. "Just wait," Bush said in an undertone.[20]

Bush and Blair held a joint press conference—one of many as their war lengthened into a bloody sectarian insurgency and false hopes of troop withdrawals had to be explained away—on May 25, 2006. "I have said to the American people, as the Iraqis stand up, we'll stand down." When he first used the phrase during a happier time he faced few serious challengers in the White House press corps. But the context had changed, and on July 20 a reporter asked how he now viewed the "big picture" and what had become of the idea that an invasion of Iraq would pave the way for a solution of questions as intractable as the Arab-Israeli dispute, because an elected government would seek new answers. The question brought this convoluted response: "It's an interesting period because of having foreign policies based on trying to create a sense of stability, we have a foreign policy that addresses the root causes of violence and instability." It is not unreasonable, given this kind of Orwellian logic, to foresee an "Iraq syndrome" that will make the Vietnam syndrome seem nothing more than a passing cloud. Against that prospect, the essays in this book take the position that history is too important to be left to the manipulations of Washington think-tank theorists and their sponsors. In the first chapter, David Elliott discusses the basic theme of the book. "Several months after the occupation of Iraq, Rumsfeld was again queried about the Vietnam parallel and again rejected it. 'It's a different era,' he said. 'It's a different place.'" We begin with an investigation of that assumption.

1

Parallel Wars? Can "Lessons of Vietnam" Be Applied to Iraq?

DAVID ELLIOTT

As the invasion of Afghanistan temporarily sputtered in late 2001, reporters asked Secretary of Defense Donald Rumsfeld if the United States might be getting into another Vietnam. "All together now: Quagmire!" Rumsfeld mocked.[1] Several months after the occupation of Iraq, Rumsfeld was again queried about the Vietnam parallel and again rejected it. "It's a different era," he said. "It's a different place."[2]

True on both counts. And yet the term "quagmire" hasn't gone away, and the Vietnam parallels have proliferated.

Melvin Laird, secretary of defense in the Nixon administration, wrote in *Foreign Affairs*, "The Vietnam War that I saw, first from my seat in Congress and then as secretary of defense, cannot be wrapped in a tidy package and tagged 'bad idea.' It was far more complex than that: a mixture of good and evil from which there are many valuable lessons to be learned. Yet the only lesson that seems to have endured is the one that begins and ends with 'Don't go there.' The war in Iraq is not 'another Vietnam.' But it could become one if we continue to use Vietnam as a sound bite while ignoring its true lessons."[3]

Uses and Misuses of Analogies

I teach a course on U.S. foreign policy and a course on the Vietnam War. Until 2004 I made great efforts to avoid linking Iraq and Vietnam. The "lessons of Vietnam" are numerous but often contradictory. Perhaps the most salient of these is to be very careful in applying analogies. Yuan Foong Khong, a former student at the Claremont Colleges, now at Oxford, wrote a classic book titled *Analogies at War*, in which he painstakingly analyzed the various ways in which analogies were misused by U.S. officials during the Vietnam War. The book appeared in 1992, just as U.S. foreign policy decision makers were grappling with the new and unfamiliar terrain of the post–Cold War world. Khong analyzed in detail how and why decision makers resort to analogies when confronted with novel problems. They serve as a cognitive filter that transforms the unfamiliar into something recognizable and reduces complexity to manageable proportions. The pitfalls of this conceptual screening process are many, however. The wrong analogy may be chosen—perhaps Kennedy and Johnson would have been better served by cautions about the French experience in Indochina than by bracing lessons from Munich and Korea. Or a potentially useful analogy may be misinterpreted or misapplied, as in the case of the misguided application of British experience in the Malayan Emergency to Vietnam.

Here is a brief reviewer's summary of Khong's book:

> In this splendid study, Yuen Foong Khong has laid open the weakness but easy attraction of reasoning by analogy in the making of foreign policy decisions. Reasoning by analogy has characterized much post–Second World War international discussion, especially in the United States. Now "no more Vietnams" has joined "no more Munichs" and "no more Koreas" in the standard package of policy rationalizations. . . . The importance of this volume is not merely its help in explaining American decisions leading to the Vietnam war. It is also a useful pointer to the use of the most frequently cited foreign policy analogy in the United States today: "no more Vietnams." As Yuen Foong Khong shows in his conclusion, Vietnam has led to the drawing of a number of "lessons" for policy-makers. One is that interventions must only occur where American interests are vital; the other is that short, sharp interventions with a certain exit route and a high probability of "winning" are essential.

One might argue that this lesson, as summarized by the reviewer, should have cautioned against launching a war of choice, based on shaky premises, with no Plan B in place if the optimistic scenario did not work out. However, as the reviewer prophetically noted in 1993, "[Khong] argues that reasoning by the analogy of Vietnam will be no more successful than reasoning by the analogies of Munich and Korea."[4]

So let us again emphasize Secretary Rumsfeld's caution that Iraq is not Vietnam. And yet the Vietnam analogies have become part of the debate about the conflict in Iraq. We should try to understand why this has happened, before moving to the more obvious issue of whether these analogies shed any light on America's current problems in Iraq.

The Vietnam analogies actually predated the American invasion and occupation of Iraq. The most often cited was the parallel between the Gulf of Tonkin Resolution and the congressional preauthorization of the use of armed force to overthrow the Saddam Hussein regime. The similarities most often mentioned were the blank-check nature of the congressional authorization of military action and the allegations of presidential deception to gain congressional assent.[5]

One important nonparallel is the nature of the decision-making process in the two conflicts. It is clear that both President Kennedy and President Johnson were pulled reluctantly along the path of escalation in Vietnam, while in Iraq the impetus for escalation came from the top. Because of presidential reluctance to raise the stakes in Vietnam, the decision-making process was prolonged and complex. In Iraq, it is hard to speak of a decision-making process. A senior official in the Bush administration later said, "There was no debate about the wisdom of going to war. . . . No discussion of pros and cons, of what might happen, no planning for the unexpected. It was just something we were going to do."[6] Bob Woodward's book on the planning of the Iraq invasion revealed that there was never a formal meeting to ratify or even discuss the merits of the idea, and that neither the secretary of state nor the secretary of defense was ever specifically asked if he agreed with the wisdom of this policy. Clearly Iraq will not go down as a model of good decision-making process for future generations.

The decision-making process in Vietnam was also flawed in many respects. Assumptions were not challenged, analogies were misused, options were not fully developed or explored, estimates of success were too optimistic, costs and benefits were not assessed, fallback plans were not often specified—all parallels with the Iraq process. Yet if the best and the brightest did not, in the final analysis, come up with the right answers to the Vietnam conundrum, it was not for lack of discussion and debate. The very incrementalism that many conservatives saw as the fatal flaw of Vietnam decision making at least guaranteed an extended process of deliberation.

"Vietnam"—Shorthand for "Failure"

Once the Iraq invasion had apparently succeeded—leading President Bush to declare "mission accomplished"—the Vietnam references tailed off. As many conservative commentators noted, the invocation of "another Vietnam" is based on the identification of "Vietnam" with defeat. The term "Vietnam" is shorthand for "failure." Throughout much of 2003, U.S. officials, the Congress, and dominant public opinion were not inclined to label Iraq a failure, and the press was therefore generally cautious in invoking memories of Vietnam. When Vietnam was mentioned in the press during this period, it was usually done to suggest that the parallels were invalid or of limited usefulness, or to point to lessons of Vietnam that should not be repeated. So it is not surprising that the use of Vietnam parallels for criticism of the Bush policy reemerged in public discussion around the time the media began to question the view of Iraq as a success story in 2004.

Vietnam analogies started to appear in public discussion even during the invasion of Afghanistan, and sporadically surfaced in the debate about the wisdom of invading Iraq and in the immediate aftermath of that invasion. H.D.S. Greenway of the *Boston Globe* wrote in early April 2003:

Comparisons with Vietnam have their limits. The United States will not lose this war, for no other reason than there are no safe havens such as north of the 17th parallel provided for the Vietnamese. But there is no hiding that the Pentagon was taken by surprise by the stiff resistance of guerrilla-like irregulars, as evidenced by Washington spending most of a week playing down what men in the field have been saying. This, too, has its echoes with Vietnam. . . . What this all comes down to is—and there is no kinder word—hubris. . . . Already officers in the Gulf are comparing Rumsfeld to Robert McNamara, the secretary of defense and architect of Vietnam who sent his soldiers into battle when he knew nothing of the Vietnamese.[7]

Yet even critical and seasoned observers initially were cautious about invoking the Vietnam parallel in Iraq.

An official acknowledgment that the United States is now involved in a guerrilla war in Iraq is no surprise and not immediate cause for alarm, military and foreign policy experts say. "You're always well-advised to acknowledge reality," said Boston University Professor Andrew Bacevich, a former U.S. Army colonel and Vietnam veteran. Central Command chief Gen. John Abizaid had just given the first official description of the Iraqi conflict as a guerrilla war, and indicated he might request more troops. "It suggests it is bigger than they had led us to believe," Bacevich said, but added, "None of that means it's Vietnam, that we should get ready for the Tet offensive, or that we should call it a quagmire." Bacevich warned, "If it turns out there is a substantial portion of the Iraqi people who hate the Americans and want them gone, then it gets ugly."[8]

The *Christian Science Monitor* spelled out the reasons for its editorial view that "Iraq is not like Vietnam" in late August 2003.[9] This view was also editorially expressed by papers in Pittsburgh and Chicago around the same time.[10] The *Chicago Sun-Times* cited evidence of progress and concluded that the main danger in Iraq was that panicky U.S. press coverage might turn victory into defeat—invoking a widespread interpretation of the Tet offensive in Vietnam as the point at which more resolute prosecution of the Vietnam War might have turned the tide, but was derailed by ill-informed negative press coverage. In an article subtitled "A Tet Moment for Iraq," John O'Sullivan said, " 'Remember the Tet Offensive' is the mantra I've been repeating to myself as gloomy media accounts of the deepening U.S. quagmire in Iraq crowded the airwaves and news pages . . . we are at a moment like the Tet offensive. This time we had better make sure that, whatever decision we make, it is based on understanding the reality of the conflict."[11]

By November 2003 the issue of Vietnam parallels heated up in the U.S. press. Craig Whitney, the assistant managing editor of the *New York Times* and a former *Times* bureau chief in Saigon during the Vietnam War, wrote: " 'QUAGMIRE,' 'attrition,' 'credibility gap,' 'Iraqification'—a listener to the debate over the situation in Iraq might think that it truly is Vietnam all over again." "But," Whitney cautioned, "Iraq is not Vietnam, and 2003 is not 1975 or 1968. Saddam Hussein was driven out of power and his regime collapsed last spring. There is no independent sanctuary named "North Iraq" for his Baath Party henchmen to fight from, no Soviet Union to keep them supplied with arms and fuel, no equivalent of Laos or Cambodia in the Middle East for whole divisions of his loyalists to hide in, no Ho Chi Minh Trail that suicide bombers can use to drive to Baghdad. Nor is there an allied Iraqi government yet, elected or otherwise."

Whitney added that the terms of the American discussion about Iraq are often similar to the arguments about Vietnam, "and small wonder: although the Vietnamese Communists won the war in 1975, nobody won the battle about it here at home. That may be why, when boiled down to their essence, parts of the current debate seem to be almost as much about Vietnam as about Iraq, as Senator John McCain pointed out in a speech to the Council on Foreign Relations in Washington."[12]

A number of other newspapers also expressed doubt that the Vietnam parallel was valid.[13] The *Washington Post* took a more equivocal stance in early October 2003 with an article asking, "Is Iraq Another Vietnam Quagmire?" and answering, "No and yes."[14] By the end of the month the tone had changed. "Vietnam It Isn't," editorialized the *Washington Post* on October 30.[15]

Iraq Setbacks and Shifting Public Opinion Affect the Invocation of Vietnam Parallels

It would take more careful research to identify the exact point at which the fusion of a perception of Iraq as a failure and the escalation of cautionary Vietnam analogies in public discourse took place. They were not uncommon in the months of 2003 following the invasion, but these negative voices were held in check by the unrelenting official optimism from Washington and Baghdad, until fissures began to appear within the administration, the military in Iraq, and the occupation officials themselves. Two related factors combined to intensify the debate over the relevance of Vietnam analogies. The first was the recognition that the hostilities were not merely a mopping-up operation and that U.S. military forces were likely to be in Iraq for a long time. From this flowed the second issue about the nature of the war—was it a full-blown insurgency, and if so, what did that mean? The question about the nature of the war had been brushed aside by those in the Bush administration who thought that the U.S. military presence in Iraq would be brief and, therefore, that the nature of the war was an abstract and irrelevant philosophical question. When soldiers and officials realized they were in it for the long term, the Vietnam tropes of quagmire, light at the end of the tunnel, and exit strategies became more prevalent.

At the higher levels it took a while for the realization that there would be no early or easy departure from Iraq to sink in, but the reality became increasingly clear at the lower levels by early 2004. Tom Ricks's exhaustive account of this period observes that "a year on the ground had brought a new realism to the troops' assessments of the situation. Few expected overnight solutions anymore, as many troops had in Iraq during the spring of 2003."[16] As Ricks's book *Fiasco* reveals, there was some internal discussion of the specter of insurgency within the Bush administration in the second half of 2003, but top officials dismissed the idea, and it did not become a burning topic until the spring of 2004. It was at this juncture that the issue of how to cope with a growing insurgency surfaced. For nearly a year following the Iraq invasion, the administration maintained that the low-level resistance came from isolated "dead-enders"—followers of Saddam Hussein who had not reconciled themselves to the loss of power and privilege—and outside agitators. The spread of armed opposition to the occupation raised the question of how and why it had happened, and what to do about it. Ricks writes, "By the late winter of 2003–4, it was clear that the U.S. effort, both in pacification and reconstruction was faltering. But it wouldn't be until spring [2004] that it would become clear just how troubled it was."[17]

If a turning point in the widespread acceptance of the Vietnam parallel with Iraq could be found, it would be in the spring of 2004, specifically in April–May, around the time of the disastrous setback in Fallujah. As argued earlier, "Vietnam" simply was shorthand for "failure," and it was at this time that the Iraq venture came to be perceived as a failure by the American people; not surprisingly, the press followed close behind. Ricks quotes a military officer in May 2004 as stating that three things had gone wrong that spring. First was the Abu Ghraib prisoner abuse scandal. Second was the Marine setback at Fallujah (compounded by political mismanagement from Washington, as Ricks makes clear), which antagonized the Sunni population. Third was "the confrontation with Moqtadr al Sadr which alienated much of the Shiite population. The United States had indeed dug itself into a deep hole and didn't know how to climb out of it."[18] It is not surprising that in May 2004 "the majority of people surveyed by the Washington Post/ABC poll said the war in Iraq was not worth fighting. It was the first time that the majority of respondents in that poll felt that way. General Zinni came to a similar conclusion. 'I have seen this movie,' he said in April 2004. 'It was called Vietnam.'"[19]

The tone of press coverage shifted along with public opinion. "In the wake of the unraveling of the Bush administration's rationales for invasion, and the tarring of the U.S. military presence, expert opinion in the United States began to catch up with the facts on the ground. The op-ed pages of the *New York Times*, the *Washington Post*, and the *Los Angeles Times* in May 2004 looked like almost the reverse of the 2002 and 2003 stampedes that culminated in the gushing reviews of Powell's presentation to the UN."[20] An excellent example could be drawn from Ricks's own paper. Richard Cohen, who had editorially rebutted the idea of Vietnam parallels with Iraq in the *Washington Post* the previous October, repeated the obvious differences between the two cases in April 2004 (desert versus jungle environment, etc.). But in the wake of the al-Sadr debacle he wrote, "In almost every way but one, Iraq is not Vietnam. Here's the one: We don't know what the hell we're doing. . . . For now, it does not matter that this uprising is containable or that Sadr may well be little more than a thug. What matters is that he was able to organize an insurrection right under our noses and put up a more than credible fight. Calling him a thug, as we are wont to do, does not change matters. This remarkable fact, to use the current argot, is sooooooo Vietnam. Once again, we are feeling our way in the dark." Concluding his diatribe, Cohen stated one of the most important elements of the Vietnam comparison: "The lesson of Vietnam is that once you make the initial mistake, little you do afterward is right."[21]

Another Echo of Vietnam: Using Spin to Defuse a Growing Credibility Gap

If "Vietnam" had become a synonym for "failure," it also evoked an image of a credibility gap and official mendacity, which is the inevitable consequence of denying failure. The *New York Times* reported in July 2004, "For Mr. Bush, the country is about evenly divided on approval of his presidency, according to the latest poll. But there are some ominous signs that Mr. Bush is beginning to suffer from a Johnson-style 'credibility gap' after sending the country to war to root out weapons of mass destruction and links to Al Qaeda, and being unable to prove either one. When asked by The New York Times and CBS News in June whether Mr. Bush was being completely honest about the war in Iraq, 20 percent of voters said he was mostly lying and 59 percent said he was hiding something. Only 18 percent thought he was telling the entire truth."[22]

The White House used time-honored political tools to attempt to shape the message about Iraq. As Confucius said, a vital aspect of legitimizing power is "rectification of names"—gaining control over political discourse by asserting the right to assign labels, and therefore meaning, to political events. In traditional Chinese thought, the power to define the categories into which social life was organized was an essential attribute of political power. Fung Yu-lan discusses this in his classic study of Chinese philosophy, citing an ancient text that says, "'Should a true King arise, he must certainly follow the ancient terms and make new ones.' . . . Thus the invention of new names and determination of their meaning is a function of the ruler and his government. Hsun Tzu says: 'When the kings had regulated names, the names were fixed and the actualities distinguished. Their principles were thus able to be carried out and their will could be known. They thus carefully led the people to unity. Therefore, the making of unauthorized distinctions between words, and the making of new words, so as thus to confuse the correct nomenclature, cause the people to be in doubt, and bring much litigation, was called great wickedness. It was a crime like that of using false credentials or false measures."[23]

In addition to labeling the active opponents of the U.S. occupation of Iraq "dead-enders" to deny them the legitimacy of the status of combatants, and to underline the hopelessness of their futile resistance, the Bush administration refused to call the resistance an insurgency, for fear of awakening the ghosts of Vietnam and raising the prospect that America would once again be stalemated in an unwinnable conflict. Subsequently the White House engaged in a similar exercise in semantics in denying that the sectarian conflict in Iraq amounted to a "civil war."[24] This was a repeat of earlier administrations' denials that the struggle in Vietnam was not a civil conflict but was, rather, aggression from the outside. The Vietnam War spawned an entire lexicon of circumlocutions (such as "protective reaction strike") that also reflected the government's attempt to control political debate at that time.

After the invasion of Iraq and "mission accomplished," an early straw in the wind that portended a reversion to analogies in public discourse came from within the government. This was the remarkable decision by someone in the Pentagon to show the classic 1965 film *The Battle of Algiers* by Gillo Pontecorvo. According to the Pentagon flyer that announced the screening of the film, the movie showed "how to win the battle against terrorism and lose the war of ideas. . . . Children shoot soldiers at point blank range. Women plant bombs in cafes. Soon the entire Arab population builds to a mad fervor. Sound familiar?"[25]

Despite the efforts of the Bush administration to stamp out the use of terminology that might serve as a reminder of Vietnam, some supporters of the administration's invasion of Iraq took the offensive and introduced a revisionist view of the Vietnam War as a success, and therefore as a useful model for Iraq. One of the early op-ed discussions of counterinsurgency in late 2003 noted, "Talk of counterinsurgency strategies inevitably summons up the trauma of Vietnam. It tends to paralyze analysis by turning every American small war into a replay of Vietnam and every casualty into a quagmire. But it shouldn't. Even in Vietnam, classic counterinsurgency strategies and tactics proved successful—when given time and effort. There is no reason to believe they cannot work in Iraq where the insurgency problem is not as large or difficult, where there is no country like North Vietnam providing major assistance to guerrillas."[26]

Rediscovering Counterinsurgency

As we will see, many who made policy recommendations on how to achieve success in Iraq chose to deal with the troubling Vietnam experience by historical revision, turning failure into remembered success. Even Thomas Ricks's otherwise perceptive book *Fiasco* implies that the adoption of a grab bag of general counterinsurgency principles and doctrine (unity of command, denial of sanctuary, restraint in use of firepower), along with a repertoire of tactics used against insurgents over the centuries, would offer some chance of success in Iraq. It is noteworthy that many of the examples of successful counterinsurgency tactics cited by Ricks are from bygone colonial days or failed attempts to cling to the remnants of empire.[27] He might have mentioned the many accounts of the British failure to pacify Iraq after World War I.[28]

Notwithstanding the complex lineage of counterinsurgency, Ricks states that "it isn't clear why U.S. commanders seemed so flatly ignorant of how other counterinsurgencies had been conducted successfully. The main reason seems to be a repugnance, after the fall of Saigon, for dwelling on unconventional operations." He cites a U.S. military officer's conclusion that "scholars are virtually unanimous in their judgment that conventional forces often lose unconventional wars because they lack a conceptual understanding of the war they are fighting."[29] Yet to understand the nature of the conflict may also be a reason for not fighting it, on the grounds that it is unwinnable or unnecessary. Still, many who accepted the objectives of the war in Iraq but had become concerned about the adverse turn of events there looked to counterinsurgency as a way of salvaging the situation.

Counterinsurgency is presented by Ricks and a number of military officers advocating a more innovative response in Iraq as the only approach that is appropriate to the nature of the conflict. It is true this has the merit of at least acknowledging that there is an insurgency and that conventional military measures would be ineffective in dealing with it. But all too often counterinsurgency is viewed as a tool kit of tactics or a grab bag of miscellaneous past experiences in dealing with insurgencies. This is reflected in the revised Army manuals discussed by Ricks, and the belated effort of the commander of U.S. forces in Iraq, General Casey, to develop a more explicit and appropriate statement of strategy and tactics.[30] The laundry list character of this exercise is clear from the itemization of the "nine unsuccessful characteristics" of U.S. military operations in Iraq—the reverse of the nine factors that could lead to success.

The problem with these historical compendiums of counterinsurgency experiences is that they miss the most important point—that each insurgency has a distinctive political and socioeconomic character, which usually renders the tool kit approach ineffective or irrelevant. In fact, it detracts from understanding the crucial underlying political issues central and distinctive to each conflict. This does have one advantage for the Bush administration, however: it keeps the focus off the political reasons for the invasion and occupation and views the problem as mainly one of restoring stability. Far from contributing to a better understanding of the "nature of the conflict," as Ricks argues, it detracts from a realistic appraisal of the key issues of the struggle.

By the end of 2003, some journalists were beginning to notice the revival of interest in counterinsurgency, and the accompanying revisionism to make it applicable to Iraq. The *Boston Globe* reported that "some military experts believe the whole idea of guerrilla warfare has been oversold . . . recently, a diverse school of revisionists—including military analyst Lewis Sorley, former CIA director William Colby, and maverick liberal journalist Michael Lind—have picked up on the idea that the Viet Cong were in fact defeated as a popular insurrection, although their North Vietnamese ally won a conventional war against exhausted South Vietnamese and American forces."

Nevertheless, the author cautioned:

> As the specter of protracted guerrilla warfare raises its head in Iraq, it's worth recalling the mixed lessons of the past. Successful counterinsurgency involves a deep familiarity with the local culture, which is difficult to gain on the fly. Gaining political legitimacy is the key to successfully defeating an insurgency, yet building such popular support can take years if not decades. Moreover, there's an inevitable tension between obtaining security for one's troops and winning popular support. Iraq, with its shadowy enemy of uncertain ideology, is very different from Vietnam. However, the troubling legacy of that conflict should cast doubt that there will be any easy or quick solution this time either.[31]

Despite the showing of *The Battle of Algiers*, the Pentagon itself was more focused on present tactics and capabilities than on historical lessons. By the beginning of 2004, the military was split between two opposing views of dealing with the conflict in Iraq. One was the "kick down the doors" approach, using commandos and special-mission units such as Delta Force and the Navy SEALs. The other was a more nuanced "winning hearts and minds" approach to counterinsurgency. The official Pentagon position was that the two approaches were complementary, but one well-informed reporter wrote that "according to a classified Defense Department policy briefing on the war against the al Qaeda terrorist network and the Baathist insurgents in Iraq, the Bush administration is moving away from work with insurgents and favoring more direct action strikes."[32]

But events soon forced a reconsideration of this position. By the spring of 2004, it was apparent that the opposition to the occupation had escalated. *New York Times* reporters James Risen and John Burns wrote in April 2004:

> United States forces are confronting a broad-based Shiite uprising that goes well beyond supporters of one militant Islamic cleric who has been the focus of American counterinsurgency efforts, United States intelligence officials said Wednesday.

That assertion contradicts repeated statements by the Bush administration and American officials in Iraq. On Wednesday, Secretary of Defense Donald H. Rumsfeld and Gen. Richard B. Myers, chairman of the Joint Chiefs of Staff, said that they did not believe the United States was facing a broad-based Shiite insurgency.

But intelligence officials now say that there is evidence that the insurgency goes beyond Mr. Sadr and his militia, and that a much larger number of Shiites have turned against the American-led occupation of Iraq, even if they are not all actively aiding the uprising.[33]

Belatedly, the Army recognized that it had made a mistake in trying to efface memories of the Vietnam War by literally throwing away the hard-won experience gained from that conflict.

The Army's historical memory contains a gap. "After Vietnam," recounts retired Army Colonel Robert Killebrew, "the Army just walked away from unconventional war." Understandably eager to put the most painful experience in its history behind it, and less understandably convinced that its conventional operations actually succeeded in Vietnam, the Army reverted to training for the conventional wars it knew best. (In this, it was assisted by canonical texts like Colonel Harry G. Summers's *On Strategy*, a selective reading of the Vietnam War in which the author criticizes policymakers for relying too heavily on counterinsurgency tactics.) With the exception of the early '80s, when it enjoyed a brief vogue during the war in El Salvador, counterinsurgency all but disappeared from the Army's vocabulary. So much so that, according to an unsparing report by Army War College scholar Conrad C. Crane, when instructors planning a course on the topic went searching for lesson material at the Army's Special Operations School during the 1980s, "they found that the staff there had been ordered to throw away their counterinsurgency files."[34]

Faced with the reality of an expanding insurgency, the Army issued a field guide to counterinsurgency warfare. "The Army field manual on counterinsurgency operations is the first since the early Vietnam era, and the first ever intended for the kind of regular Army units now embroiled in battles in Iraq, as opposed to the Special Operations forces who have taken the lead in previous counterinsurgencies."[35]

Colonel John Nagl is the most prominent Army specialist on counterinsurgency, having taught the subject at West Point, written a book on the subject (*Learning to Eat Soup with a Knife*), and practiced it in the field in Iraq. A *New York Times* profile in January 2004 wrote that

the portions of his book that focus on Vietnam stress the erroneous and muddled thinking of American military and political elites, especially Gen. William Westmoreland, who (as the historian Max Boot recounts), when asked his solution to the Vietcong, replied with one word: "firepower." As a counterpoint in his study, Nagl quotes Marine Gen. Victor (Brute) Krulak, who concluded: "You cannot win militarily. You have to win totally, or you are not winning at all." For Nagl, Vietnam stands as an encyclopedia of what shouldn't be done. Foremost in the do-not-repeat category are the indiscriminate use of firepower, the resort to conventional tactics to fight an unconventional threat and the failure to implement an effective "hearts and minds" campaign. The preferred strategy has been referred to as "total war," though the phrase is often misunderstood as referring to a scorched-earth strategy.

John Waghelstein, a retired Special Forces colonel who led the team of American advisers in El Salvador, defines total war as meaning "you use all the elements of national power. It's at the grassroots level that you're trying to win. You can kill enemy soldiers—that's not the only issue. You also need to dry up their support."[36]

The evidence that top U.S. officials did not understand that they were confronting an insurgency is compellingly presented by Ricks. But it does not necessarily follow that those who did grasp the threat of insurgency to the U.S. occupation were correct in invoking counterinsurgency remedies from the past. The Combined Action Platoons (CAPS) may have achieved some brief and limited success in a few villages in Vietnam but had little or no impact on the overall course of the conflict. Other counterinsurgency "lessons" favorably cited by Ricks include the writings of a French military theoretician of counterinsurgency, David Galula, who also enjoyed a vogue during the early Kennedy years among U.S. counterinsurgency buffs.

While theorists such as Galula did note the centrality of controlling the population, his view of revolutionary war did not, as Ricks implies, lead to a "hearts and minds" approach to pacification. Although civic action was part of his plan, it was obedience to French authority, not "freedom" or political persuasion, that Galula sought. In a 1963 lecture at the Rand Corporation, which had brought him in to advise on counterinsurgency in Vietnam, Galula proudly recounted his methods and achievements in Algeria.

> A thorough census was the first step toward controlling the population. Control also meant that my soldiers had to know every villager by sight. I committed villagers to the French struggle by requisitioning their labor and paying them for their work. I opened a dispensary. I opened a school. Reflecting on who might be our potential allies in the population, I thought that the women, given their subjugated condition, would naturally be on our side if we emancipated them. I took care that the children were kept busy in school and in organized outdoor games. In March 1957, I was well in control of the entire population. The census was completed and kept up to date, my soldiers knew every individual in their townships, and my rules concerning movements and visits were obeyed with very few violations. My authority was unchallenged.[37]

As an American civil affairs officer in Iraq pointed out, "the objective is to gain control of the population, and then to win their support."[38] Galula temporarily achieved the first objective, but not the second. In addition, the question of how these objectives can be reconciled with the aim of turning control over to Iraqis remains an unresolved problem for counterinsurgency enthusiasts. Recall the maxim cited earlier: "Gaining political legitimacy is the key to successfully defeating an insurgency."

Considering the outcome for the French in Indochina and Algeria, the U.S. military was probably better advised to watch Gillo Pontecorvo's *The Battle of Algiers*. The French "revolutionary war" school of counterinsurgency theorists did in fact focus on controlling the population, but, in the words of Roger Trinquier, "it is not necessary to have the sympathy of a majority of the people in order to rule them. The right organization can turn the trick."[39] No wonder a specialist on French politics lamented, "It was a tragic day for the French army, the Fourth Republic, and de Gaulle—to say nothing of countless Algerian Muslims—when some do-it-yourself military theoreticians stumbled across the writings of Mao Tse-Tung."[40]

While Ricks's book has been justly praised for documenting the follies and blunders of the Bush administration in Iraq, it also perpetuates the myth that there could have been a smarter way to achieve the same objective.

> It isn't clear why U.S. commanders seemed so flatly ignorant of how other counterinsurgencies had been conducted successfully. The main reason seems to be a repugnance, after the fall of Saigon, for dwelling on unconventional operations. But the cost of such willful ignorance was high. "Scholars are virtually unanimous in their judgment that conventional forces often lose unconventional wars because they lack a conceptual understanding of the war they are fighting," Lt. Col Matthew Moten, chief of military history at West Point, would comment a year later.[41]

This assertion would come as a surprise to the many scholars of the Vietnam War and other "insurgencies" who point to the underlying political issues as the factors that decided the outcome, rather than the application of refined military techniques. Indeed, the very mantra of "winning hearts and minds"—often cited by military proponents of counterinsurgency—is a reflection of this key point. No U.S. strategist in Vietnam ever devised a method of "winning hearts and minds"—and none of the counterinsurgency enthusiasts lauded by Ricks seems to have a plan for winning the hearts and minds of Iraqis under conditions of military occupation. Recall Richard Cohen's statement that "the lesson of Vietnam is that once you make the initial mistake, little you do afterward is right. If the basic policy is flawed, the best tactics in the world will not salvage it."

Let us return to the issue of the belated alleged discovery of a winning strategy in Vietnam. Lewis Sorley and others have recently advanced the view that after Tet the United States found a general (Creighton Abrams) and a strategy (clear and hold) that would have produced a different outcome had they appeared earlier in the war. Even so, many of these revisionists argue, the military conflict was essentially won by 1970 or 1971. It is, however, important to note that what Abrams favored was not counterinsurgency but intensive conventional U.S. small-unit operations backed by massive firepower. The resulting depopulation of large areas of Vietnam's countryside and the flow of refugees into areas controlled by the Saigon government was interpreted by many as "success" in pacification. Nonetheless, Abrams is now invoked by some who believe that his methods would bring success if applied to Iraq.

An article by the *Boston Globe*'s Matt Steinglass has a useful summary of the contending views on the subject of the applicability of American pacification techniques tried in Vietnam to Iraq.

> Supporters of the American invasion and occupation of Iraq have often argued that it has little in common with the Vietnam War. But judging by President Bush's new "National Strategy for Victory in Iraq," unveiled Nov. 30 [2005] and promoted in a series of recent speeches, the administration itself may have started to see some parallels. The document envisions a three-pronged security strategy for fighting the Iraqi insurgency: "Clear, Hold, and Build." It is no accident that this phrase evokes the "clear and hold" counterinsurgency strategy pursued by the American military in the final years of the Vietnam War.

Steinglass notes that two prominent journalists, the *Washington Post*'s David Ignatius and the *New Republic*'s Lawrence Kaplan, have reported that influential military strategists inside and outside the Pentagon "have been pushing to resurrect 'clear and hold' in Iraq, claiming that the US effort to suppress the Viet Cong was actually a success." This view is based in part on *A Better War*, the 1999 book by Lewis Sorley which asserts that General Creighton Abrams found a winning strategy after he replaced General Westmoreland as military commander of U.S. forces in Vietnam by changing the "search and destroy" strategy to a "clear and hold" strategy. In Sorley's view, this strategy change "virtually wiped out the insurgency. By late 1970, Sorley writes, 'the war was won.'"[42]

The *Globe* article comments that "the idea that the strategy that beat the Viet Cong could work in Iraq elides a fundamental question: Did 'clear and hold" actually beat the Viet Cong? For most historians of the war, not to mention for those who fought on the winning side, the answer is no. And the lessons for Iraq are far from clear."[43] My own research suggests that it was not a carefully crafted military strategy of counterinsurgency that led to the apparent "pacification" of the Mekong Delta and many other areas of Vietnam by 1971, but a policy of rural depopulation that emptied much of the countryside—probably not a tactic that should be repeated in Iraq, or even one that is relevant to the more urbanized Iraqi society.[44]

Counterinsurgency advocates such as Nagl deplore the indiscriminate use of firepower and are definitely on the "hearts and minds" side of the

Pentagon; nonetheless, Nagl is critical of some advocates of restrained fire-power, such as General James Conway of the Marines. Instead, Nagl stresses the importance of local knowledge and local forces. "The formation of 'indigenous' forces, as they are called, is considered a paramount element of successful counterinsurgency. In his book, Nagl emphasizes that one of the many shortcomings of American policy in Vietnam was America's inability to build a capable South Vietnamese fighting force. 'Vietnamization,' when it finally came along in 1969, was too little, too late. During one of our discussions, Nagl explained the use of Iraqi forces as a matter of efficacy and necessity."[45]

Vietnamization and Iraqification

Thus, as in Vietnam, insurgency has led to a focus on counterinsurgency, and the limitations of conventional U.S. forces in implementing counterin-surgency have in turn revived another staple of the Vietnam era, indigeniza-tion of the military effort—called Vietnamization then and Iraqification now. One form of Iraqification would have been to implement the original idea of turning over a decapitated regime to the people who had previously staffed it. Paul Bremer, in charge of the U.S. occupation, emphatically re-jected this and set U.S. policy on a course that would greatly complicate the reversion of sovereignty to Iraqis. Indeed, Bremer seemed completely op-posed to even the most limited forms of Iraqification. Ricks describes a meeting between Ambassador Bremer and a retired Marine colonel in July 2003. "'Mr. Ambassador, here are some programs that worked in Vietnam,' said the colonel, referring to popular forces that had been used successfully as village militias in Vietnam. It was the wrong word to put in front of Bremer. 'Vietnam?' Bremer exploded. '*Vietnam!* I don't want to talk about Vietnam. This is not Vietnam. This is Iraq!' "[46] Ricks clearly empathizes with the colonel's conclusion from this exchange that "the top U.S. officials in Iraq really didn't fathom the nature of the conflict they faced."[47]

I won't go into the details of Vietnamization and Iraqification, but sim-ply note a few questions raised by these issues. The first is the issue of com-parability of cases. Despite all the problems of Vietnamization, many stemming from the colonial origins of most of the officer corps engaged in a nationalist conflict, these problems pale in comparison to the problem of reintegrating former Baathist officers into a force that seems to be dissolv-ing in a cauldron of ethnic strife. A thorny problem for Iraq, which was less of an issue in Vietnam, was the question of whether or not the arming and training of an army would end up creating a force that might turn on its patron.[48]

Another issue is the question of whether or not indigenization aimed at building a new political system can succeed prior to the construction of the political basis of that system. Apart from the already difficult task of reintegrating former Baathist officers into the army, the problem of sectarian militias creates a formidable challenge. Indigenization first stresses building up a local army, which seems to be viewed as a means to achieve a desired political end, but in both Vietnam and Iraq the United States viewed the desired end somewhat differently than its nominal allies did. By the time indigenization replaced the goal of a solution based on U.S. military victory in both countries, the main U.S. objective had become face-saving extrication because of declining American political support. This inevitably leads to one of the most intriguing parallels between Vietnam and Iraq—the concept of the "decent interval"—a face-saving formula for U.S. extrication from a conflict it felt it could no longer win.

But before we address the "decent interval," let us deal with two other matters related to indigenization. The first is the issue of what strategy U.S. troops should pursue if the object is no longer a military victory and the main objective becomes turning over the fighting to the local allies. The second is how the Vietnam version of indigenization and the accompanying post-Tet military strategy has been recast as a success. Without going into detail, let me simply say that based on my own research and personal observation during the Vietnam War, it is difficult for me to agree that the United States belatedly found a winning military strategy after Tet, or to believe the somewhat contradictory second revisionist point that Vietnamization was a great success. Indeed, if it was the discovery of an effective US military strategy after Tet that was the main reason for turning the tide in Vietnam, what does this say about the role played by Vietnamization in the later years of the Vietnam War?

Melvin Laird, who as Nixon's secretary of defense was an ardent advocate of de-Americanization of the war—later known as Vietnamization—has recently claimed that Nixon's policies achieved victory in Vietnam. Laird is quite open about the stakes in characterizing the experience of indigenization in Vietnam. To accept Vietnamization as a failure would be to cast doubt on the future of Iraqification. Laird writes, "The truth about Vietnam that revisionist historians conveniently forget is that the United States had not lost when we withdrew in 1973. In fact, we grabbed defeat from the jaws of victory two years later when Congress cut off the funding for South Vietnam that had allowed it to continue to fight on its own. . . . I believed then and still believe today that given enough outside resources, South Vietnam was capable of defending itself, just as I believe Iraq can do the same now. From the Tet offensive in 1968 up to the fall of Saigon in 1975, South Vietnam never lost a major battle."[49] Clearly Laird has not reflected on (or does not agree with) General Krulak's maxim "You cannot win militarily. You have to win totally, or you are not winning at all."

The question of whether South Vietnam's army could defend itself was answered conclusively in 1975. Laird's self-serving attempt to blame the U.S. Congress only serves as a reminder to would-be local partners of the United

States that total dependency has its costs, especially when national interests diverge. Was it really helpful to the Army of the Republic of Vietnam (ARVN) to shape them in the image of the U.S. Army, so that the dependency on U.S. air support and bountiful logistical supplies was built into the organization, precluding development of a self-reliant armed force and leaving the South Vietnamese at the mercy of the American electorate? It was not only Congress that pulled the plug after it tired of bearing the costs of Vietnam, it was the American people. We should reflect long and hard about whether democracy is compatible with Empire and, if not, which we value most.

"Decent Interval" Redux

The immense costs of the Iraq War will probably likewise be dramatically reduced once the direct U.S. stake is reduced. An April 2006 report stated, "The cost of the war in Iraq will reach $320 billion after the expected passage next month of an emergency spending bill currently before the Senate, and that total is likely to more than double before the war ends, the Congressional Research Service estimated this week. . . . Even if a gradual troop withdrawal begins this year, war costs in Iraq and Afghanistan are likely to rise by an additional $371 billion during the phaseout, the report said, citing a Congressional Budget Office study. When factoring in costs of the war in Afghanistan, the $811 billion total for both wars would have far exceeded the inflation-adjusted $549 billion cost of the Vietnam War." The article also pointed out, "Such cost estimates may be producing sticker shock on Capitol Hill. This year, the wars will consume nearly as much money as the departments of Education, Justice and Homeland Security combined, a total that is more than a quarter of this year's projected budget deficit."[50]

It is not hard to imagine what will happen to the budget for Iraq's reconstruction in the event the bulk of U.S. forces are withdrawn. As in Vietnam, the issue is competing priorities in a transformed strategic environment. Indeed, Laird himself notes how the decline in American stakes affected the outcome.

> The truth is, wars are fluid things and missions change. This is more the rule than the exception. It was true in Vietnam, and it is true in Iraq today. The early U.S. objective in Southeast Asia was to stop the spread of communism. With changes in the relationship between the Soviet Union and China and the 1965 suppression of the communist movement in Indonesia, the threat of a communist empire diminished. Unwilling to abandon South Vietnam, the United States changed its mission to self-determination for Vietnam.[51]

This shifted the stakes from stopping the spread of world communism to the survival of a noncommunist Vietnam—a desirable objective but not a life-or-death concern of the United States. Even before the geostrategic context of Vietnam changed (because of the Sino-Soviet split and the belated recognition that Vietnam was the last of the wars of decolonization and not the first of the global revolutionary wars of national liberation that had spooked President Kennedy), the United States did not place a high priority on salvaging the interests of its local Vietnamese partners. In fact, the United States was complicit in the overthrow of Ngo Dinh Diem, an ally of nine years' standing, in what was arguably the key turning point in American involvement in the war. Shortly after that, John McNaughton, Robert McNamara's chief deputy for the Vietnam War, gave short shrift to the importance of local allies in U.S. calculations. He observed that U.S. aims were "70 percent—To avoid a humiliating defeat (to our reputation as a guarantor). 20 percent—To keep SVN (and then adjacent) territory from Chinese hands. 10 percent—To permit the people of SVN to enjoy a better, freer way of life. ALSO—to emerge from crisis without an unacceptable taint from methods used. NOT—to 'help a friend,' although it would be hard to stay in if asked out."[52]

Laird offered the following view of President Bush's responsibilities with regard to Iraq in light of a similar shift in the strategic context of the conflict.

> The current President Bush was persuaded that we would find WMD in Iraq and did what he felt he had to do with the information he was given. When we did not find the smoking gun, it would have been unconscionable to pack up our tanks and go home. Thus, there is now a new mission, to transform Iraq, and it is not a bad plan. Bush sees Iraq as the frontline in the war on terror—not because terrorists dominate there, but because of the opportunity to displace militant extremists' Islamist rule throughout the region. Bush's greatest strength is that terrorists believe he is in this fight to the end. I have no patience for those who can't see that big picture and who continue to view Iraq as a failed attempt to find WMD. Now, because Iraq has been set on a new course, Bush has an opportunity to reshape the region. "Nation building" is not an epithet or a slogan. After the attacks of September 11, 2001, it is our duty.[53]

But the signs of abandoning this grand plan for reshaping the Middle East have been obvious for some time, and are another reason that the United States' long-term support for Iraqification may be in doubt.[54]

The first sign was the departure of Paul Bremer and the abandonment of de-Baathification. In fact, Iraqification itself was an acknowledgment that Iraq's political future would have to be shaped by the forces in Iraq and not by Washington's preferred exiled leaders. The reconstitution of the Iraqi army was a link to the past as well.[55]

The *Washington Post*'s Robin Wright reported in August 2005 that the United States had lowered its sights on what could be achieved in Iraq and quoted an administration official as saying that it was "shedding the unreality that dominated the invasion."

The Bush administration is significantly lowering expectations of what can be achieved in Iraq, recognizing that the United States will have to settle for far less progress than originally envisioned during the transition due to end in four months, according to U.S. officials in Washington and Baghdad. The United States no longer expects to see a model new democracy, a self-supporting oil industry or a society in which the majority of people are free from serious security or economic challenges, U.S. officials say. "What we expected to achieve was never realistic given the timetable or what unfolded on the ground," said a senior official involved in policy since the 2003 invasion. "We are in a process of absorbing the factors of the situation we're in and shedding the unreality that dominated at the beginning."[56]

This more sober evaluation was, not surprisingly, accompanied by increasingly explicit talk of extrication from Iraq.[57] And, also not surprisingly, another ghost from the Vietnam era resurfaced: the concept of the "decent interval." During the Vietnam War, this was a term used to indicate that the United States was prepared to accept defeat in Vietnam, so long as American responsibility for it was obscured by a "decent interval" between the U.S. withdrawal and the ultimate South Vietnamese collapse.[58] The philosophical underpinnings of the U.S. withdrawal from Vietnam went through three clear stages. First was the recognition, following the Tet offensive of 1968, that a U.S. military victory was not possible. Second came the hope that Vietnamization—the use of the Vietnamese military to carry on the war—would succeed where American troops could not. This was the notion of Vietnamization with victory. The third stage, which led to the Paris peace agreements, was the acceptance that the Saigon forces might not win—Vietnamization with the possibility of defeat.

In June 2005, without fanfare, the United States entered an analogous third stage in Iraq. In an October report on the downscaling of U.S. expectations in Iraq, the *Los Angeles Times* quoted General George Casey, the U.S. military commander in Iraq, who said the reduction of the number of U.S. troops would "take away one of the elements that fuels the insurgency, that of the coalition forces as an occupying force."[59] The article also reminded us that there had been a preview of this new attitude as early as June 2005, when Rumsfeld said, "If [the insurgency] does go on for four, eight, 10, 12, 15 years, whatever . . . it is going to be a problem for the people of Iraq."[60]

A problem for the people of Iraq?

Someone once explained to me why the term "no problem" is prevalent in so many cultures. It means, he said, "I don't have a problem—*you* have a problem." This seems to be the implication of Rumsfeld's comment. During the war in Vietnam, the idea of a U.S. exit in which a face-saving interval would elapse before the South's defeat seems to have originally been formulated by one of LBJ's "wise men," Truman's secretary of state, Dean Acheson. Acheson later wrote, "I took it that the purpose of [American] efforts was to enable the GVN [government of Vietnam] to survive and to be able to stand alone at least for a period of time, with only a fraction of the foreign support it had now. If this could be accomplished at all or only after a very protracted period with the best that present numbers could do, it seemed to me that the situation was hopeless and that a method of disengagement should be considered."[61]

Perhaps it is still premature to call forth the ghosts of Vietnam. But the parallel between the intelligent but arrogant Robert McNamara, who proudly accepted the responsibility for "McNamara's War," and the similarly overbearing Donald Rumsfeld is hard to ignore, as anyone who has read *Dereliction of Duty*—H.R. McMaster's indictment of McNamara's flawed judgments imposed on a compliant military leadership—will readily appreciate. This book became something of a rallying point for the Vietnam-era officers who vowed it would never happen again. It left a strong impression on officers such as General Eric Shinseki, who sacrificed his military career to speak truth to power—that the planned forces for Iraq would be inadequate.

Is it irony or destiny that McMaster was at ground zero of the counterinsurgency struggle in Iraq? The *Los Angeles Times* article reports that "the U.S. commander of the Tall Afar operation, Army Col. H.R. McMaster, said Sept. 13 [2005] that it would be some time before the town had enough trained Iraqi troops to keep insurgents from filtering back. 'Is there enough force here right now to secure this area permanently?' McMaster was quoted as saying. 'No. Are there opportunities for the enemy in other areas within our region? Yes.'"[62]

The underlying motive for a disguised exit in Iraq, as in Vietnam, is that the policy has failed, and delay in facing the consequences will only make things worse for all concerned. But let us be clear about the consequences: Colin Powell's Pottery Barn rule (you break it, you own it) does not apply to situations such as Iraq and Vietnam. As the Vietnamese did before them, the Iraqis will pay the bill for America's misguided intervention.

There are also voices within the administration that warn against premature withdrawal. The most startling prediction of chaos and civil war came from U.S. ambassador Zalmay Khalilzad, who, in trying to maintain support for a more extended U.S. presence, made the remarkable admission that "the 2003 toppling of Saddam Hussein's regime had opened a 'Pandora's box' of volatile ethnic and sectarian tensions that could engulf the region in all-out war if America pulled out of the country too soon."[63]

This stark prediction is reminiscent of the Nixon talk of a "bloodbath" in the event of a too-hasty U.S. withdrawal; however, in contrast to Vietnam, it has a frightening plausibility. But if the U.S. troops merely fuel the insurgency and divert the Iraqis from finding their own mutual accommodation, and if the political support in the United States for prolonged involvement in Iraq is slipping, what is the alternative? In the end, the rationale boils down to what it was in the latter years of the Vietnam War: we have to stay there because we are there. One lesson of Vietnam is that this rationale wears thin when the electorate deems that costs are excessive. The more sophisticated version of this is the credibility argument—that a messy withdrawal would damage America's reputation and influence in the world. But that, of course, is what the "decent interval" is designed to mitigate by placing the blame elsewhere. Moreover, the credibility argument is also heavily dependent on public belief in a plausible plan for success. If "stay the course" succeeds only in ratcheting up the stakes for the United States with ever-greater peril of failure, it will be a hard sell. Indeed, just prior to the November 2006 midterm elections, the Bush administration seemed to disavow the term.[64] The appointment of James Baker to devise yet another "plan" prior to the midterm election (as in the case of Nixon's 1968 "plan," Baker piously asserted that the details could not be revealed prior to the election so as not to "politicize" the issue) is another indication of the retreat from "stay the course."[65]

The "Plan" Is the Plan: A Last-Ditch Effort to Maintain Public Support

Mustering the public's backing is the concern that underlies President Bush's decision in late 2005 to apply a lesson of Vietnam to Iraq. The conventional wisdom view is that public support for the Vietnam War (and all conflicts) slipped when the casualties rose to a level that demoralized the American public. Duke University political scientist Peter Feaver and his co-author Chris Gelpi impressed the Bush administration with a study "of poll results from the first two years of the war," in which Dr. Gelpi, Dr. Feaver, and Jason Reifler, then a Duke graduate student, took issue with what they described as the conventional wisdom since the Vietnam War— that Americans will support military operations only if American casualties are few. They found that public tolerance for the human cost of combat depended on two factors: a belief that the war was a worthy cause, and even more important, a belief that the war was likely to be successful."[66] What followed was a concerted PR attempt to convince the American public that the Bush administration did, in fact, have a plan and a victory strategy.

This resulted in a slick brochure titled "National Strategy for Victory in Iraq" in November 2005, but it did not stem the rising tide of public unease with the prospects in Iraq. Robin Wright of the *Washington Post* wrote:

> President Bush's "strategy for victory" catalogues progress in Iraq over the past 32 months, but also omits or glosses over complications, problems and uncertainties in the most ambitious U.S. military intervention since Vietnam. . . . Little is new in the

35-page document, titled "National Strategy for Victory in Iraq," which covers three broad fronts: security, political development and economic issues. The interpretation it yields depends heavily on viewing the glass half-full rather than half-empty—and doing so in defiance of daily suicide bombings, abductions or deaths. Unspoken is the critical element of the timing of the strategy's release.[67]

Like President Nixon's purported "plan" for winning the Vietnam War, touted in the 1968, and the belated change in military strategy, the current attempt to repackage Iraq, is probably too little, too late. In war as in politics, timing is everything. "'There's a lot that the administration's critics won't disagree with, but it's late,' said Robert Malley, director of the International Crisis Group Middle East program. 'I don't think the president has the luxury of time to implement a sound policy, both because of the stress on the military but also because of the problem of the trust of the American public and political elite.'"[68] Whatever the future holds, the future of Iraq will probably not be scripted by the Bush "plan," which was mainly designed to reassure the American public that there *is* a plan.

The "plan" is not undergirded by a consensus on strategy and tactics. The controversy between advocates of "kick down the door" counterinsurgency and the partisans of "winning hearts and minds" continues, and so does the indecision about the strategic implications of military tactics. The "kick down the door" approach implies more American troops, while the "hearts and minds" advocates generally favor a reduction in the visibility of occupying forces. By the time the Bush "plan" was cobbled together in late 2005, the voices calling for a sharp reduction in the number of U.S. forces in Iraq had grown louder.

Perhaps the major flaws in the idea that proclaiming a "plan" will retain support for the war in Iraq are (1) that the "plan" is constantly changing, and (2) whatever the "plan" is at the moment, it often contradicts other real or declared elements of Bush's Iraq policy. The idea of "clear, hold, and build" implies that it will be Americans who stay on "until the job is done"—which appears to downplay Iraqification and renders creating a "decent interval" more difficult. As increasing instability in Iraq raises still more doubts about both U.S. pacification and Iraqification, the administration has tried yet another tack. In his September 2006 speech in Salt Lake City, the president raised the stakes (thus undermining the "decent interval" strategy).

The *New York Times*' David Sanger noted that

President Bush's newest effort to rebuild eroding support for the war in Iraq features a distinct shift in approach: Rather than stressing the benefits of eventual victory, he and his top aides are beginning to lay out the grim consequences of failure.

It is a striking change of tone for a president who prides himself on optimism and has usually maintained that demeanor, at least in public, while his aides cast critics as defeatists.

But in his speech on Thursday in Salt Lake City—the first in a series to commemorate the Sept. 11 anniversary—he picked up on an approach that Gen. John P. Abizaid, Vice President Dick Cheney and others have refined in the past few months: a warning that defeat in Iraq will only move the battle elsewhere, threatening allies in the Middle East and eventually, Mr. Bush insisted, Americans "in the streets of our own cities."

Sanger observed that this theme recalls a Vietnam-era staple:

It is reminiscent of—updated for a different war, and a different time—President Lyndon B. Johnson's adoption of the "domino theory," in which South Vietnam's fall could lead to Communism's spread through Southeast Asia and beyond. In the case of Iraq, Mr. Bush's argument boils down to a statement he quoted from General Abizaid, his top commander in the Middle East: "If we leave, they will follow us."

Readers can draw their own conclusions about the merits of the original domino theory and/or its application to Iraq. Sanger perceptively notes another implication of this shift in political approach—it contradicts the spirit and political intent of the "plan."

Missing from Mr. Bush's latest speeches, at least so far, is detail about the progress of his previous plan, the "Strategy for Victory." . . .

The Pentagon's latest report to Congress about progress on that strategy painted a mixed but largely grim picture, especially about the rise of sectarian violence and the failed effort to create an effective Iraqi police force. So why not announce a new change of strategy? A senior official said this week that the president could only talk about a change of strategy so many times, without looking as if he is constantly casting about for solutions.[69]

"What they [the public] really want to hear is a plan, and a plan that addresses the new problem, the sectarian violence," David Frum, a former speechwriter for George W. Bush, said in an interview. "It doesn't help to talk about the consequences of failure unless the public thinks some measure of success is possible. . . . For now, with a critical election looming in just 10 weeks and nervous members of his own party searching for an argument they can sell back home, he is trying to focus voters not on the high price of winning but on the harder-to-define cost of letting the dominoes fall."[70] In politics, as in war, "live by the sword, die by the sword." The fundamental problem that the vagaries of the "plan" as it has been buffeted by the realities of Iraq reveals is that when a foreign policy venture is driven by domestic politics, strategic clarity and consistency cannot be achieved, and the link between military means and political ends is severed.

Disengagement Without Withdrawal?

The debate that had started out with a focus on counterinsurgency in 2004 morphed to a discussion of Iraqification and finally centered around something approximating the "decent interval" concept of the Vietnam era. By 2006 this debate had added another dimension, and yet another Vietnam parallel: the "enclave" strategy. A newspaper columnist for the *Cincinnati Inquirer* who is a self-proclaimed "amateur military strategist" thought he detected a whiff of the old (but never implemented) proposal for maintaining a long-term U.S. military presence in Vietnam in remarks by Senator John McCain at the American Enterprise Institute (AEI) in November 2005. "As a lifelong student of American history, including our military history," wrote Nick Clooney,

> I thought I saw a glimpse of a solution from, of all places, the Vietnam War. I suggested we study closely the proposal back then of Gen. James Gavin, a World War II hero and the father of the "air cavalry" use of helicopters. Gen. Gavin wrote, and then testified before Congress, that we should employ an "enclave" policy. A few areas should be fortified as American strong points, much like the "Green Zone" in Baghdad now. There should be no American patrols or "sweeps" in country. Those duties should be left to the people who are defending and building their own nation.

The advantage of this approach, Clooney argued, was that the United States could maintain forces to discourage outsiders from meddling in Iraq's chaos, but that these troops would "be removed as a rallying point for insurgents.[71]

Senator McCain's precise views on Iraq strategy are hard to determine from his vague and often contradictory statements, but he did make a point in the AEI speech that could be interpreted as advocating a consolidation of forces and retreat into an enclave. After a trip to Iraq he said, "I'll tell you what one of my assessment was and that I've complained bitterly about, I'd like to be able to land at the airport at Baghdad, by the way, without throwing up because the airplane has to spiral down, it's a good thing I'm an old pilot, but land at the airport in Baghdad and get into an automobile and drive to the Green Zone. That's what I'd like to be able to do. That would be a sign that we are achieving some success. It sounds a little bit sarcastic, but if we're not able to do that, then clearly we're not going to be able to expand our security capabilities."[72]

Clearer evidence of the resurgence of the "enclave" strategy comes from several journalistic accounts of the role played by massive U.S. "super bases" isolated from the Iraqi population, which seem tailor-made for an enclave strategy. Although Marines are still being used for aggressive patrols in populated areas, one reporter concludes that "the Pentagon appears to be moving the overall U.S. military effort in the opposite direction across much of the country. Army units are being concentrated in 'super bases' that line the spine of central Iraq, away from the urban centers where counterinsurgency operations take place. The two approaches underscore an increasingly high-profile divergence—some say contradiction—on how best to use U.S. forces in Iraq, and are evidence of a growing debate in the upper ranks about the wisest course of action." As the authors of this article point out, this enclave strategy is complicated by competing objectives, which could be summarized as a "choice between a smaller force and an effective one. . . . 'The key to counterinsurgency is presence among the population,' [a U.S. officer] said. 'What do mass concentrations of American forces on a large base do? If we put all our troops there and they're out of sight, what has that accomplished?'"[73] Nonetheless, the "super bases" have become the most central aspect of the U.S. military presence in Iraq.

Further evidence of a move toward an enclave strategy is contained in an *Atlantic Monthly* article, evocatively titled "Hunkering Down," which revealed that U.S. generals in Iraq were requesting official records from the 1970s relating to the U.S. withdrawal from Vietnam. "The message was explicit: we're going to be staging another withdrawal soon, from Iraq; once it begins, it could spin easily out of control; so we need a plan for an orderly exit now." But Kaplan doubts that a total pullout is likely in the foreseeable future.

> The most tangible sign of these measures is the far-flung network of Forward Operating Bases, or FOBs. There are more than seventy FOBs scattered across Iraq, many of them elaborate renovations of Saddam Hussein's former network of military bases and presidential palaces. Some bases consist of just a handful of barracks, but more than a dozen of them are vast complexes reminiscent of the West German garrisons from Cold War days. . . .
>
> There's nothing provisional about these places. They're often referred to as "enduring bases," and there are plans to keep them operating, in American hands, even if all our combat regiments go home. . . . It's clear that we're getting out of Iraq, and soon, yet it's equally clear that we're staying, in a fairly big way. We are simultaneously engaged yet disengaging, hunkered down yet packing up.[74]

The fusion of the "decent interval" strategy and the enclave strategy suggests a novel variation on the Vietnam experience: disengagement without withdrawal. Of course, the consolidation into enclaves could also be a preparatory step in total extrication, but it does leave open the option of maintaining a long-term troop presence. This still leaves open fundamental questions, such as the diplomatic and political strategy the enclaved troops would support (a unified or divided Iraq?) and many questions about how many troops would be required, how much it would cost, how politically sustainable this approach would be, and how the troops would be employed in emergency or crisis situations and, most importantly, how this would affect the attitudes of people in Iraq and the Middle East toward the United States. As in Vietnam, the key decisions on these issue will be largely determined in the heat of electoral battle in the United States.

Facing Reality

Are there any significant lessons to be learned from the Iraq conflict that might be reinforced or validated by the experience of Vietnam? Perhaps the first is that we should carefully consider the ageless wisdom of the maxim of Sun Tzu in *The Art of War*: know your enemy, know yourself. To this Maxwell Taylor, once Kennedy's chief military adviser on Vietnam and then ambassador in 1964–65 added, "First, we didn't know ourselves. We thought we were going into another Korean War, but this was a different country. Secondly, we didn't know our South Vietnamese allies. We never understood them, . . . and we knew even less about North Vietnam. . . . So, until we know the enemy and know our allies and know ourselves, we'd better keep out of this dirty kind of business."[75]

With regard to the prospects for Iraqification, we might ask who our local allies are, what interests they share with us, and how probable it is that these shared interests will lead to a desirable outcome for the United States. Interviews conducted by the Rand Corporation with top South Vietnamese military officers and civilian officials after the war revealed a widespread contempt for the South Vietnamese leaders by those who served them, and the paralyzing impact of the American embrace on the nationalist credentials of those who did not want a Hanoi-dominated future.[76]

Another parallel between Vietnam and Iraq that may or may not achieve the status of a lesson is "don't re-fight the last war, but don't forget it either." In the 1980s the Army threw away its files on counterinsurgency in Vietnam as if this could eliminate the traces of an unpleasant institutional memory. Events were to prove that these historical experiences were not so easily disposed of. More recently, the Pentagon's 2006 four-year military plan relegated the still-unresolved Iraq conflict to the dustbin of history. As a newspaper subhead put it, "A four-year blueprint for the military reflects a view that the [Iraq] war is an anomaly. There's talk of robots and drones, but no force buildup."[77]

But perhaps the most important parallel is the lesson about the limitations of American power as an instrument of global transformation. It is remarkable how quickly America's humbling defeat in Vietnam was eclipsed by the triumphalism that followed the end of the Cold War and, more recently, reshaped into an imagined victory.

The idea that history can be shaped to conform with American ideals and interests has deep roots—in manifest destiny and in Wilsonianism, among other things.[78] Neal Sheehan memorably linked the confidence and World War II triumphalism with America's misadventures in Vietnam in his book *A Bright and Shining Lie*. More recently, a number of commentators have observed the characteristic confidence and optimism of President Bush that replaced the humility he had advocated in 2000. Ron Suskind's 2004 *New York Times* profile of Bush, titled "Without a Doubt," noted that "George W. Bush, clearly, is one of history's great confidence men. That is not meant in the huckster's sense, though many critics claim that on the war in Iraq, the economy and a few other matters he has engaged in some manner of bait-and-switch. No, I mean it in the sense that he's a believer in the power of confidence. At a time when constituents are uneasy and enemies are probing for weaknesses, he clearly feels that unflinching confidence has an almost mystical power. It can all but create reality." And Suskind recounted the striking denigration of the "reality-based community" by a top Bush associate.

> The aide said that guys like me were "in what we call the reality-based community," which he defined as people who "believe that solutions emerge from your judicious study of discernible reality." I nodded and murmured something about enlightenment principles and empiricism. He cut me off. "That's not the way the world really works anymore," he continued. "We're an empire now, and when we act, we create our own reality. And while you're studying that reality—judiciously, as you will—we'll act again, creating other new realities, which you can study too, and that's how things will sort out. We're history's actors . . . and you, all of you, will be left to just study what we do."[79]

This may have been the "arrogance of power" that Senator Fulbright detected in the Kennedy and Johnson administration, but the Nietzschean hubris far exceeds the Brahman self-assurance of the best and the brightest and their faith in rational analysis.

Eventually reality collided with the administration's confident portrayal of its Iraq policy. The most striking indication of this was Ambassador Khalilzad's admission that American intervention had opened a "Pandora's box" of disastrous unintended consequences. In November 2005 congressional Republicans distanced themselves from the administration, and in December 2005 advisers convinced the president that faith and optimism were not enough and that he would have to present something that had at least the appearance of a plan for success. But one of the lessons of Vietnam is that no plan, however brilliant, can survive the collapse of political support for it if it cannot be implemented. Another is that the collapse of political support is usually the consequence of a combination of factors. In Vietnam it was the collapse of the initial stated rationale and the downgrading of Vietnam's strategic importance to the United States, which had a powerful impact on the costs Americans were willing to bear to see it through. Along with the collapse of the strategic rationale came the disillusionment with the leadership that had carried us into war. The credibility gap and loss of trust in America's leaders was a sad legacy of the Vietnam War, and history seems to be repeating itself.

Intervention or Deterrence?

Despite the many parallels, there are fundamental differences between the two cases. The end of the Vietnam War did not topple dominoes, but was followed by a period of spectacular growth in Asia and, ironically, the falling-out of Communist neighbors in Indochina and the containment of Vietnam by China. By contrast, the invasion of Iraq has stirred up forces that may destabilize the most volatile region in the world, which is also the area most essential to the functioning of the world's industrial economies.

Robert Jervis long ago boiled down the experience of the twentieth century into two opposed lessons about conflict.[80] He termed World War I the spiral escalation model and World War II the deterrence model. Adam Gopnik, in a recent article on the historiography of World War I, describes it as follows:

> The last century, through its great cataclysms, offers two clear, ringing, and, unfortunately, contradictory lessons. The First World War teaches that territorial compromise is better than full-scale war, that an "honor-bound" allegiance of the great powers to small nations is a recipe for mass killing, and that it is crazy to let the blind mechanism of armies and alliances trump common sense. The Second teaches that searching for an accommodation with tyranny by selling out small nations only encourages the tyrant, that refusing to fight now leads to a worse fight later on, and that only the steadfast rejection of compromise can prevent the natural tendency to rush to a bad peace with worse men. The First teaches us never to rush into a fight, the Second never to back down from a bully.[81]

The Vietnam War was launched by believers in the deterrence model of World War II and the lessons of Munich. Ironically, the Vietnam War was later transformed into an updated version of the lessons of World War I— about escalation spiraling out of control, and unintended consequences. The architects of the Iraq invasion were all passionate believers in the Munich lesson who lived to prove that the "Vietnam syndrome" had been expunged from the American memory. But, like the best and brightest, their historical role will probably be to disinter the lesson they hoped to bury.

2

"I'm with You": Tony Blair and the Obligations of Alliance: Anglo-American Relations in Historical Perspective

ALEX DANCHEV

Utility is an impermanent thing: it changes according to circumstances. So with the disappearance of the ground for friendship, the friendship also breaks up, because that was what kept it alive. Friendships of this kind seem to occur most frequently between the elderly—and between those in middle or early life who are pursuing their own advantage. Such people do not spend much time together, because they sometimes do not even like one another, and therefore feel no need of such an association unless they are mutually useful. For they take pleasure in each other's company only insofar as they have hopes of advantage from it. Friendships with foreigners are generally included in this class.[1]

There are three kinds of friendship, Aristotle tells us: friendship based on utility, friendship based on pleasure, and friendship based on goodness. Of these three, only the last is perfect, as he says, for "it is those who desire the good of their friends for the friends' sake that are most truly friends, because each loves the other for what he is, and not for any incidental quality." In other words, the friendship is essential rather than circumstantial, dedicated rather than calculated, persistent rather than evanescent. It does not wait on time and tide, terror and tyranny, suicide attack or simmering stockpile. It rests on character, and specifically on goodness, a scarce commodity. Friendships of this kind are rare, adds Aristotle, because men of this kind are few. "And in addition they need time and intimacy; for as the saying goes, you cannot get to know each other until you have eaten the proverbial quantity of salt together. Nor can one man accept another, or the two become friends, until each has proved to the other that he is worthy of love, and so won his trust. Those who are quick to make friendly advances to each other have the desire to be friends, but they are not unless they are worthy of love and know it." To demonstrate worthiness of this sort is no easy task, individually or internationally. To maintain the conviction is even harder. "The wish for friendship develops rapidly," Aristotle concludes appositely, "but friendship does not."[2]

The "special relationship" between Britain and America is a subtle case of friendship between foreigners posited on perfection. International relations in general are not known for their goodness, nor even their disinterestedness, as Aristotle himself underlined, yet the claims made for this particular relationship are founded on virtue. Anglo-American apologetics echo Aristotelian ethics. The special relationship is an unusually self-conscious one. It creates its own myths and propagates its own legends. What is special about it is its capacity to do this—to invent and reinvent itself, to exploit its mythical potential—which may be as close as we get to its occult essence. The special relationship is a shimmering illusion lost in never-never land, marooned somewhere between a monumentalized past and a mythical fiction, to borrow Nietzsche's terms; and it continues to cast its spell.[3] More conventionally, it is a community of belief, whose celebrants dwell in high places. The stories they tell each other to sustain that belief are of consuming interest.

One such story was told by Tony Blair to Bill Clinton, his first best friend, at a White House dinner in February 1998. It was framed by Blair as a story of "those great days of America and Britain standing together" in the Second World War. It turns on a fact-finding visit to Britain by Harry Hopkins, FDR's eyes and ears, in January 1941. The outcome of this visit would be critical in determining the president's assessment of Britain's chances of survival and the attitude he would take toward its buccaneer prime minister, as Winston Churchill well understood. The climax is reached at a farewell dinner—taking salt together is a rich seam of the tradition. As Blair recounted it:

> On the last evening before he left to take home a message to America he gave a speech to the dinner and sitting next to Churchill he said: "I suppose you wish to know what I am going to say to President Roosevelt on my return." And then Harry Hopkins said he would be quoting a verse from the Bible: "Whither thou goest, I will go, and whither thou lodgest, I will lodge. Thy people shall be my people and thy God my God." And Hopkins paused and then he said: "Even to the end." And Churchill wept.[4]

And Clinton in his turn wept, as Blair surely intended. (The tearjerker is also part of the tradition. Milking emotion is one of the prerequisites of the special relationship.) Their weeping was incommensurable—if Churchill had nothing to offer but blood, toil, tears, and sweat, Clinton had merely the toil of the Monica Lewinsky scandal—but the point was made. For the British, standing together is a kind of shibboleth. It is a proof of loyalty and of dependability. Fifty years ago Oliver Franks observed wisely: "In the Anglo-American relationship British policy has to pass the test: can the British deliver?"[5] The obligations of alliance are acutely felt by the weak.

In the beginning was the antifascist annunciation. The tale of Harry Hopkins is a moral tale. It tells of a good war, a war of indubitable legitimacy, that is the fount and origin of Anglo-American self-regard and raison d'être. It is told, and retold, for a purpose. Rigorous analysis of the grounds for a special relationship has always been too difficult. Adepts have opted instead to testify, like evangelicals. Ever since 1941 the relationship has led a double life: on one hand, a hole-and-corner affair, secret and taboo, regularly disavowed; on the other, backslapping bonhomie, brazen self-promotion, razzmatazz, showtime! In brief, private observance and public performance. For prime ministers and presidents, public performance would not be complete without the evangelical set-piece—the speech—a cocktail of primitive faith and popular history, emotionally charged, full of solemn incantation, shameless glorification, and ritual invocation of the household god Winston. "There is a union of mind and purpose between our peoples which is remarkable and which makes our relationship truly a special one. I am often asked if it is special, and why, and I say: 'It is special. It just is and that is that!'" Thus Margaret Thatcher, in characteristic vein, addressing the rubicund Ronald Reagan at the British embassy in Washington in 1985. In all this testifying, a sort of rhetorical equiprobability has been smuggled in. Specialness is goodness. Goodness is specialness. Good men (and good women) make good wars. Being good is doing good, together. "As Winston once said," Thatcher went on proprietorially, as if they were personally acquainted, "'The experience of a long life and the promptings of my blood have wrought in me the conviction that there is nothing more important for the future of the world than the fraternal association of our two peoples in righteous work, both in war and peace!' No one could put it better than that."[6]

Tony Blair is a devil for righteous work. "We are the ally of the US not because they are powerful, but because we share their values," he admonished a gathering of British ambassadors in January 2003. "I am not surprised by anti-Americanism," he continued snappishly, "but it is a foolish indulgence. For all their faults, and all nations have them, the US are a force for good; they have liberal and democratic traditions of which any nation can be proud." On this argument, utility is subsumed in goodness. "Quite apart from that, it is massively in our self-interest to remain close allies." Pleasure is off, apparently, unless it is a certain uppishness. "Bluntly there are not many countries who wouldn't wish for the same relationship as we have with the US, and that includes most of the ones critical of it in public."[7] Stephen Potter, the original satirist of Hands-Across-the-Seamanship, should be living at this hour. "It is not our policy continuously to try to be one-up, as a nation, on other nations; but it is our aim to rub in the fact that we are not trying to do this, otherwise what is the point of not trying to do this?"[8]

No European leader of his generation speaks so unblushingly of good and evil. "A force for good" is quintessential Blair, and something of a Blairite mantra. If the United States is a force for good, Washington is worthy of love. For the prime minister, this means making a conquest of the tenant of the White House, whoever that may be. In love and Anglo-American relations, reciprocity is the key. Britain too is a force for good, naturally, and also the British Army.[9] This is goodness militant. Tony is a true believer in the mission of the moment. Blazing sincerity is integral to his self-image, or self-construction. Like his folksy friend George (his next best friend), with whom he often looks so uncomfortable, he advertises himself as "a pretty straight sort of guy." He speaks with seeming frankness: *frank-seeming* is his métier, as the writer Alan Bennett has remarked: "That Tony Blair . . . will often say 'I honestly believe' rather than just 'I believe' says all that needs to be said." *Time* magazine's correspondent at the Hutton Inquiry made a similar observation: "In two and a half hours of apparently frank testimony—always thoughtful and reasoned, passionate when passion was called for—Blair gave a masterful performance."[10]

Articulacy he can do—"his brilliantly articulate impersonation of earnest inarticulacy." Authenticity is another matter.[11] A dash of missionary zeal, meanwhile, is all part of the service. "I feel a most urgent sense of mission about today's world," he told Congress in July 2003. "September 11th was not an isolated event, but a tragic prologue. Iraq, another act; and many further struggles will be set upon this stage before it's over."[12]

Doing good in the world is for Blair an ethical imperative and a practical necessity. At the George H.W. Bush Presidential Library in April 2002—when Iraq was still only a gleam in the eye—he set out his stall in front of "41" for the benefit of "43," in language the latter could understand:

> The only purpose of being in politics is to strive for the values and ideals we believe in: freedom, justice, what we Europeans call solidarity but you might call respect for and help for others. These are the decent democratic values we all avow. But alongside the values we know we need a hard-headed pragmatism—a realpolitik—required to give us any chance of translating those values into the practical world we live in. The same tension exists in the two views of international affairs. One is utilitarian: each nation maximises its own self-interest. The other is utopian: we try to create a better world. Today I want to suggest that more than ever before those two views are merging.
>
> I advocate an enlightened self-interest that puts fighting for our values right at the heart of the politics necessary to protect our nations. Engagement in the world on the basis of these values, not isolation from it, is the hard-headed pragmatism for the 21st century. . . .

If necessary the action should be military, and again, if necessary and justified, it should involve regime change. I have been involved as British Prime Minister in three conflicts involving regime change. Milosevic. The Taliban. And Sierra Leone, where a country of six million people was saved from a murderous group of gangsters who had hijacked the democratically elected government.[13]

The emphasis is interesting. One of Blair's deepest concerns is said to be untutored unilateralism, to coin a phrase, and its baleful consequences. He told the journalist Peter Stothard, who shadowed his every move for the fateful month of March 2003, that if he was not there side by side with the president he feared America would rush in, topple Saddam, and rush out again, careless of the stability of the country it left behind. The same theme is threaded through his speeches. "Prevention is better than cure," he argued beforehand. "The reason it would be crazy for us to clear out of Afghanistan once we had finished militarily is that if it drifts back into instability, the same old problems will re-emerge. Stick at it and we can show, eventually, as in the Balkans, the unstable starts to become stable." In sub-Churchillian mode, after the fact: "Finishing the fighting is not finishing the job." Most succinctly, six months on: "We who started the war must finish the peace."[14]

But there would be no more loose talk of regime change, not from this quarter. That was ruled out of order by the attorney general (Lord Goldsmith). The infamous Downing Street memorandum of a meeting of the prime minister's inner circle in July 2002 reveals among other things the attorney general's pithy advice "that the desire for regime change was not a legal basis for military action."[15] Oratorically, the prime minister fell into line. Clandestinely, he continued on his chosen course. Iraq, too, was sold as a good war, but it was precisely the selling, or the mis-selling, that gave it a bad name. It was in fact a war of the worst kind, a war of false pretenses; manufactured, as one might say, and of doubtful legality. Tony Blair was a party to the intrigue that brought it about. This was a war made in Washington, to be sure, and yet to all intents and purposes it was an Anglo-American intrigue—a sniff of the old exclusivity. Blair fulfilled the time-honored role of accomplice-in-chief.

In essence, he connived at a deception. The nature of the deception emerges with chilling clarity in the Downing Street memorandum, ironically, in a contribution from "C," the chief of the Secret Intelligence Service (Sir Richard Dearlove), recently returned from talks with the cousins: "Military action was now seen as inevitable. Bush wanted to remove Saddam, through military action, justified by the conjunction of terrorism and WMD. But *the intelligence and facts were being fixed around the policy*."[16] This last formulation (a neat one) was subsequently corroborated by the president himself in another leaked memorandum, of a tête-à-tête at the White House in January 2003, when he coolly informed the prime minister that "the dip-lomatic strategy had to be arranged around the military planning."[17]

At both of these meetings, the internal British one in July 2002 and the Anglo-American one in January 2003, the explicit assumption was that the United Kingdom would take part in any military action. British spear-carriers were not strictly necessary, as the secretary of defense made unpalat-ably plain at the time ("there are workarounds"), but Washington needed a fig leaf of legitimacy for this fight.[18] London supplied it. That was its function. Churchill once said that all he expected was compliance with his wishes after reasonable discussion. Much the same is true of Washington and the special relationship. Compliance is expected; enthusiasm is supererogatory. The British prime minister, "that simpering little whore" in the immortal words of Hunter S. Thompson, is not exactly a harlot; British troops are not exactly mercenaries.[19] But the Hessian option was more nearly a reality in Iraq than in Vietnam. Whether or not the British Army is a force for good, it is a stake in the game. The stake bought a say, of a sort. It bought access—face time—and kudos, at least in some circles. These are the traditional marks of favor in the relationship. Under the present imperium they are in short supply. Twice blessed, Tony Blair strutted on the world stage in the role of cheerleader and whipper-in. The memorandum of the second meet-ing records his fealty: he declared himself "solidly with the President and ready to do whatever it took to disarm Saddam."[20]

When it came to military action, Blair had form. He was proud of that, as his speechifying indicated.[21] He had also learned some lessons—he thought—on how to manage Anglo-American relations, in particular the delicate business of being best friend. Tony Blair is now firmly ensconced in the public mind as the president's poodle. (In the British public mind, that is, and more weakly in the international one; in the United States he has not yet lost his sheen. In this as in other respects, there is a parallel with Marga-ret Thatcher.) He himself has been conscious of the "poodle factor" from the outset. "If [terrorism] is the threat of the 21st century, Britain should be in there helping to confront it," ran one apologia, "not because we are America's poodle, but because dealing with it will make Britain safer." He put a somewhat more sophisticated argument to the assemblage of ambassadors:

> The price of British influence is not, as some would have it, that we have, obediently, to do what the US asks. I would never commit British troops to a war I thought was wrong or unnecessary. Where we disagree, as over Kyoto, we disagree. But the price of influence is that we do not leave the US to face the tricky issues alone. By tricky, I mean the ones which people wish weren't there, don't want to deal with, and, if I can put it pejoratively, know the US should confront, but want the luxury of criticizing them for it. So if the US act alone, they are unilateralist; but if they want allies, people shuffle to the back.[22]

Disobedience, however, is not his forte. ("We keep waiting for his *Love Actually* moment," lamented one of his ministerial colleagues, "and it never comes.")[23] Even before 9/11, perceptive observers noted his chronic lack of leverage, together with his promiscuous warmth, his serial devotion, his eager demeanor, his reluctance to challenge, even in private, and drew the inevitable conclusion about a relationship less special than spaniel. "In Washington today," wrote the distinguished commentator Hugo Young in February 2001, "Tony Blair will do what history tells him. It isn't possible to imagine him doing anything else. He will shake George Bush by the hand, and set about getting as close to him as a weekend in Camp David permits." "Some day soon," he added a year later, "Washington will eat him for breakfast, along with the morality it then spits out." By September 2003, in his last, coruscating column, Young was measuring the tragedy of Tony Blair— trust evaporated, credibility vanished—and pondering bleakly "our country and what becomes of it in abject thrall to Bush and his gang."[24] Others, equally perceptive, and if anything even more vituperative on the subject of Bush and his gang, conceive of Blair as a minstrel for the American cause, in John le Carré's sardonic phrase: not so much a poodle, more a seeing-eye dog. "Your little Prime Minister is not the American President's *poodle*, he is his *blind dog*, I hear," jeers one of the characters in le Carré's tract for the times, *Absolute Friends*.[25] Lap dog or guide dog, the canine analogy may be more complex than it first appears, but the power relationship it proposes is as apt as it is unambiguous.

The guide dog barked in 1999. Blair boldly went to the Economic Club of Chicago, the citadel of isolationism, to deliver a speech entitled "Doctrine of the International Community." It was an important speech on an important subject. At the heart of it was the conundrum of humanitarian intervention. "The most pressing foreign policy problem we face is to identify the circumstances in which we should get actively involved in other people's conflicts." He offered five considerations:

First, are we sure of our case? War is an imperfect instrument for righting humanitarian distress; but armed force is sometimes the only means of dealing with dictators.

Second, have we exhausted all diplomatic options? We should always give peace every chance, as we have in the case of Kosovo.

Third, on the basis of a practical assessment of the situation, are there military operations we can sensibly and prudently undertake?

Fourth, are we prepared for the long term? In the past we talked too much of exit strategies. But having made a commitment we cannot simply walk away once the fight is over; better to stay with moderate numbers of troops than return for a repeat performance with large numbers.

And finally, do we have national interests involved? The mass expulsions of ethnic Albanians from Kosovo demanded the notice of the rest of the world. But it does make a difference that this is taking place in such a combustible part of Europe.[26]

The bones of Blair's argument had been provided on request by Law-rence Freedman, professor of war studies at King's College, London, one of a small coterie invited to covert coffee mornings on international affairs to help Blair prepare for government.[27] Given two days to work it out, Freed-man turned for inspiration to a previous effort to codify the conditions un-der which the use of military force might be warranted: the so-called Weinberger Doctrine (1984).

> The United States should not commit forces to combat overseas unless the particu-lar engagement or occasion is deemed vital to our national interest or that of our allies. . . .
>
> If we decide it is necessary to put combat troops into a given situation, we should do so wholeheartedly and with the clear intention of winning. . . .
>
> If we do decide to commit forces to combat overseas, we should have clearly de-fined political and military objectives. . . .
>
> The relationship between our objectives and the forces we have committed—their size, composition, and disposition—must be continually reassessed and adjusted if necessary. . . .
>
> Before the United States commits combat forces abroad, there must be some reasonable assurance we will have the support of the American people and their elected representatives in Congress. . . .
>
> The commitment of US forces to combat should be a last resort.[28]

The Weinberger Doctrine was precipitated by a disastrous U.S. peace-keeping mission in Lebanon, a bloody failure capped by a humiliating re-treat, well remembered by Osama bin Laden.[29] More fundamentally, it embodied the consolidated lessons of the Vietnam War. As a template for decision makers, it was designed to avert either fate—debacle or quagmire. The subtext of the Weinberger Doctrine was "never again."

Given the course of events in Iraq, it is richly ironic that Tony Blair's guidance on the good intervention owed something to American determi-nation on no more Vietnams. Not the least of the ironies concerns the vexed question of exit strategy. Blair's public pronouncements tended to give the impression that he considered talk of exit strategy so much hot air—prevarication or (worse) pusillanimity on Washington's part. Another por-tion of the Chicago speech, addressed specifically to Anglo-American resolve over Kosovo, contained this grandiloquent sound bite: "Success is the only exit strategy I am prepared to consider." This might possibly find an echo in Bushite absolutism on winning the war on terror, but Clinton and his people were not amused. Official Washington is impatient with exhorta-tion. An undercurrent of mockery crept in. The president's henchmen be-gan to refer to Blair as "Winston." The deputy secretary of state, Strobe Talbott, was heard to say privately that Winston was "ready to fight to the last American."[30]

Blair told one intimate that Kosovo could be his Suez. The ghost of Suez (1956) haunts British decision makers, even those too young to remember it.[31] (Tony Blair was three.) Suez was traumatic: the special relationship was unhallowed, the prime minister (Anthony Eden) undone, the job unfinished. The lesson drawn by military men savored of the inquest on Vietnam. "What Suez lacked was coherent ministerial resolve," reflected the chief of the Defence Staff at the time of the Falklands War (1982). "There were too many changes of mind, and changes of course, whereas I think the background to success of the Falklands was that we set our objective, and we stuck to it, absolutely, throughout."[32] As for the politicians, the lesson drawn by Margaret Thatcher is a representative one. "We should never again find ourselves on the opposite side to the United States in a major international crisis affecting Britain's interests."[33] In plain language, never go to war without the Americans, an injunction very nearly flouted by Thatcher herself over the Falklands. In that little war the U.S. secretary of state, Alexander Haig, tried rather desperately to mediate, but even as he shuttled vainly between London and Buenos Aires he was clear that, whatever attitude the Americans took toward British belligerence, they would not repeat Suez, as they put it. "By which they meant they would not pillory us, even if they did not agree with us," Sir Nicholas Henderson has explained. "They would not put us in the dock, as they had done in 1956 over Suez, and bring us to our knees." In other words, they would not let their ally down. They might be equivocal, but they could not be impartial. They would do their bit. Notwithstanding the naysayers, they did.[34] The obligations of alliance are occasionally felt by the strong.

Blair came of age politically in the Falklands War. He was first selected as a candidate in a parliamentary by-election in 1982, at the very moment of decision. He supported the dispatch of the task force, with reservations. "At the same time I want a negotiated settlement and I believe that given the starkness of the military option we need to compromise on certain things. I don't think that ultimately the wishes of the Falkland Islanders must determine our position."[35] For all the idealism, the moralism, and the evangelism, there has always been a strong dose of pragmatism in Tony Blair. As prime minister, he often seemed to combine a Gladstonian impulse with a Palmerstonian itch—savior of a fallen world, with a gunboat. Ideologically, he travels light. What matters is what works, as he is fond of saying. "What works" is another Blairite mantra. On the Falklands, he was by no means alone in fearing that the military option might not work. On Iraq, twenty years later, a similar consideration applied. At the Downing Street meeting in July 2002, with his trusted advisers around him, he was most insistent. "If the political context were right, people would support regime change. The two key issues were whether the military plan worked and whether we had the political strategy to give the military plan the space to work."[36]

Evidently the idea was to develop the political strategy in concert with

Washington. The special relationship is a cardinal belief, in Blair's words, but it is also a political project, a feature of pragmatism for the twenty-first century. Utility rears its ugly head. The ardent pursuit of specialness had a party political rationale. For Tony Blair, the messiah of New Labour, tightness with a Republican president and a Republican administration would effectively neutralize the Conservative opposition. Labour, adept and ambidextrous, could work with Democrats and Republicans alike; even the neocons had no need of the Cons. The nub of the work was national security. New Labour, unlike old Labour, could be trusted with the defense of the realm. Another plank of the opposition platform had collapsed. The Conservatives supported the Iraq War—they could find no way to oppose it—but their support was redundant. In fact, their redundancy was all but complete. They had been outflanked, or blindsided, and they knew it. They were reduced to internecine impotence. The project of specialness through adhesiveness had done its worst. As formulated by the prime minister's foreign policy adviser, David Manning, "At the best of times, Britain's influence on the US is limited. But the only way we exercise that influence is by attaching ourselves firmly to them and avoiding public criticism wherever possible."[37] At home, the limpet strategy was a calculating power play.[38] In electoral terms it was a consummate success. Blair or Bliar, new or shopsoiled, Labour won three straight general election victories, in 1997, 2001, and 2005, an unprecedented feat.

Home and abroad are intertwined. In Anglo-American relations a friend in need is a friend in political difficulty. Asking for help in these circumstances is allowed and understood. So is an element of gamesmanship. Playing on domestic political difficulties is part of the repertoire. According to the well-informed Bob Woodward, Blair asked Bush for help during their tête-à-tête in January 2003. The pitch was that a second UN resolution was for him an absolute political necessity. "Blair said he needed the favor. Please." Bush heard, in his fashion. He called it "the famous second resolution meeting."[39] He tried, up to a point. It did not happen. Politically, however, extra-specially, as one might say, it was perhaps the conspicuous effort that was needed as much as the resolution itself.

For it is also a question of pragmatism in the world. Blair recapped for the documentary filmmaker Michael Cockerell: "The reason why we are with America in so many of these issues is because it is in our interests. We do think the same, we do feel the same, and we have the same—I think—sense of belief that if there is a problem you've got to act on it."[40] Anglo-America is the sphere of clarity and action; Europe, turgidity and vexation. The White House has the capacity and the will—and latterly the faith. "We're history's actors," one of Bush's senior advisors memorably said to the journalist Ron Suskind, "and you, all of you, will be left just to study what we do."[41] But not Tony Blair. Blair the renegade from the reality-based community, Blair the interloper with the patter and the air-portable brigades,

Blair the biddable best friend, would be in on the act. Tony was "our guy." He talked the talk and walked the walk. He had *cojones*, the president announced; he was someone "who does not need a focus group to convince him of the difference between right and wrong."[42] The others—Jacques, Gerhard, even Vladimir—had their own issues to deal with. Tiger shooting was not their cup of tea.[43]

Blair was committed. Commitment, he argues, is the crux of the matter. Michael Cockerell asked him if the special relationship depends in part on whether the British are prepared to send troops, "to commit themselves, to pay the blood price." He replied, unhesitatingly, "Yes. What is important though is that at moments of crisis they [the Americans] don't need to know simply that you are giving general expressions of support and sympathy. That is easy, frankly. They need to know, are you prepared to commit, to be there when the shooting starts?"[44] On this analysis the special relationship is a sanguinary affair. The price of influence, as Tony Blair would have it, must be paid in blood. The influence gained is wholly imponderable—under Blair, minimal—but an acceptable contribution is something akin to a promise of consideration. The corollary is simple. No contribution: no consideration.

This is an old lesson in Anglo-American relations. It was pressed on Tony Blair's Labour predecessor Clement Attlee (his polar opposite in stance and style) by the magisterial Oliver Franks, British ambassador in Washington, at the outbreak of the Korean War in 1950. The question arose of a British military contribution, in particular, a token ground force. Franks took it upon himself to write a personal letter to the prime minister. The burden of his argument was twofold. First, "the initial British reaction to any major question is the most important from the American point of view." If the initial reaction appeared negative, or merely consultative, "then we are 'against it' no matter what happens afterwards. The reverse applies." Second, "the Americans will to some extent—I know this to be true of the Defense Department—test the quality of the partnership by our attitude to the notion of a token ground force." This token, therefore, was a token of commitment, and also a token of friendship. Franks disclaimed any attempt to suggest what the outcome should be: the implication was clear enough. That course of action did not commend itself to London. But Attlee himself was convinced. He put it to his colleagues that they could not expect to maintain a special relationship purely on the strength of wise counsel. Disinterested advice was inappropriate. Sympathy was not enough. The chiefs of staff swallowed their scruples and decided to send a brigade group of British troops to fight alongside the Americans. Nothing less would do. The cabinet endorsed the decision as "a valuable contribution to Anglo-American solidarity." The argument advanced by Oliver Franks carried the day.[45]

It was a lesson well learned.[46] And yet, the next Labour prime minister appeared quite deliberately to unlearn it. Throughout the Vietnam War,

Harold Wilson steadfastly (or serpentinely) refused to make any contribution of that sort, resisting all blandishment and intimidation—resisting even the formidable, almost physical persuasive power of the president, Lyndon Johnson. Wilson was not short of suggestions for a token ground force. When he offered to fly to Washington for talks in 1965, fearing further escalation, Johnson told him to mind his own business. "I won't tell you how to run Malaysia and you don't tell us how to run Vietnam," adding that Britain should "send us some folks to deal with these guerrillas." When Wilson brought up Attlee's talks with Truman on Korea (in 1950), Johnson pointed out that Britain had troops in Korea but not in Vietnam.[47] "A platoon of bagpipers would be sufficient," the president informed him when they met the following year, "it was the British flag that was needed." As the secretary of state, Dean Rusk, put it to the British journalist Louis Heren in 1968, "All we needed was one regiment. The Black Watch would have done. Just one regiment, but you wouldn't. Well, don't expect us to save you again. They [the Russians] can invade Sussex, and we wouldn't do a damned thing about it."[48]

Johnson did not like to be denied. He was resentful. Wilson started low in his estimation and sank lower. The U.S. ambassador to London, David Bruce, confided to his diary the president's "antipathy" for the prime minister.[49] Barely concealed contempt might be nearer the mark. There was something of the weasel about Wilson, he thought, weasel words, weasel gestures. On another occasion when London asked for a meeting, the president's response was well-nigh unprintable. "We got enough pollution around here already without Harold coming over with his fly open and his pecker hanging out, peeing all over me." When they talked, the obligations of alliance hung heavy between them. Without soldiers in the field, Britain was "willing to share advice but not responsibility," Johnson reminded him, as if to anticipate Tony Blair.[50] Nevertheless, LBJ forbore trying to take advantage of the chronic weakness of sterling to strong-arm Wilson into a deal—dollars for troops, or less crudely, loans to support the pound in exchange for a token ground force, a move advocated by the national security adviser, McGeorge Bundy, who considered that "it makes no sense for us to rescue the pound in a situation in which there is no British flag in Vietnam," and advised the president to indicate directly that "a British brigade in Vietnam would be worth a billion dollars at the moment of truth for sterling."[51]

Johnson's patience was sorely tried. Wilson had the irritating habit of presenting himself as a restraining influence on the United States, another traditional Anglo-aspiration. In June 1966 the British government publicly dissociated itself from the bombing of gasoline, oil, and lubricant installations in Hanoi and Haiphong. Tricked out in parliamentary language, "dissociation" looked uncommonly like posturing (and propitiating the Labour left wing). To Washington this was nothing other than a craven case of shuffling to the back. It rankled. McGeorge Bundy's successor, Walt Rostow, inveighed against "an attitude of mind which, in effect, prefers that we take losses in the free world rather than the risks of sharp confrontation."[52] The prime minister almost had to beg for an audience with the president, but he was permitted to indulge his penchant for peacemaking. Over the winter of 1966–67 he was given a long enough leash to involve himself in a series of diplomatic initiatives with Moscow, in the person of the Soviet premier Alexei Kosygin, only to find the rug pulled from under him by a combination of inattention, exasperation, and suspicion on the part of the White House. Harold Wilson was apt to claim a privileged position and a special insight into both superpowers—the dream of Britain as moderator exercises a continuing fascination—but one of the many difficulties of his situation was that, if anything, the claim had more justification with Moscow than with Washington. When he floated the idea of a mission to Hanoi, an idea that emerged during his talks with Kosygin, it was time to call a halt to Harold's incontinent freelancing. The draft reply prepared for the secretary of state ran as follows: "Thank you, we are grateful for your steadfastness, persistence, skills, etc., etc., in talks thus far. Believe, in light of our various private ongoing efforts such a trip would be counter-productive at this time. Will keep in close touch. Thanks again, etc., blah blah blah."[53]

On the face of it there is a stark contrast between the limpet strategy adopted by Tony Blair and the jellyfish strategy adopted by Harold Wilson. In November 1967 the foreign secretary, George Brown, recommended to the cabinet the continuation of "our present policy of committed detachment." He concluded: "Uncritical alignment behind the Americans would be an act of folly."[54] Under the Blair regime such a sentiment would have been unthinkable, or at any rate unspeakable, for any holder of high office. "Committed detachment" was for Blair and his cohorts not merely oxymoronic but obviously moronic. Cabinet ministers were powerless to object. The cabinet as a collectivity was supine. In March 2002 the prime minister gave them their instructions: "I tell you that we must steer close to America. If we don't we will lose our influence to shape what they do."[55]

Wilson certainly demonstrated the impossibility of a relationship at the same time close and arm's length.[56] His only commitment was detachment. Exactly when and how Blair committed himself to Bush is unknown, and perhaps unknowable in terms of time and date and precise wording, but the most striking thing about his modus operandi is the care he took to reassure the president of his good intentions.[57] The dominant motif of his most private protestations in the long lead-in to the Iraq War is the reiterated pledge "I'm with you." He so averred in a personal letter to the president in July 2002; at the "cojones meeting" in September 2002; and, repeatedly, during a decisive telephone conversation in March 2003, in which Bush gave him a chance to opt out—if it would avert the fall of his government—and Blair declined, with a little touch of Harry in the night. "Thank you. I appreciate that. It's good of you to say that. But I'm there to the very end."[58]

Wilson offered Johnson no such reassurance. The reverse applies, as

Oliver Franks might have said. Johnson must have felt that he could well do without him. But he would surely have appreciated that brigade.

Beyond the protestations of faithfulness, however, there is a curious affinity of fate. Both Blair and Wilson ran their own show. Both focused their attention on the president. The relationship between prime minister and president is a combustible one. It is as high-maintenance as it is high-risk. Closed doors and personal diplomacy are prone to arouse suspicion. George Brown suspected Wilson of doing a deal with Johnson behind his back. Did Tony Blair's senior colleagues feel similarly? They have been careful to cover their tracks, but among the defense secretary's contributions to the Downing Street cabal of July 2002 is the remark that "if the Prime Minister wanted UK military involvement [in Iraq], he would need to decide this early." The decision was Blair's, certainly, but they were all in it together. In the circumstances, one might have expected a more plural construction (*we* rather than *he*), and even a degree of encouragement. Was there perhaps an element of distancing here?[59]

Covering his tracks never held much appeal for George Brown. Barbara Castle recorded his tirade in her diary:

> "God knows what he [Wilson] has said to him [Johnson]. Back in 1964 he stopped me going to Washington. He went himself. What did he pledge? I don't know: that we wouldn't devalue, and full support in the Far East. Both those have got to go. We've got to turn down their money and pull out the troops: all of them. I don't want them out of Germany. I want them out of East of Suez. This is the decision we have got to make: break the commitment to America. You are left-wing and I am supposed to be right-wing, but I've been sickened by what we have had to do to defend America— what I've had to say at the dispatch box." "Vietnam?" "Yes, Vietnam, too. And I know what he'll say this time: let's get over this again, then he'll go to Washington and cook up some screwy little deal."[60]

Wilson did no deal, yet he was deeply compromised by Vietnam. He acquired a reputation for deviousness unparalleled in British politics. He stood accused of an unsavory mix of duplicity, complicity, and mendacity. He had been cast as an apologist for a calamitous American war; he appeared now to have become an apologist for himself. There was a strong sense of hopes betrayed. Disenchantment set in, and even a certain distaste.[61] So much had been expected of Harold Wilson. It was a shame, according to some. Others felt differently. From their perspective it was worse than a shame. It was a disgrace.

If such an accounting exaggerates the wickedness of Harold Wilson, it describes no political career so well as that of Tony Blair. In an almost poetic sense, Iraq is Blair's Vietnam. Scheherazade-like, the folly continues to unfold. For Iraq the end is not yet in sight. For Tony Blair it has already arrived.

3

Forlorn Superpower: European Reactions to the American Wars in Vietnam and Iraq

WILFRIED MAUSBACH

Temperatures were near freezing when I stepped out of the Alexanderplatz subway station on February 15, 2003. Among the vast crowd that instantly engulfed me, however, nobody was paying much attention to the wind and sleet. Half a million people had turned out in Berlin that Saturday to join millions more in Amsterdam, Barcelona, Cologne, London, Madrid, Paris, Rome, and scores of other European cities to voice their opposition to U.S. president George W. Bush's apparent determination to go to war with Saddam Hussein's Iraq. Pouring past the dilapidated hulk of the Palast der Republik, once home to Communist East Germany's parliament, and onto the magnificent Unter den Linden boulevard, the marchers slogged toward the Brandenburg Gate, for decades the epitome of the Cold War divide between East and West, where signs in English, French, German, and Russian had warned "You are now leaving the American sector," that is, the free world. Not far from the Brandenburg Gate, a small side street intersects with Unter den Linden. The spot where the U.S. embassy has set up its provisional quarters, Neustädtische Kirchstrasse has been sealed off and fortified ever since the attacks on the World Trade Center and the Pentagon on September 11, 2001. Glancing at the street entrance, I noticed that someone had attached a familiar-looking placard to the police railings. In English, French, German, and Russian it read, "You are now leaving the civilized sector."

Almost to the day thirty-seven years earlier, West Berlin saw its first noteworthy demonstration against American foreign policy. On February 5, 1966, about 2,500 mostly young people peacefully marched to protest American actions in Vietnam. Afterward a few dozen of them assembled in front of the Amerikahaus, the cultural center operated by the United States Information Agency. Members of the Socialist German Students League (Sozialistischer Deutscher Studentenbund, or SDS) threw nine raw eggs at the center's façade. When they tried to pull down the Stars and Stripes, however, other protesters intervened and some minor tugging ensued before the American flag—obviously to everyone's content—came to a standstill at half-mast.

The incident created an uproar in the West Berlin press. Willy Brandt, then governing mayor of West Berlin, sent a letter of apology to the U.S. city commandant, and the federal government in Bonn promptly released a statement of displeasure and disapproval. The episode set students and authorities on a course of confrontation that plunged the country into a state of unrest for the remainder of a turbulent decade, culminating in a wave of domestic terrorism that kept police and intelligence services occupied for a quarter century. At the same time, the American war in Vietnam provided the major catalyst and principal common denominator for a global youth revolt that transformed the world and bequeathed continuing cultural cleavages to subsequent generations.

Compared to these tectonic tremors, the sea of marchers filling the streets in Berlin in 2003, joined by millions of protesters in hundreds of cities across Europe and around the world, seem to have hardly caused a ripple four years on. Yet the ominous placard at the entrance to the U.S. embassy in Berlin is emblematic of a new and potentially powerful sentiment largely absent from the protests of the 1960s. Europeans harbor a renewed urge, not solely caused but certainly abetted by the war in Iraq, to define themselves against the United States. America appears as a convenient "other" against which Europe can develop a clearly circumscribed image of itself. If this partly subterranean trend is about to gain strength, the Stars and Stripes might be taken down all the way in Europe after all.

Different Worlds

A comparison of European reactions to the American wars in Vietnam and Iraq cannot help but start by enumerating some of the fundamentally different circumstances that prevail in the first decade of the twenty-first century in contrast to the 1960s. Back then, Europe was held to be both the locus and the focus of the Western alliance's confrontation with the Soviet Union. While the United States' nuclear umbrella and forward deployments guaranteed the freedom and security of Western European nations, the latter's tanks and troops, economic resources, and diplomatic support in turn secured a precious if sometimes precarious global preponderance of power for their American protector. With the collapse of Communism in the early 1990s, Europe has ceased to be a prime strategic concern for the United States. At the same time, Europeans feel no longer dependent on Washington for their security. Consequently, America's focus has shifted away from Europe, while Europe's focus has shifted inward.[1] The challenge to overcome the division of the continent without jeopardizing the successful integration begun by its western part during the Cold War impelled the European

Union to admit ever more countries, while at the same time proceeding on the path to a more perfect union. The inevitable frictions between enlargement and consolidation contributed to an increasingly checkered outlook on the world beyond Europe, including transatlantic relations. Meanwhile, the Republican revolution of 1994, carrying with it the bitter divisions of Vietnam and the cultural wars of the 1960s and 1970s, fractured the bipartisan consensus that had characterized American foreign policy throughout the Cold War. With the ascendance of Republicans to the White House and executive branch in 2001 and the simultaneous negotiations to expand the European Union from fifteen to twenty-five member states, then, the nascent twenty-first century witnessed not only a transformed international order but also elites on both sides of the Atlantic breaking away from the moorings of a time-honored alliance.

Profound changes have occurred, however, not only on the playing fields for diplomats but also on those for dissenters. Copiers, fax machines, and above all the Internet have revolutionized the logistics of protest. Todd Gitlin, a longtime liberal activist and leading figure of the Students for a Democratic Society—the American SDS—back in the 1960s, pointed out that recent antiwar activists have managed to multiply the size of protests twentyfold in six months, whereas it took the anti–Vietnam War movement four and a half years to accomplish the same feat.[2] European organizers were indeed stunned by the number of marchers that turned out on that first coordinated day of protest against the Bush administration's Iraq policy. On the other hand, it seems that today's protests are apt to evaporate as quickly as they evolve. Cable news and online magazines are of a much more fleeting nature than the nightly news and venerable papers of the 1960s, impeding activists' efforts to build on individual events, no matter how impressive. Interestingly, there has not been a single large-scale demonstration in Europe against American policies toward Iraq since February 15, 2003.

This leads us to a final and often forgotten yet significant difference between European protests against the wars in Vietnam and in Iraq. In the latter case, Europeans were protesting a war that had not yet begun. Unlike Lyndon B. Johnson, who did not have to worry about a United Nations organization defunct because of the Cold War stalemate and who, consequently, did not bother to announce to the world his intention to send Marines ashore at Danang in March 1965, George W. Bush, prodded by his secretary of state, Colin Powell, finally decided to take his case to the UN, all the while proceeding with a buildup of forces in the Persian Gulf that seemed to reveal his determination to go to war anyway. The dense drama unfolding on the banks of New York's East River in the span of a few weeks in early 2003, followed by a heavy dose of "shock and awe," stands in stark contrast, at any rate, to the Johnson administration's gradual escalation that steadily led the United States into a quagmire in Vietnam. During the 1960s and early 1970s, therefore, antiwar activists in Europe as well as the United

States engaged in prolonged protests to end a war that seemed to go on forever, whereas in 2003, Europeans mounted a one-time concerted effort to stop a war from happening in the first place. That having failed, demonstrators returned to their everyday routines. Be it out of fatigue and frustration or because the daily carnage reported from Iraq stems mostly from Arab insurgents rather than from American B-52s, a European movement against the ongoing war is hardly discernible.

In spite of these general differences, there are a number of similarities in European reactions to the wars in Vietnam and Iraq. They become apparent once we take a closer look at the particular conditions and circumstances surrounding those wars. Perhaps surprisingly, these similarities start with European reactions to the respective American presidents.

Texans

The British historian Timothy Garton Ash has called George W. Bush "a walking gift to every European anti-American caricaturist."[3] And indeed, from the very beginning the European press had a field day poking fun at the Texas governor and presidential candidate, portraying the race against Al Gore as a campaign of cowboy versus brain. The Texas Black Tie and Boots Gala on the eve of Bush's inauguration provided ample opportunity to depict in flashy colors how country music, snakeskin boots, and Stetsons found their way into Washington.[4] Most important, the president's whole demeanor perfectly matched European stereotypes of the trigger-happy Wild West gunslinger. His waggish quip "Some folks look at me and see a certain swagger, which in Texas is called 'walking'" was good for reinforcing outdated European clichés of the Lone Star State rather than depicting the president as a regular guy.[5] To many Americans, Bush's contrived confident stride, his arms swinging loose from the shoulders in deliberate forward-and-back movement, might represent the body language of the down-home Texan. To Europeans, it suggests that he has watched one too many John Wayne movies. The president's trademark smirk and his penchant for leaning forward when speaking, narrowing his eyes, and pointing fingers all seem to say, "Have gun, will travel." Said Hans-Ulrich Klose, the vice chairman of the Foreign Relations Committee in the German parliament and an outspoken critic of Chancellor Gerhard Schröder's confrontational course in the Iraq crisis, "Much of it is the way he talks, this provocative manner, the jabbing of his finger at you. It's Texas, a culture that is unfamiliar to Germans."[6]

Of course, it was not only how George W. Bush spoke but also what he said that alienated Europeans. In their eyes, his dead-or-alive, with-or-against-us, bring-'em-on macho rhetoric clearly identified him as the equivalent of the schoolyard bully. The America that he represented seemed to be increasingly distasteful, immature, and often simply scary. In a program satirizing politicians on the French channel Canal Plus, Bush appeared as a joker whose disjointed jabbering was totally muddled save for occasional orders to bomb or execute someone. Many Europeans felt that the American president was suffering from "Mad Cowboy Disease," and his junking, a few short weeks into his first term, of the Kyoto Protocol on global warming quickly earned him the label "Toxic Texan."[7]

Taking their cue from the American media, Europeans ridiculed the president for his malapropisms and mangling of the language. Reports that he finds it difficult to read documents longer than two pages, that he has trouble processing complex information, and that he has an extremely short attention span seemed to confirm the impression that this man was ill-suited for the job of world leader.[8] In light of these sentiments, it added only insignificantly to European misgivings that the president had hardly any knowledge of the world outside of the United States and that he was quoted as finding "this foreign policy stuff" a little frustrating.

It is hard to believe today that the reputation of the American president in Europe was only slightly better when 1963 turned to 1964. Many Europeans expressed doubts and uncertainties concerning Lyndon B. Johnson's ability to effectively handle foreign affairs in a time of great flux. One observer, deploring a lack of foreign policy interest and initiative on the part of the president, surmised that Johnson was confounding the world stage with Texas local politics. British prime minister Alec Douglas-Home adjudged that John F. Kennedy's successor knew nothing of foreign policy. A German emissary came away feeling that LBJ, unlike JFK, did not speak the language of Europe. General Charles de Gaulle, taking the president's measurement at Kennedy's funeral, contemptuously spoke of a "cowboy-radical."[9]

For his part, Lyndon Johnson wished that the rest of the world would go away so that he could get ahead with the needs of Americans. "Foreigners are not like the folks I am used to," he said half jokingly. His relationship with Embassy Row was insecure to the point that national security adviser McGeorge Bundy had to plead with him to spend an hour a week with foreign diplomats. While his staff considered emphasizing the president's proclivity for personal, or "Texas hill country," diplomacy as a way to enamor him with ambassadors and world leaders, others were clearly wary of such a strategy. As the *Washington Post*'s *Parade* magazine reported, "To old-style diplomats, schooled in the niceties of protocol and the delicacies of double talk, Johnson was almost a caricature of a wheeling-dealing American politician. His Texas folksiness, shoulder hugging, hand wringing and homely speech lacked the finesse they admire." With the Vietnam War dragging on, problems of etiquette on the diplomatic parquet gave way to a much stronger aversion by large sections of the European public for whom LBJ came to represent the quintessential "ugly American"—an assessment shared by many later historians.[10]

In terms of outward appearance, to be sure, Lyndon Johnson eschewed any of the contemptuousness and unilateralism that so maddened Europe-

ans with George W. Bush more than thirty years later. Quite to the contrary, his unceasing efforts to be attentive, appreciative, and reassuring even
led some Europeans to complain that an attitude of "let's reason together"
would not solve every problem. Yet beneath this demonstrative receptive-
ness there lurked a hidden pool of paternalism, derision, and resentment.
Johnson and his aides clearly perceived themselves as guardians patiently
enduring the unreasonable demands of unruly children while trying to keep
them from getting into trouble. Every time he went to the men's room, the
president complained, he was asking the Danes, Belgians, and Germans for
permission. After a meeting with Ludwig Erhard, LBJ told his aides that the
German chancellor had been "all over me. He was ready to go in the barn
and milk my cows if he could find the teats." There was only one way to deal
with the Germans, Johnson proclaimed: "You keep patting them on the
head and then every once in a while you kick them in the balls."[11]

Remarks such as these reveal that Lyndon Johnson was a much rougher
and brusquer personality than his fellow Texan George W. Bush. Johnson's
press secretary George Reedy described his former boss as "a miserable
person—a bully, sadist, lout and egotist." In private meetings with aides,
congressmen, and world leaders alike, LBJ often cast off his public joviality
and subjected his opposite number to the notorious "Johnson treatment."
One longtime administration official described this as "a practiced routine,
which consisted of a lot of touching; hands on shoulders, hands on knee caps,
hands clasped and wringing; fingers tugging on lapels, fingers tugging on his
own ears; and all the while, the honey of his voice dripping from the large
mouth fixed in a crooked smile." Being exposed to this therapy in sometimes tempestuous meetings, several European leaders would probably have
much preferred the impromptu back rub that George W. Bush gave German chancellor Angela Merkel at the G8 summit in St. Petersburg in 2006—
but then again, they were of course all men back then.[12]

Overall, however, European statesmen, though certainly taken aback,
seem to have been more impressed or intimidated by the "Johnson treatment" than incensed or annoyed. In any case, their original skepticism gradually gave way to a general recognition that JFK's successor had developed
a good grasp of foreign policy. And indeed, although European complaints
that LBJ was neglecting his closest allies because of Vietnam never faded
away, the Johnson administration, as Tom Schwartz has recently demonstrated, successfully handled a host of intricate transatlantic problems ranging from the withdrawal of France from NATO's military structure to global
monetary issues and nuclear proliferation. In a time of transition, it thus
managed to hold the Atlantic alliance together. If this did nothing to improve the president's reputation among those fierce antiwar critics that
made up a minority of the European populace, at least it solidified his standing with the continent's political elites.

One of the most significant differences between the 1960s and the early 2000s is that this clear divide between elites and criticasters in the assessment of the American president is gone. To be sure, after 9/11 a groundswell of international sympathy temporarily blurred the image of George W. Bush as a cowboy in charge of a rogue superpower. Instead of shooting from the hip, the president reacted patiently and proportionately. Suddenly, he had the look more of the righteous marshal Wyatt Earp than of a sinister gunslinger. Even leftist dailies had to acknowledge that Bush had proven European cowboy clichés wrong by showing himself to be cooperative, eager to learn, and flexible. In fact, to a large majority of Europeans who approved of and supported the inevitable showdown with the Taliban in Afghanistan, the scene still had the rather reassuring look of a sheriff and a posse driving the bad guys out of town.

Yet this belated honeymoon lasted barely seventeen weeks. When the president's January 29, 2002, State of the Union address rang in a new phase in the war on terror by denouncing an "axis of evil" that included Iraq, Iran, and North Korea and by hinting at the possibility of preventive war against these countries, the gun-toting cowboy was back in European chat rooms and editorials. Throughout the following year, Bush's popularity in Europe— if any—continually deteriorated. A former British cabinet member called him "the most intellectually backward American president of my political lifetime" and saw him "surrounded by advisers whose bellicosity is exceeded only by their political, military and diplomatic illiteracy." Favorable views of the United States plummeted in Britain from 75 percent in mid-2002 to 48 percent in March 2003. Over the same period positive views declined from 70 to 34 percent in Italy, from 63 to 31 percent in France, and from 61 to 25 percent in Germany. Of those respondents who had unfavorable views of the United States, more than half in Britain and Italy, more than two-thirds in Germany, and more than three-quarters in France said the problem was not America in general but President Bush. Whereas Germans had given George H.W. Bush a mark of +1.1 on a popularity scale from +5 to −5 during the Gulf War of 1991, his son got a result of −2.7 in February 2003—a worse rating than any German politician had recorded in more than a quarter century. Significantly enough, such negative assessments were not confined to the general public and chattering classes but extended into elite circles. At the Davos World Economic Forum, a gathering of Europe's top CEOs, an American journalist found the level of hostility toward the Bush administration "absolutely stunning. That includes a visceral dislike of Bush in particular, who attracts adjectives I've never heard flung at a sitting president. These were not leftists; they were the cream of European capitalism."[13] This near unanimous thrashing of George W. Bush in Europe resulted not only from his demeanor, of course, but also from the style and substance of his diplomacy.

Allies

With the ruins of the World Trade Center and parts of the Pentagon still smoldering after the terrorist assaults on September 11, 2001, NATO for the first time ever invoked its Article V, declaring the attack on the United States an attack on all members. Responding to this unprecedented step, U.S. defense secretary Donald Rumsfeld dispatched his deputy, Paul Wolfowitz, to tell America's closest allies that this would not be necessary because "the mission would define the coalition." The Western alliance that triumphed in the Cold War and that had been trumpeted for more than half a century as a close-knit and true Atlantic community based on a common civilization many hundreds of years old found itself casually "downgraded to a farm team from which the United States in the future would cherry-pick 'coalitions of the willing.'" Europeans, whose nouveau aversion to war stems from the still-living memory of millions of loved ones lost on the battlefields of World War II, could not but feel profoundly snubbed by this condescending rejection of a solemn offer. Months later, Javier Solana, NATO's former secretary-general and now the EU's foreign policy chief, could hardly hide his outrage when he reminded an American journalist that "NATO invoked its most sacred covenant, that no one had dared touch in the past, and it was useless! Absolutely useless! At no point has [Central Command commander in chief] Gen. Tommy Franks even talked to anyone at NATO."[14]

The Bush administration's insensitivity was rooted only partly in the conviction that the Europeans had little to offer given the widening gap of military capabilities since the end of the Cold War. Neither was it solely due to experiences of friction during NATO's air campaign in the Kosovo war. To a considerable extent, it stemmed from a generally negative view of the utility of multilateral action, which was seen as unnecessarily impeding American decision making and freedom of action. In fact, the administration was pursuing what Philip Gordon and Jeremy Shapiro have called an "if you build it, they will come" doctrine that eschewed any prior consultation and presumed that allies would fall in line if and when the United States had unilaterally determined the course of action.[15]

Along with this take-it-or-leave-it unilateralism, American leaders fancied themselves in the role of the tragic yet defiant loner. Thus, Donald Rumsfeld could see nothing wrong in being lonesome at the outset as long as one was doing the right thing. The president himself declared that "at some point we may be the only ones left. That's okay with me. We are America." This kind of rhetoric not only reinforced European stereotypes of the Lone Ranger, it also clearly signaled that the Bush administration had little patience with the views of America's European allies.[16]

The Lone Ranger attitude, to be sure, was not invented by the Bush administration. During the 1961 Berlin crisis, for example, Kennedy's foreign policy aide Walt Rostow sent a memorandum to the president arguing that "we should prepare ourselves for what you might call a High Noon stance. (You recall Gary Cooper dealt with the bandits alone.) . . . I do believe we must be prepared in our minds for the possibility of a relatively lonely stage; and we should accept it without throwing our sheriff's badge in the dust when the crisis subsides." Neither were European complaints about a lack of consultation anything new. Europeans were also accustomed to the fact that the Atlantic alliance was by no means a relationship of equals. As a German Foreign Office memorandum that responded to General de Gaulle's 1958 scheme of a Franco-British-American triumvirate within NATO remarked, "The political strength of the present western alliance is based on respect for the equality of each member state . . . , with these member states in turn voluntarily acknowledging the leadership role of the United States." Yet throughout the Cold War there was always a recognized need for compromise, particularly in matters pertaining to Europe. As Rostow acknowledged in his memorandum to JFK, it was standard practice for the United States to put to its European allies "our own strong positions; if these are accepted—well and good; if not, we may have to adjust our positions backward." Compare this to how Secretary of State Colin Powell explained George W. Bush's style of diplomacy: "The President . . . makes sure people know what he believes in. And then he tries to persuade others that is the correct position. When it does not work, then we will take the position we believe is correct, and I hope the Europeans are left with a better understanding of the way in which we want to do business."[17]

The current secretary-general of NATO, Jan de Hoop Scheffer, has suggested that one of the problems in the run-up to the Iraq war was that the North Atlantic Council was underused as a mechanism for political consultation. The same cannot be said of the 1960s and America's deepening involvement in the Vietnam War. Although the Johnson administration, to be sure, did not contemplate involving NATO in its decision making about Vietnam, it expended considerable efforts to rally the alliance behind its policies in Southeast Asia and it used the North Atlantic Council to drum up both moral and material support for its positions.

Since 1960 the United States had been trying to shift NATO's center of gravity and involve member states in problems all around the world. As Undersecretary of State George Ball noted, however, if Washington planned to achieve a wider sharing of responsibility, "we must give other nations an opportunity to express their views while worldwide policies are being developed." Accordingly, Secretary of State Dean Rusk suggested discussing Communist efforts in various parts of the world, most notably Southeast Asia, within NATO, where—as one American official lamented—"Viet Nam was still seen as a 'US problem' rather than as a problem for the entire Alliance." In each and every meeting of the North Atlantic Council from 1964 to 1967, therefore, Rusk tried to beat into the heads of his colleagues that the whole free world had a stake in the struggle in Southeast Asia, which he took to calling "the western flank of NATO in the Pacific Ocean." Although the Americans knew that there was no way to get NATO directly involved in Vietnam, they still used the alliance's consultative mechanisms to seek greater Allied support through participation in military advisory or economic and technical assistance activities.[18]

In the spring of 1964, with Vietnamese morale reaching a new low and French calls for neutralization increasingly attracting attention, the Johnson administration resolved that it had to "get more flags flying in South Vietnam." Rusk sent out a circular telegram to U.S. ambassadors in allied countries, urging them to promptly call on foreign ministers of their host countries and obtain a principle aid commitment. Details were to be left to follow-up high-level discussions, but the secretary of state did not fail to already include a list of suggested contributions for each country. "The basic objective," ambassadors were informed, "is to have Free World Governments display their flags in Viet Nam and indicate their recognition of the fundamental nature of the struggle there."[19]

Secretary of Defense Robert McNamara took the opportunity of a trip to Bonn in May to ask for the assignment of a German medical unit to Vietnam. The German defense minister did actually show some willingness to dispatch a reserve sick bay with close to one hundred soldiers to Vietnam, but the Foreign Office quickly intervened, pointing out that at most a civilian hospital operated by the German Red Cross was conceivable, lest the German public get the impression that regular army units were being sent to Vietnam.[20]

Combat forces, to be sure, were by no means Washington's first priority. While Henry Cabot Lodge, the American ambassador in Saigon, felt it psychologically "most important that others share with the US the casualties of the US effort here," he revealed the real reasoning behind the administration's "more flags" campaign by emphasizing "the great potential impact on US public opinion which foreign sharing of the dangers could have." The flags were needed in Vietnam, then, not for military reasons but for symbolic ones. They would demonstrate to the American public that the whole Western world was committed to the struggle and at the same time boost the morale of the South Vietnamese. To lend additional credibility to the operation, U.S. officials asked South Vietnamese prime minister Nguyen Khanh to put out his own request for help, conveniently furnishing a draft speech along with the suggestion.[21]

The players were slow, however, to take the field. After a while, an impatient Lyndon Johnson fired off an indignant cable himself to American envoys in eleven key allied countries. Noting that it had now been nine weeks since Rusk had sent out his instructions to seek assistance, the president professed to be "gravely disappointed by the inadequacy of the actions by our friends and allies in response to our request that they share the burden of Free World responsibility in Viet Nam." What America was doing in Vietnam, the president wrote, represented "disinterested sacrifices by the people of the US on a scale never before known in history. The American people should not be required to continue indefinitely alone and unassisted, to be the only champions of freedom in Viet Nam today." As for the scale of allied contributions, LBJ expected especially the larger countries to "think in terms of many hundreds of men each, not handfuls." He impressed upon his envoys that there was "no other task imposed upon you in your current assignment which, to my mind, precedes this one in its urgency and significance," and he warned that he wanted to "see evidence of your success in the very near future."[22]

Even though LBJ provided his ambassadors with additional backup by sending Henry Cabot Lodge, who had just returned from his assignment to Saigon, on a whirlwind tour of European capitals, results remained sobering. All that Lodge could muster were expressions of sympathy for America's dilemma and noncommittal assurances of help. Although he publicly tried to put a good face on the matter, Lodge made no secret of his frustration during a stopover in London. While Lodge was still on his beat, a State Department research memorandum found that, so far, contributions had mostly taken the form of small-scale grants of economic and technical assistance. And Lodge's trip did little to overcome European resistance to more meaningful contributions. When an eight-man Italian medical team reached Saigon on October 11, 1964, a CIA situation report called this "a significant breakthrough." Considering LBJ's strong desire to see people from third countries on the scene, the president was probably not much impressed by this news, or by later reports that German personnel in Vietnam numbered just twelve toward the end of 1964. As the year closed out, an aide to the president had to acknowledge that contributions from other countries did not amount to much. Although Ambassador Lodge had obtained "a number of half-hearted commitments" from European allies, "few actual contributions have materialized."[23]

In fact, European governments were highly skeptical of the course pursued by Washington in Southeast Asia. Although only the French dared to openly voice their opposition to American policy, others—notably Denmark and Belgium—privately criticized its direction or expressed grave doubts about the war. In Germany, a staunchly pro-American chancellor used every opportunity to express his solidarity, but opinions in the Foreign Office were much more ambivalent. A memorandum drafted in preparation for Lodge's visit, for instance, argued that the talks should be used "to convey the Federal Government's view that it was time to look for a political solution to the Vietnamese conflict." In London, meanwhile, Whitehall combined rhetorical support for American policy with opposition to a larger British role in Vietnam and a tacit preference for negotiations. British policy makers decided not to broach this preference prior to the U.S. elections, however, deeming the subject to be too sensitive for frank discussion.[24]

If, as Fredrik Logevall has argued, European reservations in conjunction with U.S. election-year politics forestalled a decision to take the war to North Vietnam in 1964, these considerations gave way to a reinforced determination to stand firm in Southeast Asia as soon as Lyndon Johnson had been reelected in a landslide. Moreover, the president now displayed a renewed touchiness toward criticism. When Harold Wilson, propelled by the prospect of escalation, finally sought a frank discussion with Johnson in February 1965, the president told him in no uncertain terms to mind his own business. Wilson's Canadian counterpart, Lester B. Pearson, after criticizing America's Vietnam policy in a speech in Philadelphia, was invited to join LBJ at Camp David, where he found himself grabbed by the lapels and dressed down by an angry president who seemed "forlorn at not being understood better by friends." This sense of loneliness and abandonment was echoed by congressional leaders, who wondered "why we are there all alone" and "why can't we get some of our friends in there with us," complaining that "our allies really do not give a damn about Communist aggression in Southeast Asia."[25]

With the deployment of ground troops to Vietnam in 1965, Washington redoubled its efforts to enlist allied help, increasingly also alluding to an interest in military personnel proper. Although American allies in the Asia-Pacific region understandably bore the brunt of these requests, European nations were by no means immune from similar solicitations. Thus, officials in the White House and the Pentagon even pondered blackmailing the British into providing a brigade by threatening to discontinue American backing for the pound sterling. The CIA as well as the State and Treasury Departments, however, were strongly opposed to such a scheme. The agency pointed out that pressure on Britain to increase its military commitment in Vietnam beyond the British Military Mission there would probably provoke London to "insist on a quid pro quo with respect to Malaysia," which would "certainly outweigh the usefulness of an increased British role in Vietnam." Undersecretary of State George Ball, for his part, assumed that London would rather devalue its currency than commit any troops. He argued that ventilations of giving the British "an extra billion dollars for one brigade" amounted to "making mercenaries out of the soldiers." Secretary of the Treasury Henry Fowler concurred, making it plain that "he did not want to be a party to anything of this sort." Eventually, the objective of postponing the British withdrawal east of Suez and of stabilizing British commitments to NATO kept Washington from exerting sustained pressure on London for a larger contribution in Vietnam.[26]

The British were not the only Europeans seeing themselves confronted with stronger American demands. When the newly arrived German military attaché worked the circuit of U.S. and South Vietnamese officers in

Saigon in May 1965, he was stunned to find his opposite numbers stoutly anticipating a German military contribution. It took, he reported home, "repeated reminders that German troops were entirely subordinated to NATO to rebuff ardent queries about a German battalion." Not surprisingly, rumors would intermittently flare up in Germany purporting that German troops were about to be sent to Vietnam. Usually such reports would create an uproar given the fact that 81 percent of respondents opposed such an operation even if it included only volunteers. In fact, sentiment against a German involvement in Vietnam was not confined to the question of soldiers. At one point, the country's best-selling tabloid exclaimed in Dr. Seuss–like fashion, "No, Sir! The Germans do not want to go to Vietnam! Not with orderlies, not with technicians—we don't want to go at all. To Vietnam—No, Sir!"[27]

Yet U.S. officials were not so easily swayed. In the winter of 1965, with the White House facing the prospect of asking Congress to foot the bill for yet another substantial increase in troops, LBJ was more adamant than ever that he wanted to see more flags flying in Vietnam. Responding to a White House request for an optimistic assessment of where foreign combat forces could be obtained, the Pentagon reasoned that by "selling our souls and raising hob in various ways" it might be possible to get a German division of 20,000 soldiers. When Secretary of State Rusk met his German counterpart—incidentally called Gerhard Schröder, but who had no familial or political kinship to the subsequent chancellor—at a NATO meeting, he "pointed out to him that the full revelation to the Congress of the extent of our requirements in Viet-Nam will raise major questions about what others are doing." It was therefore "of the utmost importance that Germany find a way to send considerable numbers of people to South Viet-Nam." Rusk advised LBJ that he had been "very disappointed" with Schröder's "very negative" reaction and "general attitude." In view of Chancellor Erhard's impending visit to Washington, Rusk recommended that "we should marshall a strong case for Erhard and put to him some very specific suggestions as to units or type of personnel that we strongly want from the Federal Republic. I would advise against combat units as such but it is important that we get some Germans into the field." Accordingly, the German-American talks shortly before Christmas 1965 witnessed some remarkable encounters. When the German defense minister, meeting with his U.S. counterpart on December 20, inquired whether Bonn could help by purchasing U.S. jet transporters and then leave them to the Americans by way of lend-lease, McNamara snapped that he "did not need planes but crews." After dinner on that same day, Erhard got his share of the notorious Johnson treatment. Congress, the president began, would ask him what other nations were doing in Vietnam. His problems would be more understandable if other nations were involved. He was not asking for combat troops but for a medical unit or a construction battalion. When Erhard responded with talk of legal restrictions, the president exploded. The American ambassador to Germany, George McGhee, later recalled that LBJ's "tall, rangy figure towered over the comparatively small figure of the chancellor. Gesticulating and speaking in a strong, strident voice, Johnson alternately wheedled and threatened. He put his whole body into his demands. I was shocked by the emotion and vehemence behind his argument. . . . He recounted all we had done for Germany. Now was the time for Germany to pay us back." According to the memorandum of conversation, Johnson thundered, "If I can get legislation to put 200,000 more men in Vietnam, surely the Chancellor can get two battalions to Vietnam. If we are going to be partners, we better find out right now." McGhee remembered that Erhard "appeared increasingly uncomfortable, verging on fright," and indeed the chancellor found nothing to say but to admit meekly that "it isn't fair to take your security in West Berlin and not help you in Vietnam."[28]

The impression Johnson made on the German chancellor can be gauged from the hectic activity in Bonn immediately following the return of Erhard's party. On December 22, the cabinet convened at the chancellery to discuss how to react to the American pressure. Discussion centered on providing a hospital unit or a hospital ship. An interministerial working group was formed to consider this as well as additional projects, at the same time undertaking to make the charitable organizations a partner in the endeavor. This was deemed to be crucial for three reasons: first, to recruit the necessary volunteers; second, to sow the seeds of sympathy with South Vietnam throughout West German society; and third, to underline the purely humanitarian nature of Bonn's contribution. To be sure, this time the Germans really meant business. On January 12, 1966, Erhard's press secretary announced the decision of the German cabinet to outfit a hospital ship and dispatch it to South Vietnam as soon as possible. In early March the cabinet disregarded objections by Treasury Secretary Rolf Dahlgrün and established a special item in the budget for aid to Vietnam. Meanwhile, the German embassy in Washington sought advice from American officials on possible new projects, explaining that "what it needed was some spectacular impact project that would provide useful benefit for the recipient as well as some publicity for [the German] government." At the end of the year, German authorities congratulated themselves on having successfully walked the tightrope. The embassy in Saigon reported that several political expectations linked to Vietnam aid had been realized: "The U.S. has given up the desire for a military or paramilitary German contribution; . . . the hospital ship *Helgoland*, at first planned as an excuse, has turned out to be the best idea in terms of German humanitarian aid." In February 1967, the interministerial committee resolved that the Federal Republic was no longer in an "alibi situation vis-à-vis the United States."[29]

By that time, however, Washington had practically abandoned all hope to elicit a really meaningful contribution from its European allies. In fact, the Johnson administration had been unable to keep allied governments from progressively distancing themselves from American policies in Vietnam. In Britain, both Prime Minister Wilson and his defense minister, Denis Healy, had dissociated themselves from bombing runs on Hanoi and Haiphong and had promised antiwar critics in the Labour Party that they would suspend arms sales to the United States for use in Vietnam. In Germany, Erhard's successor, Kurt Georg Kiesinger, made it quite plain that—although he would not publicly criticize Washington—he did not intend to morally or politically support United States policy in Vietnam any longer, as Erhard had done before. In Italy, Pietro Nenni, chairman of the Socialist Party within the center-left coalition, told U.S. vice president Hubert H. Humphrey, "Europe does not understand America any longer, America is not understanding Europe. The root of the discord is the Vietnam War." Recapitulating the discussions on Vietnam within the Atlantic alliance for the incoming Nixon administration, U.S. ambassador to NATO Harlan Cleveland concluded that after 1967, European governments "contributed with their silence, and used our briefings in NAC as a source of facts and ideas to use in facing down those who used Vietnam as an instrument of domestic politics in their own countries."[30]

In marked contrast to the Bush administration's handling of the run-up to the Iraq war some thirty-plus years later, however, Washington did not leave it entirely up to allied governments to face down critics of American policies. Rather, the Johnson administration complemented its courtship in the councils of power with a plentiful dose of public diplomacy—the art of explaining the United States and its policies to ordinary people abroad. The United States Information Agency (USIA), the government body entrusted with telling America's story worldwide, related the drama of Vietnam to European audiences through film showings, television interviews, pamphlets and press materials, lectures, and discussion groups. In a letter to USIA field offices, the agency's director, Carl Rowan, informed public affairs officers in foreign capitals that he had "assured the President that USIA will spare no resource or effort . . . to impress upon other nations that communist aggression and subversion in Southeast Asia is indeed a menace to Free World security and . . . to create in the minds of our audience a sense of individual identification with the struggle against communism in Southeast Asia." Rowan took advantage of Ambassador Lodge's European trip to demonstrate to LBJ that he intended to keep his word, boasting that the agency was "seeking to give maximum exposure to the Lodge presentation. . . . In Germany he is scheduled for an off-the-record briefing of the foreign press in Bonn, an appearance on the country's top news-feature television show, *Panorama*, and a press conference in Munich after he sees Chancellor Erhard. In addition, USIS is arranging for showings of *Troubled Harvest*, a

15-minute USIA film on Viet-Nam specially prepared for the European audience and rushed to the field August 14. Reports so far show that the film is being scheduled for network TV showings in Austria, Denmark, Spain and the Netherlands, with probable similar use elsewhere, especially in those countries to be visited by Mr. Lodge."[31]

According to USIA's own account, the telling of the Vietnam story took on new proportions in 1965, when the agency's press and publication service "transmitted some 600 news stories, backgrounders, columns, texts of speeches, and editorial summaries for USIA posts to place in local publications around the world." The agency was especially proud of "a dramatic and poignant color film" called *The Night of the Dragon*. Gobbling up by far the most funds for a single item in USIA's 1965 budget, the film intercut actual battle scenes with a detailed illustration of South Vietnamese civilians bravely continuing their normal day-to-day activities. It was distributed in twenty-three languages to 110 countries, with special screenings in U.S. cultural centers for local opinion leaders. USIA also aided British, German, and Dutch television representatives to prepare programs on the Vietnam situation. American informational activities were not always a matter of supply and demand, however. In meetings with officials from the German government's Press and Information Office, for example, the Americans confronted their guests with a detailed wish list that included sending a hand-picked group of correspondents to Vietnam and paying for their travel. In addition, as stipulated in a memorandum of understanding, the Americans would "provide the FRG with the talking points and arguments that we are using on Viet Nam, and the Germans will draw upon these as appropriate for their own statements and releases." Starting in 1966, USIA also sponsored regular visits by foreign journalists to Vietnam. Defending these measures before the Senate Foreign Relations Committee, Rowan's successor, Leonard Marks, pointed out that the Smith-Mundt Act of 1948 forbade only domestic informational activities by the government—which led the committee's chairman, Senator William Fulbright, to wryly remark, "You are forbidden to brainwash Americans, but not others."[32]

However questionable some of the Johnson administration's public diplomacy might have been, at least the United States was trying to persuasively communicate its policies and ideals. By the turn of the century, however, the Cold War's panoply of public diplomacy had been dismantled and the remnants of USIA incorporated into the State Department. Fragmented and underfunded, U.S. information programs were incapable of having any bearing on European public opinion, nor was there apparently any interest on the part of the Bush administration to exert any influence on the masses abroad. Sure enough, an attempt would have been warranted, for what lies at the heart of the recent transatlantic conflagration is an entirely different understanding of the struggle to be waged.

Wars

Writing in the *Washington Post* on the first anniversary of September 11, Francis Fukuyama deemed it "one of the most notable features of international politics . . . how the United States has become both utterly dominant and lonely." Pundits and politicians wondered how the tremendous outpouring of sympathy right after the terrorist attacks—complete with a moving show of solidarity by more than 200,000 Germans at the Brandenburg Gate and a leading French newspaper proclaiming that "we are all Americans now"—could have evaporated so quickly. When President Bush, in the margins of a meeting with European Union leaders in 2006, was pressed by foreign journalists to explain why so many Europeans have come to dislike the United States, he proffered the estimation that "for Europe, September the 11th was a moment; for us, it was a change of thinking."[33]

There is more than a kernel of truth in this statement. For many Americans, glued to their television screens as the Twin Towers came tumbling down, that Tuesday may have been the most horrifying single day in their nation's history. The unprecedented assault on the continental United States, followed by anthrax attacks that terrified the country for weeks, raised the specter of unconscionable villains ready to employ weapons of mass destruction to potentially kill hundreds of thousands of Americans. Since 9/11, for the first time ever, Americans feel more directly threatened than Europeans. And thus they resolutely agreed when President Bush, nine days after the attacks, declared war on terrorism, vowing to "direct every resource at our command—every means of diplomacy, every tool of intelligence, every instrument of law enforcement, every financial influence, and every necessary weapon of war—to the disruption and to the defeat of the global terror network."[34]

Europeans, by and large, also agreed. At an emergency summit in Brussels, European Union leaders gave unanimous backing to U.S. plans to launch military strikes in retaliation for the terrorist attacks. Large majorities of ordinary citizens, asked if their own countries should support a U.S. military assault, answered in the affirmative: 80 percent in Denmark, 79 percent in Britain, 73 percent in France, 58 percent in Spain and Norway, and—perhaps for the first time since World War II—even a majority of Germans. For the time being, Europeans were willing to turn a blind eye even to Bush's Manichean "either you are with us or you are with the terrorists" rhetoric. Impressed by the determined yet measured tone of his speech, in which political and judicial action figured at least as prominently as military means, European editorialists praised the president for constructing a framework for the investigative and military work that lay ahead. As one paper concluded, "Bush has done a lot to assure the world that the rampant attacks on America will not result in an unrestrained response."[35]

Yet while Europeans accepted that a first military strike was inevitable, signs of a philosophical chasm were discernible already at this early stage. Thus, the staunchly pro-American *Economist* wondered whether "the awe-inspiring firepower at the disposal of American generals . . . can be used effectively in what Mr Bush calls a 'war' against global terrorism." Minuscule as they were, these scare quotes indicated a world of difference. In fact, many European leaders as well as their fellow citizens refused to use the term *war* in talking about the events. After all—as Simon Serfaty, director of European studies at the Center for Strategic and International Studies—has pointed out, "war is remembered as a way of life for the former European great powers, and terror is a recurring accident that can be defeated when it erupts and must be forgotten after it has been defeated." Europe's dislike for characterizing the response to international terrorism as a war grew when, after the Taliban had been wiped out in Afghanistan, it became clear that the Bush administration had no intention of sheathing the sword and turning to the sheriff's handcuffs and the judge's gavel. The crucial turning point for Europeans was the president's State of the Union address in January 2002. Bush's identification of an "axis of evil" and his hints at preventive war convinced Europeans that their American partners were set to reduce the struggle against terrorism to its military aspect. The first military strike, it seemed, would be followed by a second one, and then a third, and so on and so forth. Even worse, Europeans came to feel that the Bush administration's incessant talk of America as a nation "at war" represented nothing but a pretext for military interventions abroad, curtailments of civil rights at home, and the abrogation of international law on an unprecedented scale.[36]

To Europeans, America was anything but "at war." As Reinhard Bütikofer, political director of the German Green Party, tried to explain, "In this country, you have all these emotions that make even the word 'war' very different for Americans and Germans. America has its 'wars' against drugs and illiteracy. . . . Germans associate war with the near-total destruction of their cities and homeland." Half a year after the terrorist attacks, the German ambassador in Washington confessed that he had to constantly remind his backstops in Berlin "that the United States still considers itself to be at war," whereas "most Germans don't feel they are at war, with all the terrible connotations of destruction, defeat, and occupation" that it held for them.[37] If Germans think of war, they think of alarms driving them into cellars and air raid shelters almost every day for three years at a time; they think of the trials of organizing the most basic needs of life in bombed-out cities among broken pipes and tons of rubble. The British think of their own ordeal under the constant threat of German bombers throughout the summer of 1940. Russians think of a murderous war that raged on their soil for almost four years, leaving behind an unfathomable scene of destruction and more than 25 million dead. The Dutch think of the echo, day in and day out, of German boots on the cobbled streets of their occupied hometowns as they were cowering behind drawn curtains. No, Europeans did not believe that Americans were "at war." At the same time, their own collective memories of war made them obtuse to the profound impact that September 11 had on the American psyche.

On top of these differing perceptions came the conviction that—war or not—Bush's so-called axis of evil, North Korea, Iran, and Iraq, had not much to do with the struggle against terrorism. Whereas every other American believed that there was an Iraqi hand in September 11 either by Saddam Hussein himself or in the person of one or more of the hijackers, and whereas a large majority of Americans in the run-up to the war felt that Iraq was abetting terrorist plans to attack the United States, Europeans failed to see any such connections. Melvin Laird, secretary of defense in the Nixon administration, has recently argued that the spread of radical fundamentalist Islam is as real today as was the spread of Communism in the 1960s. He believes, therefore, that "Iraq was a logical place to fight back," and asserts that U.S. troops are fighting in Iraq "to preserve modern culture, Western democracy, the global economy, and all else that is threatened by the spread of barbarism in the name of religion." His successor Donald Rumsfeld, to this day, is still talking about the Iraq war and the broader antiterrorism effort in the same breath, calling the Iraq war the "epicenter" of the struggle against terrorism. Many Europeans believe, quite to the contrary, that Iraq with its despotic yet secular regime was one of the least logical places to fight militant Islamism and that it is now an epicenter of Islamist terrorism not despite but because of the American intervention. In fact, U.S. experts and even the nation's intelligence services have gradually come to share that assessment.[38]

Interestingly, there were similar disagreements about the nature and purpose of the Vietnam War during the 1960s. While the Johnson administration tried to convince its allies that South Vietnam was the victim of a carefully conceived plan of Communist aggression to destroy its political fabric and take over the country, sizable and vocal minorities in Europe argued that the conflict in fact represented a civil war in which the United States had no business. In the spring of 1965, American policy makers undertook great efforts to fix their interpretation of events in Southeast Asia firmly in the minds of Western publics. The State Department issued a white paper on Communist aggression in Vietnam that was carried in full to more than one hundred countries via USIA wireless file. A sixteen-page booklet called "Liberation or Conquest" exposed the Vietcong as a puppet organization created and directed by North Vietnamese leader Ho Chi Minh. At NATO meetings, U.S. representatives, while acknowledging that the struggle in Vietnam had some of the characteristics of a civil war, insisted that it was "basically an aggression mounted and directed, supplied and equipped from Hanoi by the North Vietnamese regime." However, when they tried to incorporate their view of "wars of national liberation" as simply one more form of Communist aggression into NATO communiqués, the French balked, pointing out that they perceived the conflict as a civil war with outside interference from both sides. A plurality of people in France agreed, as did sizable minorities in Britain, Italy, and West Germany. A special USIA report compiling survey data gathered between 1965 and late 1969 concluded, "Vietnam is not generally seen in Cold-War terms by the people of [West European] countries."[39]

In much the same way, most Europeans have never seen Iraq in "war-against-terror" terms. Yet, whereas during the 1960s, political and other elites throughout Europe—with the exception of France and some Scandinavian countries—were prepared to give America the benefit of the doubt or, at any rate, to voice their misgivings in private, in 2002–3 governments in France, Germany, Belgium, and (to a lesser extent) Turkey teamed up with their own citizens as well as overwhelming majorities in almost every other European country to openly confront American policy.[40] Clubbing together with Vladimir Putin's Russia, they represented a remarkable roadblock on the Bush administration's path to topple Saddam Hussein by force.

Sentiments

Americans do not like foreigners to get in their way. The French had already learned this during the 1960s when de Gaulle's vocal criticism of U.S. policy in Vietnam had led women to return French-made handbags to New York department stores and Chicago restaurant owners to stop serving French wines, while more imaginative minds stuck pins into de Gaulle voodoo dolls. Paris experienced a déjà vu of such reactions after its foreign minister, Dominique de Villepin, on January 20, 2003, hinted at France's readiness to use its veto in the United Nations Security Council in order to block military action against Iraq. Two days later, French president Jacques Chirac, meeting with German chancellor Gerhard Schröder on the occasion of the fortieth anniversary of the Franco-German Friendship Treaty of 1963, reemphasized that warning and at the same time forged a common antiwar position with Europe's most populous country. The Bush administration's obvious determination to wage war on Iraq no matter what allowed Chirac to accomplish what de Gaulle, his much-admired paragon, had failed to achieve forty years earlier—to pry Germany loose from the United States. In fact, throughout 1963 and 1964, Germany's acquiescence in American policies in Vietnam had critically contributed to frustrating the hopes that de Gaulle had placed in the Elysée Treaty.[41]

Now, however, the two countries ganged up against the United States, provoking much of American media to switch into full campaign mode. A doctored front-page photo in the *New York Post* replaced the heads of the French and German representatives to the UN with weasel faces. In the *Wall Street Journal*, Christopher Hitchens described Chirac as a "positive monster of conceit" and "a rat that tried to roar." Capitol Hill cafeterias had to wipe the "French" from fries and toast on their menus. A Nashville morning talk show called for "a boycott of all things French, from Perrier to champagnes to wines and French w-h-i-n-e-s, French berets, French pastries," and made an exception for French kissing only because of Valentine's Day. Shock jocks near Atlanta offered people the chance to demolish a Peugeot for ten dollars. Even those who vented their anger in less destructive ways complained in letters to the editor about France and Germany conspiring against the United States on the global stage and about their cynical enthusiasm for supporting America's enemies. As Justin Vaïsse summed up, "In unfriendly American eyes, France is a cowardly and effete nation that never met a dictator it couldn't appease. It is immoral, venal, anti-Semitic, arrogant, insignificant, and nostalgic for past glory. It is also elitist, dirty, lazy, and it is anti-American." In light of all this, it is hardly surprising that bumper stickers appeared reading "Iraq now, France next," and that the French ambassador in Washington wondered whether the media was not conveying the impression that, in fact, this order had to be reversed.[42]

Underlying these vitriolic attacks was a deep well of American mistrust about Europe. Many American commentators, obviously still mired in notions of the continent as the palladium of scheming feudal courts and unscrupulous power politics that their ancestors had fled, could not imagine that European opponents of the war were driven by anything other than avarice and cynicism. In their view, U.S. foreign policy, benign and idealistic to the core, had infuriated Europeans by upsetting "their cherished balance of power." In a somewhat self-contradictory fashion, Europe's "coalition of the unwilling" was seen as either a chorus of cowards or a bunch of slick Machiavellian plotters pursuing self-serving geopolitical ambitions. Even usually perceptive commentators like the *Washington Post* columnist Anne Applebaum, in speculating about the causes for European recalcitrance, cited a decades-old pacifism, the left-leaning media, and American failure to communicate—all factors extraneous to the substance of U.S. policy, whose integrity seemed beyond question. On Fox News, viewers learned that "Americans on the left and right believe morals matter and that foreign policy should not serve merely economic and territorial aims," as it allegedly did in France and Germany. Accordingly, the U.S. government put forward a "respectable" and "perfectly plausible" legal argument, while its critics engaged in "resolute obscurantism" and "made a mockery of the truth." It was often repeated and widely believed that France's ostensibly significant trading relationships with Iraq in particular explained the Elysée's intransigence. In spite of the fact that—from 1997 through 2002—neither exports to nor imports from Iraq exceeded 0.3 percent of France's commerce, or 0.05 percent of its GDP, more than a few Americans insisted that the French position on Iraq was all about oil.[43]

Ironically, this mirrored the prevalent charge hurled at the United States from the other side of the Atlantic. "No Blood for Oil" was the rallying cry of protesters across Europe, ennobled by a front-page story in Germany's leading news magazine calling petroleum the propellant of war, and by politicians who daubed it on placards brandished at a session of the European parliament. Most Europeans obviously felt that the Bush administration's foreign policy could be reduced to what Walter Russell Mead has called Hamiltonianism, i.e., interventionism driven by economic interest, or—more prosaically—fighting a war to fill the tanks of American SUVs. Yet, while 75 percent of respondents in France and 54 percent in Germany believed that the Iraq war centered on oil, not a single European government embraced this dubious view, and many commentators expressly rejected it.[44]

What alarmed European elites much more than America's putative hunger for "the black gravy" was the casual manner in which President Bush and his supporters rode roughshod over international law in unilaterally determining that Saddam Hussein presented a clear and present danger to the United States that justified preventive war. It did not help that the administration proffered a checkered assortment of vindications for an apparently precooked policy, finally settling on the issue of weapons of mass destruction for reasons that—as Deputy Secretary of Defense Paul Wolfowitz explained—had "a lot to do with the U.S. government bureaucracy." To be sure, even French and German intelligence suggested that prohibited weapons programs existed in Iraq. Yet policy makers in Paris and Berlin wondered whether a country slightly more than twice the size of Idaho, more than 6,000 miles from American shores, ranked 127th on the UN's Human Development Index, with a per capita GDP of less than a twentieth of that of the United States, ravaged by successive wars and subject to daily American and British patrols of no-fly zones covering approximately two-thirds of its territory, forced to permit renewed and more robust UN inspection teams on the ground really posed an imminent threat to the national security of the world's sole remaining superpower. As the French ambassador to the United States put it, "Saddam is in his box, and the box now is closed with the inspectors doing their job in the box."[45]

With the actual existence of WMDs in Iraq presumed but not proved and both the inclination and the capacity of Saddam Hussein to employ any of these weapons against the United States highly dubitable, the Bush administration's case ultimately rested on the argument that the Iraqi dictator would pass such weapons on to terrorists. However, the president and his aides, in spite of tremendous efforts, consistently failed to prove any links between Saddam and al-Qaeda. European critics of the impending war concluded, therefore, that the United States was claiming a right to wage pre-ventive war in order to eliminate even an imagined or invented threat from "a hostile regime that has nothing more than the intent and ability to de-velop WMDs." As even American observers have pointed out, this would, in effect, have granted Washington "the right of arbitrary aggression," and would have "amounted to the death notice of a rules-based international system." When the invasion of Iraq commenced with a massive bombard-ment on March 20, 2003, one British observer confessed his fear of being back "to the Hobbesian world in which right is measured only by might." Many Europeans felt that the United States was denouncing the standards of civilized behavior and relapsing into premodern modes of conduct. As the French defense minister, Michèle Alliot-Marie, put it, "We live, after all, no longer in prehistoric times, when he who carried the biggest club knocked down the other in order to snitch away his mammoth's ham."[46] Similar no-tions of a transatlantic cultural chasm and, indeed, of European cultural superiority, would surface frequently in the months ahead.

During the 1960s it was inconceivable that the Western allies would ex-change similar barbs across the Atlantic. Even when de Gaulle's position on Vietnam had become openly and publicly hostile to that of the United States and he suspended French participation in NATO's unified command and kicked U.S. troops out of the country in 1966—partly due, as American of-ficials acknowledged, "to his belief that the U.S. was headed straight for war with China"—the Johnson administration shrugged off the general's ma-neuvers. In public at least, LBJ never lost his diplomatic decorum, and he managed to keep his differences with de Gaulle from disrupting the entire alliance. During the dispute over Iraq, on the other hand, pundits and policy makers on both sides of the Atlantic exchanged what one observer has called "an unprecedented burst of rhetorical venom."[47] Then again, not even de Gaulle, in spite of his public criticism, much less any other European leader of the 1960s, actively tried to block American actions in Vietnam, as France and Germany did in the UN Security Council forty years later.

In fact, Europeans did quarrel much less with Washington's reasoning for fighting in Vietnam than they did with its arguments to invade Iraq. Although the American legal position with regard to both the 1954 Geneva Agreement and the provisions of the SEATO Treaty was anything but in-disputable, its vocal critics were mainly confined to fringe groups on the far left. Only when larger parts of the population ceased to see Vietnam exclu-sively through a Cold War lens and began to conceive of it as a civil war did they start to call the legitimacy of the American engagement into question. Even then, however, it was first and foremost American actions *in* the war rather than justifications *for* the war that accounted for the rising criticism. Just like many Americans, Europeans were repelled by television coverage of carpet bombings and the resulting heavy physical destruction and loss of civilian lives within both North and South Vietnam. They were disturbed by reports and photographs in the world press of atrocities committed by U.S. troops and their South Vietnamese allies. They were, in short, increasingly drawing the conclusion that the United States was waging a dirty war against a small and ravaged nation in Southeast Asia for no good reason.

European public opinion clearly turned against the Vietnam War in the winter and spring of 1967. In February, U.S. actions still commanded some predominance of support in Britain and Italy while opinion in Germany was almost evenly divided. By May, however, support had been substantially reduced in Britain and cut almost in half in Germany, Italy, and France, where it had never been strong to begin with. In all four countries majorities or substantial pluralities now opposed U.S. actions. In West Germany, the net favorable—calculated by deducting the percentage of negative answers from positive ones—which had been solidly in the affirmative during the early years of the war, went from +6 in February 1967 to −35 in May and −39 in December. Peace activists began to compare American actions in Vietnam to German atrocities during World War II, and an International War Crimes Tribunal—presided over by Bertrand Russell and Jean-Paul Sartre—convened in Stockholm, Sweden, and Roskilde, Denmark, to charge the United States with genocide. Not surprisingly, such accusations were reinforced by the My Lai massacre. And while some observers ascribed the particularly ferocious German reaction to the carnage to an urge to serve Americans with the same sauce they had dished up to Germans after 1945, many other Europeans expressed their dismay as well, calling for the United States to heed the rules of warfare and the standards of civilized conduct in Vietnam.[48]

For an overwhelming majority of Europeans, to be sure, American atrocities in Vietnam represented deplorable yet isolated incidents, incapable of calling into question a common culture and shared values. At the dawn of the twenty-first century, however, Europeans seem to be less inclined to look upon similar transgressions in Afghanistan, Iraq, and Guantánamo as inescapable concomitants of war. Instead, they have started to wonder whether the United States is not about to betray a common cultural heritage.

Values

In Iraq, as in Vietnam, American warfare has projected overwhelming and advanced technological resources against outgunned enemies, while at the same time having to contend with a confusing and treacherous situation on the ground. In Iraq, as in Vietnam, this combination has resulted in appalling human rights abuses.

The most infamous of the abuses in Vietnam occurred in March 1968, when soldiers of Charlie Company, 11th brigade, Americal Division, massacred several hundred villagers in the hamlet of My Lai. Thirty-seven and a half years later, in the early morning hours of November 19, 2005, troops of Kilo Company, 3rd battalion, 1st Marine Regiment, entered the desert city of Haditha and butchered twenty-four civilians, including women and children, in what a London editorial called "My Lai on the Euphrates." Although the number of victims was far smaller this time, some parallels were unmistakable. As in My Lai, the perpetrators had sustained painful losses in the days and months leading up to the atrocity. Inflicted by an invisible and elusive enemy, these losses had frustrated soldiers. Their nerves were all on edge. Nor was this true only for the localities in which these particular incidents happened. In fact, reports that troops involved in the carnage at Haditha saw the events as part of the normal course of combat evoked Colonel Oran K. Henderson's assertion in 1971: "Every unit of brigade size has its My Lai hidden some place." Recalling the repercussions of My Lai, commentators on both sides of the Atlantic wondered whether Haditha would turn the American public against a war that was corroding American values.[49]

It is a strange coincidence that the same journalist who uncovered the My Lai massacre in 1969, Seymour Hersh, also disclosed the single most damaging episode of the American occupation in Iraq, namely the Abu Ghraib prison scandal. The repugnant pictures that shocked the world in the spring of 2004 became even more disturbing when Hersh and others revealed that they were rooted in decisions made at the highest level of the political leadership.[50] Already before the disquieting paper trail began to accumulate, there was a near-unanimous call from the European press for the U.S. secretary of defense, Donald Rumsfeld, to resign. Even conservative papers like the German *Die Welt* and Spain's *ABC* joined the chorus. The cover of the British *Economist*, displaying one of the most ghastly pictures emanating from Abu Ghraib—a hooded man with outstretched arms, wired as if for electrocution—carried a headline uncharacteristically blunt for Europe's most venerable newsmagazine: "Resign, Rumsfeld." Inside, a full-page editorial reasoned that the image might well acquire the same iconic status as the famous photograph of a naked girl running toward a camera during the Vietnam War, and it lamented that the abuse at Abu Ghraib "forms part of a culture of extra-legal behavior that has been set at the highest level." It was this realization that most disturbed European opinion leaders—not that soldiers under duress would violate human rights but that the civilian leadership seemed to condone if not wantonly accept this kind of conduct.[51]

To be sure, many Europeans acknowledged that the American government condemned the incidents, launched several investigations, and put the perpetrators on trial. Yet the Bush administration's assurances rang ever more hollow with each new report of prisoner mistreatment and each new internal memorandum trying to circumvent both U.S. and international law that was leaked to the press. There already had been a short flare-up of European human rights sensibilities over the treatment of detainees at the U.S. naval base at Guantánamo Bay, Cuba, in early 2002. Darkly fore-boding, a British commentator had warned back then of "the gulf this [treat-ment] is opening up between two cultures that imagine they have everything important in common." And even the conservative *Daily Telegraph* ad-monished Washington to treat its prisoners in the war on terror according to the Geneva norms, lest it would endanger the "distinction between ci-vilised society and the apocalyptic savagery of those who would destroy it." However, dismissed even by reputable American papers as the clamor of "America-bashers in the European press and human rights community," the outcry quickly subsided when the Bush administration promised that detainees would be treated "consistently with the principles of the Geneva Conventions."[52] Indeed, only four months after 9/11, many Europeans still accepted that there would inevitably be some initial irregularity in Ameri-can efforts to cope with a novel situation.

Abu Ghraib, however, brought these earlier qualms back with a ven-geance, serving as a poignant reminder that—more than two years into the campaign—America's detainees were still being denied any semblance of Western justice. In addition, there was mounting evidence that the Bush administration's protestations that prisoners would be treated "consistently with the principles" of international law had never referred to the letter of the law but merely to its spirit—with the Bush administration reserving the right to single-handedly interpret that spirit. Thus, it turned out that the first wave of international outrage had hardly abated when President Bush signed an order determining that, in fact, "none of the provisions of Geneva apply to our conflict with al Qaeda in Afghanistan or elsewhere throughout the world." In the following months and years, lawyers from the White House, Justice Department, and Defense Department spared no ink petti-fogging the question of torture. In August 2002, a memorandum signed by Assistant Attorney General Jay S. Bybee asserted that nothing constituted torture short of the exertion of "serious physical injury so severe that death, organ failure, or permanent damage resulting in a loss of significant body functions will likely result." In December 2002, Secretary Rumsfeld ap-proved counter-resistance techniques for interrogations at Guantánamo that included stripping, hooding, stress positions, sensory deprivations, and the use of attack dogs. An April 2003 working group report went so far as to argue that President Bush's constitutional authority as Commander-in-Chief in fact overrode any legal limits on prisoner interrogations. In other words, the President of the United States in his capacity as military leader is above the law, whereas those he high-handedly designates as "enemy combatants"—a category unknown to and a concept highly contentious in international law—are beneath, i.e. outside of, the law.[53]

It should not come as a surprise, then, that European commentators perceive a common heritage to be in danger. The rule of law, after all, has long been considered a fundamental tenet of western democracies, and abolishing torture was a central aim of the eighteenth-century Enlightenment, which shaped both Western European and American civilization. Now, however, Europeans smell a new form of American exceptionalism—an exeptionalism that claims an exemption from civilized norms when it comes to terrorists or suspects of terrorism, relegating these human beings to a rung one step below mankind. David Rose's report about the plight of five British citizens in Guantánamo—published in a German paperback edition even before the English original appeared—is subtitled "America's War on Human Rights."[54]

Most disturbing, the American political system seems to be unwilling or unable to reverse this trend. While the infamous August 2002 memorandum was withdrawn in the wake of the Abu Ghraib scandal and Donald Rumsfeld quickly rescinded his approval of questionable interrogation techniques (making them subject to his personal approval on a case-by-case basis), the Bush administration has continued its efforts to establish esoteric differences between abuse or mistreatment and torture, and it has fought attempts to rein in CIA interrogators tooth and nail. With the Military Commissions Act, signed into law by President Bush on October 17, 2006, the U.S. Congress has largely caved in to the executive branch's desires, stripping noncitizens of habeas corpus rights and granting the White House the right to interpret—without any review by the courts—the Geneva Conventions and to determine the rules for interrogations. Although the law includes a ban on the harshest treatment of detainees, senators and the administration have already disagreed on whether that would include, for instance, the technique of "waterboarding," in which prisoners are immersed in water until they nearly drown. The ongoing debate is astounding to most Europeans, in particular since, as François Heisbourg of the Foundation for Strategic Research in Paris has pointed out, the technique "harkens back to one of the favorite practices of the Gestapo—the bathtub torture, which was a synonym for waterboarding." Meanwhile, the instigators of America's new exceptionalism have been rewarded instead of being held accountable. Secretary of Defense Donald Rumsfeld was kept on for the second term until his November 8, 2006, resignation. Alberto Gonzales has been promoted to the highest law enforcement job in the country. Jay S. Bybee is now a federal judge at the U.S. Court of Appeals for the Ninth Circuit. All this might well ensure that the question of human rights will remain for some time to come what Harvard's Andrew Moravcsik perceives it to be, namely "the single most severe irritant in U.S.-European relations . . . testifying to a widening divergence between U.S. and European identities."[55]

Drift?

The French philosopher Jacques Derrida, surveying the curtailment of fundamental rights and the violation of human rights in the course of America's global war on terrorism, accused the Bush administration of "state terrorism." Not coincidentally, it was also Derrida who—together with Germany's leading philosopher, Jürgen Habermas—instigated a series of articles about European identity in reputable German, French, Italian, Spanish, and Swiss dailies in the wake of the Iraq War. Arguing that the mass demonstrations on February 15, 2003, in Berlin, London, Madrid, Paris, Rome, and many other cities had signified "the birth of a European public sphere," Habermas and Derrida set out to delineate the constituents of a European identity. They found them in a strong secularism in politics, a relatively large trust in the civilizing power of the state and its capacity to correct the excesses of capitalism, a heightened sensitivity to the potential brutality of state power as reflected in the ban on capital punishment, and a belief in the mutual limitation of sovereignty.[56] It is, of course, easy to detect the foil against which this catalog has been contrived: the conspicuous role of religion in American politics, America's allegedly merciless capitalism and continuing application of the death penalty, and—last but not least—the Bush administration's crass unilateralism. European intellectuals, then, have begun to employ America as a convenient "other" against which the blueprint of a closely circumscribed common European identity can be created. Thus, if the Vietnam War did afford individual European countries the opportunity to recalibrate aspects of their national identity,[57] then the Iraq War and its concomitants seem bound to expedite the emergence of common European identity.

The indignation aroused among large parts of the European public by American human rights violations in Afghanistan, Iraq, and Guantánamo, and the growing unease among political and intellectual elites about developments within the American political system, could become a potentially powerful catalyst for efforts to construct a common European identity by setting the continent apart from its increasingly strange-looking ally across the Atlantic. To be sure, European governments have enacted antiterrorism legislation of their own that infringes on individual rights. Several countries also seem to have tacitly tolerated, if not cooperated in, the CIA's program of extraordinary renditions, which has widely been denounced as outsourcing torture. European politicians have repeatedly called for Guantánamo to be closed but have on various occasions blocked the return of their own citizens from the detention facility. A German citizen recently released from Guantánamo has even accused German Special Forces of participating in his mistreatment while he was in American confinement.[58] Yet if more reports on American atrocities should surface and—more importantly—if the U.S. government continues in its unapologetic maceration of the rule of law, these indications of European complicity might not keep Europeans from assuming the mantle of the true champion of Western civilization, developing a new sense of mission apart from or even directed against the United States. Should that happen and should it become impossible for Europeans to see their values reflected also in the Stars and Stripes, then the American flag would have forfeited its raison d'être in Europe.

4

Manufacturing the Threat to Justify Aggressive War in Vietnam and Iraq

GARETH PORTER

One of the most chilling parallels between Vietnam and Iraq is the way in which the war planners deliberately created threats out of whole cloth to justify going to war. They felt they had to have a serious threat, because without it, political resistance would have been too strong, whether inside the government, outside it, or both. A comparison of the two cases underlines a common characteristic of aggressive war in a democratic system.

But the comparison also reveals both a fundamental difference in the politics of Vietnam and Iraq and an enormous difference in the sophistication and skill with which deceit and manipulation were used to ensure the necessary political support for war. The neoconservatives who engineered the United States into aggressive war on Iraq faced a much tougher task in obtaining the necessary official public compliance to open the path to war than did the national security advisers to Kennedy and Johnson on Vietnam. In the early twenty-first century there was no longer an enemy perceived to be malevolent and all-powerful, and the attentive public was no longer automatically inclined to support military force when the government called for it. But the Bush war planners were much more self-conscious, systematic, and disciplined in their approach to creating the story line they needed to go to war than the war planners of the Kennedy-Johnson era.

Those differences are an indication of how much the system for waging aggressive war has evolved in the more than four decades between Vietnam and Iraq. In the end, however, it is still the commonality of the two cases that stands out. Those who were pushing for aggressive war had to conjure up a threat, because nothing in the region of interest supported a case for the use of force, and they knew it. In both the 1953–65 period of the Cold War and again in the post–Cold War era (1991–2006), the United States was overwhelmingly dominant in military terms, both globally and in the regions in question. In the 1954–62 period, China was known by U.S. policy makers to be militarily weak and was on the defensive, seeking to accommodate capitalist and even feudalist regimes in the region in the hope of containing U.S. military influence in the region, especially in East Asia. The Communist movements in Southeast Asia, except for those in Vietnam and Laos, were either small and weak or supportive of the noncommunist regime. In the Persian Gulf and the Middle East in 2001, no regional state was threatening to dominate the region.

U.S. intelligence was well aware of these realities in both cases. When they are not put under intense political pressure to bend their analysis to policy, professional intelligence analysts generally have no difficulty distinguishing between the real geopolitical and military situation in a given region and an official line put out for public consumption. That is why the war planners had to do an end run around the intelligence community in the 1960s and again in the early years of the twenty-first century. In the case of Vietnam, they either pretended that the intelligence estimates on the issue did not exist or made a slight obeisance to them but then asserted something completely different; in the Iraq case, they went even further, putting intense pressure on the intelligence professionals while using fabricated evidence both to skew intelligence and to construct a case for public consumption.

Vietnam and the "Loss of Southeast Asia"

In the era of the Eisenhower and Kennedy administrations, the United States was the overwhelmingly militarily dominant power in East Asia. By the early 1960s, the U.S. Navy's Seventh Fleet had 140 ships, including seven aircraft carriers, in the region, and the U.S. military had major air and naval bases in Japan, Okinawa, Korea, and the Philippines from which it could launch attack air attacks against China and was constructing new bases in Thailand from which it could strike deep into China as well. The U.S. military and political posture toward China was one of explicit and overt threat to the regime, backed up by a system of bases and alliances that physically surrounded China.[1] The most immediate threat to the Chinese regime was the 100,000 Nationalist Chinese troops based on offshore islands backed by the U.S. Seventh Fleet, which ostentatiously sailed up and down the Taiwan Strait only a few miles from the mainland. The Nationalist troops constantly maneuvered in the Taiwan Strait with the participation of U.S. officers and provoked incidents with Chinese Communist troops.[2]

From the mid-1950s through the early 1960s, apart from this aggressive U.S. policy toward China, East Asia offered a remarkably peaceful setting, in which the threat of Communist revolution engulfing Southeast Asia was, at worst, extremely remote. Not only was China turning away from support for Communist movements in the region, but it was seeking to establish normal ties with regimes of all stripes, including military allies of the United States.[3] The Communist parties of Southeast Asia, except for those in Vietnam and Laos, were either too weak to threaten incumbent regimes or had a strong stake in preserving the bourgeois nationalist regime (as in the case of the Indonesian Communist Party). Even the Communist regime in North Vietnam, which maintained the objective of reuniting the country divided by the establishment of a U.S.-protected client regime in the South, followed the injunction of Soviet premier Nikita Khrushchev as well as Mao Zedong to maintain peace and wait for more favorable circumstances to take action on the issue, at least until 1959.[4]

But the Eisenhower administration took advantage of the absence of threat from the Communist states and movements to focus on the objective of consolidating client regimes in South Vietnam, Laos, and Thailand, which would then cooperate with the United States in its broader Cold War strategy in regard to China and North Vietnam. In South Vietnam and Laos, the strategy took the form of ignoring the Geneva Accords, consolidating the power of pro-U.S. regimes, and seeking to destroy the South Vietnamese Communist movement left behind after the Geneva agreements and the Lao Communist movement as well as Lao neutralism. Meanwhile, Washington was exploiting its alliance with the Thai military to get four major air bases in Thailand from which U.S. bombers could hit targets in China and North Vietnam.[5] As for the government in North Vietnam the Eisenhower administration called the "Viet Minh," the policy was one of destabilization by denying its legitimacy, discouraging other noncommunist states from having relations with it, and undertaking actions to "probe weaknesses of the Viet Minh and exploit them internally and internationally whenever possible."[6]

The Kennedy administration continued the policy of surrounding and threatening China, as new international and internal Chinese developments made the Communist regime even more vulnerable to such external pressures. Washington was aware that the emergence of serious conflict between Mao's China and Khrushchev's Soviet Union in 1961–62 left the Chinese Communist regime without the prospect of Soviet support in the event of confrontation with the United States. Meanwhile, the widespread famine and unrest caused by Mao Zedong's disastrous Great Leap Forward program of the late 1950s weakened the Chinese military. Nationalist China's Jiang Jiexi and his CIA allies were pressing in spring 1962 for the United States to support an airborne invasion of the Chinese mainland by several teams of 200–300 Nationalist Chinese commandos. And a secret November 1962 policy paper on China said the United States should avoid any action that would "reduce pressures operating on the regime," including "pressures resulting from our military presence in the Taiwan Strait, Korea and Southeast Asia."[7]

In this regional setting of a U.S. posture that was on the offensive against China, South Vietnam and Laos threatened a breach in the U.S. Cold War system in East Asia. Communist movements had taken up arms and had gained control over large parts of the countryside, replacing the tenuous authority of pro-U.S. governments. The national security bureaucracy, led by the Joint Chiefs of Staff (JCS), immediately pressed Kennedy for a commitment of U.S. forces in Laos, and a strike against North Vietnam and/or China, if they should intervene. In the summer and fall, after Kennedy had rejected their advice to intervene in Laos, Kennedy's advisers began calling for the deployment of U.S. troops to South Vietnam as well. In October, the JCS gave Kennedy a plan for the deployment of 170,000 troops, 128,000 of which were to deal with the potential intervention of North Vietnam and China. A mission to South Vietnam, led by White House advisers General Maxwell Taylor and Walt W. Rostow, recommended the introduction of 8,000 troops, to be followed by more later on.

As the date for a crucial National Security Council meeting on the issue of military intervention in Vietnam approached, the national security advisers struggled over how to convince Kennedy, who they knew was already skeptical about committing military forces in Southeast Asia, that it was necessary for U.S. national security. They recognized that they would have to portray the struggle in South Vietnam as having a significance extending to the entire Southeast Asian region in order to have any chance of success.

But they had a serious problem: the intelligence community had already told a completely different story in an estimate issued in the first weeks of the new administration. That National Intelligence Estimates (NIE) had underlined the relative stability and security that would remain in noncommunist Southeast Asia even in the event that Laos and South Vietnam were both lost to Communist movements. The estimate projected no "falling dominoes"—no states going Communist or even allying with the Communist China—if that happened. It concluded that the result of the loss of Laos would be that Thailand, then a military ally that was allowing the United States to build major air bases to bomb China and North Vietnam, would "almost certainly incline . . . toward accommodation to Communist power in Southeast Asia" and cause other states in the region to feel a "strong temptation to take a neutral position between the two power blocs." A Communist victory in South Vietnam, it said, would have the same effect, only "more severe."[8] In other words, there would be less willingness to follow the same policies of hostility toward China and North Vietnam as in the past.

This was hardly a shocking analysis, given the general unwillingness in the region to unnecessarily antagonize China. After all, the very Thai military leaders who had made their deals with the United States in order to get U.S. largesse had secretly reached an agreement with China in 1956–57 on eventual normalization of relations and even encouraged the Thai press to criticize the hard-line U.S. policy toward China.[9] And Burma, Cambodia, and Indonesia were already committed to a neutralist posture in the Asian Cold War, so the intelligence assessment was essentially predicting no change in their policy. As for the Philippines, where the United States had major air and naval bases, the last presidential candidate to challenge the country's Cold War anti-China policy had been humiliated in the 1957 election, with the help of a CIA dirty tricks campaign that had distributed free condoms with holes in them in the candidate's name.[10]

The intelligence finding thus provided no basis for making a case for going to war in South Vietnam, and Kennedy's advisers knew it. Furthermore, they knew that Kennedy was aware of the intelligence analysis, so they couldn't completely ignore it. But Secretary of Defense Robert S. McNamara and his deputy Roswell Gipatric had to come up with a threat that would justify the recommendation that they were joining the JCS in making for "the introduction of U.S. forces on a substantial scale" and a warning to Hanoi of "punitive retaliation" if it continued to support the Vietcong.

McNamara may have believed the formula they used to dramatize the stakes in South Vietnam was clever, perhaps even artful. But it was rather amateurish. "The fall of South Vietnam to Communism," he wrote in a memorandum to Kennedy on behalf of Gilpatric and JCS on November 8, 1961, "would lead to the fairly rapid extension of Communist control, or complete accommodation to Communism, in the rest of mainland Southeast Asia and in Indonesia." Except for the use of the word "accommodation," it had nothing in common with the intelligence analysis. And it offered no evidence to support that heavy-handed language. Three days later McNamara and Secretary of State Dean Rusk sent Kennedy another variant of that formula, describing the dire consequences of failing to defeat the Communist uprising in South Vietnam: "We would have to face the near certainty," they wrote, "that the remainder of Southeast Asia and Indonesia would move to a complete accommodation with Communism, if not formal incorporation within the Communist bloc."

Kennedy knew this was just a ploy—a tactic in the bureaucratic game being played by those who were pushing for war. Expecting them to haul out the old falling-domino argument to support their recommendation for a commitment of U.S. troops to South Vietnam, Kennedy told Arthur Krock, a longtime family friend and confidant, on October 11, 1961, he doubted that the United States should intervene in "civil disturbances caused by guerrillas," such as in South Vietnam. And he expressed doubt that the falling-domino theory "has much point any more because . . . the Chinese Communists are bound to get nuclear weapons in time, and from that moment on they will dominate South East Asia."[11]

When the showdown at the National Security Council meeting came, Kennedy again expressed doubt that South Vietnam was worth a war, and not one participant tried to argue the case that Southeast Asia would be lost in the event the war in South Vietnam was lost. The pro-war hawks in the administration never tried to fabricate such a threat to Southeast Asia again before Kennedy was shot down in Dallas.[12]

Shortly after Lyndon Johnson become president, the same coterie of national security advisers—McNamara, Rusk, National Security Adviser McGeorge Bundy, and Taylor—went into action again to revive a domino theory that none of them took seriously themselves. They considered Johnson to be relatively unsophisticated and lacking in self-confidence on foreign affairs and therefore more credulous about the threat to Southeast Asia they needed to create.

The occasion for the resuscitation of a theory that had long been discredited within the executive branch was the first effort by the national security advisers to get Johnson's approval for the idea of bombing North Vietnam. In late February McNamara ordered his assistant secretary, William P. Bundy, to draft a paper supporting that recommendation to Johnson. But again, those who wished to build a case for catastrophic consequences of giving up the U.S. power position in South Vietnam to the Communists had a problem: only days before, the intelligence community had issued a new Special NIE that had presented a more forceful refutation of the domino theory. It reaffirmed previous intelligence estimates that the defeat of the South Vietnamese government would "have a serious effect on the future willingness of government in Southeast Asia to adopt anti-Communist, rather than neutralist stances." But it carefully distinguished this impact from the idea that noncommunist Southeast Asia would simply give up and join the Communist side. The primary effect, it observed, would be a series of "livable settlements with the Communists"—an outcome very different from the dire consequences predicted by the domino theory.[13]

Bundy thus had to either acknowledge that the threat that the United States would face in Southeast Asia if it did not go to war in Vietnam was one of neutralism, not Communism, or simply pretend that the new intelligence estimate didn't exist. He chose the latter course, and engaged in an exercise in creative writing on Southeast Asia. "Unless we can achieve [our] objective in South Vietnam," his draft paper warned, "almost all of Southeast Asia will probably fall rapidly under Communist dominance (all of Vietnam, Laos and Cambodia), accommodate to Communism so as to remove effective US and anti-Communist influence (Burma), or fall under the domination of forces not now explicitly Communist but likely then to become so (Indonesia taking over Malaysia)." Bundy portrayed Thailand as certain to come under "grave pressure," the Philippines as becoming "shaky," and an unexplained threat to the rest of East and South Asia and the Pacific all the way to New Zealand as "greatly increased."[14]

As Bundy knew very well, such claims were directly contradicted not only by the CIA's analysis but by State Department reporting as well.[15] In fact, this alarmist line was quite different from what Bundy had written on the same subject only a few weeks earlier, which had merely portrayed Thailand and Malaysia as likely to become "shaky"—a term that was deliberately vague in order to imply more than could be stated explicitly.[16] This description of a menacing situation in the region after defeat in South Vietnam drafted by Bundy on March 1 was what Johnson's national security advisers evidently believed was necessary to get Johnson's acquiescence to their war plan.

Lyndon Johnson rejected the bombing program recommended by Mc-Namara, but in late May, Rusk, McNamara, and McGeorge Bundy all returned to the idea that Johnson would be responsible for the Southeast Asian dominoes falling if he failed to take resolute action against North Vietnam. Johnson complained to his friend Senator Richard Russell (D.-Ga.) that his advisers had been trying to convince him that Vietnam would be "a domino that will kick off a whole list of others" and that therefore "we've just got to prepare for the worst."[17]

Instead of accepting the argument, however, Johnson sought the views of the CIA's intelligence analysts on the question "Would the rest of Southeast Asia necessarily fall if Laos and South Vietnam came under North Vietnamese control?" Since that subject had already been addressed in the CIA's early February estimate on mainland Southeast Asia, Johnson's request makes it clear that McGeorge Bundy had deliberately kept that strategic information out of the president's hands, the better to deceive him by ginning up a nonexistent threat in Southeast Asia.

The memorandum that the director of the CIA's Office of National Estimates sent back to the White House a few days later reaffirmed the CIA's earlier conclusion that Southeast Asia would not follow South Vietnam and Laos into the Communist camp. "With the possible exception of Cambodia," the memorandum said, "it is likely that no nation in the area would quickly succumb to Communism as a result of the fall of Laos and Vietnam," it said. Nor, it added, would the further spread of Communism in the area be "inexorable." It observed that "any spread which did occur would take time—time in which the total situation might change in any number of ways unfavorable to the Communist cause." The memo also rejected the notion that Southeast Asian countries would "bandwagon" to the Communist side. The analysts anticipated that Thailand's military cooperation with the United States would be "reduced," but said the Thais would shift to a "neutralist position" rather than a pro-Communist one. As for the Philippines and Japan, the memo said they would maintain their policy of military cooperation with Washington, despite increased internal political pressures for neutralism.[18]

The CIA memo soon became known in the intelligence communist as the "Death of the Domino Theory Memo."[19] When William Bundy heard about it, he began backing off his earlier concoction. Bundy was no longer working for McNamara but was now assistant secretary of state for East Asian affairs and thus, in theory, the administration's leading policy maker on the region. On June 15 he wrote a paper making it clear that the problem in Southeast Asia would be a wave not of Communism but of neutralism.[20]

However, Bundy's rejection of the falling-domino scenario he had previously drafted didn't prevent him from suggesting that it be used to drum up public support for an aggressive U.S. war against North Vietnam. Bundy and State Department official Michael Forrestal recommended in late July that Democratic candidates and their supporters be prompted to argue during the electoral campaign that "preventing Communist domination of South Vietnam is of the highest importance to U.S. national security." The campaign line they advocated would have argued that if South Vietnam was lost, "Burma and India to the west and the Philippines to the east" would also go Communist.[21] That was a line which Bundy himself did not believe, but about which he evidently had no compunction, as long as it was directed at a presumably gullible public rather than a president who was now privy to the CIA's analysis of the issue. The idea was never taken up by the Democratic Party.

The Joint Chiefs of Staff, like Johnson's civilian advisers, were determined to get Johnson's approval for a bombing campaign against North Vietnam. They were also sure enough of their political authority to simply ignore the CIA estimate that stood in their way. Meeting with Johnson and his other advisers in early September, JCS chairman General Earle G. Wheeler suggested that failure to prevail in South Vietnam would lead to abject surrender by noncommunist Southeast Asia to China. He told Johnson the JCS agreed unanimously that "if we should lose South Vietnam, we would lose Southeast Asia," adding, "Country after country would give way and look toward Communist China as the rising power of the area." Both Rusk and CIA director John McCone, who betrayed his own Office of National Estimates, then associated themselves with the JCS view.[22]

This was the same bandwagon argument—the idea that noncommunist countries would be "lost" by aligning themselves with China against the United States—that the CIA had debunked, but it now had the power and prestige of the JCS behind it. The coterie of civilian advisers bent on war was ready to exploit this new asset in their campaign to get Johnson's approval for war against North Vietnam. But William Bundy suddenly became a new problem for them. In October, he wrote a forty-two-page analysis underlining the difference between states making accommodations with China and becoming "vassal states" of China. And in November, Bundy, who was coordinator of a working group drafting papers in support of a new recommendation to the president for bombing North Vietnam, wrote the paper on U.S. objectives and strategic stakes in South Vietnam himself. In that paper, he acknowledged that the loss of South Vietnam would threaten the ability of the United States to continue pursuing the same hard-line policy of isolation and pressure on China, but not the survival of a noncommunist and independent Southeast Asia.[23]

Johnson's principal advisers—McNamara, Rusk, and McGeorge Bundy—could not allow William Bundy to continue to make an independent argument that interfered with their political strategy for getting presidential approval of their bombing plan. They resorted to hardball tactics to eliminate that analysis from the paper that would go to Johnson. On November 24, those three, along with Undersecretary of State George Ball, McCone, and Wheeler, reached a "consensus" to dismiss William Bundy's analysis of the strategic stake. They cited the alarmist view of the JCS's response to Bundy's draft, which referred to the "early loss of Southeast Asia and the progressive unraveling of the wider defense structures" as inevitable consequences of the loss of South Vietnam.[24] Johnson's key advisers, determined to go to war in Vietnam, hoped that the president would be swayed by the political weight of the alliance of national security bureaucracies standing behind this hyped-up description of the threat.

Saddam and the "Mushroom Cloud"

Just as war in Vietnam was rooted in the determination of the U.S. national security elite to maintain the dominant power position the United States held in East Asia, the roots of the war in Iraq lie in the collapse of the Soviet Union and the emergence of the United States as the sole superpower in 1991. But during the first post–Cold War decade, U.S. power in the region was far less dominant than it had been during the high tide of U.S. power in East Asia. As a result of the 1991 Gulf War, the U.S. military obtained a semipermanent role in Iraq by creating no-fly zones for Saddam's forces in both the north and the south patrolled by U.S. planes based in Kuwait and Saudi Arabia. Beginning in 1998, those zones provided a vehicle the Clinton administration could use to carry out increasingly aggressive bombing operations against military targets in Iraq.

Nevertheless, the United States lacked permanent bases, and its access to facilities in the Gulf remained politically tenuous, given Saudi sensitivities about the U.S. military presence. And all across the region Arab governments were generally unsympathetic to U.S. policy in the Middle East—especially its close relationship with Israel. The United States had no political-military allies in the region providing major bases from which it could project power into the rest of the region. That constrained U.S. political-military influence in the Middle East.

There was thus a wide chasm between the complete U.S. military dominance globally and its relatively limited military presence in the Persian Gulf. That gap frustrated the neoconservatives and hard-line officials from past Republican administrations who had attacked détente and advocated victory over the Soviet Union in the Cold War. This group of former top national security officials—led by Dick Cheney, Paul Wolfowitz, and Donald Rumsfeld, and including Richard Perle and Douglas Feith—believed the United States had both the might and the right to pursue far more ambitious political-military objectives in the Middle East and elsewhere than the Clinton administration had done in its eight years in office.[25]

They advocated a more deliberate exploitation of U.S. military supremacy in the world to change the Middle East to conform to U.S. interests. Their focus was on Iraq, where the United States was already in a powerful position to go after Saddam Hussein's regime. Because of the ruinous Iran-Iraq War, the U.S. Gulf War in 1991, and the U.S. economic sanctions against Iraq, the country had experienced a precipitous economic and military decline. It had lost 60 percent of its ground combat divisions and its tanks. Its military spending had fallen by 85 percent. And its arms imports had declined by 95 percent, making it impossible to keep its military ready for combat, much less modernized.[26] This loss of economic and military resources made Iraq a tempting target for regime change through military force for the neoconservatives.

In 1998 Wolfowitz drafted a letter calling on Bill Clinton to take over Southern Iraq for an anti-Saddam provisional government, protect it with U.S. airpower, and then expand the zone until Saddam was overthrown. Five other men who would later be named to the five top national security jobs in the Bush administration—Donald Rumsfeld (secretary of defense), Douglas Feith (undersecretary of defense for policy), Zalmay Khalilzad (National Security Council staff), Richard Armitage (deputy secretary of state), and John Bolton (undersecretary of state)—were among the signatories to the letter.[27]

But regime change in Iraq was only the beginning of much larger military ambitions nurtured by the neoconservatives in the Gulf region, in line with a global posture of exploiting U.S. supremacy to the hilt. A white paper on national defense released in 2000 by the Project for the New American Century (PNAC), with which the leading neoconservative figures were closely associated, laid out a "blueprint for maintaining global U.S. preeminence, precluding the rise of a great power rival, and shaping the international security order in line with American principles and interests." It was straightforward about the objective of gaining a new military position in the Middle East with which to project its power. "The U.S. has for decades sought to play a more permanent role in the Gulf regional security," it said. "While the unresolved conflict with Iraq provides the immediate justification, the need for a substantial American force presence in the Gulf transcends the issue of the regime of Saddam Hussein." It noted the difficulty that "Saudi domestic sensibilities" presented for the maintenance of bases in Saudi Arabia, hinting broadly that Iraq was the place this "permanent Gulf military presence" would have to be located. Such a presence was necessary, it said, even "should Saddam pass from the scene," because "Iran may well prove as large a threat."[28]

The neoconservatives viewed the overthrow of Saddam as opening the way for just such a major increase in U.S. military presence, which they would use to transform the region. Rumsfeld informed a National Security Council meeting on February 1, 2001, that getting rid of Saddam was the administration's top priority. He hinted at the administration's broader aims in the Persian Gulf region, saying, "Imagine what the region would look like without Saddam and with a regime that's aligned with U.S. interests."[29]

Then came the terrorist attacks of September 11, 2001. Those attacks promised to sweep away the domestic political constraints on the use of U.S. military power in a wave of national fear and support for decisive military action against terrorists. But it was not Osama bin Laden and al-Qaeda that interested the Bush administration's top officials but Saddam Hussein and Iraq. Within five hours of the American Airlines plane crashing into the Pentagon, the neoconservative team began urgent planning for an attack on Iraq. Rumsfeld told his aides, according to one official's notes, that he wanted the "best info" available to "judge whether good enough to hit SH [Saddam Hussein] at the same time, not only OBL [Osama bin Laden]." According to the notes, Rumsfeld said he wanted to "go massive . . . sweep it all up, things related and not." General Greg Newbold, the senior staff officer for the Joint Chiefs of Staff, recalls that a few days later, "you could still smell the smoke in the corridors" when Douglas Feith upbraided him for saying he was working hard on tracking down al-Qaeda in Afghanistan. "Why are you working on Afghanistan?" Feith said. "You ought to be working on Iraq."[30]

The military planning for further use of force against other regimes in the region also began immediately. A few days after 9/11, General Wesley Clark, who commanded the NATO bombing campaign in the Kosovo War, visited with old friends at the Pentagon and was told that there was "a list of states" that Rumsfeld and Wolfowitz wanted to "take down." Two months later, a senior military officer in the Pentagon told Clark that the plan to attack Iraq "was being discussed as part of a five-year campaign plan" that would involve a total of seven countries in the Middle East and even the Horn of Africa: Iraq, Iran, Syria, Lebanon, Libya, Sudan, and Somalia.[31] The Bush administration's first special envoy to Afghanistan, James Dobbins, has confirmed that U.S. military planning after 9/11 was based on "an intention that the U.S. would retain troops in Iraq—not for Iraq stabilization, because that was thought not to be needed, but for coercive diplomacy in the region." The two main targets of that coercion, according to Dobbins, were to be Iran and Syria.[32]

Beyond Iraq, the primary target for regime change was the Islamic Republic of Iran. In January 2003, two months before the Iraq invasion, officials in the Near East and South Asia bureau (NESA) and the Office of Special Plans under Douglas Feith were discussing "going after Iran" once the Iraq war had ended, according to Lieutenant Colonel Karen Kwiatkowski, who was working in NESA at the time.[33]

But how could the Bush administration sell an aggressive war against Iraq to the American people when there was no evidence linking Saddam to the events of 9/11? Ten days after the attacks on the World Trade Center and the Pentagon, the U.S. intelligence community told George W. Bush in his daily, thirty- to forty-five-minute early-morning national security briefing that there was no evidence linking Saddam's regime to the attacks, and hardly any evidence even of a significant link between Saddam and al-Qaeda. The same information was then incorporated into CIA analyses on contacts between Iraq and al-Qaeda, which went to Bush, Cheney, Rumsfeld, and national security adviser Condoleezza Rice, among others.[34]

But Bush was persuaded by his top national security officials to pay no heed to what the CIA had told him. Cheney, Rumsfeld, and Wolfowitz hated the CIA at least as much as they did their foreign enemies, because agency officials had dismissed their theories about Saddam and al-Qaeda and had opposed their efforts to push their Iraqi client Ahmad Chalabi's agenda over the years.[35]

They had to create a link in the minds of Americans between Saddam's Iraq and the greatest fears Americans had after 9/11, which was that terrorists would explode a nuclear weapon in U.S. cities or introduce a biological weapon such as anthrax. They would have to convince Americans that Saddam was mixed up with al-Qaeda and that there was a serious danger that he would give such weapons to al-Qaeda.

That is what the Bush administration set out to do, employing a complex and multipronged strategy to shape intelligence, media coverage, and public opinion to conform to a line that would be compatible with their interest in going to war against Saddam. Within days of the attacks, Wolfowitz and Feith had set up a secret office to provide the information the administration would need to do so. Eventually given the odd-sounding cover name Policy Counterterrorism Evaluation Group, the office was officially responsible for studying "the policy implications of relationships among terrorist groups and their sources of support." Although it was referred to within the Pentagon as the "Iraqi intelligence cell," it was staffed not by intelligence officers but by loyal neoconservatives: David Wurmser, a close friend and protégé of Richard Perle, and Michael Maloof, another Perle protégé going back to Cold War days. In fact, Wurmser was one of the architects of the neoconservative vision of an Iraq under the exile Ahmed Chalabi. He had written a book in which he proposed an alliance between Jordan and Chalabi's Iraqi National Congress (INC) to redraw the map of the Middle East, and had thanked not only Perle and Feith but Ahmed Chalabi himself for their help. The point of the exercise was to come up with the evidence to support a policy that the neoconservatives had been determined to advance for years.[36]

For zealous neoconservatives to comb through every intelligence report for something that could be used to support the threat they wished to conjure up was a perversion of intelligence analysis. As Paul Pillar, then the national intelligence officer for the Middle East, later observed, "In the shadowy world of international terrorism, almost anyone can be 'linked' to almost anyone else if enough effort is made to find evidence of casual contacts, the mentioning of names in the same breath, or indications of common travels or experiences."[37]

Even as they were putting Wurmser to work assembling evidence to be used to support the Pentagon's war plans for Iraq, the neoconservatives were also encouraging a program that would plant the key pieces of information the administration would use to build its case. The chosen instrument for doing so was that same Iraqi National Congress of Ahmed Chalabi, which fully expected to be the primary beneficiary of a U.S. war on Saddam's Iraq. Chalabi had long enjoyed cozy relations with Perle and Wolfowitz, and, through them, with the entire neoconservative network. The INC had been set up in exile and was operating in northern Iraq under the protection of the U.S. no-fly zone. Perle, Wolfowitz, and Feith had already agreed that Chalabi and the INC "government in exile" would be installed in power once Saddam's regime was destroyed, even though the CIA had long considered him a liar and the State Department charged that he had siphoned off money that was supposed to go to the Iraqi resistance. Perle ran the Defense Policy Board, and when it convened a week after the September 11 terrorist attacks, Chalabi was the featured speaker, with Rumsfeld attending part of the session.[38]

The INC had always been in the business of planting false information about Saddam. Former CIA operative Robert Baer, who had worked with Chalabi in the mid-1990s, went with him in 1994 to visit a "forgery shop" in a town in Kurdistan. Baer described it as "something like a spy novel. It was a room where people were scanning Iraqi intelligence documents into computers and doing disinformation."[39]

A major objective of Chalabi's operation by the late 1990s was to plant defectors claiming that Saddam had an enormous active bioweapons program, a spectacular anti-Saddam story: an alleged fleet of biological weapons labs on wheels. The story was apparently inspired by Israeli intelligence, which had been telling UN weapons inspectors for years that Iraq had mobile biological weapons labs disguised as ice-cream trucks. In 2000, an Iraqi defector surfaced in a German refugee camp claiming to have been recruited by Saddam's regime to design and build such mobile bioweapons labs. German intelligence gave him the codename "Curveball."

But, as was revealed later, the "defector" was the brother of one of Chalabi's top aides, and another Iraqi defector, who had actually worked with him, said Curveball had never worked on such a program. Even though DIA did not know that, they believed he was lying and that he had been coached by the Chalabi group on what to say. When no such mobile labs could be found by the UN inspectors, they concluded that Chalabi and the defectors whom he had offered were liars.[40]

After he began to get funds through the State Department under the 1997 Iraq Liberation Act, Chalabi had turned his attention to the media, hiring the giant public relations firm Burson-Marsteller to help set up meetings between the INC and journalists. But after 9/11 and the beginning of urgent planning for a U.S. invasion of Iraq the INC became much more systematic about planting stories in the foreign press—an indication that Chalabi was being prompted by his friends in the Pentagon and Vice President Cheney's office. By June 2002, the INC had already succeeded in planting no fewer than 108 stories in foreign media, nearly half of which were U.S.-based, about Saddam's alleged weapons of mass destruction and support for al-Qaeda terrorists, according to a memo the group submitted to Congress.[41]

The Chalabi disinformation operation also simultaneously fed directly into the Bush administration's system for shaping government intelligence and for manipulating public opinion. The INC was sending its defector stories directly to Feith's group in the Pentagon and to Cheney's office in the White House. Feith channeled the stories to DIA and also used them to write a long, detailed summary of the alleged intelligence linking Saddam to both al-Qaeda and to WMD, which was sent directly to Congress.[42] Meanwhile, far from maintaining an arm's-length relationship with the neoconservative advisers who were using these reports, Chalabi stayed in close touch with his old friend Richard Perle.[43] Chalabi was, in short, an integral part of the neoconservative team preparing the case for war.

Over the next year, Feith's and Cheney's offices were putting intense pressure on intelligence analysts to integrate their propaganda lines into their analysis and to discredit the CIA for failing to do so. Cheney himself visited the CIA several times during the summer of 2002, and officials from both Feith's and Cheney's offices went back to analysts again and again to question them about specific issues and to request that they "reexamine" their conclusions on both Saddam's link with terrorists and on weapons of mass destruction.[44] The CIA's ombudsman told the Senate Intelligence Committee that he had spoken with approximately twenty-four individuals about whether they had been pressured to change their analysis in regard to Saddam and al-Qaeda. About half a dozen specifically used the word "pressure," and several others implied that that they had been pressured.[45] The Kerr Group report, written as part of an evaluation of the prewar intelligence and analysis on Iraq, also referred to the "constant stream of questions [by policymakers to intelligence analysts] aimed at finding links between Saddam and the terrorist network." It further noted, "Some in the Intelligence Community and elsewhere hold the view that intense policymaker demands in the run-up to the war constituted inappropriate pressure on intelligence analysts."[46]

The single issue on which Feith's office pushed the the intelligence analysts hardest was the allegation that September 11 hijacker Mohamed Atta had met in Prague with a senior Iraqi intelligence officer in April 2001. It was based on a story leaked to the press by an unnamed Czech official in October 2001, and Cheney declared in December 2001 that the meeting was "pretty well confirmed." The problem with the story was that the FBI could find no records showing any travel by Atta to Prague, but it did obtain credit card and phone records that put Atta in Virginia when the meeting was alleged to have taken place. U.S. intelligence officials were very certain that there was no evidence to support the claim.[47]

Nevertheless, Feith and Wolfowitz refused to back off the story, which they clearly viewed as the keystone of their case. In mid-2002, Wolfwitz's office took the argument constructed by Feith's office and turned it into a slide-show briefing that criticized the intelligence community for its failure to find that Saddam was allied with al-Qaeda. The Atta-Iraqi Prague meeting was still a prominent theme in the slide show.[48]

In 2002, Rumsfeld and Wolfowitz felt so strongly about forcing the intelligence analysts to accommodate their position that they apparently considered trying to ram another "Team B" operation, such as the one the anti-détente hardliners had used to make the estimate on Soviet strategic forces tilt toward the neoconservative view in 1976 (just after Rumsfeld had become secretary of defense and Cheney chief of staff in the Ford White House), down the CIA's throat.[49] Rumsfeld found the briefing slide show prepared by one of Wolfowitz's aides "excellent" and asked the briefers to provide "some possible next steps to see if we can illuminate the differences between us and CIA." The briefers reported that there was a possibility of "setting up a small group with our people combined with their [CIA] people" and to "have a session in which each side might make the case for their assessment."[50]

The White House began intensive planning for the "Iraq rollout" in July and determined that the best time to launch a "full-scale lobbying campaign" on the coming war was the day after Labor Day when Congress reconvened. As White House chief of staff Andrew H. Card Jr. explained to the New York Times, "From a marketing point of view, you don't introduce new products in August."[51] A "White House Iraq Group," which included Bush's political strategist Karl Rove, national security adviser Condoleezza Rice, Vice President Cheney's chief of staff, Lewis "Scooter" Libby, and communications adviser Karen Hughes, began meeting in August to plan in detail how the message on Iraq would be shaped in the national media.[52]

The decision was made over the summer that the main theme had to be that Saddam was on his way to making nuclear weapons he would use to threaten the United States. In September 2002 another story deliberately planted by top administration officials provided the introduction to the administration's main message for the next few months. On Sunday, September 8, the *New York Times* published a story by Judith Miller and Michael Gordon that Saddam had attempted to purchase "specially designed aluminum tubes, which American officials believe were intended as components of centrifuges to enrich uranium." The story failed to report the degree to which this interpretation was opposed by most analysts in the intelligence community. But an even more significant quote was the one from an unnamed administration official expressing worry that "the first sign of a 'smoking gun' . . . may be a mushroom cloud."[53]

This was the fearful image that the White House Iraq Group had planned as the central theme of its campaign to play on the nation's post-9/11 fears. The unnamed official quoted in the article was obviously Condi Rice, who was a key member of the group that was determining the day-to-day strategy for manipulating the media. Later that same day, Rice dropped that mask of anonymity when she again invoked that image, declaring on CNN, "We don't want the smoking gun to be a mushroom cloud."[54] Also that day, Cheney, appearing on NBC's *Meet the Press*, cited the *Times* story to buttress the administration's case that Saddam was on his way to producing nuclear weapons.[55]

Rove's White House group felt confident that it could get away with a campaign based on statements not supported by the intelligence analysis because there was no official intelligence estimate that could be leaked to the press by disgruntled officials at the CIA. An NIE on Iraq would have been the normal procedure under the circumstances, but unless the neoconservatives could insert their own people into the process, the war hawk leadership were determined to avoid it.

But a new threat to the plan surfaced when the chairman of the Senate Select Committee on Intelligence, Bob Graham (D-Fla.), met with CIA director George Tenet on September 5, 2002. Graham was stunned to learn that no NIE on Iraq had been requested or prepared. When Graham used the rarely employed senatorial authority to direct the completion of such an NIE, Tenet objected, making the lame excuse that the intelligence analysts were too busy with other assignments to analyze Saddam's capabilities and intentions regarding WMD. Graham insisted, and only then was the process of producing an NIE on Iraq's WMD begun.[56]

The final struggle between intelligence analysts and the war party in the administration came over what would be included in Colin Powell's speech to the United Nations in early February 2003. When preparations for the speech began in December, CIA and DIA officials had already begun to warn their superiors that the defectors being promoted by Chalabi's organization with claims about mobile bioweapons labs, especially Curveball, were "fabricators." Curveball's German handlers had warned that his information was vague and impossible to verify and that he was not psychologically stable. The head of the CIA's clandestine services, James L. Pavitt, said, "My people were saying, 'We think he's a stinker.'" But the CIA's weapons specialists were taken in by Curveball, believing the defector's descriptions were too detailed to be fabricated. In December 2002, the chief of the CIA's European division, Tyler Drumheller, took his objections to Curveball's story directly to Tenet's chief deputy, John E. McLaughlin.

But the leadership of the agency was under heavy pressure from the White House not to reject Curveball's testimony. After a final warning to Tenet's office about Curveball as an unreliable source, based on the testimony of the Defense Intelligence officer who had quizzed the informant, the CIA Iraq desk officer wrote to CIA colleagues, "The Powers That Be probably aren't interested in whether Curve Ball knows what he's talking about." The next day the phony story about mobile biological weapons labs was the centerpiece of Secretary of State Colin Powell's dramatic statement to the UN Security Council.[57]

The same political pressures were brought to bear on behalf of other key elements of the neoconservative story line. Intelligence analysts had refused to include anything about alleged efforts by Iraq to purchase uranium in its classified reports, but the White House managed to get it into the speech anyway.[58] Powell's staff did balk at including the notorious story of the Atta-Iraqi meeting. After it had been removed from the speech, Deputy National Security Adviser Stephen J. Hadley put it back in, obviously at the behest of Cheney and the Pentagon, only to have Powell take it out again. That item did not appear in the speech.[59]

Conclusion

The two processes of fabricating threats to justify aggressive war occurred in situations that were fundamentally similar. Both the national security advisers of the Kennedy-Johnson period and the top national security officials in the George W. Bush administration had secret agendas in planning to use force. The public was led to believe that the United States was only interested in responding to aggression from another power in East Asia or in the Middle East. But in reality the national security policy makers were in both cases pursuing strategies for getting or maintaining regional dominance. In the Vietnam era, the United States had already achieved such dominance in East and Southeast Asia, and the policy makers saw the use of force in Vietnam as a means of holding together its empire of bases and alliances by dissuading any states from dropping out of the U.S. system. In 2001, on the other hand, the neoconservatives and their allies in the military had been unable to establish in the Persian Gulf the kind of permanent military presence and political-military dominance the United States had enjoyed in East Asia in the 1950s and 1960s. That was what the Iraq War was aimed at changing.

But neither of these two sets of regional power ambitions was a politically acceptable basis for war. So the policy makers had to create a threat of such gravity that it would make the public—and in the Vietnam case, even the president of the United States—accept their preference for war.

What is more striking, however, is how much the coterie of officials bent on war and its way of achieving its goal had changed over four decades. The coalition of military men and civilian advisers who were determined to push through their project for war in Vietnam did not put pressure on the intelligence community. In fact, as Tom Hughes, then the director of intelligence and research in the State Department, recalls, both McGeorge Bundy and Rusk not only did not object to intelligence that contradicted their position on the issue but actually protected dissenters.[60] That tolerance did not extend, of course, to William Bundy's dissenting view when the presentation of the principals in the administration to Johnson was at stake. But it contrasts with the group in the Bush administration, which was openly in conflict with the intelligence community.

The techniques used by the Bush administration team to advance its plan to create a threat out of whole cloth were a world apart from the amateurish approach of the Kennedy- and Johnson-era officials. The latter had hoped to take advantage of Lyndon Johnson's presumed ignorance and simplemindedness about such matters by putting forward the long-discredited domino theory, but when that appeared unsuccessful, they fell back on the political authority of the JCS to make the sale to Johnson. The neoconservatives, on the other hand, had a sophisticated, multipronged plan involving influencing the intelligence process while also shaping press coverage and public opinion. And one of the keys to all three layers of the plan was the exploitation of their Iraqi client's ability to create "facts" on the ground.

It may be debated whether the war planners were acting with complete cynicism or actually believed in the threats they were helping to create. In the Vietnam case it can be concluded that the arguments advanced to Kennedy and Johnson were purely instrumental, rather than reflective of the actual beliefs of the officials making them. In the case of Iraq, the thought processes of the officials involved are more difficult to penetrate. On one hand, their ability to distinguish between reality and what they wanted reality to be was obviously weak. On the other hand, they appear to have embraced an ethic in which any tactic necessary to achieve their goal was justified. What we know with certainty is that they created the facts they needed, just as another group of war planners had done four decades earlier.

5

Wise Guys, Rough Business: Iraq and the Tonkin Gulf

JOHN PRADOS

Among those at the summit of the administration of George W. Bush, only Secretary of Defense Donald H. Rumsfeld actually had a chance to vote on the 1964 Gulf of Tonkin Resolution, which marked a key passage on the American road to war in Vietnam. That war, citizens have been authoritatively informed, was the work of "the best and brightest," the coterie of senior policy makers in the Kennedy and Johnson administrations who believed in the mission of waging an anti-communist crusade in Southeast Asia.[1] Americans, Rumsfeld and his Bush administration colleagues among them, have had decades to ponder and absorb the lessons of Vietnam. And we are not talking about dummies here, those who need guidebooks to mundane facts of history or the dynamics of international relations. Indeed, much was made at the outset of George W. Bush's presidency about the luster and qualifications of his own top people.

Today, when public discourse is filled with comparisons between the Vietnam conflict and the Bush war in Iraq, it is useful to contrast the two along this additional dimension: the employment in both cases of congressional sanction short of declarations of war and administrations' use of deceptive measures to obtain those approvals. This essay will briefly survey the mind-sets of officials in the policy-making circles in each case, the formulation of a purpose (war), and the attainment of the instrumental goal (the initiation of hostilities). Because the Bush administration's actions frame the most immediate national experience, the essay will treat them first. It will then present equivalent data for the Vietnam conflict. Finally, drawing on both cases, the discussion will turn to questions of what they show with respect to issues of presidential power, checks and balances in constitutional government, and tendencies with regard to war and peace.

Wise Guys

Don Rumsfeld had been in on the ground floor at the Gulf of Tonkin because at the time he was a member of the House of Representatives from Michigan. His colleagues in George W. Bush's administration were younger. With few exceptions they had observed the Vietnam War, not fought it. Rumsfeld himself had discovered Bush's vice president, Richard B. Cheney, whom he had hired to Cheney's first Washington job, at the Office of Economic Opportunity, and shepherded through to Gerald R. Ford's White House, where Cheney got his own sea legs as Ford's last chief of staff. Cheney had held student and parental draft deferments during the Vietnam era and never went to war. President Bush himself had joined the Texas Air National Guard and avoided Vietnam service.

The exceptions were the leaders of the Department of State. Secretary of State Colin L. Powell, a retired general, had commanded infantrymen in Vietnam and been a staff officer, then had risen to senior staff positions during the Reagan years and been Chairman of the Joint Chiefs of Staff during the first Gulf War of 1990–91. The secretary's Vietnam experience had been at the fore when as a top general he articulated what became known as the "Powell Doctrine," dictating that any future U.S. military intervention be attempted only with the full support of the American people, and then only if it had clearly defined political and military goals, regularly reviewed, and if those goals were sought with decisive force.[2] Powell's deputy secretary, Richard L. Armitage, had been a naval officer and special warfare adviser in Vietnam. He did not produce grand theories, but he did ably second his boss. The secretary's chief of staff was yet another former military officer, Colonel Larry Wilkerson, a highly disciplined acolyte.

The second tier of Bush's national security managers were all individuals with strong policy views, some of them defense intellectuals or international relations theorists from the high Cold War years, others with business or legal backgrounds. In Rumsfeld's Pentagon the key figures were deputy secretary Paul Wolfowitz, undersecretary for policy Douglas Feith, assistant secretary Stephen Cambone, and policy adviser Richard Perle. Wolfowitz and Perle had been colleagues in political maneuvers on ballistic missile defenses as far back as 1969, and Wolfowitz had been a member of the notorious "Team B" that produced a conservative critique of U.S. intelligence on the Soviet Union late in the Ford administration, when Rumsfeld served as secretary of defense for the first time. Cambone had been Rumsfeld's staff chief when the latter chaired a national commission on ballistic missile threats to the United States in the late 1990s. Feith and Wolfowitz had collaborated on the staff of Richard Cheney when he, too, served as secretary of defense during the first Bush presidency.

Vice President Cheney inserted the fresh wrinkle that characterized presidential decision making in George W. Bush's cabinet room. Cheney had detailed knowledge and set purposes in a White House where the president possessed little more than visceral feelings. Cheney could give shape and momentum to projects, and Bush appreciated that. It is often remarked that Richard Cheney became the most powerful vice president in U.S. history, but for that to happen President Bush had to permit it. Cheney built his own miniature version of a National Security Council (NSC) staff, complete with area specialists and senior managers; a hint of its importance is that I. Lewis "Scooter" Libby, its boss, was simultaneously Cheney's chief of staff. Seconded by career diplomat Eric Edelman, with legal advice from conservative lawyer David Addington, the Cheney security staff ably backed up the vice president's intention to act. As Colin Powell put it, "He determined, with the president's permission, that he would play a different role than previous vice-presidents."[3]

Vice President Cheney's freedom of action widened due to the weakness of the NSC staff proper, headed by Condoleezza Rice. The first woman to serve as national security adviser, Rice would be hampered in several ways. Though an NSC staff veteran from the first Bush administration, where she held the portfolio for Russia under security adviser General Brent Scowcroft, Rice was outclassed by Vice President Cheney and cabinet officers Rumsfeld and Powell, all of whom had been NSC principals in previous administrations. Rice had also determined to stay close to the president, usually a good recipe for a security adviser, except that in this White House the line of action ran through Cheney's office. In addition, Rice's effort to reduce the NSC staff and restrict it to coordinating functions, and her refusal to stake out policy positions at National Security Council and other key meetings, militated against her developing bureaucratic weight. Moreover, some of Rice's staff, notably her senior director for South Asian affairs, Zalmay M. Khalilzad, shared the views of the activists. In fact, there is no evidence that Rice herself held views that were any different. In addition, Rice's deputy, Stephen Hadley, had his own lines of communication direct to Cheney, in whose office he had worked during the first Bush presidency. It was sometimes even said that Hadley was Cheney's spy on the NSC staff. Finally, President George W. Bush's reluctance to discipline his senior officials when they were caught out while running policy maneuvers, such as conducting a cabal between the vice president's office and the office of the secretary of defense, robbed Rice of significant authority. In short, the path lay open for policy activism.

Not only was there an open path, there was a clear vision shared by key people who became Bush officials. Conservative thinkers formed a lobbying group/think tank called the Project for a New American Century (PNAC) in the spring of 1997. Donald Rumsfeld was among its founders. In January 1998 the group sent an open letter to President Bill Clinton urging him to implement "a strategy for removing Saddam's regime from power."[4] Among its signatories were Rumsfeld, PNAC co-founder William Kristol, Richard L. Armitage, John Bolton, Zalmay Khalilzad, Richard Perle, and Paul Wolfowitz. Their lobbying proved instrumental in congressional passage of legislation mandating U.S. support for anti-Saddam Iraqi exiles, and numerous PNAC figures turned up among George W. Bush's campaign foreign policy advisers. Richard Cheney at the time was CEO of a corporation (Halliburton) doing substantial business with the Clinton administration and could not afford to take such a political position, but he too joined the Bush campaign and emerged as the vice presidential candidate. Existing evidence suggests that after entering the Bush administration Cheney was slower to make up his mind about an Iraq operation but that he did so by late 2001; once on board, the vice president proved to be the activist among activists for the Iraq invasion.

A key distinction between the Iraq War and the Vietnam conflict exists and should be noted: unlike the circumstances Washington faced in Southeast Asia, in 2001 there was peace between the United States and Iraq. In Southeast Asia the Kennedy and Johnson administrations ramped up a preexisting involvement, but in Iraq no such involvement existed. Triggering a war involved not only conjuring a casus belli but inducing Americans to subscribe to the Bush administration's interpretation of the situation. The major exploitable issue centered around Saddam's efforts in the 1970s and 1980s to develop an Iraqi program to create weapons of mass destruction, including chemical, biological, and nuclear weapons. Iraq succeeded with the first two types, and used them in its war with Iran that took place between 1980 and 1988, as well as against a Kurdish minority agitating for independence or at least autonomy.

The issue of Iraqi weapons was never clear-cut. Simple assertions regarding the chemical and biological ones obscured the extent to which U.S. exports of production technology and precursor materials had assisted Saddam's efforts. In fact, the U.S. president at the time, Ronald Reagan, had tilted toward Saddam in the Iran-Iraq war, assisting the Iraqis with intelligence, some military advice, and U.S. naval protection for Iraqi efforts to circumvent an Iranian blockade of Saddam's oil exports. Reagan had actually employed Donald Rumsfeld as an emissary to Baghdad.

In addition, claims about Iraqi weapons telescoped the impact of the Gulf war of 1990–91, fought after Saddam attacked his neighbor Kuwait. That was the war conducted by President George H.W. Bush, with Richard Cheney as secretary of defense and General Colin Powell as chairman of the Joint Chiefs of Staff. At the time and afterward it was a major proposition in U.S. accounts of its military victory that American airpower had destroyed Saddam's infrastructure for creating weapons of mass destruction. Moreover, that war ended with a United Nations Security Council resolution—accepted by Baghdad—that permitted UN weapons inspectors to enter Iraq and destroy any vestiges of Saddam's weapons programs that remained. The lifting of UN economic sanctions against Iraq became contingent on the completion of that task.

This is not the place for a detailed recounting of the weapons inspections. In brief, the history of the 1990s was a record of Iraq's grudging response to the UN inspectors, efforts to preserve knowledge of techniques while acquiescing in the destruction of weapons and manufacturing capacity. The Iraqis tried to shut out the UN where they could, but the inspectors did a good job of ferreting out residual Iraqi capabilities and eliminating them. The whole thing began as an adversarial process and deteriorated from there, punctuated by a series of U.S. covert operations designed to overthrow Saddam. In 1998 the Iraqi leader expelled the UN inspectors for a second and final time, after which the United States and Great Britain responded with a series of sharp attacks aimed at destroying Saddam's suspected weapons infrastructure. At that time there were intelligence uncertainties regarding what weapons capabilities Saddam might still have, but there was no hard evidence he had any at all, and there was a concrete record of the accomplishments of the UN weapons inspectors plus bomb damage assessments of the effects of the Anglo-American air attacks.

The Clinton administration in its last years had kept a watchful eye on Iraq but considered Saddam contained. The Central Intelligence Agency (CIA) produced assessments indicating that Iraq might be reconstituting its weapons infrastructure while admitting it lacked any means of knowing the real state of affairs. By the time the George W. Bush administration came into office in 2001 there existed no hard data on Iraqi weapons, only a series of Iraqi insinuations on its forces contrasted with a body of evidence from UN inspections. Even had Saddam had such weapons, he had not threatened the United States. Then came the September 11 terrorist attacks on the United States. That same day Secretary Rumsfeld, meeting with the current Joint Chiefs of Staff chairman, General Richard B. Myers, said his instinct was to respond by attacking Iraq. At Camp David on September 17, when President Bush held discussions among his NSC-level officials on plans to assault terrorist bases in Afghanistan, Paul Wolfowitz put on the table the idea of adding Iraq to the target list. Bush quickly agreed and added orders to plan for an Iraq operation to the directive he subsequently issued on Afghanistan.[5] Rumsfeld then told General Tommy Franks, commander in chief of the U.S. Central Command (CENTCOM), responsible for all military activity in South Asia, "By the way, don't forget about Iraq."[6]

Late in November, with a military campaign in Afghanistan in full swing, President Bush asked Rumsfeld about his options on Iraq. Secretary Rumsfeld then visited CENTCOM headquarters for a private conversation with General Franks, instructing him to update U.S. contingency plans for Iraq. Franks had just designated the command that would conduct any Iraq operation; now he turned to planning one. Rumsfeld issued similar planning orders to the JCS on December 1. Three days after Christmas, following several reviews of the plans with Rumsfeld, General Franks went to the Bush ranch in Crawford, Texas, where he presented his first formal briefing of the Iraq invasion option to George W. Bush.[7]

Vice President Richard Cheney's footprints first appear on January 2, 2002. Accompanied by Scooter Libby, he met with CIA director George J. Tenet and top agency officers to review possibilities for a covert operation to topple Saddam. Within a month the CIA was presenting a completed plan to Rumsfeld. Officials also took the first steps to neutralize anticipated opposition. Paul Wolfowitz demanded that the CIA investigate Hans Blix, the director of the UN's weapons inspection unit, on the suspicion that Blix had previously pulled punches as an international inspector of nuclear programs. (The CIA could find no evidence against Blix.)[8]

In a move aimed at the CIA itself, which Bush officials viewed with a certain disdain, a shadowy Pentagon intelligence unit in Douglas Feith's office, the Policy Counterterrorism Evaluation Group (PCEG), began to reevaluate agency reporting on state sponsorship of terrorism. The PCEG not only worked for Feith but also had direct links to Cheney's office and was said to produce some of its papers at the direction of the vice president. Staff openly called themselves the "cabal" and bragged of their channels to Cheney.[9] This report aimed to prove the existence of a terror alliance between the 9/11 plotters and Saddam Hussein's government. By calling into question the CIA's analysis, the cabal hoped to put pressure on the CIA to produce conclusions that would buttress its own predilections for action. It is noteworthy that when Hans Blix visited the Bush people in Washington on January 10, Condoleezza Rice told him that "she did not think it would be beyond Saddam Hussein to use or transfer weapons of mass destruction."[10] Rice hoped, she said, to get the international community to focus on Iraq.

The point here is not to recite the preparation of the Iraq option in exhaustive detail. Rather, it is to show how early concrete preparations began, in fact even before President Bush included Iraq among the "axis of evil" states he excoriated in his January 2002 State of the Union speech. Revised versions of the CENTCOM war plan would be briefed to Bush repeatedly during 2002—in early February, April, May, June, and a final plan early in August. Evidence indicates that the key decisions had been made by the time Bush met with British prime minister Tony Blair at the Crawford ranch in early April. President Bush issued orders for specific war preparations and for deployment of forces in June and July.

Americans knew nothing about any of this until February 2002. Just prior to the second CENTCOM war plan briefing for Bush, Secretary Powell told the press the administration was considering all its alternatives, and he told a congressional committee that regime change in Iraq was the policy, though the president allegedly had *no* war plan on his desk. On February 13 Bush himself told a news conference, "I will reserve whatever options

I have, I'll keep them close to my vest."[11] Just before the Crawford summit with Blair in April, President Bush went further and said on television, "I've made up my mind that Saddam needs to go. That's about all I'm willing to share with you." This time Bush himself used a formulation identical to Powell's—one he would reiterate many, many times until the very eve of the Iraq invasion—and said he had no war plans on his desk.[12]

Between Powell's remarks in February and those of the president in early April, Bush had signed the directive authorizing the CIA covert operation; the CIA's director, George Tenet, had secretly met with Iraqi Kurd leaders to enlist them, answering their doubts about U.S. purpose by assuring them that this time America was *really* on the march; Vice President Cheney had visited European and Persian Gulf states to line up allies; and British leader Tony Blair had taken quiet soundings in Washington to verify Bush's seriousness and determine his own course. The administration also very consciously attempted to build a policy basis for aggressive war in the form of a new national security strategy that provided for the conduct of so-called preemptive war.[13] President Bush introduced the strategy in his commencement address at West Point at the beginning of June.

Dick Cheney's trip ought to have been a warning to the Bush administration. Among the Europeans, only Blair seemed to be on board. As for the others, only the Gulf state of Qatar was willing to participate, and it would go no further than permit U.S. bases to support a war. In May President Bush himself went to Europe and achieved mere flickers of interest from minor East European states anxious to ingratiate themselves with Washington. In France and Germany he felt obliged to defuse European fears by insisting he had no war plans on his desk. Meanwhile, Donald Rumsfeld sent Paul Wolfowitz to Turkey to secure transit rights and approval for a U.S. northern front against Saddam. Istanbul wanted no part of the project. General Franks was more successful with the king of Jordan, but there too participation would amount to bases, not forces. The American public viewed these developments with the gradually dawning realization that Bush might actually be up to something. By July Congress was sufficiently concerned that it held hearings on the administration's plans for Iraq. Donald Rumsfeld told Congress that airpower alone would not defeat Iraq and ground forces would be required. In short, by midsummer it had become apparent to the White House that a massive sales job would be necessary if there was to be a war against Saddam Hussein.

The problem became crystal clear on August 4, when retired General Brent Scowcroft appeared in a television interview to warn against attacking Iraq, as he feared that such an attack would undercut the U.S. war on terror. Scowcroft was a figure of special importance: national security adviser to two presidents, including George Bush's father, of whom Scowcroft was an intimate friend; manager of the first Iraq war; mentor of Condi Rice; and the chairman of the new Bush administration's Foreign Intelligence

Advisory Board. Scowcroft's opposition indicated that George W. Bush's own political party was not united behind war. The very next day President Bush created an interagency entity called the White House Iraq Group (WHIG), chaired by Bush political guru Karl Rove, for the specific purpose of selling the notion that Iraq posed an urgent menace to the United States. Scowcroft articulated his arguments in more detail in an article that appeared in the *Wall Street Journal* ten days later: "The central point is that any campaign against Iraq, whatever the strategy, cost and risks, is certain to divert us for some indefinite period from our war on terrorism. Worse, there is a virtual consensus in the world against an attack on Iraq at this time . . . [requiring] the U.S. to pursue a virtual go-it-alone strategy."[14]

Condi Rice answered Scowcroft the same day, telling reporters the United States did *not* have the option of ignoring Iraq, as if there were not an ongoing United Nations negotiation with Baghdad about resumption of weapons inspections. Vice President Cheney struck the next blow in a speech on August 27, thundering that "we now know" that Saddam had resumed efforts to acquire nuclear weapons while rejecting the argument that UN inspections could stop him. On August 29, the day President Bush signed the order to deploy forces for war, he spoke to Tony Blair on the telephone and they agreed to give the public information that would paint Saddam as a grave and gathering danger. The first WHIG paper, never published, made Iraqi nuclear weapons the main issue. On September 6, after meeting with Tony Blair, Bush declared, "It's the stated policy of this government to have regime change. And it hasn't changed. And we'll use all tools at our disposal to do so." The president also trivialized objections to his course, saying, "I don't know what more evidence we need."[15]

The selling of the Iraq war represented nothing less than a propaganda campaign aimed at the American people. Guided by the WHIG, the campaign thus had three components. One was a series of leaks of national security information to friendly journalists, then promptly confirmed by administration officials speaking on the record. An example was the leak to the *New York Times* of the claim that Iraq had sought to acquire certain aluminum tubes to enrich uranium for nuclear weapons, promptly confirmed by Condi Rice, who declared that "we don't want the smoking gun to be a mushroom cloud," and by Vice President Cheney. Secretary Rumsfeld then added his assent.[16] As each of these commentators had to be aware, the purpose as well as the nuclear-technology potential of these tubes was hotly disputed within the intelligence community *at the very time* they were making categorical assertions otherwise.[17] Another example was leaks on Saddam's alleged ties to al-Qaeda terrorists, largely drawn from the overblown reporting of the Feith PCEG staff who worked for Rumsfeld. The second component was a series of closely coordinated speeches, both by the president and by surrogates such as Rumsfeld, Wolfowitz, Rice, and others, drumming in the theme of an Iraqi threat. These speeches often occurred in tandem, several at a time, with the surrogates using almost identical phrase-ology. White House spokesmen then "expanded" on the themes of the speeches by reiterating the same language, and answered every question by reference to the texts. In the wake of the Iraq War there have been repeated compilations by observers tabulating dozens, even hundreds, of assertions of threat, numbers possible only because of the systematic "public informa-tion" strategy the Bush White House pursued.

The third component of the Bush strategy requires separate comment because, in the wake of the Iraq War, huge amounts of energy have been devoted to blaming the CIA, portraying the run-up to the war as a simple "intelligence failure." As the official investigations have confirmed, there were intelligence failures on interpreting Iraqi weapons of mass destruction programs. These were failures of analysis. There was also a failure to collect enough information, an overreliance on sources providing false data, and a tendency to dismiss intelligence that did not fit with preconceived notions. The failures were in the direction of claiming Iraqi capabilities that did not exist, and thus helped promote Bush administration objectives. The failures were encouraged by CIA director George Tenet, who wanted intelligence to please Bush. But neither the CIA nor the intelligence community as a whole presented a unified view, nor were they wrong on every issue. The CIA and National Security Agency dissented on the charges that Saddam was allied to al-Qaeda; the Defense Intelligence Agency took a more relaxed view on alleged Iraqi chemical weapons; the State Department and Department of Energy intelligence units rejected the claim that Iraqi aluminum tubes were for a nuclear weapons program; the Air Force scoffed at statements that Iraqi unmanned aerial vehicles had been designed as delivery systems for chemical and biological weapons; the CIA insisted that U.S. troops in Iraq would not ultimately be seen as liberators.

The Bush White House actually did two things, not one: not only did it pick out the most menacing bits of the reporting and feature them to sug-gest that the intelligence confirmed the charges against Saddam Hussein (while saying nothing about the other reports) but it also took measures to suppress dissent. Vice President Cheney repeatedly pressed analysts to redo their reports, went to the CIA a dozen times to further that effort, and sent Scooter Libby to the agency's headquarters more times still. Another of the old PNAC crew, John Bolton, chose this time in the summer of 2002 to kick up a separate fight with the CIA, demanding the firing of senior analysts on the same staff that would compile the Iraq National Intelligence Estimate (NIE). The administration thus simultaneously encouraged a certain type of intelligence reporting and attempted to discipline those who took a differ-ent view. These actions had to have had a chilling effect on the intelligence analysts.

Clinching evidence of Bush distrust of the intelligence community re-sides precisely in the case of the Iraq NIE. In fact, *the Bush administration never asked for an Iraq NIE.* Do not be misled by after-the-fact administration claims that the intelligence estimates supported its course on Iraq. This is in fact the only time (excluding contingency operations) since the system for creating national intelligence estimates was created in 1950 that a president did not ask U.S. intelligence for its considered estimate before launching a war. *The Bush White House was afraid of what an Iraq NIE might say.* Absent a written judgment in a national estimate, Bush and his surrogates were free to claim anything they wanted about Saddam's weapons. With a written opinion, the possibilities for contradicting Bush's charges abounded. Every one of the things the intelligence agencies disbelieved about Iraqi weaponry would feature among Bush administration accusations against Saddam.

Both official investigations of the Iraq intelligence, one by Congress and the other by a presidential commission, confirm that the NIE was requested by Congress, not the administration (again the only time in U.S. history a prewar NIE has resulted from a request by the legislative branch of government). When it emerged, the CIA's faulty assumptions and Tenet's anxiety to please resulted in a paper that mostly supported the administration's claims. The NIE was immediately made the basis for a white paper, similar to the public document produced in the same time frame by Tony Blair's government in the United Kingdom, that was released to Congress and the American people. The CIA white paper was shorn of all its qualifiers and dissents. When members of the Senate Select Committee on Intelligence asked for more of the nuanced text in the original to be released, Tenet combined a small increment of this material with additional inflammatory allegations of links between Saddam and al-Qaeda, an issue of prime importance at the Bush White House and one with which the CIA specifically *disagreed.* It is impossible to escape the conclusion that the Bush administration manipulated the U.S. intelligence system in furtherance of its goal of initiating war against Iraq.

This intelligence work played out within the political context of President Bush's move to secure approval for the use of force. The doubts evidenced over the summer of 2002 trumped the White House's desire to rely solely upon the president's authority as commander in chief to order hostilities. Secretary of State Colin L. Powell convinced Bush that United Nations approval was necessary since the war would take place within the legal framework of UN resolutions on Iraq passed at the time of the Gulf War and afterward. President Bush spoke at the UN General Assembly on September 12—again making assertions about Iraqi weapons of mass destruction—and asked for a Security Council resolution. After this speech almost two-thirds of Americans surveyed in opinion polls supported Bush's proposed war, but support fell to just 33 percent when the question was posed in terms of a unilateral U.S. war on Iraq. That made necessary some form of recognition from the Congress. It was in this connection that senators asked for an NIE on Iraq. But most members of Congress would rely on the CIA white paper—the propaganda product—for their information, which was repeatedly cited as fact. By several accounts only a handful of representatives and senators actually read the NIE itself. In the middle of debate, on October 7, President Bush gave a speech in Cincinnati with his most detailed recitation yet of a litany of charges against Saddam Hussein. One more outrageous charge against the Iraqis—that they had sought to buy uranium ore in Africa—was kept out of the text only by dint of last-minute CIA intervention. It is likely that the record will ultimately show that George Tenet told Stephen Hadley, the NSC deputy responsible for clearing the draft, that he could not hold the CIA in line if this charge appeared in the Cincinnati speech. A few months later, after passage of the congressional war resolution and a UN Security Council resolution covering new weapons inspections and threatening further action if obstructed by Iraq, and as if there had never been any CIA objection to the uranium ore allegation, the charge reappeared in another Bush speech, his 2003 State of the Union address, where its presence eventually caused a huge controversy.

Prodded by allegations of Iraqi perfidy, and unimpressed by Saddam Hussein's September 17 agreement to readmit UN weapons inspectors, the Bush administration and Congress hammered out a joint resolution to approve the use of force. Bush's own draft text went to Capitol Hill two days *after* Baghdad agreed to the inspections, an additional commentary that goes to the point that *nothing Iraq could have done short of preemptive surrender would have avoided this war.* The resolution passed the House of Representatives by a vote of 296 to 133 and the Senate by 77 to 23. The Authorization for Use of Military Force Against Iraq Resolution became Public Law 107-243. No part of the law permitted war for the purpose of regime change, to bring democracy to Iraq, or to force any other internal changes in that country's territory or behavior. The operative language in Section 2 allowed for the use of armed force to defend the United States against the "threat posed by Iraq," and to "enforce all relevant United Nations Security Council resolutions regarding Iraq."[18] If Iraq posed no threat to the United States, that provision had no force. If Iraq had no weapons of mass destruction, under the existing Security Council resolutions Baghdad would be considered disarmed and the resolutions fulfilled, and the authorization for force voted by Congress would expire. Thus the Bush administration's legal authority to wage war flowed directly from the existence of Iraqi weapons of mass destruction and nothing else. Deception—of the public, of the Congress, and of world opinion—was central to the Bush administration's enterprise. Since the fresh Security Council resolution passed on November 8 also had the purpose of ridding Iraq of weapons of mass destruction, and no more, President Bush derived no additional authority from it. Equally important, additional action, such as war, under that resolution required a further Security Council determination, a judgment that Washington proved unable to obtain.

At this writing, more than three years into the Iraq War, with more than 20,000 American casualties (killed and wounded) and perhaps twice that number of Iraqi dead, the hubris displayed by President Bush and his colleagues is painful to behold. These policy makers played as rough as Mafia wise guys. Not only did they depend on deception—and then changed their story even more as their original justifications collapsed—they failed to plan for the Iraq occupation, failed to respond to an incipient resistance, failed at the task of reconstructing the country destroyed in this maneuver, botched the Iraqi political realignment they wanted, failed at the alleged goal of making Iraq the basis for a democratic revolution in the Middle East, and all the while claimed victory, "mission accomplished." Today the United States pays more for war in Iraq than that country's own gross domestic product, and before this book is published the dollar cost of the Iraq war will exceed that for Vietnam. All of that is apart from the question of whether the Iraq war was even legal under U.S. and international law, which it was not. The Iraq experience gives new meaning to the idea of "the best and the brightest."

The Best and the Brightest

One way in which the Vietnam War is an obvious comparison to the Iraq War is that in both cases, legal authority, such as it was, was secured in a manner that involved deception. In Vietnam the deception resulted from the Gulf of Tonkin incident in August 1964. The incident, a naval clash in waters off the northern Vietnamese coast, was followed by a U.S. air attack on North Vietnam launched by President Lyndon B. Johnson's administration, and then an approach to Congress for a resolution authorizing the use of force.

Much confusion surrounded the Gulf of Tonkin incident, both then and later. There had been a naval battle between North Vietnamese torpedo boats and the U.S. destroyer *Maddox* on August 2, though the retaliation and push for the congressional resolution came after an alleged second attack, reports of which are now known to have been false. This analysis is not another tour of the particulars of the Gulf of Tonkin incident, which have been exhaustively examined elsewhere,[19] and illuminated further by the release in 2005 and 2006 of the original National Security Agency dispatches that document its reporting at the time.[20] The focus here will be on what LBJ's top policy makers, the best and the brightest, did at the time with the information they had. The record shows a rush to war, cloaked by protestations in the opposite direction.

As Lloyd Gardner, one of the foremost historians of Lyndon Johnson and his presidency, concludes of this period, "Johnson portrayed himself throughout the 1964 campaign as the peace candidate," against Republican opponent Barry Goldwater, who unabashedly promoted a war policy.[21] (In a campaign speech at Manchester, New Hampshire, LBJ declared, "I have not thought that we were ready for American boys to do the fighting for Asian boys.")[22] George C. Herring, another leading historian of the American war in Vietnam, similarly observes that "the President was not prepared to employ American military power on a large scale early in 1964 . . . he had no enthusiasm for a massive engagement of American forces on the Asian mainland."[23] Lyndon Johnson had an ambitious domestic policy agenda he called the Great Society, and feared that war in Vietnam would threaten the accomplishment of his other important goals.

But Johnson also faced an evolving crisis situation in Vietnam. He felt the United States had commitments in Southeast Asia and that these commitments were not to be walked away from. In particular, the regime in power in South Vietnam was shaky, in danger of collapse in the face of a North Vietnamese–backed insurgency or internally from a succession of military coups d'état, and LBJ's advisers constantly offered the course of injecting additional doses of U.S. force as a part of the solution to that problem. The president acquiesced. At the NSC on March 17, 1964, among a welter of other Vietnam recommendations from Secretary of Defense Robert S. McNamara, the Joint Chiefs of Staff advised that U.S. air forces in Southeast Asia should be raised to a new standard of preparation, ready to mount attacks on North Vietnam within twenty-four hours rather than the seventy-two hours then programmed. President Johnson approved.[24]

This kind of thinking permeated the actions of the best and the brightest. The very next day, the president's NSC staffer for Southeast Asia, Michael Forrestal, reported to LBJ's national security adviser, McGeorge Bundy, the view of the Joint Chiefs' special assistant for counterinsurgency and special operations that if the United States could not "make the high jumps in South Vietnam, we should pole-vault into the North."[25] In a cable to the president on March 19, U.S. ambassador to South Vietnam Henry Cabot Lodge insisted that "if [North Vietnam] thought that the US had the *will* to use just what we have out here in Southeast Asia . . . they would see they cannot afford a Viet Cong victory . . . The price would be too high."[26] The president was aware of this thinking and not resistant to it, except for ruling out the "overt" use of force. Thus, to Lodge's missive LBJ replied he was taking steps to ensure the ambassador saw the latest Washington planning papers on applying pressure and power against North Vietnam. Before the end of the month Forrestal and others would have begun developing a "political scenario for pressures on the North."[27] This sub-rosa policy development continued even while President Johnson, on the campaign trail, positioned himself as the peace candidate.

The top-secret "covert" program of pressures against North Vietnam was already under way, prefigured in a directive President Johnson had issued in November 1963 and specifically approved in January 1964. This was Operations Plan (OPLAN) 34-A. The 34-A attacks on North Vietnam had begun a few weeks later. The political scenario of March 1964 envisioned the covert U.S. attacks building up to open attacks by South Vietnam made with covert U.S. support. Among the elements of the scenario were that Washington would mount a public information campaign to increase awareness of and support for its course in South Vietnam, would release information in the form of a white paper intended to demonstrate North Vietnamese aggression against South Vietnam, and would send a signal to Hanoi through an intermediary to cease and desist or face the consequences. Presidential speeches would explain the necessity for direct action against the North. President Johnson, under this plan, would have a series of meetings with congressional leaders, at first simply speaking of the threat, but ultimately asking for "Congressional support and possibly a Congressional resolution."[28]

President Johnson actually had some of the congressional leaders attend an NSC meeting with him in early April but did not press for approval of the use of U.S. force. Declassified documents clearly show that work on the "political scenario" continued, and that officials realized there would be serious domestic problems in moving directly to overt U.S. military action. The documents show that this work became a regular track in U.S. policy planning that went on in tandem with the OPLAN 34-A operations. Moreover, the planning continued even as Washington rejected efforts by French president Charles de Gaulle to preserve peace by neutralizing Southeast Asia. The Americans also enlisted as an intermediary Canadian diplomat J. Blair Seaborn, who actually met with North Vietnamese leaders in June. By that time President Johnson already had an interagency group actively preparing additional elements for his escalation, including target lists for attacks on North Vietnam and drafts of the text for a congressional resolution that would authorize the use of force in Vietnam. That text was ready when the Tonkin Gulf incident took place. In short, for a period of at least five months the Johnson administration had quietly prepared the ground for an escalation that the president was publicly saying he wanted no part of. The specific measures envisioned in the summer of 1964 were not as extreme as what the Bush administration wanted to do in 2002, but the process was similar.

The escalation planning versus public posture of peaceful intent amounted to one deceptive element in Johnson administration actions on Vietnam. But a second feature in the Vietnam case was a direct deception carried out in the context of the Tonkin Gulf incident. Without dwelling on the particulars of the supposed combat action in the Gulf, suffice it to say that there were two key issues. The first pertained to the August 2 skirmish and whether the North Vietnamese could link the *Maddox*'s electronic intelligence intercept mission to the OPLAN 34-A raids, which had struck a nearby island on the Vietnamese coast just hours before the appearance of the destroyer. Washington officials recognized the linkage. Mike Forrestal, chairing LBJ's Vietnam coordinating committee, mentioned it in an August 3 memo. William P. Bundy, the brother of the national security adviser and a Pentagon member of Forrestal's group, did so also. Secretary McNamara discussed the linkage directly with the president in a phone conversation on the morning of August 3 and advised that congressional members be told of the connection.[29] They were not. A few days later, during congressional hearings on the proposed legal authorization for force, McNamara would be formally asked about the linkage. He denied that any existed.

Declassified documents plus the records of President Johnson's phone calls on August 4 show that the National Security Agency warned of new, imminent attacks on the *Maddox* and an accompanying warship but that these warnings were based upon translation errors and misinterpretation of the times the North Vietnamese had sent the messages. Relying upon this erroneous information, LBJ and his advisers prepared to bomb North Vietnam in reprisal. Then the warships in the Gulf of Tonkin sent initial reports that they were under attack. Based on mistaken evaluations of sonar contacts, panicked visual sighting reports from lookouts, and radar malfunctions, the U.S. Navy's own on-scene commander warned against reading too much into his initial dispatches. Aircraft sent to the battle area also reported seeing nothing. Washington's Pacific theater commander, Admiral U.S. Grant Sharp, conceded some uncertainty about the reality of this supposed battle but wanted to go ahead with the bombing. Washington's best and brightest concurred. President Johnson approved the mission. Operation Pierce Arrow, the first open U.S. bombing of North Vietnam, took place as a result. The president simultaneously asked Congress to give him authority to use force in the war. Despite his private doubts, Johnson insisted that the "battle" of August 4 had been a real one.

The other key deception in the Tonkin Gulf incident then became the effort to hold the line on claims that the August 4 incident, the one upon which U.S. military action had actually been predicated, had in fact taken place. Despite the gradual emergence of discrepant information, the Johnson administration continued to insist that there had been two attacks on American vessels in the Tonkin Gulf. So, to a lesser degree, did the U.S. government under later presidents.

In the meantime, the best and the brightest moved immediately to secure a legal authorization for the use of force in Southeast Asia. Congress responded by passage of the Gulf of Tonkin Resolution. When President Johnson's draft text for a resolution arrived at the Senate on August 5, Senator Wayne Morse (D.-Ore.) rose to object that the authorization for force violated the provision of the Constitution (Article I, Section 8) that reserves to Congress the power to declare war. His objection was ignored. Morse demanded that the Senate Foreign Relations Committee at least hold full hearings on the issue. Senator J. William Fulbright, chairman of the committee, countered that the United States faced an emergency situation and needed to act immediately. Very abbreviated hearings were held. Hurried as this process was, the questions of whether there was a relationship between the OPLAN 34-A raids and the destroyer patrol, whether the *Maddox* had violated North Vietnamese territorial waters, and what the real mission of the *Maddox* was nevertheless surfaced at the hearings. The Johnson administration misled Congress on every point and said nothing of the doubts that already existed inside the executive branch as to whether the second incident—the event used to claim a pattern of aggression and catalyze the resolution—had even happened.[30]

The Gulf of Tonkin Resolution passed Congress on August 7, 1964. In the Senate only Senator Morse and Senator Ernest Gruening (D.-Alaska) voted against the resolution, which passed by a vote of 88 to 2. The House of Representatives approved it unanimously, 416–0—if Donald Rumsfeld was present on the floor at that moment (which cannot be determined), he voted in favor. The operative language in Section 2 of the resolution (which became Public Law 88-107) states, "The United States is, therefore, prepared, as the President determines, to take all necessary steps, including the use of armed force, to assist" the nations of Southeast Asia.[31] The grant of authority was not qualified except as to area (it applied to member or protocol states of the Southeast Asia Treaty Organization).

The Johnson administration did feel misgivings as to what it had accomplished and how. On at least two occasions officials considered going back to Congress for a more specific and explicit delegation of authority to wage war in Vietnam. Both times that course was rejected out of fear that legislative sentiment would no longer favor approval. In 1967, while serving as undersecretary of state, Nicholas deB. Katzenbach termed the resolution a functional equivalent of a declaration of war.[32] Meanwhile, the underlying stipulations the Johnson admnistation had made steadily disintegrated to the point that consensus on whether there had been a second incident evaporated. In 1970 Congress repealed the resolution. By then Richard Nixon was president, and from that time to the end of the major U.S. combat role in Vietnam, in early 1973, he waged war for the putative reason of recovering American prisoners, relying upon his constitutional prerogatives as commander in chief. Shortly thereafter, in 1973, Congress passed the War Powers Act (P.L. 93-148), over Nixon's veto, intending to prevent anything like Vietnam from ever happening again.

A final irony in this tale lies in the fact that the Vietnam War ultimately ended on the watch of President Gerald R. Ford, when Don Rumsfeld was doing his first stint as secretary of defense. Near the end, yet another battlefield episode occurred about which Washington was tempted to dissemble.

During the final evacuation of Saigon in March 1975, the White House announced that all Americans had left the country when in reality over a hundred U.S. Marines were still on the ground awaiting helicopter airlift. The secretary of state, Henry Kissinger, wanted to blame the Pentagon's national military command center for the snafu, which happened because he himself had assumed that because the ambassador had left, the rest of the Americans were gone. Rumsfeld insisted on putting out the real story. He has been quoted as saying, "This war has been marked by so many lies and evasions that it is not right to have the war end with one last lie."[33] It would have been good if Rumsfeld had applied that Vietnam lesson to Iraq policy in the Bush administration.

Analysis

For all their differences, there is an eerie convergence between the Iraq and Vietnam cases, at least along the dimensions analyzed here. In both cases an American president permitted—and actively participated in—deliberately misleading Congress and the American people on an issue of war and peace for the purpose of obtaining legal authority to conduct hostilities. In the Vietnam case the deception involved masking particulars of an incident whose true circumstances would have undercut the Johnson administration's demand for the grant of authority to make war. In the Iraq case the deception involved making up an "imminent" threat, contriving an image of an aggressive adversary out of whatever claims and charges could be patched together. In both cases a time element was inserted to galvanize Congress, and efforts were made to cloak the U.S. moves under the mantle of multinational action. The Bush administration's maneuvers on Iraq actually seem the more egregious because they started a war where no prior conflict existed, where the deception was open-ended and based upon no events whatsoever, and because the Bush administration "gamed" the system, domestic and international, playing Congress and the United Nations off against each other.

The full record of the Bush administration's manipulation remains shrouded in the secrecy of classified documents that will not see the light of day for some time. But the Vietnam case shows that these kinds of efforts are not casual, serendipitous misstatements of a day. Rather, the second case demonstrates that the problem is systemic. Faced with obstacles to desired courses of action, presidents are tempted to resort to deceptions. They are calculated. Just as Johnson's best and brightest crafted their scenario to lay the groundwork for escalation, it is highly likely that a similar planning process occurred under George W. Bush. It is distressing that presidents do not level with the American people, and more so that such manipulative techniques are ever considered acceptable. This situation must change if democracy is to survive. Indeed, that a president (George W. Bush) who makes fostering democracy his international goal relies on this kind of deception is an additional indictment of his actions.

Congress did learn something from Vietnam. In passing the War Powers Act it attempted to prevent further international misadventures. That law explicitly reaffirms the location of the war powers within Congress, as provided by the Constitution. It also restricts the president's power as commander in chief to actions pursuant to "(1) a declaration of war, (2) specific statutory authorization, or (3) a national emergency created by attack upon the United States, its territories or possessions, or its armed forces."[34] It is past time for the lawyers—and lawmakers—to stop splitting hairs arguing why the War Powers Act does not apply in each successive instance, and start enforcing the law.

In the 2002 Iraq war resolution the example of the Gulf of Tonkin had not been entirely forgotten. That was one reason the resolution that passed was more circumscribed, predicated on enforcing a United Nations mandate and requiring periodic reports from the president. Congress tied the grant of authority to a second body, the United Nations Security Council. The executive branch proceeded to claim powers from a broader swath of UN resolutions that it asserted were activated as a result of its own deception, as well as to rely upon the commander-in-chief clause as if no restrictions on this exist. A similar arrogation of power based on deceit has characterized Bush's conduct of the entire war on terror.

6

Gulliver at Bay: The Paradox of the Imperial Presidency

ANDREW J. BACEVICH

Here is the central paradox of American politics in the midst of the so-called Global War on Terror: as the executive branch seemingly accrues ever more power, its capacity for effective governance diminishes. Under the administration of George W. Bush, the imperial presidency has returned with a vengeance. Meanwhile, when it comes to solving actually existing problems—whether reforming social security or balancing the budget, responding to natural diasters or stabilizing Iraq—the president has repeatedly failed to deliver. Indeed, precisely where Bush's power ought seemingly to be greatest—when acting in his capacity as wartime commander in chief—he appears most feeble.

Pundits frequently refer to the occupant of the Oval Office as the Most Powerful Man in the World. Yet if power implies the ability to control events or to determine outcomes, the power wielded by President Bush, however vast in a nominal sense, ends up in practice being quite limited. In theory, he can order a nuclear attack capable of destroying any nation in the world; in reality, just tracking down the conspirators who plotted 9/11 poses a daunting challenge.

To some extent, we have gotten what we asked for. Americans have long evinced a pronounced preference for bold and assertive executive leadership along with a disdain for Congress as the refuge of hacks and boodlers. Especially in moments of crisis, we count on strong presidents to save the day. Time and again throughout U.S. history—the Civil War and the Great Depression providing classic examples—presidents untroubled by constitutional niceties have exploited this inclination to expand the powers claimed by the executive branch. Based on the way that Americans have chosen to remember Abraham Lincoln and Franklin Delano Roosevelt, the chief executive who disregards the system of checks and balances and interprets his authority expansively is less likely to face impeachment than to be enshrined as a Great Man.

As a consequence, long before George W. Bush emerged as the victor in the disputed election of 2000 and long before the Republican Party established its present-day ascendancy, the White House had emerged as the holiest of holies in American political life. Back in the 1930s, Democrats intent on circumventing a Congress that obstructed progressive reforms established the template for what became the modern presidency. Soon enough, however, Republicans found that template to their liking, even as they spouted conservative bromides about the danger posed by Leviathan.

Consecutive national security emergencies, first World War II and then the Cold War, cemented this cult of the presidency. By the time of John F. Kennedy's storied inauguration in 1961, the chief executive was no longer the first citizen of the Republic; he had achieved the status of elected monarch. In national politics, the White House had become the glittering prize, with proximity to the Oval Office defining status and clout. The election of Bill Clinton just about completed the transformation of the president from public servant to celebrity. Hollywood, the capital of celebrity culture, affirmed this verdict, with the television networks cranking out worshipful series with names such as *The West Wing* and *Commander in Chief.*[1]

Granted, from time to time, presidents have overstepped their bounds, triggering efforts to curtail the scope of executive authority. Seldom, however, has the backlash had much of a permanent effect. The War Powers Resolution, passed over presidential veto in the midst of the infamous Watergate scandal, illustrates this point. Belatedly settling accounts with Richard Nixon (and perhaps Lyndon Baines Johnson), the Congress attempted through this measure to reassert a legislative voice in decisions to undertake or sustain military intervention abroad. When it came to reducing the prerogatives of the commander in chief, however, the practical impact of the legislation proved to be essentially nil. As one historian has written, subsequent presidents "routinely ignored, evaded, or otherwise minimized the reach of the law."[2] When they wished to use force, occupants of the White House during the 1980s and 1990s simply did so, either asserting virtually unlimited authority to act as they wished or demanding and receiving from a compliant Congress a mandate for intervention.[3] In the run-up to 1991's Operation Desert Storm, for example, while President George H.W. Bush indicated that he would welcome a congressional endorsement of his declared intent to eject Iraq from Kuwait, he made it clear that he was going to war regardless of what the Congress did or did not do.

By the end of the twentieth century, the War Powers Resolution had become a dead letter. So too had the proviso from Article I, Section 8 of the Constitution explicitly assigning to the Congress the power to declare war. Ever since 1945, as one observer has written, especially as related to war and the use of force, "Presidents have regularly breached constitutional principles and democratic values" and gotten away with it.[4]

Before assessing the use and abuse of presidential power during the administration of George W. Bush, it is important to recall this history. The imbalances afflicting present-day American politics at the national level and the distortions inflicted on the Constitution since 9/11 did not spring out of nowhere. They have been a long time coming, encouraged and nurtured in plain sight over the course of decades. If we have an outsized presidency today, it's because, with only occasional exceptions, both political parties, the press, influential interest groups, and the majority of the American people have endorsed its growth and because a dysfunctional Congress has largely forfeited its constitutional responsibilities, especially in matters relating to national security.

Having said all that, it is also true that the administration of George W. Bush has taken the imperial presidency to a new level. As the authors of a recent Cato Institute study have written, the Bush administration has engaged in a "ceaseless push for power, unchecked by either the courts or Congress" and informed by "presidential indifference to constitutional safeguards and principles." Gene Healy and Timothy Lynch charge the Bush White House with promoting a definition of exeuctive power that includes "a president who can launch wars at will."[5] From this conception come vast claims of presidential prerogatives not only to start wars but also to expand them, to engage in massive domestic surveillance, to order the abusive treatment of prisoners, and to detain indefinitely and without trial individuals (including American citizens) said to pose a threat of national security. To justify these claims, the Bush administration cites the overriding imperative of national security. In essence, "keeping America safe" in an age of international terror provides a universally applicable, all-purpose cover story.

Here lies the political significance of 9/11: the unspeakable events of September 11, 2001, which killed thousands, left many thousands more bereft, and horrified countless millions who merely bore witness, suggested to men of ambition in the inner circles of the Bush administration an opportunity. They seized upon that opportunity with alacrity. These men did not fear a "Global War on Terror." They welcomed it, certain of their ability to bend war to their purposes. Two purposes in particular stood out: first, removing any last constraints on the use of U.S. military power, and second, concentrating authority to employ that power in the upper echelons of the executive branch and especially the White House. They conceived of a preventive war with Iraq as the means to achieve those twin objectives.

Advertised as necessary to prevent Saddam Hussein from passing weapons of mass destruction to terrorists, the actual rationale for the Iraq War had next to nothing to do with the threat posed by Saddam Hussein. In this regard, when Deputy Secretary of Defense Paul Wolfowitz famously remarked that the Bush administration had advertised Saddam's WMD program as its casus belli because it was "the one issue that everyone could agree on," he hinted at a more complex truth.[6] Weapons of mass destruction offered little more than a convenient pretext for a war of choice conjured up to serve a multiplicity of ends.

In fact, neither the Baath Party regime nor the Iraqi army, crippled by defeat and well over a decade of punishing sanctions, threatened anyone except the Iraqi people. The hawks within the Bush administration understood this quite well. They hankered to invade Iraq not because Saddam was strong and dangerous but because he was weak and vulnerable, not because he was implicated in 9/11 but because he looked like an easy mark.

The war's architects viewed Iraq less as a destination than as a point of departure. In their eyes, 2003 was not 1945. It was 1939—not a climax but the opening gambit of a vast enterprise largely hidden from public view. Allusions to Saddam as a new Hitler notwithstanding, they did not see Baghdad as Berlin. It was instead Warsaw, a preliminary objective. The war's most determined proponents—Vice President Richard Cheney, Secretary of Defense Donald Rumsfeld, and Wolfowitz himself—saw toppling Saddam less as an end in itself than as the first phase of a campaign expected to run through many more. In Iraq they intended to set precedents, thereby facilitating other actions to follow.

Although President Bush portrayed himself as a reluctant warrior who considered armed conflict a last resort, key members of his administration had other views. They were determined that nothing should get in the way of a showdown with Saddam. "In crafting a strategy for Iraq," Undersecretary of Defense Douglas Feith insisted to one baffled U.S. general, "we cannot accept surrender."[7] The object of the exercise was to remove impediments to the subsequent employment of American power. For this, merely promulgating a doctrine of preventive war would not suffice; actually implementing that doctrine was imperative.

The principal players in this game had their eyes fixed on two very different fronts. One of those fronts, of course, was the Persian Gulf. As Bush administration hawks saw it, the weak and feckless Clinton administration had allowed the once-dominant U.S. position in the region to erode throughout the previous decade. Taking down Saddam promised to restore U.S. preeminence, yielding large economic and political benefits.

In the near term, such a demonstration of American assertiveness would ease concerns about access to the energy reserves on which the prosperity of the developed world depended. A "friendly" Iraq would reduce the need to cater to Saudi Arabia, whose friendship was looking increasingly problematic given the fact that fifteen of the nineteen 9/11 hijackers had been Saudis. In the longer term, Iraq could serve as a secure operating base or jumping-off point for subsequent U.S. efforts to extend the Pax Americana across the broader Middle East, a project expected to last decades. Here lay the ultimate strategic rationale for war: invading Iraq would set the stage for the further employment of U.S. power aimed at eradicating the conditions breeding violent Islamic radicalism. As applied to Iraq, "liberation" was a code word; the real aim was more akin to pacification and control.

By planting the Stars and Stripes in downtown Baghdad, Michael Gordon and Bernard Trainor have written, the advocates of war intended not only to "implant democracy in a nation that had never known it" but to "begin to redraw the political map of the region." As "a demonstration of American power for Syria and other wayward regimes," Operation Iraqi Freedom would show the consequences of defying the world's sole superpower. Even beyond the Middle East, Saddam's demise was likely to have salutary effects, letting "other adversaries know they should watch their step."[8]

But embarking upon this bold venture required first the removal of obstacles at home. This was the second front, in many respects more challenging than the first.

As George W. Bush's more bellicose lieutenants saw it, the principal constraints on the use of American power lay within the U.S. government itself. In a speech to Defense Department employees just a day prior to 9/11, Rumsfeld had warned of "an adversary that poses a threat, a serious threat, to the security of the United States of America." Who was this adversary? Some evil tyrant or murderous terrorist? No, announced the secretary of defense, "the adversary's closer to home. It's the Pentagon bureaucracy."[9]

In fact, the internal threat was by no means confined to this one bureaucracy. It encompassed much of official Washington. It included the Congress and the Supreme Court, each of which could circumscribe presidential freedom of action. It extended to the Central Intelligence Agency and the State Department, which the hawks viewed as obstreperous and hidebound. It even included the senior leadership of the U.S. military, especially the unimaginative and excessively risk-averse Joint Chiefs of Staff. All of these could impede the greater assertiveness that Cheney, Rumsfeld, and Wolfowitz had yearned for even before September 11. In order to make headway on the foreign front, each and every one of these sources of opposition on the home front had to be neutralized.

So unleashing American might abroad implied a radical reconfiguration of power relationships at home. On this score, 9/11 came as a godsend. In its wake, citing the urgent imperatives of national security, the hawks set out to concentrate authority in their own hands. September 11, 2001, inaugurated what became in essence a rolling coup.

Nominally, the object of the exercise was to empower the commander in chief to wage his Global War on Terror. Yet with George W. Bush a president in the mold of William McKinley or Warren G. Harding—an affable man of modest talent whose rise in national politics was attributable primarily to his perceived electability—Cheney and his collaborators were really engaged in an effort to enhance their own clout. Bush might serve as the front man, but on matters of substance, theirs would be the decisive voices. Gordon and Trainor describe the operative model this way: "The president would preside, the vice president would guide, and the defense secretary would implement," with Wolfowitz and a handful of others, it might be added, lending the enterprise some semblance of intellectual coherence.[10]

In the event, step one—bringing the Congress to heel—proved to be remarkably easy. Executive cajolery and chicanery were unnecessary; the Congress simply took itself out of the game. Immediately after 9/11, the Senate and House of Representatives issued the executive branch the equivalent of a blank check. A joint resolution passed on September 14, 2001, not only authorized the president "to use all necessary and appropriate force against those nations, organizations, or persons" that had perpetrated 9/11, but also called upon him "to prevent any future acts of international terrorism against the United States."[11]

The notorious Gulf of Tonkin Resolution of 1964 was a straitjacket compared to this spacious grant of authority. Using the prevention of "future acts of international terrorism" as a rationale, creative lawyers employed by the Bush administration proved able to justify any action up to and including torture.[12] Even when the subsequent Bush initiatives produced massive intelligence failures, operational ineptitude, and dubious practices such as warrantless wiretaps and the wrongful detention and abuse of detainees, the White House had little difficulty fending off legislative meddling.

As if to drive home its contempt for the Congress, the White House also began claiming the prerogative of disregarding any legislative action that it did not like. On at least 750 occasions during his first five years in office, President Bush issued so-called signing statements voiding legislative provisions with which his administration happened to disagree.[13] Most notoriously, when the Congress in late 2005 roused itself long enough to ban torture as an instrument of U.S. policy, Bush asserted that as commander in chief, he would abide by this stricture only so far as it suited him to do so. As David Golove, professor of law at New York University, has remarked, the signing statement amounted to Bush saying, "I will comply with this law when I want to, and if something arises in the war on terrorism where I think it's important to torture . . . I have the authority to do so and nothing in this law is going to stop me."[14]

As a result of all this, the aftermath of 9/11 saw the system of checks and balances all but collapse. Today, individual legislators still quibble and gripe, but as an institution, the Congress today hardly amounts to more than a nuisance. With regard to national security, its chief function is simply to appropriate the ever more spectacular sums of money that the war on terror requires and to rubber-stamp increases in the national debt ceiling. This, of course, it routinely and obligingly does. As long as the Congress stayed firmly in Republican hands, President Bush rightly considered executive accountability to be no more than a theoretical proposition.

Nor, thus far at least, have the courts interfered with this presidential muscle flexing. The U.S. Supreme Court historically has shown little inclination to encroach on presidential turf in time of war. Any prospect of the present court confronting this president was seemingly nipped in the bud by the fortuitous retirement of one justice followed by the death of another. In appointing John Roberts and Samuel Alito, President Bush elevated to the high court two jurists with proven track records of giving the executive branch a wide berth on matters relating to national security.[15]

Within the executive branch itself, however, a somewhat different story occurred. There, efforts by Cheney and Rumsfeld to consolidate authority in their own hands encountered fierce resistance.

During the months leading up to the Iraq War, Rumsfeld and his aides waged a bureaucratic battle royal to marginalize the State Department and to wrest control of intelligence analysis away from the CIA. Colin Powell became one casualty of that bruising fight. George Tenet, eased out as CIA director, was another. Whether that battle ended with the demise of Powell and Tenet is another matter. With Rumsfeld by 2006 under siege while Condoleezza Rice enjoys Bush's confidence as Powell never did, and with efforts to silence the CIA having yielded a criminal indictment of the vice president's former chief of staff, any declaration of victory on behalf of the Cheney-Rumsfeld axis might be a tad premature.

Still, the overall conclusion is as clear as it is disturbing. To the extent that any meaningful limits on executive power survive, they are almost entirely bureaucratic. The president has more to fear from a disgruntled leaker in the intelligence community than from the Congress of the United States. In effect, the Bush administration has eviscerated the Constitution.

Yet in a sense all of these battles were peripheral. The really pivotal action was occurring within the Department of Defense itself. The coup that Cheney, Rumsfeld, and Wolfowitz engineered was after all a military one. This was true not in the sense that the intent was to empower the officer corps—quite the contrary—but rather in the sense that the coup leaders all subscribed to the conviction that armed might held the key both to advancing U.S. global ambitions and to investing supreme power in the president/ commander in chief. Indeed, to persuade Americans to see this president's principal identity or function as being commander in chief was to remove encumbrances on his power (and by extension on their own power).

Quasi-permanent global war offered these hawks the prospect of converting that conviction into reality. The idea was not to declare war on 9/11 and then turn things over to the generals who would deliver victory. Rather, the idea was to declare war and then to use the ensuing conflict as a vehicle for achieving their own purposes. Hence, the importance they placed on calling the shots in that war. Determined to have a decisive voice in deciding when and where U.S. forces would go into battle, they also wanted to dictate *how* those forces would fight. This implied shifting the boundary that defined civil-military relations—with war against Iraq the instrument for effecting that shift.

The team that Donald Rumsfeld recruited to assist him in managing the Pentagon contained an unusual number of military zealots. These men believed in the utility of force. They did not shrink from committing their fellow citizens to war. Indeed, they viewed the prospect with considerable enthusiasm.

In addition to Wolfowitz and Feith, the group included Stephen Cambone, Lawrence Di Rita, William Luti, and on a part-time basis Richard Perle, who chaired the Defense Policy Board. During the 1980s, in the service of Ronald Reagan and then George H.W. Bush, many of them had had a hand in rebuilding the armed forces, kicking the Vietnam syndrome, and winning the Cold War. They had, in their own minds, raised American influence and prestige to heights not seen since the end of World War II. Yet they had left office in 1993 with the nagging sense that their mission was unfinished.[16] Although the hegemony of the world's sole superpower was real enough, it fell short of being absolute and unquestioned.

Then came the era of Bill Clinton: eight years of drift and stagnation camouflaged by the vaporous talk in which the "Man from Hope" specialized. With his misguided notions of foreign policy as a variant of social work, Clinton had repeatedly misused America's armed forces. Kowtowing to his own generals, he had failed to push through the reforms essential for perpetuating U.S. military dominance. Beguiled by his own rhetoric about globalization, he had ignored threats brewing in East Asia and the Middle East. In the Clinton years, American power had atrophied even as new dangers proliferated.

For the zealots, these were wilderness years. Apart from publishing an occasional op-ed piece or signing the odd manifesto, they were stuck on the sidelines, watching with dismay. For them, the Bush restoration of November–December 2000 came not a moment too soon, seemingly offering the chance to reverse this slide toward decline and disarray. Although they had made little headway in promoting their agenda during the administration's first months, the propitious onset of the Global War on Terror promised to change all that. For those intent on establishing beyond doubt and beyond challenge the supremacy of American arms, an expansive, amorphous, open-ended war seemed made to order.

When it came to cementing U.S. military dominion, the secretary of defense and his closest associates viewed the Pentagon brass less as part of the solution than as part of the problem. Based on what they had seen during the Clinton years, Rumsfeld and Wolfowitz were both concerned that the Joint Chiefs of Staff had gotten too big for their britches. Civilian control of the military had grown tenuous.[17] The new secretary of defense and his deputy took office intent on putting the generals in their place.

This proved to be easier said than done. Prior to 9/11, the generals pushed back. Inside "the Building," Rumsfeld's ideas, along with his imperious manner, touched off a nasty round of civil-military conflict. Questions of personality aside, disagreement centered on what national security aficionados call "transformation," the secretary's vision for redesigning U.S. forces so as to make them lighter, more agile, and (by no means incidentally) more readily available for use.

As Rumsfeld and his disciples saw it, senior military officers (especially those in the U.S. Army) were still enamored with the Powell Doctrine of overwhelming force. The Powell Doctrine was rooted in an appreciation of quantity—employing lots of tanks, lots of artillery, and lots of "boots on the ground." Rumsfeld's vision of a new American way of war emphasized quality—relying on precise intelligence, precise weapons, and smaller numbers of troops, primarily elite special operations forces.

Implicit in the Powell Doctrine was the assumption that the wars of the future would be large, uncertain, expensive, and therefore infrequent. Implicit in Rumsfeld's thinking was the expectation that future American wars would be brief and economical, all but eliminating the political risks of opting for force. The secretary of defense believed that technology was rendering obsolete old worries about fog, friction, and chance. Why bother studying Karl von Clausewitz when "shock and awe" could make a clean sweep of things?

For Rumsfeld and his coterie, here lay the appeal of having a go at Iraq. Operation Enduring Freedom in Afghanistan had proved something of a test drive for their ideas. The secretary of defense was counting on a swift victory over Saddam to fully validate his vision and to discredit once and for all the generals who were obstructing his reforms.

So Rumsfeld was intent on having the war fought his way. In the run-up to Operation Iraqi Freedom he exerted himself to marginalize the Joint Chiefs of Staff. The secretary of defense had little use for professional military advice and so, in planning the war, the chiefs played essentially no role. The compliant JCS chairman, General Richard Myers, so much under Rumsfeld's thumb that he was said by Senator John McCain to be "incapable of expressing an independent view," remained an onlooker.[18] When one member of the Joint Chiefs dared to dissent—army General Eric Shinseki suggesting that occupying Iraq might require several hundred thousand troops—Wolfowitz retaliated with a public rebuke and Rumsfeld pushed Shinseki into instant oblivion.

Rumsfeld's chosen military interlocutor was General Tommy Franks, commander of United States Central Command. In a best-selling memoir published after his retirement, Franks portrays himself as a folksy "good old boy" from west Texas who also happens to be a military genius.[19] More accurately, he was Rumsfeld's useful idiot—a coarse, not especially bright, kiss-up, kick-down martinet who mistreated his subordinates but was adept at keeping his boss happy. Franks knew that he was not really in charge, but he pretended otherwise. Appreciating the "political value in being able to stand at the Pentagon podium and say that the Bush administration was implementing the military's plan," Rumsfeld was happy to play along.[20]

So the hawks not only got their war but got it their way. The war plan that Rumsfeld bludgeoned Franks into drafting conformed to their requirements. It envisioned a relatively small force rushing toward Baghdad at breakneck speed, swiftly toppling the Baathist regime, and just as quickly extricating itself. Underlying these expectations were three key assumptions: that the regular Iraqi army wouldn't fight, that the Iraqi people would greet arriving U.S. and British troops as liberators, and that major Iraqi institutions would survive the war intact, facilitating the rapid withdrawal of all but a small contingent of occupying forces.

In the event, these assumptions proved fallacious. When the Anglo-American attack began, the anticipated mass defection of Iraqi forces did not occur. The Iraqi army fought, albeit poorly (although some U.S. troops found even this level of opposition disconcerting). Iraqi irregulars—the Fedayeen—offered a spirited resistance that caught allied commanders by surprise. Meanwhile, the welcome given to allied forces as they traversed southern Iraq proved to be spotty and less than wholehearted. Worse still, when Baghdad fell, Iraq's political infrastructure collapsed, creating a vacuum and giving rise to mass disorder.

Dismissed by the administration as mere blemishes on an otherwise perfect campaign, each of these developments—especially the appearance of irregular forces—proved a portent of things to come. Rumsfeld was slow to respond to these warnings. Entranced with his vision of warfare rendered precise by precision weapons, he had little patience with facts that did not suit his preconceptions. Persuading himself that the fall of Baghdad signified victory, he could not see that the war for Iraq had only just begun.

Buying into Rumsfeld's delusions, Bush on May 1, 2003, declared an end to "major combat operations," the first in what would become an unending series of missteps. In fact, on April 24, 2003, an incident in Fallujah—

troops from the 82nd Airborne Division firing into a crowd of angry demonstrators—had kick-started the insurgency. Heavy-handed U.S. tactics added fuel to the fire. Gordon and Trainor quote one senior officer in the 4th Infantry Division: "The only thing these sand niggers understand is force and I'm about to introduce them to it."[21] President Bush's chosen proconsul, L. Paul Bremer, compounded the problem by dissolving the remnants of the Iraq army, thereby providing the insurgents a pool of potential recruits. As Franks made his escape, command in Iraq devolved upon Lieutenant General Ricardo Sanchez, an officer of indifferent ability who was poorly prepared for the challenges he faced and unable to forge an amicable relationship with Bremer. From there it was all downhill.

The subsequent course of the Iraq War—seemingly endless and perhaps unwinnable—left Rumsfeld's once towering reputation in shreds and largely discredited his "transformation" project. "Shock and awe" survived only as something of a bad joke, akin to "new world order" or "end of history." Events made it clear that from the outset Rumsfeld's grand plan to transform the U.S. military had been at odds with the administration's grand plans to transform the broader Middle East. Imperial projects don't propser with small armies that leave quickly; they require large armies that stay.

The war also suggested that extending the Pax Americana across the broader Middle East was likely to be substantially more difficult and costly than the advocates of imprinting liberal democracy on the Islamic world imagined. Indeed, a prudent reading of the Iraq experience might suggest that the World's Sole Superpower possesses neither the wisdom, nor the will, nor the resources required for such an enterprise.

But what does the Iraq War tell us about the power of the imperial presidency? There can be no doubt that the imperial pretensions of those around the president got us into this mess. But what can George W. Bush, employing all the influence and authority at his command, do to get us out?

Remarkably little, it turns out. Apart from incessant jawboning—promising success just around the corner, touting the latest "turning point," and warning against the dangers of insurgent "isolationism" should popular support for the war flag—the Most Powerful Man in the World has demonstrated an inability either to win the Iraq War or to extricate the United States from Iraq in a timely way. Having chosen after 9/11 to fight his Global War on Terror without mobilizing the country—neither increasing the size of the armed forces nor changing U.S. domestic priorities.—he finds himself unable today to raise the additional resources that "victory" would require. He has yet to identify the "second front" that will seize the initiative from the enemy. He has yet to devise the Manhattan Project that will deliver decisive results. He has yet to form the Grand Alliance that will rally the world in support of the cause. In terms of shaping the course of the Iraq War, the photographer who recorded the abuse of Iraqi detainees by U.S. troops at Abu Ghraib has wielded greater influence than has President Bush.

By the summer of 2006, political observers were transfixed by the slow but steady decline in the president's approval rating as measured by the opinion polls, as if the number reported actually meant anything. What mattered was not that George W. Bush had become the least popular president since Richard Nixon or Harry Truman. What mattered was that neither he, nor his administration, nor the vast apparatus of the federal government could do anything to get the nation out of its fix. Here lay the ultimate expression of what the rolling coup of 2001–2003 had wrought.

7

Class Wars

"You bet your goddamn dollar I'm bitter. It's people like us who give up our sons for the country," said a firefighter whose son was killed in action. "Let's face it: if you have a lot of money, or if you have the right connections, you don't end up on a firing line over there. . . . I think we ought to win that war or pull out. What the hell else should we do—sit and bleed ourselves to death, year after year?" His wife jumps in to add, "My husband and I can't help but thinking that our son gave his life for nothing, nothing at all."[1]

These may sound like voices from our own time, perhaps from grieving parents who joined Cindy Sheehan in August 2005 as she took up vigil in Crawford, Texas, to demand (unsuccessfully) that President George W. Bush interrupt his five-week wartime vacation long enough to offer her a personal justification of the war in Iraq that had killed her own son. Actually, those voices come from another war, almost four decades ago, and the lost son died in Vietnam.

The specter of the Vietnam War so haunts American memory that there is no keeping it repressed, try as we might. Every foreign military intervention since the 1970s has triggered debates about the significance of its contested legacy. Indeed, even prior to the "shock and awe" that initiated the U.S. invasion of Iraq in March 2003, antiwar activists evoked the nightmare of that long-ago war to rally some 10 million global protesters on February 15 in their efforts to prevent Bush's preemptive war.

Of course, some Iraq-Vietnam analogies are strained to the point of absurdity. The histories of the two countries are vastly different, as are the political and social goals that moved their people to take up arms against Americans and American-backed forces. The United States entered Vietnam in the wake of French colonial defeat to create and support a proxy South Vietnamese government against a nationwide Communist movement led by the widely revered Ho Chi Minh (who was supported by China and the Soviet Union). The revolutionary nationalism that triumphed in Vietnam was the culmination of many centuries of anticolonial struggle that had served to unify anti-foreign forces. By contrast, the U.S. occupation of Iraq followed the rapid overthrow of a despised dictator, and no Iraqi faction has demonstrated the potential to unite the nation, which was cobbled together by British imperialism after World War I.

The most striking and useful analogies between the American experiences in Vietnam and Iraq focus not on the particularities of those very different nations, but on the rhetoric and policy of American officials. It can deepen our understanding of the present to explore, for example, how U.S. policy makers in both wars used broad, abstract threats (global Communism/global terrorism) to justify wars against forces that posed no direct challenge to U.S. security; or to examine the lies and distortions (the Gulf of Tonkin incident/weapons of mass destruction) used as pretexts for war; or to look at the fatuous claims of selflessness (fatuous because the United States would never support a government in South Vietnam or Iraq that did not allow for a strong American military and economic presence); or to scrutinize the routine official claims of progress in the face of ongoing resistance.

Another, perhaps less noticed, connection between the wars in Iraq and Vietnam is that in both cases the United States sent a disproportionately working-class military to kill and die while asking or demanding virtually no sacrifices from more privileged Americans at home. Despite the differences between the Vietnam-era draft and the current all-volunteer force, both systems put most of the dirty work of warfare in the hands of people with significantly fewer choices and opportunities than their wealthier peers and sent them to fight undeclared wars on false pretexts. The insistence that volunteers must understand the risks of military service falls apart as soon as one considers the violence done to consent by a war that bypasses constitutional checks and balances (never mind international prohibitions against unilateral attacks on sovereign nations), and by the use of "stop-loss" orders to extend "volunteer" terms of service far beyond their contracted limits.

While the class composition of the military then and now is probably similar, there are significant differences in age, gender, and marital status. The average age of American troops in Iraq is about twenty-seven, while in Vietnam it was significantly lower, about twenty. The higher figure in Iraq is largely attributable to the use of the National Guard and reserves, units that tend to be older than regular army recruits, while in Vietnam very few reserve forces were activated for combat duty overseas.

American forces in Iraq also include many more women than in Vietnam. In 1970, women accounted for 1.4 percent of the armed forces, and most servicewomen were nurses or clerical workers. Now women make up almost 15 percent of U.S. forces and fill all but about 10 percent of military occupational specialties. More than 61 American servicewomen were killed in Iraq by October 1, 2006, compared to eight during the entire Vietnam War.[2]

According to Charles Moskos, a military sociologist at Northwestern

University, the most significant demographic difference between American forces in Vietnam and Iraq is marital status: fewer than one in four of the troops in Vietnam were married, compared to more than half in Iraq. In keeping with that disparity, many more soldiers today have children (including the 10 percent of women soldiers who are single mothers).[3]

The long-term social and political impact of these differences is not yet clear, but it is certainly evident that many Americans with complex family responsibilities are serving multiple tours in a harrowing war zone under enormous strain. Those conditions may well produce a crisis of military morale equivalent to the latter years of the Vietnam War, when the average soldier was a young, single male who served a one-year tour of duty.

The Vietnam-Era Military

In 1964, just prior to the major American escalation in Vietnam, the National Opinion Research Center (NORC) surveyed thousands of active-duty enlisted men and found that only about 20 percent had fathers with white-collar jobs. In the army it was only 17 percent. "White-collar" is a fuzzy term, including everything from underpaid, underappreciated salespeople to corporate executives, but it remains synonymous with at least middle-class status, and in the 1960s 44 percent of American men held those jobs, more than twice the figure for soldiers' fathers. According to the NORC survey, almost 70 percent of American enlisted men had fathers who did either blue-collar or farm labor, and an additional 10 percent had no father at home. Thus, the first major combat units sent to Vietnam in 1965 were overwhelmingly drawn from the working class.[4]

As American troops levels escalated dramatically in the mid-1960s, draft quotas shot up accordingly. As they did, the military began to slash its admissions standards to fill the quotas. Beginning in 1965, the military began to draft hundreds of thousands of men who had scored in the lowest two categories (IV and V) on the Armed Forces Qualifying Test, the military's mental aptitude test, the kind of men who would have been routinely rejected in the years before the Vietnam buildup. Most were from poor and broken families, 80 percent were high school dropouts, and half had IQs of less than 85. Even these lower standards were further dropped with the institution of Project 100,000. Begun in 1966 by Secretary of Defense Robert McNamara, Project 100,000 was touted as a liberal effort to uplift the "subterranean poor" who had "not had the opportunity to earn their fair share of this nation's abundance." Under this program, the military would admit 100,000 men each year that had previously been rejected for flunking the aptitude test. Almost none received the remedial training and education they were promised. Despite the high-minded rhetoric, Project 100,000 merely served to send many poor, terribly confused, and woefully uneducated boys to Vietnam, where their death rate was twice as high as it was for

American forces as a whole. This was a Great Society program that was quite literally shot down on the battlefields of Vietnam.[5]

Meanwhile, more prosperous young people tended to find refuge from the draft in college, where they received student deferments, and in the National Guard and reserves (which, it began to be clear by 1965, would not be mobilized in great numbers for duty in Vietnam). The wealthy and well-connected also had greater success than their less privileged peers using notes from family doctors to receive one of many medical exemptions provided by the Selective Service.

The introduction of a lottery system in late 1969 ended some of the most obvious class inequities of the draft system, but not in time to have much impact on the overall class composition of forces that served in Vietnam, since student deferments continued until 1971, troop withdrawals lowered draft calls in the early 1970s, and medical exemptions remained relatively easy for the privileged to attain.

Class inequality in military service was also revealed in the most important postwar statistical study of Vietnam veterans, *Legacies of Vietnam*. When measured against the backgrounds of nonveterans of the same generation, Vietnam veterans came out on the bottom in income, occupation, and education.[6] The point is not that *all* working-class men went to Vietnam while everyone better off stayed home. After all, this was a generation in which 27 million men came of draft age during the Vietnam War, and only about 10 percent of that total actually went to Vietnam, so even millions of working-class and poor men served elsewhere in the military or were exempted altogether from the draft. However, the key point is that the odds of working-class men going into the military and on to Vietnam were far higher than they were for their middle- and upper-class peers.

Racial disproportions among American forces drew considerable attention in the mid-1960s, as well they should. In 1965–66, African Americans accounted for more than 20 percent of U.S. casualties, about twice their representation in the American population. Civil rights leaders such as Martin Luther King Jr. drew attention to both racial and class inequalities in Vietnam service, and the Pentagon reduced the proportion of blacks exposed to combat. The percentage of African American casualties steadily declined, and by war's end, blacks represented 12.6 percent of all U.S. fatalities in Vietnam. For the war as a whole, then, the greatest inequities in military service were socioeconomic.

Working-Class War Revisited: Iraq

"We don't do body counts," General Tommy Franks announced in the early days of the Iraq War, a decision undoubtedly reflecting the memory of how embarrassing those tallies became during the Vietnam War—how they provided incentives for indiscriminate killing, how they were routinely inflated, and how meaningless they were as a measure of American progress. The military is equally wary of gathering statistics about the class backgrounds of its soldiers, information that would show precisely how the armed forces stacks up in relation to the larger society. Ever since the all-volunteer military was introduced in 1973, the armed forces have faced charges that they are at least as disproportionately working-class as they were during the Vietnam War, yet it has fallen to outside researchers to conduct whatever class analysis can be done.

Lacking truly definitive statistics, it is not an easy task. One of the few recent efforts was conducted by the National Priorities Project (NPP), a Northampton, Massachusetts, research group. First they gathered Pentagon data on the zip code tabulation areas (ZCTAs) of all of the military's 2004 recruits. Then the researchers used Census Bureau data to identify the median family income of every ZCTA. The final step was to assign each recruit the same family income as the median for his or her ZCTA. The possible shortcomings of this approach are obvious. What if the recruit's family income was different from the median? Whether rich or poor, they get assigned a median number, a method guaranteed to flatten out inequalities.

Even so, the NPP study, found that nearly two-thirds of all military recruits (64 percent) were from zip code areas with median household incomes below the U.S. median. The greatest number of recruits came from places with household incomes between $35,000 and $40,000 (just below the national median income of $43,318). The NPP study also found that the twenty counties that produced the highest per capita number of recruits all fell below the national median income.[7]

A Heritage Fund analysis uses the same data to dismiss the claim of serious class inequities in military service, pointing out that recruits from the poorest ZCTAs were underrepresented (as were those from the richest). Of course, a military that is overwhelmingly working-class and lower-middle-class is both possible and consistent with this data. And it is likely that this class profile would be tugged downward if we could determine the precise family income and occupation of each recruit. As the Heritage study concedes, "Because we lack individualized household income data, our approach does not indicate whether or not the recruits came from the poorer households in their neighborhoods."[8]

A similar methodology was used by a group of MIT scholars in the early 1990s to link American servicemen who died in Vietnam to the median incomes of their prewar census tracts. Led by Arnold Barnet, this team concluded that there were no significant class inequalities among U.S. fatalities in the Vietnam War.[9] While it is certainly plausible that fatalities, which included significant numbers of pilots and junior officers, may have reflected fewer class disproportions than the entire military in Vietnam, even Barnet's figures show that the wealthiest group in his study had 22 percent fewer fatalities than its proportionate share, while the second poorest group suffered 31 percent more deaths than its share. More significantly, it is simply misleading to *assume* that each soldier reflects the median income of his community. As James Fallows pointed out in his critique of the MIT study, even communities with high median incomes included firefighters, plumbers, store clerks, and other people whose working-class identifies are obscured by median incomes.[10]

Perhaps the most telling indication of class inequalities in the current military emerges from the crisis in military recruitment that began as casualties from the Iraq War mounted, the false pretexts of the war became more widely known, and the U.S. occupation became increasingly beleaguered. The recruitment budget was raised from $2.7 billion to $3 billion, an additional thousand recruiters were put in the field, enlistment bonuses were raised, and recruiters intensified their focus on the unemployed and economically disadvantaged, particularly from the rural South.

According to the *Washington Post*'s Ann Scott Tyson, Martinsville, Virginia, where the median income is $27,000 and more than a sixth of its citizens live below the poverty line, is "typical of the lower-income communities across the nation that today constitute the U.S. military's richest recruiting grounds." Recruiters often focus on "anchor schools," such as Magna Vista High near Martinsville, where school officials welcome recruiters and encourage students to take the military's vocational test, where half the students receive financial aid or free lunch, and where there is a large Junior Reserve Officers' Training Corps.[11]

However, recruiters are finding that many of their most likely prospects are not teenagers but people in their twenties who have tried the job market only to become discouraged enough to turn to the military. "I tried anything and everything," said Albert Deal, a twenty-five-year-old recruit, reeling off a list of unsuccessful job searches. He finally concluded that the military was "something to make a life of." Among African Americans, however, recruitment has fallen dramatically. In 2001 blacks made up more than 22 percent of the army; by 2006 this had fallen to 14 percent, still a few percentage points above the nation as a whole, but not nearly so disproportionate as before the Iraq War began.[12]

The fact that 44 percent of recruits come from rural areas and 41 percent from the South (a region with 35 percent of the nation's youth) has led some commentators to suggest that pro-military regional cultures may be as important as class in shaping the composition of today's military, the assumption being that the South is more pro-military than the Northeast, for example, where 18 percent of the nation's youth population provides only 13 percent of the army's recruits. If that is true, one might expect the military to maintain a higher level of morale and discipline within its ranks in Iraq regardless of the general population's view of the war. It might also mean that if morale does weaken significantly (and there are some signs that this is happening), there might also be a dramatic shift in national political views in areas of the nation once regarded as predictably conservative.[13]

In the face of the worst recruiting year since 1973, the Department of Defense began in 2005 to lower its admission standards, just as it had at the height of Vietnam escalation. Since the mid-1980s the military had tightly restricted the number of recruits who scored in the second lowest category of its aptitude test (Category IV). Congress forbids the military from taking recruits from Category V (the lowest nine percentiles), but the Pentagon in September 2005 raised the cap on Category IV from 2 percent to 4. Since education and economics are closely linked, the lowering of testing standards also drops the class composition of military recruits.[14]

Despite the drop in standards, the military in Iraq, at least through 2006, has a significantly higher percentage of high school graduates, well over 95 percent, at least 10 percent above the relevant age group in the larger population. And even with this dropping of standards, the military has not dipped as low as the Vietnam-era military on mental aptitude. That said, this is a military of high school graduates, with college graduates largely restricted to the officer corps. In terms of higher education, the military is substantially below the national average.

Class and Politics

Many voices of the Vietnam era are long forgotten or were never clearly heard, especially those of people such as the firefighter and his wife who opened this essay. In their place, we have a canned image of Vietnam-era working-class whites as bigoted hard-hats, superpatriotic hawks who simply despised long-haired protesters and supported their president, Archie Bunkers all.

In that stereotype lies a partial but misleading truth. A 1969 poll found that 27 percent of white male union members identified themselves as "convinced hawks," compared to 17 percent who called themselves "convinced doves" (with others somewhere in between).[15] And many working-class families were indeed appalled by the antiwar movement of those years. "I hate those peace demonstrators," said the firefighter who lost his son in Vietnam. But his hostility did not make him a hawk. He was furious because he saw antiwar activists as privileged and disrespectful snobs who "insult everything we believe in" without having to share his family's military and economic sacrifices. In virtually the same breath, however, he said about the war of his time, "The sooner we get the hell out of there [Vietnam] the better." A close analysis suggests that working-class hostility toward antiwar protesters was based more on class and cultural tensions than on political differences over the legitimacy or necessity of the American war in Vietnam. Indeed, polls of the early 1970s showed that a majority of Americans from all classes opposed both the war *and* antiwar protest.

In fact, some evidence suggests that poor and working-class Americans (and we need to remind ourselves that these large categories include men and women of a wide variety of races and ethnicities) were more profoundly disaffected by the Vietnam War than any other groups of Americans. For example, a Gallup poll from January 1971 showed that the less formal education people had, the more likely they were to want the military out of Vietnam: 80 percent of Americans with grade school educations called for a U.S. withdrawal, and 75 percent of high school graduates agreed; only among college graduates did the figure drop to 60 percent.[16]

In Vietnam itself, the mostly working-class American military made its growing opposition to the war increasingly clear as the fighting dragged on. By late 1969, demoralization and resistance within the armed forces were endemic. Desertions were beginning to skyrocket, drug use was becoming rampant, avoidance of combat routine and even outright mutinies were not unusual, and hundreds of officers were wounded or killed by their own enraged troops. By 1972, the military was in shambles. It is now largely forgotten that the U.S. pulled out of Vietnam not just because of domestic opposition to the war but also because it no longer seemed possible to field a functional, obedient army.

Ohio 1968: Is This War Worth Another Child?

Resistance within the military did not come out of the blue. Its origins were deeply embedded in that prolonged war. By the mid-1960s, for instance, many hard-fighting and disciplined American soldiers were already embittered by their commanders' war of attrition that had them "humping the boonies" as bait to draw fire from an elusive and dangerous enemy who determined the time, place, and duration of the vast majority of firefights. They often viewed their officers as ticket-punching lifers who sought promotion by jeopardizing their troops in an effort to post the highest possible enemy body counts, the chief measure of progress back in Washington. GIs, who might risk everything to save a buddy, increasingly came to view the war itself as meaningless. "It don't mean nothin'," they commonly said.

In the face of rising opposition, Presidents Johnson and Nixon sought to rally—in Nixon's famous phrase—the "silent majority" in support of the war, not by explaining the need for ever more sacrifice but by demonizing critics who threatened to turn America into a "pitiful, helpless giant." Though the Nixon administration, unlike the present one, did not have its own media machine constantly available to attack its enemies, Nixon often sent out his vice president, Spiro Agnew, as an attack dog to vilify student protesters ("an effete corps of impudent snobs") and the media ("nattering nabobs of negativism").

The cynical courting of middle America certainly encouraged working-class anger toward antiwar activists deemed elitists by the administration, but in the end it proved incapable of overcoming the rising tide of outrage among families who believed they were bearing the greatest burden in a war that lacked an achievable or worthy purpose. Already, in the long months after the Tet offensive of January 31, 1968, when as many as 500 Americans were dying every week, the most basic of all questions was beginning to well up from the heartland: was this war worth the life of even one more of our children?

You could see it, for example, in Parma, Ohio, a working-class neighborhood near Cleveland that ultimately lost thirty-five young men in Vietnam. On Memorial Day 1968 the *Cleveland Press*, a newspaper previously known for its strong support for the war, ran a startling front-page feature by reporter Dick Feagler under the headline "He Was Only 19—Did You Know Him?" It was about a Parma boy named Greg Fischer who had just died in Vietnam.

For Clark Dougan, now an editor at the University of Massachusetts Press, the news of Greg Fischer's death struck like a hammer because he had known the nineteen-year-old. They were classmates together at Valley Forge High School, where the school's principal had often come on the intercom to ask for a moment of silence because yet another former Valley Forge student had died in Vietnam. The newspaper article, Dougan recalls,

> was really asking, how many more people like Greg are we willing to waste? This is just an ordinary kid we're talking about. He wasn't an Eagle Scout, or a class president, or an all-American athlete. He was a kid who had worked in the local pharmacy. . . . I think that was the moment when "Middle America" really turned against the war. The *Cleveland Press* was part of the Scripps-Howard chain, a conservative syndicate that had strongly supported the war. So it was remarkable that this newspaper would run such an angry editorial about an American casualty. It reflected a feeling that was spreading all over working-class communities like Parma. I think a lot of World War II veterans who had been sitting around their kitchen tables saying, "You've got to fight for your country," were starting to say, "Fuck this. It's not worth Greg Fischer's life or his buddy's life."[17]

Ohio 2005: The Chickenhawk War

The author of that article, Dick Feagler, was still on the job thirty-seven years later, writing for the *Cleveland Plain Dealer*, lashing out at the war in Iraq, at those who have "a bland, nitwit allegiance to the blood and death as if the carnage in Iraq were some kind of Olympic sport."[18] As in 1968, the burden of death falls disproportionately on the working class and is showing signs of fundamentally eroding heartland support for the war. It's worth noting, though, that editorial dissent over the war in places such as Ohio is routinely coupled with deep concern about the well-being of American soldiers—their training, equipment, terms of deployment, and medical care. Like many other Ohioan columnists, Feagler often couples his attacks on the war with prayers for the troops, even telling readers how to send care packages and letters of support.

As American fatalities approached 2,000 in the summer of 2005, one could sense a sea change in public opinion similar to the turning point brought about by the Tet offensive of 1968. By August, a CBS poll found that a clear majority of Americans—57 percent—believed the war in Iraq was not worth the loss of American lives. By May 2006, 62 percent thought the war was not worth fighting (an ABC/*Washington Post* poll). By March 2006, Gallup found that 60 percent of Americans viewed the war as a mistake, and by May 2006 an ABC News/*Washington Post* poll found that 66 percent of Americans disapproved of President Bush's handling of the war, almost exactly the level reached by President Lyndon Johnson after the Tet offensive. And Bush's overall approval rating fell to around 30 percent in the spring of 2006, among the lowest presidential approval ratings in polling history.[19]

As in 1968, so in 2005 criticism began to surface throughout the nation about the inequities of sacrifice—not just that the wealthy were not doing their share of the fighting and dying, but, as *New York Times* columnist Bob Herbert pointed out, the architects of the war and "the loudest of the hawks are the least likely to send their sons or daughters off" to Iraq. "If Mr. Bush's war in Iraq is worth dying for, then children of the privileged should be doing some of the dying."[20] President Bush's five-week-long vacation that summer was only the most obvious symbol of the obscene gulf in safety between the advocates of the war and its victims. That gulf was at the heart of growing disaffection in places such as Ohio, where in August 2005 twenty marines from the same reserve unit (3rd Battalion, 25th Marines) were killed in Iraq within seventy-two hours. That unit is headquartered in Brook Park, Ohio, a working-class suburb adjacent to Parma, and the losses included fourteen men from Ohio, bringing the state's total fatalities to more than ninety.

Sam Fulwood, another *Plain Dealer* columnist, responded to these losses by recalling Bush's 2003 "bring 'em on" taunting of the Iraqi insurgents. "Two years ago, tucked in the comfort and safety of the White House's Roosevelt Room, the president challenged 'anybody who wants to harm American troops.' John Wayne couldn't have said it with more cowboy swagger. 'Bring them on.'" Well, as Fulwood concluded, with a stridency rarely seen in midwestern papers just a few months ago, "the chicken hawk got his wish."[21]

In the summer of 2005, for the first time, not just in Ohio but all over the country, media outlets started to raise a once forbidden question: should we withdraw? As the *Cincinnati Enquirer* framed it on August 7, in response to the local casualties, "Do we seek revenge? Do we continue as usual? Or do we leave?"[22] The last question, once asked in a whisper if at all, began to be asked in earnest. And when it was raised by an antiwar Iraq War Marine veteran named Paul Hackett, running as a Democrat in a special election for Congress, he came within two percentage points of winning in a district east of Cincinnati that had given George Bush a whopping 64 percent of its votes in November 2004 and has elected a Republican to the House of Representatives almost automatically for the past thirty years. It was the outspoken Hackett who attacked the president as a son of a bitch who had made the United States less secure and whose "bring 'em on" speech was "the most incredibly stupid comment I've ever heard a president of the United States make."[23]

Just a few months later, in November, Democratic congressman John Murtha of Pennsylvania, a Vietnam War veteran once known for his hawkish support of U.S. intervention abroad, called for U.S. withdrawal. In response to charges that criticism of the war might damage the morale of American troops, Murtha responded: "What demoralizes them is not the criticism. What demoralizes them is going to war with not enough troops and equipment . . . being deployed when their homes have been ravaged by hurricanes [Katrina] . . . being on their second or third deployments, leaving their families behind without a network of support."[24] And when President Bush and Vice President Cheney called Murtha's position irresponsible, he fired back sarcastically, "I like guys who got five deferments . . . send people to war, and then don't like to hear suggestions."[25]

In presidential elections, Ohio and Pennsylvania are often spoken of as bellwether states. They may also play that role when it comes to America's wars. Disillusionment with the Iraq War has soared in the American heartland not only because of mounting casualties and the obvious lack of progress in quelling the Iraqi insurgency but also because the military is strained to its limits by keeping more than 130,000 troops in Iraq (a figure that would be much higher if the military did not subcontract to private businesses so much of its rear-echelon support). Many thousands of Americans have already served two and even three tours, and untold numbers have been required to serve beyond their contractual terms of enlistment by "stop-loss" orders.

During the Vietnam era, Lyndon Johnson decided to rely almost exclusively on the draft and the active-duty military to fight the war, hoping to keep casualties (and so their impact) largely restricted to young, mostly unmarried, and powerless individuals. The reserve forces, he understood, tended to be older, married, and more rooted in their communities. Now the reserves and National Guard make up half of U.S. combat forces in Iraq, a figure that has doubled since early 2004. This increasing reliance on the reserves with their many family and community connections helps to account for the growing antiwar activism among military families that have joined groups such as Military Families Speak Out, Gold Star Mothers for Peace, and Families of the Fallen for Change.

At least as striking, and overlooked, has been the movement within organized labor to oppose the war. In July 2005, at the National Convention of the AFL-CIO in Chicago, a long line of speakers rose to denounce the U.S. war in Iraq. Brooks Sunkett, a Vietnam veteran and vice president of the Communications Workers of America, said that he had been lied to three decades ago when the government sent him to war, and "we have to stop it from lying to a new generation now." The power of antiwar sentiment from the floor moved the leadership to change the wording of their Iraq War resolution to call for a rapid withdrawal from Iraq rather than the more ambiguous "as soon as possible."[26]

> Our soldiers—the men and women risking their lives in Iraq—come from America's working families. They are our sons and daughters, our sisters and brothers, our husbands and wives. They deserve to be properly equipped with protective body gear and up-armored vehicles. And they deserve leadership that fully values their courage and sacrifice. Most importantly, they deserve a commitment from our country's leaders to bring them home rapidly. An unending military presence will waste lives and resources, undermine our nation's security and weaken our military.[27]

While the resolution does not call for an immediate withdrawal, as antiwar labor activists had hoped, it does mark the first time in the AFL-CIO's fifty-year history that it has taken a position clearly opposed to a major U.S. foreign policy or military action.[28]

During the Vietnam War, by contrast, the AFL-CIO routinely endorsed Washington's war policies. Even as late as 1970, when Nixon ordered the ground invasion of Cambodia, AFL-CIO president George Meany insisted that the president "should have the full support of the American people. He certainly has ours." Actually, labor was by no means united in support of the war, but those unions and rank-and-file members that opposed the war often did so in opposition to their own leadership as well.[29]

Soldiers, veterans, and their families have, as they did in the early 1970s, once again moved to the forefront of a growing, grassroots struggle to end an unpopular war. Cindy Sheehan's impassioned opposition to the war has not only gained extraordinary media attention but seems to have ignited a genuine outpouring of public support. Many who may have feared that public opposition to the war might be taken as unpatriotic or unsupportive of American troops have been emboldened by Sheehan's demand that her son's death, and all the others, not be used to justify further bloodshed in a war that cannot be convincingly justified by an administration distant from their lives and their suffering. As of 2006, some 400 American soldiers have reportedly deserted to Canada (despite tougher asylum laws than those prevailing in that country during the Vietnam War) and an estimated 9,000 military personnel have failed to report for duty since the war started. Further evidence of declining military support for the war came early in 2006 with a Zogby poll showing that 29 percent of U.S. troops in Iraq favored immediate withdrawal, with 72 percent calling for withdrawal within a year.

And yet a note of caution should be sounded in evaluating the prospects for anything resembling a mass GI movement against the war. The same poll found that 85 percent of U.S. troops believed the main U.S. mission in Iraq was "to retaliate for Saddam's role in the 9/11 attacks," and back at home only a few hundred people had joined Iraq Veterans Against the War.

A *Nation* article by Christian Parenti attributes the loyalty of American soldiers to continue fighting for a cause for which they had many doubts could be attributed largely to one of the principal lessons the military learned from Vietnam: the importance of unit cohesion for the preservation of military morale. The military, Parenti argues, has honed to a fine art the ability to motivate soldiers not around an abstact cause but around the duty to fight for their comrades. This idea has been around since the beginning of war but has been hammered home in the years since Vietnam, a war in which unit cohesion was profoundly compromised by the military policy of rotating most soldiers in and out of Vietnam as individuals rather than as whole units.

As result, men who might rebel "are guilt-tripped and emotionally blackmailed into serving causes they hate." Correspondence with a former student who faced a decision to do a second tour in Iraq (unlike many, he actually had a choice in the matter) convinces me that there is real substance to Parenti's argument. During and after his first tour, this student (we'll call him Robert) had come to have fundamental doubts about the legitimacy of the war. Yet he decided to volunteer for a second tour out of a sense of responsibility to the other men in his unit. "As much as I disagree with the war . . . I don't think I can watch marines go to war from the TV after having been asked to finally contribute." The "finally" in that sentence is based on Robert's belief that his first tour involved "cupcake" duty along the Kuwait border and his sense of guilt that by not serving a second tour he would be letting others risk their lives in place of him. What's more, "the problem in my mind is that I made a promise. When I joined the marines, I promised my service for my six years. I have only done four of them.

"When I weigh it in my head I have come to the conclusion that with the years on my contract and my unfailing feeling that I haven't fulfilled my responsibilities as a marine, I must agree to go. For me, it is a lose-lose situation. I have lost respect for myself for going because I know in my heart that this war is wrong, but only slightly less respect than if I would again have to watch marines go into combat without me."[30]

Of course, a growing number of soldiers are wondering why they should sacrifice for their buddies in service of a cause they can no longer support, especially when the larger society seems so unwilling to share the sacrifice. For the privileged, the Iraq War has been a time to reap the benefits of major tax cuts and still-galloping increases in top corporate salaries. As former House majority leader Tom DeLay put it in 2003, "Nothing is more important in the face of a war than cutting taxes."[31] *New York Times* columnist Paul Krugman suggests that a more precise statement of the "DeLay Principle" would be that "nothing is more important in the face of a war than cutting taxes for very, very wealthy people."

One contrast between our own time and the Vietnam era is that today we are significantly less committed to curbing the worst consequences of economic and social inequality. Though the burden of fighting in Vietnam was not equally shared, and our presidents acted as if domestic life could be as unencumbered as in the most prosperous peacetime, for much of the 1960s there was at least a significant national commitment to improving the lives of poor and working people. While the social and economic reforms of the Great Society have resulted in failures as well as successes, and its funding never came close to approximating the claims of its rhetoric, it was at least partially responsible for reducing the poverty rate from 22 percent to 13 percent between 1963 and 1973. Today working people not only supply the troops who die in our name but bear the lion's share of the economic sacrifices as we wage an apparently permanent "war on terror" without so much as a slight increase in the minimum wage.

8

The Female Shape of the All-Volunteer Force

ELIZABETH L. HILLMAN

Because of the numbers and influence of women in the ranks, the U.S. military took on a distinctively female shape in the last decades of the twentieth century. In every service, at nearly every rank and grade, in virtually every unit and at every installation, servicewomen reported for duty alongside men. As early as the 1970s, military and political leaders knew that the military could not meet its personnel needs without drawing on the female labor force. And the need for women in uniform has not let up since. The tremendous demand for military resources in the post-Vietnam era, coupled with women's push for equal opportunity, has drawn women into the military in transformative numbers. In spite of the resistance of military institutions, the post-Vietnam armed forces have become "feminized" in many key respects. "Female" issues such as promoting healthy families, ending sexual harassment, and preventing sexualized torture command the attention of military task forces and congressional committees. "Feminine" skills including compromise, negotiation, and communication are among the skills most critical to successful peacekeeping operations and even to military interrogation. And women themselves are essential cogs in the military manpower machine.

But this new gender balance, this "feminization," has caught military and political leaders off guard. The United States has not reconceived military service as a civic duty of and career opportunity for both women and men, nor has it made the military workplace safe for women. Instead, military and civilian leaders have restricted women's opportunities and reinvented a "warrior" culture of aggression and male coming-of-age.[1] Despite the integration of women and racial minorities into most of the armed forces, the U.S. military remains one of the only American institutions that can legally discriminate on the basis of sex.

In the last three decades, observers in and out of uniform have debated the wisdom and consequences of women's military service. But none can dispute the new gender demographics of the post-Vietnam U.S. military.

Those demographics reveal a startling and largely ignored truth: with the end of forcible service for men, women rescued the all-volunteer force from devastating shortfalls in the number and quality of recruits. As the Vietnam War ended, the Selective Service Act was allowed to expire. When the last draft call went out in 1973, women made up less than 2 percent of the U.S. military. Ten years later, the female presence in the ranks had increased five times over. By September 2005, women were 16 percent of the American armed forces.[2] Without them, the military would have suffered not only a shortage of personnel, but also a striking drop in the education levels and test scores of new recruits.

Much as the officials and consultants of the Vietnam era failed to appreciate the degree to which women and racial minorities would become essential military personnel, the architects of the early twenty-first century military transformation have failed to reckon with the consequences of women's heightened military participation. One of the lessons that the military has forgotten since the Vietnam War is that women saved the all-volunteer force. That rescue came at great cost—to servicewomen, to the military, and to the United States.

The All-Volunteer Force: Women as Saving Grace

In 2003, the University of Michigan won a battle in the courts to preserve its ability to consider race in student admissions decisions. It won by arguing that diversity was a compelling objective of state educational policy.[3] A turning point in that case was the amicus curiae brief signed by twenty-nine retired generals and admirals, including notable military leaders such as Admiral William T. Crowe, chairman of the Joint Chiefs of Staff from 1985 to 1989; General Norman Schwarzkopf, commander of allied forces in the Gulf War of 1991; and General Wesley Clark, supreme allied commander in Europe from 1997 to 2000. Their brief, quoted at some length in Justice Sandra Day O'Connor's opinion for the Supreme Court, stressed the negative consequences of racial disparities in the Vietnam-era armed forces and declared that affirmative action was essential to maintaining a diverse, well-qualified military.[4] That amicus brief was a direct outgrowth of the military's role as a model of successful racial integration. Active-duty as well as retired military leaders routinely invoke the rhetoric of equal opportunity in the strongest possible language.[5] The armed forces of the early twenty-first century embrace diversity as a positive good as thoroughly and publicly as any American institution.

But thirty years ago, the experts who were asked to prepare the nation for the end of conscription did not see diversity as a possibility, much less a goal. During the Vietnam War, the Department of Defense had relied on forced service, not volunteers, to fill many of the least desirable and most dangerous military occupations. The risks and hardships of serving in the

Army's ground forces rather than in the more technical, less martial forces of the air and sea services persuaded many young men to enlist in the Navy or Air Force rather than wait for a draft notice and end up in the infantry. After the war, military planners and civilian government officials underestimated the degree to which the end of the draft would also end this incentive to volunteer.[6] They also misjudged the extent of American youth's disenchantment with military service. As a result, they anticipated almost no change in the gender or racial demographics of military service in a volunteer military.[7]

The most influential expert assessment was the report prepared by the Gates Commission in 1970. Chartered by President Nixon to develop a plan to end the draft and named for its chair, Thomas S. Gates, a former secretary of defense, the commission unanimously recommended that conscription be ended.[8] The commission's report ignored women entirely, mentioning female service only in the context of alternatives to a volunteer force.[9] Instead, the report stressed the importance of increasing military pay, describing "the first indispensable step" toward a successful volunteer force as removing "the present inequity in the pay" of servicemen.[10] This emphasis on financial incentives reflected the influence of commissioners such as economists Alan Greenspan and Milton Friedman, but the commission's failure to discuss even the possible recruitment of women was nonetheless a remarkable omission.[11] Military leaders knew—and had known since at least World War II, when more than 350,000 women served in military uniforms—that women could be relied upon to fill gaps in military staffing. A 1966 Pentagon task force had studied the use of women to meet the personnel needs of the war in Vietnam, and in 1967 Congress had lifted the 2 percent ceiling on female enlistments.[12] In addition, the commissioners themselves had identified the structural factors—the evolution in military occupations and the skills that those occupations required—that soon led to many more women in uniform. The commission noted the trend toward more technical and bureaucratic military jobs, documenting how the proportion of military occupations involving ground combat had fallen from 25 percent in 1945 to 10 percent by 1974.[13] This meant that an increasing number of military positions could be filled by servicewomen without even reaching the question as to whether women should be subjected to combat situations. The commission also identified the quality of recruits as a major concern for an all-volunteer force, a problem that could logically be addressed by broadening the potential pool of recruits to include women.[14] But the commission failed to connect the dots when it came to women. The demographics of the commission itself were part of the problem: only one of fifteen commissioners, and none of the thirty-one senior staff and research leads, was a woman.[15]

The experts' botched forecast was apparent almost immediately. As soon as the draft ended, the numbers and quality indicators of male volunteers fell and the Department of Defense scrambled to recruit women. By 1972, Secretary of Defense Melvin R. Laird was establishing a task force to prepare contingencies for the use of women if the draft ended, and by 1978, the Carter administration was explicitly directing the Pentagon to increase the number of servicewomen.[16] A 1977 Brookings Institution study recommended recruiting women because it was less expensive and would reduce the pressure for more men.[17] Fifteen years after the draft ended, the number of women in uniform had increased from 1.5 percent to more than 9 percent.[18] Women's scores on military aptitude tests shored up the military's quality indicators as well as its overall numbers.[19] In fiscal years 1974 to 1976, for example, 88 percent of the women who joined the Army were high school graduates, as compared to only 52 percent of the men; in the first decade of the volunteer force, 92 percent of all women enlistees had high school diplomas, compared to only 70 percent of male enlistees.[20] One scholar bluntly wrote, "It is widely acknowledged that women were the saving grace of the volunteer concept during the 1970s."[21]

After the 1970s, women continued to enlist in larger numbers than initially expected, spurred in part by changes in military personnel policies. In order to attempt to recruit more men, the military increased pay and benefits and recognized the need to support military families and servicemembers' dependents. These changes in military policy created economic and social incentives that made recruiting and retention of skilled, reliable servicemen possible. But they also made a military career more attractive to women, especially those who lacked significant economic opportunities in the civilian sector. The military eliminated restrictions on assignments that prevented women from serving in many military occupations and relaxed restrictions that forced pregnant women to be discharged and limited the number of dependent children of recruits. These trends combined to make the armed forces a viable career choice for those seeking economic security and educational support. By the late 1990s, the number of military personnel who served for more than four years had increased significantly, one of many indicators of an increasingly career-oriented force.[22]

This sea change in military demographics made women the fastest-growing segment of veterans in the early twenty-first century.[23] In 1983, Congress established a Secretary of Veterans' Affairs Advisory Committee on Women Veterans. In 1994, a Center for Women Veterans was established in the Department of Veterans Affairs after legislation championed by Representative Maxine Waters of California.[24]

In addition to missing the gender implications of the volunteer force, government planners also underestimated the rate at which African Americans would enlist in a volunteer military.[25] The percentage of African Americans in the military nearly doubled in the first decade after the end of the draft.[26] This concurrent increase in minority and female participation led to a dramatic rise in the number of African American women in the service; by 1986, black women were 43 percent of Army enlisted women and 30 percent of the entire female force.[27] In 2005, women constituted 16 percent of the military workforce and 48 percent of the overall civilian workforce.[28] African American women, however, accounted for 28 percent of the female military presence despite being only 13 percent of the female civilian labor force.[29] In the Army, this overrepresentation of African American women was especially pronounced: black women made up 39 percent of female Army personnel on active duty in 2004.[30] In recent years, the Congressional Black Caucus Veterans Braintrust has paid particular attention to the needs of the fast-growing population of African American female veterans.[31] In many respects, African American women were at the center of the demographic transformation triggered by the end of the Vietnam War. Their experience crystallizes the role and treatment of women in the volunteer force: they helped to save the volunteer army by enlisting in disproportionately high numbers but their opportunities for military success were circumscribed by discrimination and harassment.

Women Volunteers: Fits, Starts, and Progress

Once in uniform, women were assigned, evaluated, and promoted in ways that reflected cultural assumptions about female capability. Military laws and policies structured the work environments of servicewomen and reinforced a gender hierarchy that affected civilian as well as military women. Within that hierarchy, sexual harassment and assault became a feature of the military workplace and threatened the lives and health of women around domestic and foreign military bases. Because the volunteer force needed female servicemembers, and because women needed the career stability and economic opportunities that military service offered, the ranks of servicewomen steadily grew. But the emphasis on male authority and aggressiveness that predominated in many quarters of military service left women unprotected from discrimination and abuse. Women made great strides toward becoming full participants in military service. Their success, however, came against a backdrop of continued restrictions and a repetitious debate about whether or not they belonged in the service at all.

When the Vietnam War ended, servicewomen had already won the support of many commanders and political leaders. The Defense Department Advisory Committee on Women in the Services, established by Secretary of Defense George C. Marshall in 1951 to aid in the recruitment of women during the Korean War, monitored the progress of women's service and recommended solutions to recurring problems.[32] The promotion and recruiting restrictions that had prevented women from either attaining high rank or reaching a significant proportion of the force were already gone, and by 1972, the Air Force, Army, and Navy Reserve Officer Training Corps (ROTC) programs were all open to women.[33] Admiral Elmo Zumwalt, the Navy's maverick chief of naval operations from 1970 to 1974, opened many previously closed naval occupational specialties to women during his tenure. The Air Force led the way in accommodating women's reproductive lives by allowing women with children to enlist and permitting waivers of the Department of Defense's automatic discharge policy for pregnant women. Civil courts, responding to new pressure for civil rights and expanding notions of legal equality, had also begun to push the armed forces to treat women fairly. In 1973, the Supreme Court held that the military could require servicewomen, but not servicemen, to prove their spouses were financially dependent before offering military benefits.[34] Still, in 1972, just before the draft ended, only 42,000 women served in the military, and more than 90 percent were assigned to jobs classified as medical, dental, or clerical in nature.[35]

The advent of the volunteer force brought sharp increases not only in servicewomen's numbers (more than 100,000 women were serving in 1976 and more than 150,000 by 1979) but also in their opportunities.[36] By 1976, the percentage of women in those "feminine" military classifications had dropped to 60 percent, and by 1983, it was down to 55 percent, with increasing numbers of women assigned to fields such as intelligence, supply, and equipment repair.[37] Congress opened the elite national service academies to women in 1976, and the courts continued to nudge the military in the direction of equitable gender policies, holding in 1976 that the Marine Corps' policy of mandatory discharge of pregnant Marines violated the Constitution and ordering the Navy to open additional ships to women in 1978.[38] By 2005, women accounted for about one-sixth of the active and reserve forces. They were most outnumbered in Marine Corps, where female marines were but 5 percent of the force, but they made up nearly a quarter of both Army and Air Force reserves.[39]

Progress toward equal opportunity across gender lines was not a steady march, however. As the number of servicewomen grew, gender-based restrictions on military assignments remained in place. Military leaders limited the changes wrought by women's military presence by preserving some positions as male-only. They argued that the risks involved, the physical capabilities required, or the military facilities available (such as berthing capacity on ships) would make women's presence in these positions a detriment to military effectiveness. This debate centered on the issue of appropriateness and practicability of assigning women only to noncombat jobs. Proponents of women in combat argued that the restrictions protected masculine privilege, not female bodies, while opponents pointed to the history of male participation in war fighting and the vital importance of bonding ("unit cohesion") in guaranteeing performance under fire. The Supreme Court upheld the all-male Selective Service system in 1981 on the grounds that women were not eligible for combat, demonstrating the importance of this military personnel policy.[40]

The patchwork of combat exclusion rules that evolved as Congress and the president negotiated with the services revealed widespread resistance to the full inclusion of female servicemembers. Identifying combat positions was not a simple task; some military occupational specialties were opened, closed, and reopened to women as opinions shifted about their suitability for women.[41] Lawrence J. Korb, a scholar of military affairs and an assistant secretary of defense from 1981 to 1985, once described the "combat-exclusion policy" as "the worst of all possible worlds for female military personnel" because it limited women's advancement but failed to protect them from the risks of dangerous service.[42] The arguments for and against permitting women to serve in combat positions were endlessly recycled during the first three decades of the volunteer force.[43]

Still, the trend was clearly in the direction of opening doors to women. Most military jobs are now performed by both men and women. In 1988, the Department of Defense opened about 30,000 new positions to service-women by setting a single standard (called the "risk rule") to be used in evaluating sex-based restrictions on assignments. The service of military women in the invasion of Panama in 1989 and the Persian Gulf War in 1990 and 1991 led to more pressure to lift sex-based restrictions on assignments.[44] Combat aviation opened to women in 1993, and a 1994 policy change rescinded the "risk rule" in favor of a ban on the assignment of women to units below the brigade level with a primary mission of engaging in direct ground combat.[45] Servicewomen have acted as peacekeepers in Haiti, enforced no-fly zones in Iraq, flown combat missions in Kosovo, died in terrorist attacks on the USS *Cole* in 2000 and at the Pentagon in 2001, and been wounded alongside men in Afghanistan and Iraq in the first U.S. wars of the twenty-first century.

Thirty years into the volunteer force, women shoulder the burdens of military duty but have yet to ascend to the highest ranks of military institutions. In 2005, there were 43 female flag or general officers as compared to 874 male such officers, a female representation of less than five percent, and only one woman stood among the 173 men at the two highest grades.[46] The wide gap between women's representation at the top and the bottom of the military hierarchy reflects more than the time lag between accession to duty and late-career promotions.[47]

The vestiges of the combat exclusion policy keep women off the fastest tracks to military promotion. In 2005, sex-based restrictions on women's assignments placed 15 to 20 percent of military positions off-limits for women, most of them in the infantry and special forces.[48] Women are excluded from 178 enlisted specialties (5 percent of all available specialties) and 17 officer specialties (1 percent of those available).[49] Servicewomen remain concentrated in health care and administrative occupations.[50] Although these combat exclusions cannot eliminate female casualties, they have placed disproportionately more servicemen than women in harm's way. Even in the ongoing war in Iraq, which has brought female military casualties and deaths to the front pages of U.S. newspapers, servicewomen account for only 1 percent of deaths and 2 percent of the wounded.[51] For those who served short terms in the conscript army of the Vietnam War, avoiding combat had been a way to stay alive; for those who make careers in the volunteer military, avoiding combat is still a safer way to go, but it has also become a professional liability. Women are "underrepresented in tactical operations, the area that yields two-thirds of the general and flag officers of the Services."[52] Women are also a smaller percentage of service academy graduates then men, partly because so many women are directly commissioned as nurses but also because women's presence at the academies has been carefully monitored by officials unwilling to permit too many women to populate the ranks of elite cadets and midshipmen.[53] Women of all races have lower promotion and retention rates than men, though the data vary across race lines. White women tend to leave the military before attaining high rank, while African American women—notwithstanding a widespread perception among white servicemen that minorities are favored in selection for promotion—are promoted at lower rates than the members of any other demographic category.[54] Every service except the Air Force still includes photographs in the packets considered by promotion boards, furthering the perception that race and gender are taken into account—as pluses or minuses—in the promotion process.[55]

Family responsibilities also contribute to women's underrepresentation at the highest levels of military service. Although most senior servicemen are married, husbands—and children—are scarce for women at high ranks as compared to men. At the relatively senior ranks of O–5 and O–6 (that is, lieutenant colonels and colonels in the Army, Air Force, and Marine Corps and commanders and captains in the Navy), 90 percent of men but only 55 percent of women are married.[56] Ninety-four percent of military spouses are women.[57] Even with such relatively low rates of marriage, servicewomen routinely identify family issues such as child care among their primary concerns about continued military service.[58]

Women's family responsibilities were of great concern to those who opposed the integration of women into the military infrastructure. But fears about women missing too much time for medical reasons and maternity, including pregnancy-related disabilities, have proven unfounded. Most studies of gender differences in performance point out that men miss more time for disciplinary matters such as drug and alcohol abuse than women miss for medical leave.[59] After all, the demands of family push servicemen as well as women away from the sacrifices that a military career requires.[60]

The Volunteer Force Today

Women's military opportunities have opened up dramatically since the Vietnam War, and women were critical in keeping the volunteer army afloat after the draft ended. But women's appearance in the volunteer military was not enough to meet the armed forces' relentless need for more people, more expertise, and more money. Servicewomen mitigated, but did not end, the constant pressure to recruit. The military's failure to promote gender equity in assignment and promotion policies and its inability to build a culture in which women were valued and respected as much as men have created additional problems for the volunteer force. Though the gender transformation of the volunteer military answered the question of whether women should serve, doubts about the proper extent of that service have persisted in American public discourse.[61] In the post-9/11 military, the debate continues over women's military participation, even in the face of rising demands for military personnel and declining success in recruiting.[62]

Thirty years into the volunteer military, the United States has invested enormous resources in recruiting military personnel. In fiscal year 2003, the Department of Defense spent $455 million on special incentives such as enlistment bonuses, college funds, and loan repayments.[63] In addition to these incentive programs, the United States has repeatedly increased military pay since the Vietnam era, responding to studies that stressed higher pay as a primary means of recruiting high-quality personnel.[64] These financial incentives are necessary because current military personnel policies prohibit so many potential recruits from enlisting. According to the Department of Defense, at least half of U.S. youth between the ages of 16 and 21 are not qualified to enlist, mostly because of "physical and mental deficits" such as asthma, obesity, illegal drug use, or the use of prescription antidepressants.[65] Potential recruits are also disqualified for failure to meet educational, aptitude, or moral character standards (measured by criminal convictions and evidence of "asocial behavior").[66] A recruit can also be disqualified for having too many children; if unmarried, no dependent children are allowed, and if married, a recruit may have no more than two dependent children.[67] Waivers to these requirements are permitted and are more likely during times of greatest need; in 2005, the GAO reported that waivers for physical disabilities appeared to be increasing, while waivers for character failings were declining.[68] The military's policy prohibiting service by men and women who are unable—or refuse—to hide their gay or lesbian sexual orientation also limits the pool of available military recruits. The constant need for more personnel both taxes resources and undermines morale.

The twenty-first-century U.S. military also faces an uphill battle in retaining high-quality personnel because of the conditions under which many servicemembers work and live. One recent study described the strain that the post-9/11 military actions have placed on the volunteer military as "unprecedented" because of lengthy, frequent deployments and "exposure to nontraditional, hostile combat conditions."[69] These conditions have contributed to declining interest among male high school students in military service, a shift that is especially evident among African American young men since fiscal year 2002.[70] As a result of these trends, the military has little choice but to recruit women to help to fill its ranks.

The women who heed the call to join, as well as the civilian women who live or work with servicemembers, must reckon with not only limits on advancement but also a climate of sexual harassment, assault, and violence. Some of the abuse endured by military and civilian women at the hands of servicemen takes place at home, where the stresses of military life can explode into family violence.[71] The pressures of military service are often worst at the bottom of the military hierarchy, where financial pressures are greatest and where the wives of young enlistees often find their career opportunities limited by their husbands' service.[72] Military families often face "separations, serious financial pressures, isolation from family and peer support systems, and frequent moves," all of which increase the risk of family violence.[73] Military training and combat experience may also increase the risk of domestic violence.[74] The Department of Defense has responded to public outcry and congressional mandates by establishing programs to discourage and track spousal and child abuse in military families, but the problem is far from resolved.[75]

Abuse of women also takes place in military workplaces, partly because of continued resistance to the integration of the volunteer force. Women and racial minorities struggle with being excluded, tested, and harassed more often than white men, who still dominate the ranks, constituting 58 percent of the 2005 military.[76] Servicewomen routinely hear denigrating comments about female capabilities, rebuff unwanted sexual advances, are physically harassed, and must face down assumptions that they are promoted because of, not in spite of, their gender and/or race.[77] The parade of military sexual harassment and assault scandals in the 1990s and first few years of the 2000s demonstrated that sexualized abuse had become a part of military service.[78] Servicewomen are also disproportionately censured under the "don't ask/don't tell" policy, and fear of being called a lesbian deters women from reporting unwanted sexual advances and assaults.[79] The military's zero-tolerance response to this epidemic of abuse has led some servicemen to avoid allegations of sexual harassment by avoiding women entirely, a reaction that further isolates servicewomen and limits their advancement.[80] As a 2005 task force on sexual harassment and assault at the U.S. service academies described the situation: "Although progress has been made, hostile attitudes and inappropriate actions toward women, and the toleration of these by some . . . continue to hinder the establishment of a safe and professional environment."[81]

*   *   *

In 2006, even with the help of women enlistees, the volunteer force faces constant challenges to meet its personnel needs. Despite their willingness to serve, women have not been able to rescue the U.S. military from the threat posed by the end of conscription, nor have they changed its fundamental nature. Their service has not ended the insular nature of military service, lessened the rigidity of military culture, or restored the luster of military service to attract and keep the best and brightest. They have not transformed the military's social and political order into the entrepreneurial, risk-taking environment that Secretary of Defense Donald Rumsfeld wants.[82] And neither has their presence forestalled the sexual violence so often committed by U.S. servicemembers.

Perhaps the most telling example of the success and limits of the gender integration of the volunteer force is the appearance of women at the center of the first major military scandal of the twenty-first century. Although the sexual harassment and torture of detainees in the post-9/11 wars was perpetrated by both women and men, the public faces of the American torturers indisputably belonged to two Army women, a private and a general: the derisive smile and dangling cigarette of Specialist Lynndie R. England, a young female enlistee photographed while pointing at naked detainees, and the stern visage of Brigadier General Janis Karpinski, the Army Reserve officer in charge of the prison at Abu Ghraib during the most publicized incidents of prisoner abuse.[83] Other women were also key figures in the debacle, including dozens of enlisted military police and nonmilitary interrogators. Lieutenant Colonel Diane E. Beaver, the staff judge advocate for a joint task force at Guantánamo Bay, wrote a key legal brief recommending the use of more aggressive interrogation techniques in 2002. Major General Barbara Fast, the highest-ranking woman to serve in Iraq, was the intelligence chief for the U.S. military ground commander and oversaw the interrogation centers at Abu Ghraib during 2003 and 2004. Not all of these women were punished for their roles in the scandal, but several were, most notably Karpinski, who was reprimanded and demoted, and England, who was sentenced to three years' confinement and dishonorably discharged. Servicewomen's successful integration into the intelligence, military police, and legal career fields put them at the center of detainee operations in Iraq and made them relatively easy to blame for the military's maltreatment of detainees and mismanagement of detention facilities.[84]

Whoever bears ultimate responsibility for the crimes that took place in American detention facilities in the post-9/11 wars, Lynndie England has joined the rogues' gallery of U.S. servicemembers punished for their failures in wartime. That gallery used to be exclusively male, featuring the troubled Eddie Slovik, executed during World War II for desertion; the unfortunate Claude Batchelor, a trumpet player turned infantryman who was court-martialed after the Korean War for collaborating with Communists while imprisoned in North Korea; and the notorious William Calley, convicted but barely punished for leading the horrifying massacre at My Lai. The addition of women to such a dubious military legacy suggests that women bear the impossible burdens of wartime service no more nobly or easily than men.

9

Familiar Foreign Policy and Familiar Wars: Vietnam, Iraq . . . Before and After

GABRIEL KOLKO

Crises, imminent dangers, and threats to the nation's security and vital interests have been intrinsic to American foreign policy since at least 1947. They have mobilized a reticent public and, even more important, a Congress that must perpetually approve huge sums to implement its military dimensions. In this context, reality has scant place and the images of perils are of the essence. Political leaders, indeed, themselves often come to believe illusions as facts fall to the wayside. Deliberate exaggerations, if not outright falsehoods, have been routine since President Harry S. Truman in March 1947 enunciated his classic Truman Doctrine. The only way he could convince a budget-minded Congress and indifferent public to accept his quite limited but costly program was to paint the crisis in Greece and Turkey in the most foreboding global terms. Congress and the American public are "not sufficiently aware," as Undersecretary of State Dean Acheson put it, of the need to spend the money essential for what was seen as a protracted crisis encompassing all Europe and even much of the world. George Kennan, the key theoretician of containing Soviet power and whose doctrine had immense influence, objected to the Truman Doctrine's strident tone, and even Secretary of State George C. Marshall thought the president was overstating the case. Exaggeration and the threat of nefarious dangers became intrinsic to how Washington portrayed the world after 1947, and they continue until this day despite the disappearance of the Soviet bloc.[1] They make Congress produce funds that might otherwise not be available.

From 1947 onward, in the words of Willard C. Matthias, who was for many years in charge of the Central Intelligence Agency's Soviet estimates and retired in 1973 as a senior official, "there developed a four-decade-long debate between the civilian and military intelligence agencies over Soviet intentions."[2] Massive arms spending was dependent on portraying the USSR's goals in the most ominous ways possible, which meant emphasizing

Soviet capabilities rather than intentions, and ignoring their inherently cautious, fatalist, but passive Marxist view of change and the historical process. Liberalizing tendencies in the USSR were dismissed, the gravity of the Soviet-Chinese schism was grossly underestimated, and as Matthias states it, "after 1968, our rational and balanced approach to making judgments about the Soviets came under increasing attack."[3] Needless to say, diplomatic exchanges with the Russians were frowned upon even at crucial moments of the Korean War, and negotiations were considered a last resort only.

The war in Vietnam, but also most other aspects of American foreign and military policy since 1946, must be assessed in this context. President Richard Nixon had a deep antipathy to the CIA, one that Henry Kissinger and Secretary of Defense Melvin Laird shared, and he fired Richard Helms in 1973 as director of the CIA because Helms refused to allow the Agency to serve as a cover for the Watergate break-in. President Jimmy Carter's chief aides regarded the Agency's estimates as a "nuisance," not so much inaccurate as "irrelevant."[4] Ronald Reagan appointed William Casey head of the CIA in 1981, and Casey—as one of his successors reports it—"argued, he fought, he yelled, he grumped" with his analysts and only more roughly continued what was in fact a decades-old policy.[5] He pursued his own foreign policy agenda aggressively and maintained that "our estimating program has become a powerful instrument in forcing the pace in the policy area."[6] No one, the CIA included, in 1989 had any foreboding whatsoever of the total collapse in the Soviet bloc, with its immense consequences.

Such a critical assessment of the role that objective intelligence played in the decision-making process is no longer the opinion of dissident historians but virtually the consensus of the memoirs that former intelligence officials have written. Notwithstanding many very able people in the CIA and their access to a tremendous amount of information, since 1946 there has never been an objective, disinterested intelligence system that shaped policy. Preconceived ideas or interests determined how the world was portrayed, and the outcome was disastrous, if only because action frequently bore scant relation to reality. Even more unforgivable from the government's perspective, these illusions and misconceptions often produced grave failures.

The distortion of information for political objectives became worse with time, but it preceded the Vietnam War by well over a decade and simply continues in our own day. The CIA, which often produced excellent analytic assessments, was taken seriously only insofar as its burgeoning action wing could implement foreign policies covertly. The Vietnam War evolved in this context, and erroneous and often duplicitous estimates provided the setting of every crisis since then—Iraq included. It is crucial that we regard the intelligence and information process as inherently polluted, subject to political whims. The problem has never been knowledge but policy.

The American government had capable people working on Vietnam, and they knew a great deal about that nation. George W. Allen joined the

Pentagon's intelligence service in 1949 and immediately became involved with the French effort to retain their Indochina colonies; his memoir is required reading on the entire Vietnam experience. In 1963, scandalized by the American military's myopia and mores, he moved to the CIA and soon became its leading Vietnam analyst. He met innumerable decision-makers in this capacity. When he retired from the CIA in 1979 he worked for them on contract for the next fifteen years, and the Agency cleared his book. In it he confirms how frequently crucial decisions were based on illusions and falsehoods.

Allen recounts how Eisenhower and Dulles strongly opposed France following what the Americans were then doing in Korea—signing a cease-fire agreement and making a settlement with their enemies after being stalemated on the field in battle. They wanted the French to fight harder and longer, which France refused to do. The United States opposed the Geneva accords and, "basing their views on a set of assumptions that we believed were entirely unrealistic," assumed the French mission in Indochina was foredoomed.[7] The Eisenhower administration prevented the Geneva accords' conditions on reunification elections from being implemented, and violated its military provisions. The history of the rest of the decade is well known, but every step of the way CIA analysts accurately predicted what would go wrong.

The so-called Tonkin Gulf crisis of August 1964 "astonished" Allen because he was aware that covert Saigon and American missions were taking place in the gulf and that the North Vietnamese would investigate them. At first he thought that a branch of the American military did not know what another section was up to, "but I did not realize how eagerly the administration was seeking a pretext for a major escalation" in the hope of shoring up the Saigon regime. The same was true of the Pleiku incidents of early 1965, which became an excuse for "a retaliation waiting for something to happen; the Pleiku attacks were a convenient trigger for intended escalation." It was a justification for permanently bombing North Vietnam.[8]

Robert L. Sansom and Jeffrey Race both studied the land and peasant question in Vietnam for the American government and published insightful books well before the war ended. Both asserted that land reform was a key precondition of a successful anticommunist political mobilization in the South, and both were ignored. Race describes how Washington's "policy was founded on and protected by deception and outrageous lies," and how a general told him that identifying America's errors in Vietnam was off-limits, as the Pentagon "cannot permit such subjects to be discussed." That there were structural reasons for peasant support of the Communists "simply couldn't get through" to the men at the top.[9] There were also articulate skeptics within the Pentagon who thought the war was futile, and its Systems Analysis Office published a very informative report every six weeks or so; the Joint Chiefs of Staff several times sought to close down or restrict it.

Many critics of the war worked at the Rand Corporation, and Rand employees leaked the Pentagon Papers. There was, in short, plenty of accurate information available—for those who wanted to read and use it. It simply made no difference because the vast gap between reality and policy was irreconcilable.

In 1998 the CIA released Harold P. Ford's account of 1962–68, which complements and corroborates Allen's memoir.[10] Ford makes it perfectly clear that Secretary of Defense Robert McNamara's later complaint that there were no "Vietnam experts" to whom he could turn is simply false. He refused to heed their advice whenever they warned against the series of disasters Allen and others describe. Among the many failures were the American inability to understand the Communists' military doctrine or estimate their numbers accurately—the "order of battle," which became a contention between the CIA and Pentagon. In addition, the Johnson administration unconditionally supported the venal and corrupt Nguyen Van Thieu becoming a virtual dictator and ending the chronic political instability that followed the American-endorsed assassination of Ngo Dinh Diem. The level of corruption that permeated Thieu's entire system, from the state to the army, was well known and tolerated in Washington; Allen provides additional details. And all Washington administrations trained and equipped Saigon's army to fight a conventional war according to official American doctrine. It was, of course, mainly a guerrilla war.

The myths of progress in the war were conscious falsehoods intended to manipulate public opinion and justify the futile endeavor. When Allen and other CIA analysts objected, they were told to conform. In numerous instances American officials consciously issued erroneous data, such as the hamlet evaluation statistics. At no time was truth given a higher priority than political convenience or the lies both the politicians and generals propounded. The military intelligence and CIA were constantly struggling with each other for analytic domination, and the CIA lost most of these bureaucratic turf wars. And while some politicians, military, and CIA action people—those whose hawkish policies were already predetermined—undoubtedly really believed these fairy tales, most knew that their careers depended on being optimists.

The most serious consequence of these deceptions was the so-called order-of-battle controversy before the Tet offensive began in January 1968. The lower the numbers the more progress the American military could claim, and so they refused to count the various local forces—roughly 300,000 men disappeared because admitting their existence, General Creighton Abrams argued in August 1967, would produce a "gloomy" conclusion.[11]

The CIA objected to a point but eventually had to accept the distortions; both Allen and Ford are very detailed on this particular controversy. Ultimately, General William Westmoreland unsuccessfully sued CBS for allowing a leading CIA specialist on the order of battle to expound his views. But the Communists during the Tet offensive had far larger military forces than most American officials believed they did, and their stunning attacks changed American politicians' and, even more ominous, public perceptions of reality. The Tet defeat, Allen insists, was much greater because of the "overblown psychological campaign in the fall of 1967," which was also essential for Lyndon Johnson's reelection ambitions.[12] The falsified data, in the end, were believed by those seeking initially to manipulate public opinion, and the Tet defeat was the beginning of the end for the protracted American effort to win the Vietnam War.

Lies became the rule. The public had to be led along and, as Allen recounts, "on many occasions the truth was grotesquely and deliberately distorted in order to make a point."[13] But Vietnam was only one of many examples of how foreign policies were formulated: "our policies tend to be excessively dominated by aggressive individuals or organizations, or by the interplay of bureaucratic politics, rather than by rational deliberation of national interests."[14] After thirty-odd years in this role, Allen became disillusioned.

Both Ford and Allen come to the same conclusion, to cite Allen, "that our leaders tended toward self-delusion."[15] What is most significant in both of the Allen and Ford accounts is that they were written by men with firsthand knowledge; McGeorge Bundy emerges as a villain and cynical manipulator and Robert McNamara as confused but committed to the war, a pathetic character. Critical historians had concluded this long before. But what is unique is Allen's intimate account of meetings and confrontations, revealing the mind-set of men hell-bent on the path of destruction and defeat.

The CIA has produced many unhappy people who had access to much more information than policy critics and who came to identical conclusions. Technology over the past fifteen years has vastly increased the volume of information available to the intelligence community, making research and analysis more rather than less difficult—and more liable to be irrelevant or wrong. Anyone who reads the CIA's unclassified version of *Studies in Intelligence* knows that there are a significant number of analysts who are quite candid, saying that "much of the information" the CIA gets, "to be blunt, is garbage."[16] Other memoirs, dealing with the CIA's action section or the Pentagon's special operations forces, describe endless ineptitude and confusion. Screwing up covert efforts is so common that it is practically the rule rather than the exception. But it was not only covert operations that failed. Confusion was inherent in the competing services' refusal since 1947 to subordinate their rival fiefdoms by standardizing technical communication systems and sharing basic intelligence, a deficiency that increased with time and today plagues the American military more than ever.[17]

Publicly, the CIA defended its reputation for gathering intelligence ex-

pertly and impersonally until the mid-1970s House and Senate investigations. Before then, its critics confirmed its failures mainly by deduction, but
the congressional investigations portrayed an organization that was not
merely malevolent but also simply incompetent on many critical matters. It
did not anticipate the Korean War, the Czech crisis of 1968, the October
1973 Mideast War, the 1974 Portuguese upheaval, India's explosion of a
nuclear device in 1972, the fall of the shah in 1979, and much else that subsequently took the United States by surprise. That policy predilection determines what its analysts report, or that the CIA's directors have been
ambitious careerists who often tailor their reporting, has been conventional
wisdom for decades, and what has occurred in the case of Iraq was only the
rule. Biases and political interests and ambitions, especially the pressure
to be reelected, have made policy makers reluctant to accept intelligence
they do not wish to hear—and most senior intelligence officials acknowledge these constraints. Those who make decisions want intelligence to support their goals, and if does not, then they use it selectively or ignore it
entirely because they not only have confidence in their own judgments but
have their own agendas. Very few senior intelligence officials believe that
their objectivity will prevent bad or dangerous policies from being pursued.
As one of them phrased it, "But the idea that intelligence can ignore the
political atmosphere in which it is being delivered is, again, a Panglossian
affliction."[18]

The Case of Iraq

There are great cultural, political, and physical differences between Vietnam
and Iraq that cannot be minimized, and the geopolitical situation is entirely
different. After all, the United States encouraged and materially supported
Saddam Hussein in his war with Iran throughout the 1980s because it feared
a militantly Shiite Iran would dominate the Persian Gulf region. It still does,
and if the Shia majority takes over the Iraqi government or if the federalism
written into the new Iraqi constitution leads to a real or de facto partition of
the country, one or the other of which is very probable, Iran is more likely
than ever to attain its regional geopolitical ambitions. But putting this fundamental paradox in the American position aside, which makes the transfer
of power to the Iraqi Shias and real democracy highly unlikely, the United
States has ignored the lessons of the traumatic Vietnam experience and is
today repeating many of the errors that produced defeat there.

The intelligence process worked badly in both Vietnam and Iraq. Policy
always precedes this process and definitively shapes the outcome, but precisely because both wars ended in failures we know much more about what
intelligence said—in part because whistle-blowers have much more incentive to reveal the truth. Scott Ritter, who had previously been an officer in
U.S. Marine intelligence, in September 1991 went to work for the United

Nations' weapons inspection team charged with the task of confirming whether Iraq retained weapons of mass destruction (WMDs) or means of delivering them, and American, British, and Israeli intelligence fed him their best information. Early in his mission, which involved frequent inspections of sites the UN chose, he concluded that Iraq had complied with UN disarmament criteria, which the defection of Hussein Kamal, Saddam Hussein's son-in-law, in August 1995 only confirmed. Still, every American administration from 1991 onward maintained the myth of Iraqi possession of WMDs because their real goal, Ritter concluded, was regime change.[19] As for ties between al-Qaeda and Saddam's regime and teaching the former how to use WMDs, which Bush gave as a reason for the war, from the end of September 2001 onward the president knew that the secular Iraq regime was hostile to Osama bin Laden's Islamic fanaticism. Well before the war began, the U.S. Defense Intelligence Agency identified the source of this allegation as a fabricator. The CIA, much to the irritation of the Bush administration, especially Vice President Richard Cheney and Defense Secretary Donald Rumsfeld, provided a great deal of evidence to prove that war was avoidable.[20] The real reasons for the United States embarking on war in Iraq lie elsewhere, and assigning a precise weight to them is a dubious task. Crucial, however, was a mentality, which Rumsfeld expressed to the president-elect, that the new administration should be "forward-leaning" in its foreign policy and end the Clinton administration's purported defensiveness.[21] Bush, of course, was of the same mind. Intelligence was never important in defining action, and the Bush administration not only ignored it but—as the Valerie Plame case revealed—often consciously distorted what the intelligence community was reporting.

The resemblance to Vietnam is clear, but only because all important American foreign policies have been treated in a similar manner. What was crucial was that this administration resolved before it took office to be aggressive, although it was unclear in what region of the world it would most operate, just as John F. Kennedy and Lyndon Johnson had done in the 1960s. In both Vietnam and Iraq, unexpected defeats and surprises awaited the United States, just as they awaited every nation that embarked on wars over the past two centuries.

What followed thereafter was perfectly predictable: detailed reports from many people such as Ritter or from the CIA itself, experts on Iraqi arms and politics, were essentially discarded on behalf of exceedingly dubious but convenient information, the most bizarre and unreliable of which came from "Curveball," an Iraqi whom German intelligence considered wholly untrustworthy and whose veracity only Ahmad Chalabi's network had vouched for. The CIA issued fabricator warnings on some of these people and never believed them. A year before the invasion, most of the intelligence community agreed that reports that Hussein was attempting to import uranium were false, but Bush ignored them and often cited such fictions to justify invading Iraq. The CIA's director, George Tenet, for purely career reasons told the president that the fables he wanted to believe were true, but the large majority of people at the CIA knew that Iraq had long ceased trying to develop nuclear weapons, and most opposed embarking on war there.[22] Other official experts emphatically cautioned decision makers about the chaotic future of a post-Saddam Iraq and the threat of civil war and were similarly ignored. For public purposes the CIA was purportedly the main source of the utter falsehoods the Bush administration used to justify going to war in Iraq, but in fact the Agency warned it had strong doubts about them.[23] The administration had no scruples whatsoever in doing so, but it was only following many deep-rooted precedents: Congress and the public are told whatever will win their acquiescence, but such efforts work for a time only.

In both places successive American administrations slighted the advice of their most knowledgeable intelligence experts. But America's leaders have repeatedly believed what they wanted, not what their intelligence told them. Cynicism and a contempt for the public always exist among those who covet and gain power. The extent to which self-delusion and political convenience become intertwined can be endlessly debated, and elements of both can be found in countless cases. While it is an issue that cannot be resolved definitively, and every case and individual is different, such devious procedures greatly subverted the rationality—and prudence—that intelligence is supposed to provide.

But there can be no doubt that the Pentagon in the 1960s had an uncritical faith in its overwhelming firepower, high technology, mobility, and mastery of the skies. This was a natural and timeless trait inherent in American mores, one that weapons producers have always reinforced. Social and political challenges, Washington believed, would fall by the wayside once the enemy was easily destroyed. It still has faith in weapons, and Defense Secretary Donald Rumsfeld believes the military has the technology to "shock and awe" all adversaries. But as in Vietnam, technology was exceedingly fallible in Iraq, and logistics also became even more of a nightmare because no close ports exist in Iraq. Indeed, precisely because it had become infinitely more complicated, technology in Iraq failed even more quickly, while crucial and obvious things, such as the immense water deficit, proved surprisingly time-consuming and very expensive.[24]

Both the Vietnam and Iraq wars were exceedingly costly, in part because of the reliance on the latest technology and massive firepower as well as incompetent and corrupt proxies. The Vietnam War was far more expensive than anticipated; it lasted much longer than predicted, and Johnson had to abandon much of his domestic program to pay for it. It was a major cause of the weakening of the dollar and the United States ultimately going off the gold standard.[25] The Iraq War has been very similar, also coming at the conjunction of massive budget deficits and a weakening dollar, greatly aggravating an unfavorable contextual economic position. The war in Iraq had cost at least $439 billion by mid-2006, in three and a half years exceeding well over half of what the Vietnam war cost over nine years, and estimates of its eventual long-term cost are $1 trillion or even more, making it the most expensive war in American history.

Wars in both Vietnam and Iraq were highly decentralized, and the number of troops required only increased despite the fact that firepower was also greater. When the number of American troops in Vietnam reached a half million, the public turned against President Johnson and defeated his party. In the case of Iraq the public has become hostile to the adventure, if not antiwar, much more quickly; in late 2005 nearly two-thirds of the public disapproved of the president's handling of the situation in Iraq and 58 percent believed he had not given good reasons for keeping troops there. Fifty-seven percent believed he deliberately misled the people in order to make a case for war in Iraq. By February 2006, 63 percent of the American public thought the Iraq War was not worth the loss of American lives or the cost, and 48 percent favored immediate withdrawal. Bush's job-approval rating kept on falling, hitting a low of 33 percent by the end of April 2006.[26]

What happens in a nation's political, social, and economic spheres is far more decisive than military equations. That was true in China in the late 1940s and in Vietnam in 1975, and it is also the case in Iraq today. Wars are ultimately won politically or not at all. This is true in every place and at all times. Leaders in Washington thought this interpretation of events in Vietnam was bizarre, and they paid no attention when their experts reminded them of the limits of military power. The importance of Vietnamese politics was slighted, escalations followed, and the credibility of American military power—the willingness to use it and win no matter how long it took or how much it cost—became their primary concern.

In both Vietnam and Iraq the public was mobilized on the basis of cynical falsehoods that ultimately backfired, causing a credibility gap. People eventually ceased to believe anything Washington told them. Countless lies were told during the Vietnam War, but eventually many of the men who counted most were themselves unable to separate truth from fiction. Most American leaders really believed that if the Communists won in Vietnam the dominoes would fall and the Chinese would dominate all Southeast Asia. The Iraq War was initially justified because Hussein was purported to have weapons of mass destruction and ties to al-Qaeda; no evidence whatsoever for either allegation existed beforehand or has been found.

There are about 160,000 American and foreign troops in Iraq (over 260,000 if support troops in the region are included) at the time of this writing—far more than Bush predicted would remain by this time—but, as in Vietnam, their morale is already low and sinking. Bush's ratings in the polls have fallen dramatically, especially as he has run up huge budget deficits and ignored domestic issues, such as health insurance, that greatly determine how people vote. He needs many more soldiers in Iraq desperately. Depending on the resistance or geopolitical context in the region, substantial number of American forces may remain in Iraq for many years. In Vietnam, President Nixon tried to "Vietnamize" the land war and transfer the burdens of soldiering to Nguyen Van Thieu's huge army. But Thieu's army was organized entirely to maintain him in power rather than win the victory that American forces could not attain.

The idea that the war can be "Iraqized" and the army will be loyal to America's nominal goals or be militarily effective is quixotic. As in Vietnam, where the Buddhists opposed the Catholic minority who provided the leaders America endorsed, Iraq is a divided nation ethnically and religiously, and Washington has the unenviable choice between the risks of disorder that its own lack of troops make likely and civil war if it arms Iraqis. Elections have only exacerbated these differences, not resolved them. Shiites make up three-fifths of the Iraqi population, their leaders have their own political agendas, and their taking over the army or politics will also strengthen Iran's influence and power in the region. Despite plenty of expert opinion to warn it, the Bush administration has scant perception of the complexity of the political problems it confronts in Iraq. All major Iraqi religious and ethnic groups have armed militias, but American officials increasingly regard the Shiites as the greatest single threat to their authority. Afghanistan looms as a reminder of how military success depends ultimately on politics, and how things go wrong.

"Iraqization" of the military conflict will not accomplish what has eluded the Americans, and in both Vietnam and Iraq the United States underestimated the length of time it would have to remain and cultivated fatal illusions about the strength of its friends. While appraisals of the effectiveness or size of the Iraqi army vary, the United States must prevent the Shiite majority who fill its ranks, many of whom are pro-Iranian, from becoming even more powerful. Therefore it is now incorporating Sunni officers who worked for Hussein before the war, a total reversal of its policy when it began the conflict. The Bush administration's reliance on local troops to fulfill American goals is an act of desperation, no more likely to be successful in Iraq than it was in Vietnam. Vietnam was a religiously divided nation, but Iraq is even more disunited internally, and the possibility of civil war is greater. In Vietnam the Communists rode nationalism to power because of the French and Americans, but in Iraq there is likely to be chaos. In both places, the United States will lose the war because all wars are decided by a larger social, political, and economic context, which American military power has never been able to control.

Rumsfeld's admission in his confidential memo in October 2003 that "we lack the metrics to know if we are winning or losing the global war on terror" was an indication that key members of the Bush administration are far less confident of what they are doing than they were when they embarked on war.[27] But as in Vietnam, when Defense Secretary Robert McNamara ceased to believe that victory was inevitable, it is too late to change course, and now the credibility of America's military power is at stake.

Eventually, domestic politics takes precedence over everything else. It did during the Vietnam War, and it is very likely it will also be the case with the war in Iraq. By 1968 the polls were turning against the Democrats, and the Tet offensive in late January caught President Lyndon Johnson by surprise because he and his generals refused to believe the CIA's estimates that there were really 600,000 rather than 300,000 people in the Communist forces. Nixon won because he promised a war-weary public he would bring peace with honor. Bush declared in October 2003 that "we're not leaving" Iraq soon, but his party and political advisers will probably have the last word as American casualties mount and Bush's poll ratings continue to decline. Vietnam proved that the American public has limited patience. That is more the case than ever.

There is no evidence, either from the many firsthand memoirs or the practice and conduct of post-1945 American foreign policy, that grand policy options or goals were ever influenced or defined by information—nominally, analytic intelligence—that as truthfully as possible approximated reality in all its dimensions. Were this the case, there would be far fewer defeats and failures for Washington to confront, and it would be a great deal more modest regarding its global interventions and ambitions. Respect for the parameters of reality involves decisive constraints, and the United States simply does not choose its foreign policies this way. So what is the use and function of what is termed "intelligence" in the analytic meaning of that word?

The large technical and ideological cadres that purvey intelligence, rather than becoming a source of rationality and clarity, deluge the already insupportable complexity of foreign policy formulation with data, and accurate information becomes worthless as soon as it fails to reinforce what America's political and military leaders wish to hear. Intelligence functionaries accept the constraints of the system quite willingly because it pays their salaries. These personnel transform themselves into peddlers of just one more economic activity and never transcend the policy limits that the non-technocratic ruling elites impose. This is just as true in all areas of domestic affairs as in foreign policies.

The state's intelligence mechanisms are constrained by a larger structural and ideological environment and by the inherent irrationality of a foreign policy that foredooms any effort to base action on informed insight. Even when the insight is exact and knowledge is far greater than ignorance, political and social boundaries usually place decisive limits on the application of "rationality" to actions. Political and ideological imperatives and interests define the nature of "relevant" truths. Intelligence's pretension to being objective is a hoax because those parts of it that do not reconfirm the power structure's interests and predetermined policies are ignored and discarded. There are innumerable reasons we must conclude this, not least the growing number of published insider memoirs and even the official American intelligence community's assessments. But more important is the entire experience with Iraq and the United States' failed confrontation with the Islamic world for over half a century. To expect the United States to behave other than as it has is to cultivate serious illusions indeed.

The system, in a word, is irrational. We saw it in Vietnam and we are seeing it today in Iraq.

10

Mr. Rumsfeld's War

LLOYD C. GARDNER

*I didn't come here to sit around and tweak
and calibrate modestly what's going on.*
—Donald Rumsfeld, newspaper interview, December 27, 2001

*Some people call that a quagmire. It was possibly the
fastest march on a capitol in modern military history.*
—Donald Rumsfeld addresses American troops in Baghdad, April 30, 2003

*I think the biggest problem we've got in the country is people
don't study history anymore. People who go to school in high schools and colleges,
they tend to study current events and call it history.*
—Donald Rumsfeld, television interview, March 3, 2006

These enemies are not going to quit.
—Donald Rumsfeld in Iraq, July 11, 2006

Mr. Rumsfeld's war was to be everything Vietnam was not. The quick march to Baghdad, ending with the famous pictures of Saddam Hussein's statue being pulled down by joyous Iraqis, would demonstrate that this time there would be no stalemate on the battlefield or hesitation in finishing what had to be done. Mr. Rumsfeld's war would not be Mr. McNamara's war, but neither would it be like the first Gulf War in 1991, when American troops were ordered to stand down before taking Baghdad. Gulf War I had left a brutal dictator in power, it was asserted, one whose ambitions remained fully intact, and whose willingness to use poison gas against his own people set him apart even in a region of repressive regimes, occupied lands, and suicide bombers. He had defied the United States and gotten away with it.

So while President George H.W. Bush and his top advisers proclaimed they had "kicked the Vietnam syndrome" forty ways to Sunday by expelling Iraqi forces from Kuwait, Gulf War I left others in his administration deeply dissatisfied. In their view, the outcome—after all the tedious diplomacy of building a "grand coalition" and brave talk about a "new world order"—had been to leave things pretty much where they were before the war. Iraq had been driven back temporarily, but Saddam Hussein still ruled in Baghdad, and still threatened to unleash all forms of war on his enemies near and far. Israel had been a target for Scud missiles in the war, and it was only with great difficulty that Washington had persuaded Tel Aviv not to retaliate and thereby set off a general conflagration across the Middle East. As this example demonstrated, keeping Hussein in a box was bound to be expensive (politically as well as economically), no matter what sanctions were imposed on his regime. And in the end they would not be effective. As matters stood, Gulf War I had ended like Korea in 1953—only worse. Policy makers had behaved as if the old containment rules still applied. If this was the new world order on display, there was not much to feel proud about. This harsh verdict summed up the neoconservative verdict on Gulf War I, and more generally on George H.W. Bush's overly cautious leadership. From their point of view, the lessons of Vietnam still had not been properly learned. The Cold War had been won but Vietnam still haunted the nation, inhibiting a true realization of all that had changed and all that was required of the nation's leadership and the American military to meet the new challenge of failed states and terrorism.

A new theoretical document titled "Defense Planning Guidance" had emerged in the aftermath of the Gulf War from the office of Paul Wolfowitz, Undersecretary of Defense for Policy. The principal author was his protégé Zalmay Khalilzad, a naturalized American citizen from Afghanistan. Khalilzad held a Ph.D. from the University of Chicago, where many of the neocons (including Wolfowitz) had studied with philosopher Leo Strauss—a godfather of sorts to the neocon intellectuals. Years later Khalilzad would be appointed America's ambassador/proconsul in Baghdad, where he found himself in a role similar to that played by British officials in another era, managing outlying posts of empire in Middle Eastern capitals. Author James Mann, whose highly praised book *Rise of the Vulcans* traces George W. Bush's "war cabinet," calls the 1992 draft Defense Planning Guidance "one of the most significant foreign policy documents of the past half-century." When it was leaked to the press, however, the White House insisted it be rewritten, lest assertions of America's unique responsibility to maintain world order alarm members of the grand coalition who had rallied to Bush's call, and, not incidentally, paid most of the bill to oust Iraqi forces from Kuwait in Gulf War I. Various members of the allied coalition had, in fact, reimbursed the United States for 88 percent of the total amount of $61 billion, "so the actual cost to the taxpayer was only about $7 billion, roughly the same as for the Spanish-American War, and on a per capita basis only $26.92, arguably the least expensive war in the nation's history."[1]

While such figures suggested real value in the coalition, Khalilzad's draft argued it was not likely to be repeated. Future coalitions were more likely "to be ad hoc assemblies" formed to deal with a particular crisis. They could not be the determining factor. "The United States should be postured to act independently when collective action cannot be orchestrated." Washington could not always be sure it would have partners, or desire them, but must always be sure it had freedom of action. "Our first objective is to prevent the re-emergence of a new rival. This is a dominant consideration underlying the new regional defense strategy and requires that we endeavor to prevent any hostile power from dominating a region whose resources would, under consolidated control, be sufficient to generate global power."

The 1992 draft promised that one lesson from Vietnam not to be re-peated was the bitter experience when America's formal allies in SEATO (Southeast Asia Treaty Organization) had made a dramatic showing of nonsupport, with the bitterest memories being of French president Charles de Gaulle's opposition and the virtual breakdown of the alliance. The SEATO experience was recalled, obviously, when the United States fash-ioned the "coalition of the willing," again over Paris's objection, to wage war in Iraq.

The list of tasks for the Defense Department outlined in the draft was almost endless, and even included preventing "threats to U.S. society from narcotics trafficking." The rapid growth of Pentagon assignments continued throughout the decade—largely at the expense of the State Department. Dana Priest, a first-rate reporter for the *Washington Post,* followed this story closely. In *The Mission,* she writes about the commanders in chief (CinCs) of the five regional commands the Pentagon designated to cover the world, "Proconsuls to the Empire." The boundaries of these commands are recon-sidered every two years and perhaps redrawn—another reason why ad hoc coalitions are more suitable to the overall mission of the American military. And when you downgrade formal treaties (State Department business), in favor of status-of-forces agreements (Pentagon business), you have taken a long step toward reducing the area of diplomatic decision and action. But more than that, the CinCs became the main users of training programs in host countries by the U.S. Special Operations Command, which enables each command to forge ties with counterparts in countries around the world. With a budget of nearly half a billion dollars a year, CinC headquar-ters grew to twice their Cold War size and were "lavish compared to the civilian agencies that by law and tradition were supposed to manage U.S. foreign relations." Each CinC had at his disposal a long-distance aircraft and a fleet of helicopters. Some travel with entourages of up to thirty-five staff-ers. By contrast, only the secretary of state commands a personal airplane, while all other diplomats hitch rides or travel by commercial aircraft. When a CinC arrives in a country for a conference, he is the center of attention, travels in the lead car in a motorcade, and throws lavish parties while am-bassadors stand around on the edge of the crowd. One of the most thought-ful of the CinCs, General Anthony Zinni, had a good sense of the historical precedents for his role in CentCom. "Zinni chuckled that he had become a modern-day proconsul, descendant of the warrior-statesmen who ruled the Roman Empire's outlying territory, bringing order and ideals from a legalistic Rome. Julius Caesar, Caesar Augustus—they would have understood."[2]

When Don Rumsfeld became secretary of defense in 2001, he took a very dim view of using the military to halt the production and distribution of drugs, a problem he felt had to be handled at home—primarily within the family. He also eliminated the acronym *CinC*—because there could be only one commander in chief, the president—but otherwise the burgeoning power of the Pentagon over the State Department, and eventually over all intelligence agencies, well suited his plans for consolidating power in the military headquarters of this new empire. "Ad hoc assemblies" ultimately became the "coalition of the willing," a phrase invented, appropriately enough, by Rumsfeld during the Afghan intervention against the Taliban and then adopted by President George W. Bush to describe the nations willing to follow him into Iraq in March 2003 without a second United Nations resolution.[3]

When Bush appointed him defense secretary at the age of sixty-eight, Rumsfeld was the oldest person to be selected to hold that job. He had also been the youngest when Gerald Ford picked him in 1975. In that first Pentagon go-round Rumsfeld established himself as an opponent of Henry Kissinger—and thereby won notice and praise from anti-détente conservatives for his opposition to SALT II. Even so, when he returned to the Pentagon, it was widely expected that Secretary of State Colin Powell would be the dominant figure in the administration. Bob Woodward, chief chronicler of the Bush administration, labeled Rumsfeld a "wild card," a man whose early presidential ambitions as a bright young Republican prospect never fully flowered in part, ironically, because of the rise of the Bush dynasty. Three days before 9/11 the *New York Times* all but predicted he would be soon gone. "Mr. Rumsfeld has done a lousy job of selling his military reforms to the generals and admirals, not to mention to Congress."[4]

Rumsfeld's "reforms" originated in a Hobbesian view of the world, similar if not identical to that of the authors of the Project for the New American Century (PNAC)—who had criticized George H.W. Bush for not pressing regime change in the first Gulf War. He was a signer of their open letters to President Bill Clinton in 1998 demanding that regime change be the policy of the United States government, and he served as chair of a nominally bipartisan commission appointed by House Speaker Newt Gingrich to study the need for an anti-ballistic-missile system. As could be expected, Rumsfeld's report sounded a bugle call for immediate action, while it also anticipated later events by casting a jaundiced eye on the Central Intelligence Agency. Conservative columnist William Safire championed the report as authored by nine men "with command experience [who] had the advantage denied to compartmented C.I.A. analysts." There was no time to lose, it alleged, in building a "rudimentary shield" to protect the nation against Iran,

North Korea, or Libya—one of which might build a weapon or even buy one "that will enable it to get the drop on us."[5]

Hence long before 9/11, Donald Rumsfeld's worldview encompassed a central belief in the irrationality of foreign leaders who would commit nuclear suicide by launching a missile against the United States, along with the untrustworthiness of allies or "coalitions," and the doubtful accuracy of the liberal-infested Central Intelligence Agency. To those who would call this worldview the very essence of imperial unilateralism, Rumsfeld had a ready answer—constructing a missile shield was the only way to reassure America's allies we would be there and always willing to perform our special role as guarantor of world order because we could not be held in check by a rogue state or group brandishing a nuke. The world had been enjoying great prosperity since the Cold War, he told Congress on June 21, 2001, as the free market system spread into all corners of the world. To hesitate now in building an anti-missile system was to choose "intentional vulnerability," risking everything gained thus far and putting future expansion in jeopardy.

> At present we are enjoying the benefits of the unprecedented global economic expansion—an expansion driven by information technology, innovative entrepreneurs, the spread of democracy, free economic systems, and the growth of societies that respect individual liberty and reward individual initiative. . . .
>
> In the event of a hostile threat by one of these [rogue] states, we would have three unpleasant choices: acquiesce and allow it to invade its neighbors (as Iraq invaded Kuwait); oppose the threat and put Western population centers at risk; or be forced to take pre-emptive action.
>
> Intentional vulnerability could make building coalitions against aggression next to impossible. At worst, it could lead to a rise in isolationism—something that would surely damage economic progress in our still dangerous world.[6]

Rumsfeld had a hard sell that day, but several noteworthy things stood out in this presentation. First, there was his phrasemaking, a great asset later in the run-up to the Iraq War and the giddy months of "mission accomplished." "Intentional vulnerability" was a gem, immediately putting opponents on the defensive. Overall, however, the statement connected the dots—as Rumsfeld was fond of saying after 9/11—between military policy and the continued expansion of the world economy in an orderly world. Without a missile defense system, he argued, the United States could be held hostage by a rogue state, something that would create a series of crises. Building a missile shield would be a form of preemptive war against terrorism. He jumped the gun on the "axis of evil" speech here, identifying North Korea, Iraq, and Iran as the most likely to attempt such a ploy. Unlike Soviet leaders in the Cold War, he said, who had to answer to the Politburo at least, Saddam Hussein and Kim Jong Il had unbridled power to do as they pleased. "These are very different regimes," and they were coming together:

"Just as we see growing interdependence within the free world, there is also a growing interdependence among the world's rogue states. Those states are sharing information, technology, weapons material and know-how at a rapid pace."

While he thus identified a lineup of states to put in opposition to American-led "coalitions of the willing," also known at times as the "free world," whose membership would shift from time to time as America's needs for allies waxed and waned, Rumsfeld had yet not succeeded in his missions of promoting the missile shield or shaking up the Pentagon right up to the moment the terrorists struck. Indeed, on the day before 9/11 he told a Pentagon "town meeting" the nation faced an adversary that operated across all time zones. "You may think I'm describing one of the last decrepit dictators of the world. But their day, too, is almost past, and they cannot match the strength and size of this adversary. The adversary's closer to home. It's the Pentagon bureaucracy."[7]

When the third hijacked plane smashed into the Pentagon on the morning of 9/11, it ended one phase of Mr. Rumsfeld's war and began another. In his recent presentation to Congress on a missile shield, he had used the Cold War expression "free world," which, as then, demanded an equivalent enemy, such as the "evil empire." Now he had proof it was a real force—Islamic extremists directed by "rogue states" were responsible. It was impossible to believe otherwise. In his very first meetings with Pentagon aides on the day of the attacks Rumsfeld had made up his mind about the proper response. The third plane had hit the Pentagon at just after 9:30 in the morning. At 2:40 in the afternoon, the defense secretary called for a quick review of all the intelligence data: "Judge whether good enough hit S.H. at the same time," an aide wrote in his notes. "Not only UBL [Osama bin Laden]." It apparently mattered little whether Hussein was involved in the actual attacks or not. "Go massive. Sweep it all up. Things related and not."[8]

The next day, meeting with the National Security Council in the conference room of a Cold War–era bunker known as the Presidential Emergency Operations Center, Bush announced, "We have made the decision to punish whoever harbors terrorists, not just the perpetrators." That afternoon over a secure phone from Air Force One, the president told Rumsfeld he would be responsible for organizing the war. "We'll clean up the mess," he told the defense secretary, "and then the ball will be in your court."[9]

Bush was with Rumsfeld all the way on the fundamental question of whom to blame most. Like the defense secretary, he demanded intelligence to expose Saddam Hussein as the man behind the attack and related events from years past. "I want you, as soon as you can," the president ordered the head of counterterrorism, Richard A. Clarke, "to go back over everything, everything. See if Saddam did this. See if he's linked in any way." Clarke was stunned. "But Mr. President, al Qaeda did this." "I know, I know, but . . . see if Saddam was involved. Just look. I want to know any shred." Rumsfeld even suggested at one of the early strategy sessions that there were better targets in Iraq than in Afghanistan, where the Taliban regime sheltered Osama bin Laden and his al-Qaeda minions. Clarke thought he must be joking. But Rumsfeld was never more serious. He made clear that his objective was "getting Iraq." Bush listened, but for the moment Colin Powell's objections carried the day, and the focus would be on al-Qaeda. When the meeting broke up, Clarke hastened to thank Powell for his support, but the secretary of state shook his head. "It's not over yet."[10]

Powell was right. The president had not rejected the idea of attacking Iraq, but that could wait a bit. He noted that "what we needed to do with Iraq was to change the government, not just hit it with more cruise missiles." At a pre-9/11 meeting, Treasury Secretary Paul O'Neill had recorded Rumsfeld's views on the real objective for American policy. "Imagine what the region would look like without Saddam and with a regime that's aligned with U.S. interests," he said. "It would change everything in the region and beyond it. It would demonstrate what U.S. policy is all about."[11]

From now on Powell was playing a losing hand, for 9/11 gave Rumsfeld the leverage he needed to master his competitors, especially as he could count on the most powerful vice president in history, Dick Cheney. In an interview with *Washington Post* correspondent Thomas E. Ricks, Rumsfeld described how he operated in the White House. "I reduce down the size of the room . . . I clean the damn room out." He had the president's full blessing, he said, so that people who had no need to know were not around to cause problems. "He is very taken with his own view of the world," a not-so-admiring administration official told Ricks, "and doesn't mind putting down people who disagree. . . . He can be mocking. He can be pretty abusive." The Air Force chief of staff, General John P. Jumper, put it more diplomatically. "We see the same Donald Rumsfeld the American people see."[12]

The American people saw Rumsfeld as the man at the podium—the chief spokesman not only for the Pentagon but also for all matters that concerned every aspect of the war. In Gulf War I, the chair of the Joint Chiefs took most questions from the press. Not anymore. In the first ninety days after the September 2001 attacks on the World Trade Center and the Pentagon, Rumsfeld gave a total of 111 press conferences and interviews, almost as fast as one network crew could set up after the last exited his spacious office. Word went out that Rumsfeld never sat down otherwise. He worked standing up all day long, jotting down his "snowflakes" that went out to all offices down the long corridors of the Pentagon. In the process of managing two wars, Afghanistan and then Iraq, the former Princeton wrestler and Navy pilot got a hammerlock on the generals and forced them to adapt to his vision of a military and a war-fighting strategy, he said, that would not be anything like Vietnam. When army generals complained that many more troops were needed, Rumsfeld dismissed the protest with a breezy comment that the Russians had 300,000 men in Afghanistan and were driven out as occupiers.

Rumsfeld's success as "secretary of war," a term he immediately liked when a newscaster asked him if that title did not fit better, depended to a great extent on his Pentagon team of idea men drawn from the neocon roster that moved into the Department of Defense from the conservative think tanks that had proliferated since the end of the Cold War. Heading their agenda were a whole set of objectives that had very little to do with chasing down one man, Osama bin Laden, and which included eliminating a possible military threat to Washington's ally, Israel, creating a center outside Saudi Arabia (an increasingly restive host for American troops) from which to control events in the Middle East, and making sure American access to oil resources was secure. Saddam Hussein had been useful once as a counterweight to Iran's radical Islamist regime. Indeed, Rumsfeld himself had been sent by President Ronald Reagan to Baghdad in 1984 to assure Hussein that the United States did not see him as an enemy and to advise him that Iraq had been removed from the list of terrorist-supporting states. Following his visit, the special envoy told the *New York Times,* "It struck us as useful to have a relationship, given that we were interested in solving the Mideast problems." The visit was also useful to Saddam, as he soon received shipments of helicopters and, perhaps more important, vital intelligence information on Iranian troop movements. All this was at a time, moreover, when reports of Hussein's use of poison gas in the Iran-Iraq were well known to the State Department.[13]

That crime was charged against Saddam Hussein in the run-up to the 2003 war, as Rumsfeld's loyalists such as Paul Wolfowitz, back in DOD as deputy secretary, Douglas Feith, who became undersecretary for policy, Stephen Cambone, and others such as Richard Perle, who sat on the secretary's advisory council, searched the intelligence files for that "shred" of evidence the president wanted, and listened to Iraqi exiles such as "Curveball," whose code name was well chosen, to tie up all the loose ends. While these Pentagon "intellectuals" led the way to the Iraq War from 2001 to 2003, Rumsfeld's insouciant manner endeared him to many in the media, allowing him to dodge the truly important issues, such as the creation of a special office in the Pentagon to second-guess all the other intelligence agencies, including his own Defense Intelligence Agency, over the question of Iraqi weapons of mass destruction. "I had an uncle named Lou Serett," he said in explanation, "who taught speech and persuasion at Northwestern University many years ago, and he used to say that persuasion was a two-edged sword. Reason and emotion plunge it deep."

Time magazine's special report in May 2002 on the debate within the administration over Iraq asserted Rumsfeld was so determined to find a rationale for an attack that on ten separate occasions he asked the CIA to find evidence linking Baghdad to the attacks on September 11. But every time, the intelligence agency "came back empty-handed." In an almost backhanded way, the report revealed something else—the war hawks in the Pentagon "strongly believed that after years of American sanctions and periodic air assaults, the Iraqi leader is weaker than most people believe."[14]

Such a belief ran directly counter, however, to the notion that Saddam Hussein posed a great military danger to the region or to the United States. Thus when it proved impossible to establish the link with al-Qaeda, the search for a rationale shifted to weapons of mass destruction. Since Saddam Hussein had thrown out UN inspectors at one point, it would be easier to discredit CIA assessments—a tactic Rumsfeld knew something about from his chairmanship of the 1998 commission on the need for a missile defense system. This worked beautifully, especially when the national security adviser, Condoleezza Rice, declared in a television interview that the United States did not want the proof to be a mushroom cloud. "The White House's biggest fear," quipped a top Senate foreign policy aide, "is that U.N. weapons inspectors will be allowed to go in." And when that happened, Rumsfeld had to shift his ground a bit, to argue that weapons inspections were useless in a state run by liars and cheats, who had plenty of time over a decade to hide WMDs no matter how diligent the search was. Saddam Hussein actually "cooperated" in making the American case, write Michael R. Gordon and Gen. Bernard E. Trainor in their authoritative history of the war, *Cobra II,* because he feared revealing to Iranian enemies that he had destroyed his WMD programs in 1991. "The Iraqi leader had initially calculated that he could maintain the ambiguity over his WMD program," they note, "to deter Iran, his opponents at home, and other adversaries even as he complied with the letter of the U.N. inspection demands. It was a fine line to walk and a misreading of his American adversary."[15]

It was certainly a misreading of Donald Rumsfeld. Before and after President Bush's 2002 State of the Union speech, in which he identified Iran, Iraq, and North Korea as the "axis of evil," Rumsfeld spoke about a longer list of states supporting terrorism. He always added Syria and Cuba to Bush's inventory, and noted the existence of terrorist cells in fifty or sixty countries. In this way, of course, the Great War on Terror provided a rolling list of enemies that could be expanded or contracted as need be to suit policy needs. Here truly was the formula for permanent war for permanent peace. The important point for him from the start was to depersonalize the war on terror. He liked to think about how the world looked from an observation point far away. He remarked one time that in his office in the Pentagon he kept a satellite picture of the two Koreas at night under a clear plastic cover on his desk. The South was a blaze of lights, while in the north only Pyongyang, the capital, showed up as a pinpoint against the vast dark background. The comparison intrigued him as demonstrating the differences economically and politically between the light and dark places of the world. Another time he commented, "Anyone looking down from Mars sees that the countries that are providing the greatest opportunity for people are the freer countries." To deal with the threat to Western culture, he added, meant accepting the challenge of those who "hate freedom." "It isn't just the United States, it's a way of life."[16]

The two key issues for Rumsfeld, then, were, first, that Osama bin Laden represented only an intermediate objective, and, second, that no one coalition could possibly meet all the needs of American policy, and it was dangerous to think so. One might recognize in Rumsfeld's worldview a combination of themes in American foreign policy going back quite a distance and certainly to Woodrow Wilson's famous "alter ego," Colonel Edward M. House, who identified the critical challenge to the industrial nations as bringing order to the "waste places of the earth." House had tried to persuade British and German leaders before the outbreak of the Great War to put aside their differences to reach an accord on that overarching problem. Rumsfeld talked about his own problems with France and Germany, albeit of a different nature. Their hesitations about signing on to a Bush coalition to force regime change in Iraq disappointed but did not really surprise the defense secretary and his aides. They knew that once the Taliban had been routed in Afghanistan, there would be sharp disagreements over the next steps to make the world safe from terrorism. Rumsfeld admitted there were questions floating about, but, he insisted, they emanated mostly from "old" Europe, while the center of gravity on the continent had moved eastward as states formerly part of the Warsaw Pact had now become stalwart allies of the United States.

Rumsfeld's attitude toward the effort to locate Osama bin Laden and bring him to justice, as President Bush promised the nation in Old West style in the days immediately after 9/11, shifted behind his clever ripostes at the podium as the effort began to impinge upon larger objectives of the key players in the administration. In an interview broadcast on the CBS program *Face the Nation* on September 23, the first question asked was whether the Taliban should be believed when they said they really did not know where bin Laden was. Rumsfeld was blunt: "Of course not. They know where he is." The implication was that the posse was ready to mount up and go after their man in the badlands. Only a week later, however, he had started to back away from the idea that a ground force could find the supposed author of the attacks. This time, on NBC's *Meet the Press*, the questioner was Tim Russert, who cited the bad experience of the Russians in trying to subdue the Afghan resistance. "I think the idea of thinking that a conventional ground effort in that country, when what you're looking for are needles in a haystack, I think that . . . those kinds of comments need to be given careful attention."[17]

When the first air attacks were launched in early October, Rumsfeld found himself debating Secretary of State Powell, who had been arguing that the United States could not just go into Afghanistan then withdraw, leaving a vacuum, as had happened when the Russians withdrew a decade earlier. That had produced the Taliban regime. God knew what would happen this time. Rumsfeld wanted to minimize the involvement of ground troops. When the attacks began he issued a fifteen-page directive to his generals reminding them the president had ordered a global war on terrorism, not just the al-Qaeda network or Afghanistan. It was clear as clear could be that he did not want a prolonged search for Osama bin Laden if that meant a distraction from dealing with Saddam Hussein. He would continue to do his best to link the two, even claiming nearly a year later that he had "bulletproof" evidence of the close relationship, so as to focus attention on the axis of evil. On October 24, this time talking to the editorial board of *USA Today*, he amplified what he had told the generals in his policy guidance directive. Was it necessary to get bin Laden in order to succeed? "My attitude is if he were gone tomorrow the same problem would exist. He's got a whole bunch of lieutenants that have been trained and they've got bank accounts all over and they've got cells in 50 or 60 countries." Of course that was true, as subsequent events would show, but whether the answer was attacking Iraq was not explored further. Instead Rumsfeld left the impression of a man determined to bypass bin Laden to get to the real trouble. "I don't get up every morning and say that's the end, the goal and the end point of this thing. I think that would be a big mistake."[18]

At about the same time, President Bush was in New York City for a rally near ground zero and a private meeting with business leaders about rebuilding the city. "I truly believe," he told them, "that out of this will come more order in the world—real progress to peace in the Middle East, stability with oil-producing regions." As for the possibility of preventing new attacks, "I can't tell you whether the bastards will strike again."[19]

Addressing a dinner meeting of the Center for Security Policy—one of the many right-wing think tanks that proliferated across Washington in the post–Cold War period—in early November 2001, Rumsfeld talked about how 9/11 had changed modern warfare, making a joke out of the supposedly retro nature of his reforms. "I flew over the Afghan mountains on Sunday, where some of our Special Forces are moving around on horseback, and it is a rugged, hostile environment." In news reports of the speech, however, it appeared he had ad-libbed a few additional words, smiling as he said, "Some are moving around the countryside on horseback—part of our military's transformation." Changing his prepared remarks into a clever irony was an attribute apparently acquired long after the days when, as a young congressman from Illinois, he had hired a speech coach to improve his presentations. The irony was not lost on the dinner group that night. The image of Americans operating alone in a "rugged, hostile environment" was all part of the promotion of the special forces under SOCOM, but it also struck the familiar frontier theme Bush had adopted as his metaphor for America's fight against the lawless bands around the world.[20]

Rumsfeld drew the greatest applause that night indeed when he discussed the role of coalitions. They were fine, he said, America needed help. But . . . "I used the word in the plural form," he alerted them, "not the singular." That was because in the Afghan war—and implicitly in the war against Iraq to come—the coalitions would be different. "It's important because if it were a single coalition, and a coalition member decided not to participate in one way or another, it would be charged that the coalition was falling apart." If that were allowed to happen, the weakest link in the chain would end the mission. "Which is why we don't have a single coalition, we have flexible coalitions for different aspects of the task. *In this way, the mission determines the coalition; the coalition must not determine the mission.*"

Rumsfeld paused at one point to glance back at his opposition to SALT II, saying there were times in government when tenacity and bullheadedness were essential, as when trying to keep your country from committing to a flawed treaty. The honoree of the evening, former defense secretary James Schlesinger, had continued the fight against the treaty, "and I'm thankful for that." The code words were all there in this speech. America was going after Iraq, and if necessary would do so without the United Nations Security Council imprimatur.

The short war against the Taliban came to an end (at least initially) without Osama bin Laden dead or in custody. His escape did not go unnoticed—even by a media still enthralled by the trauma of 9/11 and a Congress willing to stop asking questions at the drop of a bomb. An immediate controversy arose over the number and use of ground troops in the Tora Bora Mountains, where, American intelligence indicated, Osama bin Laden and key members of al-Qaeda had been surrounded. Rumsfeld came under fire for committing too few troops and allowing Afghan soldiers of dubious capability or loyalty to complete the action. Osama lived to fight another day but, from one point of view his escape was actually beneficial to Rumsfeld's cause, by maintaining a constant sense of peril.[21]

In a speech to American troops in Afghanistan on December 16, 2001, Rumsfeld promised that American troops would stay in the country to "find Osama bin Laden" and his lieutenants, but this would be a short-term effort. In the next sentence he declared that no Americans would be among the 3,000–5,000 peacekeeping troops stationed in Afghanistan in the postwar period. When Osama escaped from the region, Rumsfeld first said there was no evidence he was alive, and then dismissed the intelligence that he had been in the Tora Bora region in December at all as mere speculation. "Had it been verifiable, one would have thought someone would have done something about it."[22]

That was an interesting question for Rumsfeld to pose. In the weeks after the Tora Bora siege ended, Pentagon spokesmen from Rumsfeld on down minimized the importance of finding the al-Qaeda leader. "Everybody wants to know where Osama bin Laden is," said one official, reflecting a widespread attitude. "The next question is, who cares? Osama bin Laden as a center of gravity is gone."[23]

The new center of gravity was Iraq. Rumsfeld began making the case in February 2002 that arms inspections were not much use because the Iraqis had had a long time to go underground. "They've had lots of illicit things that have come in. They have advanced their weapons of mass destruction programs. They've developed greater degrees of mobility. They are very accomplished liars, as to what's going on. You could put inspectors all over that place, and it would be very difficult to find anything." The point of all these assertions was to make the case that regime change had to come first before weapons inspections would be of any use. Given that premise, there was nothing Saddam Hussein could do to avoid a showdown with the United States. President Bush, meanwhile, had given his "axis of evil" speech. The shift was almost complete.[24]

The only period during which a serious debate on the road to war appeared to have taken place was during August and September 2002. It was initiated by former national security adviser Brent Scowcroft, who wrote in the *Wall Street Journal* on August 15, 2002 that Saddam was a problem, and had regional ambitions that posed a "real threat to U.S. interests" in the Persian Gulf area. But there was no evidence of ties to terrorist groups that launched 9/11, nor was there reason to believe that he would risk his investment in weapons of mass destruction, much less his country, by handing them over to terrorists "who would use them for their own purposes and leave Baghdad as the return address."[25]

Scowcroft made a "realist" case against war, but he gave much of it away with these words: "It is beyond dispute that Saddam Hussein is a menace. He terrorizes and brutalizes his own people. He has launched war on one of his neighbors. He devotes enormous effort to rebuilding his military forces and equipping them with weapons of mass destruction. We will all be better off when he is gone." It simply was too hard, even for Scowcroft, to break through the WMD barrier. His only real argument was that it was not in the Iraqi leader's interest to share the weapons with terrorists. That left Rumsfeld merely the task of proving—actually only asserting—a connection with al-Qaeda. The most dramatic utterance in this short-lived public debate came from Scowcroft's former protégé, Condoleezza Rice. Previously termed the balance wheel in the administration, the national security adviser asserted on CNN's *Late Edition* on September 8, 2002, that there was a direct connection between Saddam Hussein and al-Qaeda. "Given what we have experienced on September 11," she began, "I don't think anyone wants to wait for the 100 percent surety that he has a weapon of mass destruction that can reach the United States." How close was he to a weapon? asked host Wolf

Blitzer. "The problem here is that there will always be some uncertainty about how quickly he can acquire nuclear weapons," replied Rice. *"But we don't want the smoking gun to be a mushroom cloud."*[26]

Rice's comment was also a stinging rebuke to Colin Powell, who had told British newscaster David Frost that it would be wrong to move without the UN cover that inspections would provide. Powell was breaking his silence, newspaper accounts said, because of Dick Cheney's recent speeches in which the vice president had asserted that the idea of more weapons inspections was "dangerous" in that it "would provide false comfort."[27]

President Bush, meanwhile, delivered a strong speech to the UN in which he said he would work with the Security Council, "but the purposes of the United States should not be doubted." Two days later, in his weekly five-minute radio talk to the nation (a Reagan innovation that had worked beautifully to capture headlines on sleepy news weekends), Bush declared that the UN must act or become "irrelevant." He also sent a resolution to Congress asking for the authority to use force. "This is a chance for Congress to indicate support, a chance for Congress to say we support the administration's ability to keep the peace, that's what this is all about."[28]

Just at this moment the Russian defense minister, Sergei Ivanov, arrived for talks with Rumsfeld at the Pentagon. With the American secretary of defense standing close by, Ivanov said he believed that UN weapons inspectors could settle the issue without undue difficulty. Both Americans and Russians have had experience in that sort of business, he said—a reference to Reagan's famous phrase "trust but verify" mantra during START negotiations. "I think we can easily establish [whether] there exist or not weapons of mass destruction technology."[29]

Rumsfeld did not interrupt Ivanov, but he told the House Armed Services Committee that Congress must act on Bush's recommendation before the UN Security Council took up the American-sponsored resolution. "Delaying a vote in the Congress would send a message that the U.S. may be unprepared to take a stand, just as we are asking the international community to take a stand." This was the classic Cold War White House ploy to put Congress over a barrel, first used with the 1947 Truman Doctrine. Bush added even more pointed "friendly words of advice" for congressional incumbents seeking re-election. "If I were running for office, I'm not sure how I'd explain to the American people—say, vote for me, and, oh, by the way, on a matter of national security, I think I'm going to wait for somebody else to act."[30]

Bush also promised that there would be deadlines within the resolution being proposed at the UN. "Our chief negotiator for the United States, our Secretary of State, understands that we must have deadlines. And we're talking days and weeks, not months and years." Rumsfeld now took the lead in setting forth an opaque distinction between weapons "inspectors" and weapons "discoverers." UN inspectors could not by any stretch succeed unless they were dealing with a cooperative regime; nobody could, for it would be asking the impossible with such a huge territory to cover. And yet, after the war began, Rumsfeld would insist that he knew the locations of the hidden WMDs—with hardly a concern for any small matters of consistency.[31]

At the end of September, Rumsfeld put the final coat of gloss on the case for war, asserting that he had "bulletproof" evidence of Iraq's links to al-Qaeda. He talked about recently declassified intelligence reports concerning the suspected ties, including the presence of senior members of al-Qaeda in Baghdad in "recent periods," reports that he said were "factual" and "exactly accurate." He could not give out details, he said, because that would jeopardize the lives of spies and dry up sources of information—and he also acknowledged (à la Condoleezza Rice) that nothing could be presented beyond a reasonable doubt, and that his information was probably not strong enough to stand up in an American court.[32]

Rumsfield's hints that he had special intelligence about the links, given what had appeared to be serious doubts elsewhere, led to some probing questions at a news conference about an article that claimed a special Defense Department team was sifting through intelligence separate from the CIA and the Defense Intelligence Agency (DIA). "I asked about this," he began, as if somewhat surprised himself to learn about it, "and I'm told that after September 11th a small group—I think two, to start with, and maybe four now, or some number close to less than a handful of people in the policy shop were asked to begin poring over this mountain of information. . . . It is not—any suggestion that it's an intelligence-gathering activity or an intelligence unit of some sort, I think, would be a misunderstanding of it." For once there was a significant follow-up question. The suggestion in the article, said the questioner, was that he was unhappy with the intelligence that he was getting about the link between al-Qaeda and Iraq. "Why would I be unhappy?" quipped Rumsfeld. "The intelligence is what intelligence is. It says their best estimates."[33]

It was a disingenuous answer. Rumsfeld had chafed at intelligence that he did not control, and the Office of Special Projects in Undersecretary Douglas Feith's office had been engaged for more than a year in an exercise to make the intelligence fit the policy. "They are politicizing intelligence, no question about it," a former CIA counterterrorism chief, Vincent M. Cannistraro, told *Washington Post* reporters. "And they are undertaking a campaign to get George Tenet [the director of central intelligence] fired because they can't get him to say what they want on Iraq."[34]

Rumsfeld replied to such comments by insisting that he and "George" couldn't have a "closer relationship." The secretary of defense actually found George Tenet's conversations of little use to his purpose, as the director "was trying to impress him" with spy tales, an aide said, without success. But even if he had found Tenet a keen reporter on questions that mattered to him, Rumsfeld had set out not only to reform the military but to extend control over all intelligence. This became clear very early on after 9/11 when former national security adviser Brent Scowcroft presented a draft memorandum to Rumsfeld and Vice President Dick Cheney detailing his own ideas for intelligence reform. It centered on creating an "intelligence library," a central location that would bring all resources together, but what especially stood out was his plan for putting the CIA in charge of everything. Rumsfeld strongly disagreed, and Scowcroft went to Cheney, who simply said he ought to take it to the president. Scowcroft looked forward to future discussions, but that was the last time he was ever to see the inside of the vice president's office.[35]

Later, when Tenet confessed that he had misled President Bush with information about Iraq's WMDs—famously calling the evidence a "slam dunk"—the White House agreed to create a new position, director of national intelligence. Rumsfeld had come into office with a desire to consolidate control over all intelligence in the Pentagon, so that the secretary would have "one dog to kick." He failed to see why, however, there was a need for a director of national intelligence, writes James Risen, "when the nation already had Don Rumsfeld."[36]

Rumsfeld's other campaign centered in SOCOM, the Special Operations Command that had evolved from the days of John F. Kennedy and the Green Berets, and the Rapid Deployment Force in the Carter years, to the full-blown command headquartered in Florida. Americans on horseback in the Afghan mountains calling in air strikes on the Taliban was a perfect example. In addition to controlling intelligence that reached Pentagon offices, and funneled out of them into policy decisions, Rumsfeld wished to mount espionage operations of a quasi-military sort. In the Reagan years, CIA director William Casey had sought a similar off-the-shelf capacity to use where Congress or some other agency such as the State Department had failed to see the imperative need to carry out covert activities in the "national interest." The result then had been the Iran-contra scandal. Rumsfeld had bigger plans.

In October 2001, a new unit under SOCOM came into being, the Strategic Support Branch, which, he hoped, would help to end his "near total dependence on CIA" detection for what is known as human intelligence, or "humint" in spook language. But he wanted the capability to carry out missions as well. A memorandum from the Joint Chiefs answering his "snowflake" query identified "emerging target countries such as Somalia, Yemen, Indonesia, Philippines and Georgia" as places where the Strategic Support Branch would be especially useful. It would be possible, another memorandum said, to recruit agents for covert actions who included "notorious figures" whose links to the U.S. government would be embarrassing if identified.[37]

As the Afghan war seemed close to an end, Rumsfeld answered questions for a newspaper interview concerning the use of SOCOM in the conflict, and hinted at where it would be useful in the future. "I can name without batting an eye, 15 or 20 places, portions of countries that are not currently under the control of a central government. That suggests that unconventional things will need to be done in concert with conventional capabilities." He also mentioned that there had been a transformation in the sizing of forces to fit potential conflicts with Iraq and North Korea, as well as the establishment of a "new nuclear posture" for "strategic offensive weapons." These were hints of the "shock and awe" approach to warfare that would provide the overall framework for SOCOM planning.[38]

A big aid to Rumsfeld in planning for SOCOM was the abrupt change in the definition of the enemy. At first President Bush referred to the 9/11 attacks as crimes, not a military action. "This is not a criminal action," Rumsfeld argued to the president, "this is war." Admiral Rowan Scarborough called the episode "Rumsfeld's instant declaration of war, and it took America from the Clinton administration's view that terrorism was a criminal matter to the Bush administration's view that terrorism was a global enemy to be destroyed." Bush issued a military order in November that characterized the 9/11 attacks as being "on a scale that has created a state of armed conflict that requires the use of the United States Armed Forces." How they would be used was up to Rumsfeld.[39]

"If Rumsfeld gets his way," asserted one of the first assessments of the future role of SOCOM, "administration hawks may soon start using special forces to attack or undermine other regimes on Washington's hit list— without the sort of crucial public debate that preceded the war in Iraq." Pentagon officials called SOCOM the "Secret Army of Northern Virginia," falling into ranks under Donald Rumsfeld's stern gaze. Asked to describe a scenario where the Strategic Support Branch might play a role, Assistant Secretary of Defense Thomas O'Connell happily obliged. "A hostile country close to our borders suddenly changes leadership. . . . We would want to make sure the successor is not hostile." Within a few weeks it emerged, in a *Washington Post* article, that Rumsfeld wanted his special operations forces to enter a country and conduct operations without explicit concurrence from the U.S. ambassador. In the Pentagon view, the article said, the campaign against terrorism is a war and requires similar freedom to prosecute as in Iraq. Rumsfeld's pressure on Bush to call post-9/11 activities a "war" instead of a "criminal action" was indeed "a very big thought," and a lot had already flowed from that idea. Chief of mission authority has been a pillar of presidential authority overseas, said an administration official familiar with the new tension between State and Defense. "When you start eroding that, it can have repercussions that are . . . risky." Colin Powell's chief aide, Deputy Secretary of State Richard Armitage, instructed his counterterrorism coordinator, J. Cofer Black, to act as point man to thwart the Pentagon's initiative. "I gave Cofer specific instructions to dismount, kill the horses and fight on foot—this is not going to happen."[40]

Donald Rumsfeld without doubt had no peer as the strongest secretary of defense since the 1947 reorganization of the military—with his closest competitor Robert McNamara. Rumsfeld owed his power in part to the evolution of America's Cold War expansion and the multiplication of American military bases around the world. This new American empire was in place well before he returned to the Pentagon in 2001. But he led the fight to control intelligence in ways that harmed national security by relying upon a group of loyalists who had highly politicized views of the Middle East, and who in turn relied upon Iraqi exiles whose personal ambitions colored every scrap of information supplied to the Pentagon. To the neocons Chalabi was the "George Washington of Iraq," but the arc of his career resembled the last "George Washington" America supported, Ngo Dinh Diem of Vietnam. Even more than the strong-willed McNamara, who thought he understood how to fight Ho Chi Minh and learned otherwise, Donald Rumsfeld *knew* his intelligence sources were good—because he had a vision of a post-Saddam Middle East welcoming American forces, as his friend Dick Cheney assured the nation, as "liberators."

The curious mix of Hobbes and Wilson that inspired such hopes for a happy outcome of war with Iraq could be seen also in Rumsfeld's embrace of "shock and awe" as the answer to the gradualism of the Vietnam War that conservatives blamed for the defeat. It was certainly true, as Lyndon Johnson often said, that almost until the last years of the war, and whether the public thought that going into Vietnam was a mistake or not, the prevalent dissenting opinion was not to get out but to find a quick way to win.

The Cold War, including Vietnam, Rumsfeld argued, had been fought like classical nineteenth- and twentieth-century conflicts—from positions of strength, basically immobile fortresses within which American forces waited to repel an attack. Despite the sad lessons of Vietnam and the experience with counterinsurgency, Americans had waged the war in Southeast Asia in a set-piece fashion, like a chess game where players meditated about moves, whereas the challenge of the new century required the speed and quick reflexes of a video game, where rapid movement counted for more than numbers. Gradualism brought nothing but disaster, whether by ratcheting up troops over a period of years or the Rolling Thunder bombing campaign that rumbled on for months and years without producing anything but good world press for the enemy. Vietnam was almost a perfect failure, straining to the breaking point the military's ability to hold together a conscript army, and the nation's tolerance for a "limited war" strategy. Bringing a force of 100,000 men to a trouble spot in three months, Rumsfeld liked to say, would yield better results than 300,000 men in six months.

While the army resisted his appeals for such heretical thinking, students at the National Defense University had already produced a book, *Shock and Awe: Achieving Rapid Dominance,* that appealed to Pentagon savants and Rumsfeld as the very antithesis of Vietnam. The principal author of *Shock and Awe* was Harlan K. Ullman, a retired Navy commander and military theorist who taught at the National War College. Winning a war, said the authors, depended upon shocking and awing civilian populations into submission. Ullman cited Hiroshima and the German blitzkrieg as appropriate strategies for victory. The book also criticized—in terms Rumsfeld would appreciate—Gulf War I as an example of a "decisive force" strategy that required time and concentrated on force-on-force warfare. Shock and awe, on the other hand, would concentrate on changing the whole environment. "The target is the adversary's will, perception, and understanding."

> Total mastery achieved at extraordinary speed and across tactical, strategic, and political levels will destroy the will to resist. With Rapid Dominance, the goal is to use our power with such compellance that even the strongest of wills will be awed.

But wouldn't this be warfare against civilian populations? The book nodded slightly in the direction of acknowledging such contentious implications:

> Rapid Dominance will strive to achieve a dominance that is so complete and victory is so swift, that an adversary's losses in both manpower and material could be relatively light, and yet the message is so unmistakable that resistance would be seen as futile.[41]

So the adversary's losses "could" be relatively light, but the key target was an enemy's will to resist, and the example of ultimate "shock and awe" was Hiroshima. As Pentagon planners worked on the "force sizing" needed to mount a "shock and awe" campaign against Iraq, Rumsfeld seized the political initiative by adding his own conditions to what the UN required of Saddam Hussein to avoid war. Security Council Resolution 1441, adopted on November 8, 2002, found Iraq in "material breach" of its obligations under previous resolutions concerning UN inspections, and demanded that Baghdad allow the inspections to resume. As Secretary-General Kofi Annan put it, "If Iraq's defiance continues . . . the Security Council must face its responsibilities." The resolution gave Iraq forty-five days to comply. When it did readmit the inspectors, Secretary Rumsfeld hastened to tell reporters what the *United States* required of Iraq. He elaborated yet again on the supposed difference between "discoverers" or "finders" and inspectors. Inspections were useless. "The burden of proof is not on the United States or the United Nations to prove that Iraq has these weapons. We know they do." Unless Saddam Hussein first came clean and admitted he had the WMDs, the inspectors were just so many tourists with special escorts. What Rumsfeld did not say, of course, was that his condition was a useless requirement, because it implied that Saddam's admission that he had the weapons and knew where they were was all that mattered. But Rumsfeld had already called the Iraqi regime a bunch of liars and deceivers, so owning up to having the weapons would have no value in validating their destruction. What the administration had offered was a Hobson's choice. An alternative to war "would be for Saddam Hussein to leave." The United States interpreted Resolution 1441—without any further UN action—as allowing members to take military action to enforce its requirements.[42]

Amidst all this heated rhetoric the expected report from Hans Blix, the chief UN inspector, hardly mattered; the American media were already in awe of Pentagon boasts about what was in store for Iraq if Saddam Hussein stayed in Baghdad. Author Harold Ullman explained the plan in quite open terms in a newspaper interview: "We want them to quit, not to fight, so that you have this simultaneous effect—rather like the nuclear weapons at Hiroshima—not taking days or weeks but minutes." Even if such talk was only meant to scare Hussein into leaving, it appeared to dismiss any protests from other nations or domestic critics that it was premature to think about the horrors of unleashing such a war, or the precedent of such threats. "You're sitting in Baghdad and, all of a sudden," continued the *Dr. Strangelove*—like interview, "you're the general and 30 of your division headquarters have been wiped out. You also take the city down. By that I mean you get rid of their power and water. In two, three, four, five days they are physically, emotionally and psychologically exhausted."[43]

Such near-apocalyptic visions were hardly likely to secure votes for a "second resolution" even if Hans Blix reported the Iraqi government had been uncooperative. But his interim report of January 27, 2003, instead reported progress with many unanswered questions still pending, and his final update before the war, on March 7, 2003, asserted that the remaining issues could be resolved not in weeks but certainly within months because of outside pressures on Iraq and the growing capabilities of the UN team. At the end of this last report he noted, "It must be remembered that in accordance with the governing resolutions, a sustained inspection and monitoring system is to remain in place after verified disarmament to give confidence and to strike an alarm, if signs were seen of the revival of any proscribed weapons programmes."

But no report by Hans Blix, whatever it said, nor the inability to get a second resolution could slow the double-time march to war. Ten days after Blix's plea for more time to complete the work, President Bush gave Saddam forty-eight hours to get out of Iraq and take his two sons with him. Rumsfeld had been arguing for more than a year that getting Osama bin Laden would not solve the problem of the terrorist threat, but now it appeared that "shock and awe" was a personal message to the Iraqi leader. Acting on supposedly good intelligence, decapitating strikes were launched on March 20 at a supposed hide-out, Dora Farms. After the fall of Baghdad it was revealed that the F-117s had dropped 2,000 "bunker-busting" bombs on an empty field. Saddam Hussein had never been there, and there was no bunker.[44]

General Tommy Franks, the overall American commander, meanwhile, fired up his commanders in a "final huddle" by showing them the opening scenes from *Gladiator*, with Russell Crowe as the Roman commander who was sent to deal with a rebellious Germanic tribe. With all the weapons at hand and ready to go, Crowe cried out to his officers, "On my signal, unleash hell." Franks had battled Rumsfeld from the outset of planning trying to secure approval of a larger force, but the secretary of defense had insisted on keeping the number to less than 150,000. If "shock and awe" worked, presumably the war would be over quickly, and the postwar problems would be easy. When the president asked Franks about military plans for that Phase IV of Operation Iraqi Freedom, the general said he would have "lord mayors" in every major city and town.[45]

Franks's response appeared to satisfy the president, even if Franks continued to have his own doubts in private, and there was little follow-up. The air attacks on Baghdad did not live up to Ullman's predictions, but were really "shock and awe lite." The targets were government buildings and the initial attacks came at night, so civilian casualties were minimal in this first phase of the war. The road to Baghdad was a short one. "The images of thousands of cheering Iraqis, celebrating and embracing coalition forces," declared Rumsfeld on April 11, 2003, "are being broadcast throughout the world, including the Arab world." They gave the lie to reports that Iraqis were ambivalent or opposed to the coalition's arrival in their country. "I think it's important that that message be seen, for America is a friend of the Arab people. And now, finally, Arab people are hearing the same message, not from U.S. officials, but from their fellow Arabs, the liberated people of Iraq."[46]

In the middle of this celebratory news conference, however, came a series of inconvenient questions that Rumsfeld answered with the famous comment, "Stuff happens"—a quip that would shadow him wherever he went all the rest of his years in office. Picking up on the theme of cheering Iraqis, a questioner asked about other pictures of raucous Iraqis carrying out antiquities looted from Baghdad museums along with similar scenes across the country. Rumsfeld tried to make light of the television images. "The images you are seeing on television you are seeing over, and over, and over, and it's the same picture of some person walking out of some building with a vase, and you see it 20 times, and you think, 'My goodness, were there that many vases?' (Laughter.) 'Is it possible that there were that many vases in the whole country?'"

But the questions kept coming. Did he think, then, that words such as *anarchy* and *lawlessness* were ill-chosen? "Absolutely. I picked up a newspaper today and I couldn't believe it. I read eight headlines that talked about chaos, violence, unrest. And it was just Henny Penny—'The sky is falling.'

I've never seen anything like it!" Here was a country being liberated from a vicious dictator, and all this newspaper could do was to show a single bleeding civilian and call it chaos. But there were more questions, and an obviously irritated Rumsfeld finally declared that you could take a television camera into any American city in recent years and film riots and looting. "Stuff happens!" It happened everywhere. "It is a fundamental misunderstanding to see those images over, and over, and over again of some boy walking out with a vase and say, 'Oh, my goodness, you didn't have a plan.' That's nonsense."[47]

This dialogue was an ironic variation on something yet unknown to the public, Secretary of State Colin Powell's warning to the president about the aftermath of "shock and awe." In Iraq, he said, Pottery Barn rules applied: you break it, you own it. The April looting did not dampen the president's ardor for declaring on board the USS *Abraham Lincoln* on May 1, 2003, "mission accomplished." After emerging from the aircraft he had helped pilot, still dressed in a flight suit, Bush told the assembled sailors on the carrier that major military operations were over. What was left were cleanup operations and the transition to democracy. Rumsfeld disputed the Powell prediction. "I don't believe it's our job to reconstruct the country," he said, suggesting that oil revenues might not be enough to repair all the damage but that there were other industries like tourism. The ruins of Babylon, for example, could be a big draw. "Tourism is going to be something important to that country as soon as the security situation is resolved. . . . In the last analysis, they have to create an environment that's hospitable to investment and enterprise."[48]

Three years later, the security situation had not been resolved. The country was on the verge of civil war—with untold thousands of Iraqis dead, and American deaths heading toward the 3,000 mark, "mission accomplished" had become a horrible joke on the "liberated" Iraqis. Rumsfeld had also tried to sidestep another "inconvenient" issue in the April 11 press conference, the seeming disappearance of the WMDs. He had said one time that he knew where they were. Eleven days into the war, on March 30, 2003, when the first flickers of doubt about the WMDs began to sneak into the mainstream media, Rumsfeld answered a question posed by ABC News this way: "We know where they are. They're in the area around Tikrit and Baghdad and east, west, south and north somewhat." In the April 11 press conference, however, he was already saying, "We are not going to find them, in my view, just as I never believed the inspectors would by running around seeing if they can open a door and surprise somebody and find something, because these people have learned that they can live in an inspection environment. . . . No. It's a big country. What we're going to do is we're going to find the people who will tell us that, and we're going to find ways to encourage them to tell us that." Still later, talking about some claims he had made, he retreated to what became a standard administration ploy: blame the intelligence. "I should have said, 'I believe they're in that area. Our intelligence tells us they're in that area,' and that was our best judgment."[49]

The statement that the only way the WMDs could be found was through interrogation, "and we're going to find ways to encourage them to tell us that," took on an ugly double meaning after the torture scandals at the Abu Ghraib prison came to light. As the months dragged on and on, "shock and awe" became "stay the course," and Mr. Rumsfeld's war began to look very much like Mr. McNamara's war after all. Calls for sending additional troops to Iraq to carry out pacification continued to be turned down; calls to set a date for troop withdrawals got the same answer. But other countries were not so determined to stick it out, and the "coalition of the willing" became a subject of mordant humor as the "coalition of the dwindling." The phrase "shock and awe" floated out into American pop culture, sportswriters seized on its cliché value for describing titanic encounters, and coaches promised fans their teams would inflict shock and awe on opponents. Inevitably, it had sex value as well, just as the Bikini atomic tests became a name for skimpy swimwear. "Madonna," read a headline of a 2006 concert review, "Delivers Shock, Awe at HP Pavilion."[50]

War protestors mocked Rumsfeld and the administration's claims, as in the lyrics of Neil Young's song "Shock and Awe":

> Back in the days of shock and awe
> We came to liberate them all
> History was the cruel judge of overconfidence
> Back in the days of shock and awe
> Back in the days of "mission accomplished"
> Our chief was landing on the deck
> The sun was setting on a golden photo-op
> Back in the days of "mission accomplished."

In Iraq, however, the phrase had not lost its original meaning, and continued to describe scenes of terror and destruction, if in a different context. "When the Americans invaded Iraq they tried to shock and awe to scare their enemy," said a Baghdad University professor. "Now Iraqis are shocking and awing each other." The death rate in the violence and sectarian warfare had reached over 1,000 per month, while Defense Secretary Rumsfeld, no longer talking about how "stuff happens," declared that withdrawing was not a strategy.[51]

While he had started out as a dedicated anti-nation-building secretary, like his ostensible boss, George W. Bush, Rumsfeld became a convert to "transformational" diplomacy, out of necessity, as the full measure of the looming catastrophe for American interests became an eyes-wide-open nightmare. When all predictions about Iraq had proved wrong, when no WMDs had been found and no connection established with al-Qaeda discovered, Rumsfeld fell back to transformation-style language and Vietnam-style attacks on the press. In a speech to the National Press Club on February 2, 2006, he spoke of an ideological battle to the finish. "Compelled by a militant ideology that celebrates murder and suicide with no territory to defend, with little to lose, they will either succeed in changing our way of life or we'll succeed in changing theirs." The insurrectionists in Iraq thus became the twenty-first-century equivalent of the nearly invisible Kremlin "agents" that drove the Cold War. It had been this agent theory of revolution, of course, that supplied the paste needed to hold together things such as the domino theory. As in the Vietnam War, these sinister figures were able to "manipulate the world's press to their advantage." While most commentators continued to see the media as reluctant to engage administration figures on controversial subjects, Rumsfeld scolded his audience as dupes who did not realize that "they [the terrorists] carefully plan attacks to garner headlines in their effort to break our will."[52]

In other talks he spoke of the reluctance of reporters to be "embedded" with American troops as something approximating treason. Calls for Rumsfeld to resign were heard from a variety of quarters. Some wanted him gone because he had failed to plan properly for the war; some wanted him gone because he had led the march to a war based upon manipulated intelligence; and some wanted him gone because he had been responsible, as head of the Department of Defense, for what had taken place at Guantánamo and Abu Ghraib. President Bush declared in the midst of the uproar that he was the "decider" and that Rumsfeld would stay. He could not very well fire him, after all, because his own career was "embedded" in the success of the war—and the Rumsfeld strategy for winning. But pressure became too great after the 2006 elections—and he did.

It will no doubt be a long time before historians have access to many of the "snowflake" memos that Rumsfeld sent to his chief Pentagon aides, but one was leaked that raised many questions about the war on terror. In an October 16, 2003, note, he asked them to give him their best thoughts on the most basic question of whether the nation was winning or losing the global war on terror. Was it the case that in the current situation "the harder we work, the behinder we get"? The analogy to *Alice in Wonderland* itself posed questions that he would have had a hard time deflecting in his usual manner at press briefings. "Today," he commented, "we lack metrics to know if we are winning or losing the global war on terror. Are we capturing, killing or deterring and dissuading more terrorists every day than the madrassas and the radical clerics are recruiting, training and deploying against us? Does the US need to fashion a broad, integrated plan to stop the next generation of terrorists? The US is putting relatively little effort into a long-range plan, but we are putting a great deal of effort into trying to stop terrorists. The cost-benefit ratio is against us! Our cost is billions against the terrorists' cost of millions."[53]

It was a "McNamara moment," reminiscent of the dawning on that earlier occupant of the spacious office in the Pentagon that all his assumptions about body counts and "metrics" of the Vietnam War were in error. After the war was long over, McNamara blamed the whole thing on the lack of understanding on each side and the fog of war. Rumsfeld's probes did not produce anything near the rueful meanderings of McNamara's post-Vietnam odyssey in search of lessons, and he quickly returned to four-square defense of the war and the strategy he had imposed on the generals.

In March 2006, he traveled to Vail, Colorado, with a small group of wounded military, twenty-four of them. It was the third year that Iraq veterans had been entertained by the Vail citizenry, as they sought to work through their injuries with special instructors to help them. "These people," he told a TV interviewer, would never have had "a chance to come to Vail, Colorado, never in their lives, to come here and spend several days and just have a fantastic time and understand that they are capable of going up on that mountain and beating the mountain." Aside from this revealing commentary about who was doing the fighting in Iraq, Rumsfeld also commented on their wounds: "They're folks who have lost legs or arms or sight and have demonstrated a determination to be able to go out and live a life, a normal life."

Asked how he would change public perception of the war—and, implicitly, his own role in pushing for an invasion of Iraq—Rumsfeld began with a long discussion of how wars had never been popular in the United States, from the time of Washington and the Revolution. "George Washington was almost fired. . . . And Franklin Roosevelt was one of the most hated people in the country. . . . He was Commander in Chief." The trouble was people did not study history anymore, and journalists ought to do a better job of providing context "rather than just running around trying to win a Pulitzer by dramatizing something that's negative that in fact is [positive]."

> The impression one gets by reading the press is that Iraq is aflame. I was over there a month I guess ago, and every time I go it is not aflame. It's not burning. There are people being killed every day. Under Saddam Hussein they had over several hundred thousand people murdered and put into mass graves. So it's not as though it was peaceful and now it's violent. It's always been violent. That's a part of the world, I'm afraid. There's been sectarian differences between the various religious sects for, you know, hundreds of years.[54]

Donald Rumsfeld was never at a loss for words, or for historical justifications—however outrageous—to explain why "stuff happens." The idea that somehow it was all inevitable from the start, as this most famous phrase from the war conjured up, seemed a last, desperate effort to avoid confronting an Iraq syndrome more devastating to American self-interests and self-perceptions than Vietnam had been, with all its consequences. The sense that fate had put the United States into a place where it could not "abandon" the Iraq mission no matter what was happening in real time was simply the dark side of the anonymous White House aide's hubris-filled comment before the war began to a journalist who had written something that had not gone down well in the executive mansion. People like the journalist, the aide said, were stuck "in what we call the reality-based community," defined as those who believed that solutions emerged from a judicious study of "discernible reality." "That's not the way the world really works anymore. We're an empire now, and when we act, we create our own reality. And while you're studying that reality—judiciously, as you will—we'll act again, creating other new realities, which you can study too, and that's how things will sort out. We're history's actors . . . and you, all of you, will be left to just study what we do."[55]

Tommy Franks had picked out *Gladiator* to inspire his commanders to unleash hell as Russell Crowe did on behalf of Rome against a rebellious Germanic tribe. Studies of the Roman Empire have long been dominated by the notion—coming from Gibbons on down—that internal corruption and abandonment of ancient values destroyed its viability. Now a new historian, Peter Heather, reverses that verdict. "The west Roman state fell not because of the weight of its own 'stupendous fabric,' but because its Germanic neighbors had responded to its power in ways the Romans could never have foreseen. There is in all this a pleasing denouement. By virtue of its unbounded aggression, Roman imperialism was ultimately responsible for its own destruction."[56]

Perhaps the study of history has indeed advanced more than Rumsfeld fears is the case. Whether that is the case or not, Secretary Rumsfeld found himself in Dushanbe, Tajikistan, one of America's new post–Cold War allies, with rich resources of oil and natural gas, strategically located near Afghanistan. Tajikistan is also known as one of the most tyrannical regimes of Central Asia. Whatever words of advice he had for the Tajik rulers about the rising tide of democratic thought in their part of the world, Rumsfeld had strong words of warning to those countries he once called part of "old" Europe, and who were now, under the aegis of NATO, sending a force to quell the resurgent Taliban. Back in the immediate post-9/11 days, it will be remembered, the defense secretary had vowed that the coalition—any coalition—would not be allowed to determine the American mission. The American forces that went into Afghanistan numbered not more than one division, and used the so-called Northern Alliance to do much of the heavy lifting during the brief campaign. Our Afghan "allies" in this mini-coalition were very enterprising people, particularly when it came to raising opium poppies. Things had now come full circle, as dramatists like to say, and Rumsfeld warned that unless Western Europe did more to help out in stopping the flow of drug money to the Taliban by halting production in Afghanistan, the whole enterprise could fail. "Western Europe ought to have an enormous interest in the success in Afghanistan, and it's going to take a lot more effort on their part" for the Kabul government to be successful. Apparently now it was the responsibility of the coalition to see that the American mission did not fail. Mr. Rumsfeld's war had opened a new front, a rear-guard action as public disillusionment with the enterprise reached the post-Tet levels of the Vietnam War.[57]

Moving on to Iraq on a "surprise" visit to American troops, Rumsfeld's comments were terse and showed considerable irritation at being questioned, his pre- and early-war tilting with reporters now a thing long past as the plane neared its destination. The Iraqis were engaged in a comprehensive review of their security requirements, he said. How long would that take? "I don't talk deadlines." What about the uproar over immunity granted to American troops that exempted them from Iraqi law, and the allegations of murder and rape? "It's being handled as it should be." Then, addressing troops at an American air base at Balad, he said the enemy had proven "persistent and ruthless," even after the loss of the terrorist leader Abu Musab al-Zarqawi. Victory depended on Iraqi unity and taking the fight to the enemy; it was political as much as military. No deadlines, no change in strategy, only more of the same. "These enemies are not going to quit." It was not a very cheering message, one delivered in the shadow of Robert McNamara.[58]

11

Zelig in U.S. Foreign Relations: The Roles of China in the American Post-9/11 World

WALTER LAFEBER

For more than 200 years, Americans have viewed China as a kind of Zelig in their foreign and economic policies.[1] In the 1780s, when the drive for an effective constitutional government threatened to be undermined by economic depression, U.S. mercantile traders looked to the China market as a potential savior. During the 1840s, just after a severe economic downturn and amidst the religious fervor of their Great Awakening revivals, Americans opened formal diplomatic relations with Peking. They believed China would become a great customer for both their goods and their Christianity. From the 1870s to the 1920s, as the United States initially stepped on the world stage as a great power, China assumed the multiple roles of a reluctant but willing accomplice who would make the central U.S. diplomatic principle, the open-door policy, work for overproducing industrialists who sought profit; frighten labor leaders who feared the "Yellow Peril's" many emigrants to the United States; and welcome Christian missionaries who desperately sought converts as protection against the supposedly threatening tenets of Darwinism. As a leading missionary privately remarked in 1927, "One would be justified in concluding that apparently China exists for the missionary, rather than the missionary for China." Many on Wall Street or in the Gary, Indiana, steel mills could have agreed with that statement in regard to their own roles.[2]

By the 1930s, internationalists pointed to China as the reason why the United States had to go to war with Japan, which had invaded China, and by the mid-1940s as the reason why, with the Chinese taking the lead, Asia would be stabilized and its markets become a mammoth magnet for American goods. For Henry Luce, the editor of *Life* and *Time* magazines, China was to be a worthy partner in creating what he termed "the American Century."[3]

But the yellow brick road to the American Century took a detour in

1949, when China came under Communist control. The half-century-old fear of a Yellow Peril became real during the Korean War of 1950–1953. Chinese troops intervened five months after the war began, killed tens of thousands of U.S. troops who had been driving toward the Korean-Chinese boundary, and thus ensured that the Americans would not end up permanently camped on China's border. Korea remained split between the two sides of the Cold War. In the 1960s, the Soviet Union seemed checked by the aftereffects of the Cuban missile crisis and the early stages of détente. China was now labeled enemy number one by President John F. Kennedy. It became a major reason why Americans would have to die in Vietnam. China, Kennedy believed, exemplified the Communist state that had no concern for human life but was committed to being a proselytizer whose central mission was to turn the impoverished, formerly colonized, newly emerging countries into Communist partners.[4]

By the early 1970s, the tragic military and political dead end in Vietnam and the possibility of exploiting a potentially highly profitable economic/diplomatic frontier in China led President Richard Nixon to open talks with Beijing leaders. In American eyes, China had turned into a high card that could be played against the Soviets (from whom the Chinese had begun splitting a decade earlier) and the Japanese (who seemed to be moving rapidly to dominate the world economy). Whatever the effects of the high card, the Soviets collapsed in 1991. At about the same time, Japan's economy began to stagger, then sharply slumped. The United States emerged in the early 1990s as the greatest by far of military powers, and the supreme economic force.

American observers with illusions and too little historical perspective began to talk about the developments in the 1990s—a U.S. military budget greater than the next twenty such budgets in the world combined, the amoeba-like spread of the American computer domination of global communications, President Clinton's virtual eradication of the huge U.S. governmental debt—as simply the preface to making the post-2000 years another American Century, to be dominated by what columnist Charles Krauthammer called the Washington-based "unipolar power." This new American Century appeared to be especially in hand because, as President George H.W. Bush announced in 1991 with the defeat of Iraq in the First Gulf War, Americans had finally "kicked" the ghost of Vietnam. They once again seemed willing to commit their lives to the use of armed force.[5] Much of the heavier kicking was done by the growing neoconservative movement, which included Krauthammer and Undersecretary of Defense Paul Wolfowitz. The neoconservatives, who believed in, among other tenets, basing policies on the willing use of ever larger U.S. military power, the all-out defense of Israel, and the spreading of American democratic principles around the globe, had begun in the 1960s–1970s as an angry, gut-driven reaction to the U.S.

failure in Vietnam. The neocons possessed a visceral dislike of the antiwar movement (especially on college campuses), which they blamed for undermining the war effort.

China now served the all-important purpose of replacing the Soviet Union as an enemy, or at least a potential enemy. It had to, for there seemed to be no other threat that could serve as justification for massive U.S. military budgets and the more than 700 bases Americans had established around the globe to contain a now nonexistent Soviet Union. As China had been conceived in Washington during the 1970s as the card to be played against the Soviets, in the 1990s it was conceived as the card that would replace the Soviets. What the Vietnam War had helped create, the supposed end of the "Vietnam syndrome" would now re-create as a suitable armed threat, at least potentially, to justify the U.S. military budgets for containing the Chinese.

The Project for the New American Century, a neoconservative think tank led by William Kristol (editor of the *Weekly Standard*, a newsmagazine that often served as a mouthpiece for the George W. Bush administration), published a widely noted call to action in 2000, *Rebuilding America's Defenses*. The ninety-page paper emphasized the need to switch American attention from Europe, where it had been focused for half a century, to other regions, especially Asia, and to build a military that could control such regions. China drew special attention: "Raising U.S. military strength in east Asia is the key to coping with the rise of China to great power status," and such a buildup "may provide a spur to the process of democratization inside China itself." An ever larger and more expensive American military could apparently have nothing but wondrous effects, and China was now to be a central target—or, as the neoconservatives seemed to phrase it, China was to be a future democracy, courtesy of the Pentagon.[6]

A founding document for these views on the need for the buildup and use of the American military was the 1992 Defense Planning Guidance. But it did not initially focus on China. Written in the Bush administration's Pentagon under the aegis of the leading neoconservative theorist, Paul Wolfowitz, the paper warned that future generations would have to prepare massively and globally to "preclude any hostile power from dominating a region critical to our interests." The final draft feared that Japan and Germany might become such "hostile" powers. When a leading German official criticized the document, Krauthammer rushed to its rescue by warning that "the alternative is Japanese carriers patrolling the Strait of Malacca, and a nuclear Germany dominating Europe."[7]

Such illusions did not preoccupy a more realistic Wolfowitz or, for that matter, the Democratic administration of President Bill Clinton. In 1995–96, Clinton had more immediate concerns. U.S. officials allowed the president of Taiwan, Lee Teng-hui, to visit the United States in a widely publicized visit. Lee vigorously attacked the belief, long propagated by Beijing and acquiesced to by Washington, that his country was "peacefully" to be brought into "one China." A number of neoconservative and conservative voices, led by the *Wall Street Journal*'s editorial page, joined Lee in denouncing Beijing's "one-China" policy. The Chinese ominously began to move forces into positions that posed a threat to Taiwan. In response, Clinton ordered U.S. naval units to protect the Taiwanese. The crisis faded away, but it was followed by a series of lesser confrontations that climaxed in 1999 with the U.S. bombing of the Chinese embassy in Belgrade during the American effort to halt an expanding Balkan conflict. Washington declared the bombing an accident. Beijing announced it was too precise (it wiped out the floors housing Chinese intelligence offices) to be accidental. The attack coincided with a U.S. congressional investigation charging two American companies with providing military secrets to China.

By 1999–2000, Krauthammer's warnings about Japanese aircraft carriers and German nuclear weapons had been discarded into the forgotten bin, where they had long belonged. The warnings issued during the winter about the Chinese by the Project for the New American Century had now taken center stage. China, Wolfowitz stated flatly during the 2000 presidential campaign, was "probably the single most serious foreign policy challenge of the coming decades." When the George W. Bush administration entered office the next year, the French ambassador to Washington surveyed some of the new officials and believed that, for the first time in American history, Europe would no longer be the focal point of Washington's diplomacy. Instead, the pivot would be the region from Northeast Asia across to the Middle East—that is, China and much of the Chinese front yard in Korea and backyard in Central Asia.[8]

A perceptive analysis of this pre-9/11 evolution was published in the winter of 1999–2000 by Owen Harries, editor of the *National Interest,* often lauded as the conservatives' most influential foreign policy journal. Harries, however, dissented sharply from many conservatives and most neoconservatives.

He began with the important axiom that describes the two-century-old U.S. involvement with the Chinese: "over the years Americans have had great difficulty thinking rationally about China. They have tended to oscillate violently between romanticizing and demonizing that country and its people." Americans, Harries claimed, saw the Chinese not in accurate historical terms but through "stereotypes" such as "China as Treasure" (that is, bottomless markets), "China as Sick Patient" (thus badly needing U.S.-style democracy and Christianity), or "China as Threat—at one time Yellow Peril, at another Red Menace, and now, in the eyes of some very vocal and not uninfluential Americans, as rival, malevolent superpower." If China did become a truly great power, Harries warned, given these long-standing stereotypes—upon which Americans ignorant of history would depend to provide the necessary background for their foreign policies—"the chances of a cool, sensible American reaction cannot be rated particularly high."

Over the previous three decades (ironically, since the Vietnam War helped trigger the U.S.-China rapprochement in 1971), Harries concluded, the international behavior of China had become unexceptionable—to the extent that its critics have to put great emphasis on the occupation of one uninhabited reef in the Spratly Islands in the South China Sea, and have to ignore the awkward fact that in recent years China has used force in the pursuit of its foreign policy much less frequently than has the United States itself. (This does not prevent other serious people from using terms such as *appeasement* and *Munich* whenever a compromise with China over any issue is put forward. A suggestion: anyone resorting to the term *Munich* should be obliged to identify the Hitler actor—that is, the insatiable expansionist—in the situation under discussion.)[9]

The great problem, of course, for anyone who hoped to equate Chinese leaders with Hitler was that U.S. corporations were rushing headlong into China, flush pocketbooks at the ready, and even some American missionary enterprises were joining the invasion in the prayerful hope of increasing the number of Chinese Christians (currently about 70 million, around 5 percent of the population). Beijing welcomed most of the business invaders, especially as a mass exodus of hundreds of millions of rural Chinese to the burgeoning cities required the massive creation of jobs if officials, caught in the vortex of the greatest internal migration in history, hoped to avoid massive political unrest. Chinese authorities have long been highly sensitive to such unrest. Centuries of their history had been reshaped by it. Beijing officials knew that rural unrest, assisted by a fresh invasion of China during the 1890s by traders and missionaries, had helped produce the 1900 Boxer Rebellion. The rebellion climaxed with the imperial powers (including the United States and Japan) invading China to free the besieged diplomatic compound in Peking. The Boxer uprising and the invasion fatally undermined the Manchu dynasty, which had ruled the country for nearly three centuries. In 1911 the Manchus fell before the first onslaught of the Chinese Revolution.

Nothing has more preoccupied recent Chinese leadership than the history of periodic mass uprisings against the central authority. In the past several centuries, these uprisings have sometimes been spurred on by the dislocations and challenges inflicted by oblivious outsiders carrying checkbooks and Bibles. Their preoccupation with this history explains why Chinese officials placed the suppression of the 1989 democratic protests in Beijing, even though it had to be done with military force and untold loss of life, over the growing ties to the United States. It also explains why they have been brutal in trying to smash the anticommunist Falun Gong quasi-religious movement, a movement whose leader found sanctuary in the West.

All this—the moves against Taiwan and attempts by pro-democracy and anticommunist groups—brought sharp, if usually limited, reaction from the

United States between 1989 and 2001. But over those years, nothing slowed the rush of Western, especially U.S., capital into the fabled China market.

This rush was the major, long-term, and politically (as well as economically) powerful drive that weakened the repeated efforts by Wolfowitz and others to contain the buildup of the Chinese military. U.S. policy, both before and after 9/11, was therefore schizophrenic. The Zelig that to Washington officials appeared to be the new Soviet-type military threat (if not now, then in a decade or two) called for focusing on Beijing as, in Wolfowitz's words, "probably the single most serious foreign policy challenge of the coming decades." But Zelig also became, once again, the great China market sought by Americans since the 1780s and—more shockingly and suddenly— the world's cheapest producer, which attracted hundreds of billions of investment dollars.

Washington officials, both Democrats and liberals, but especially Republicans and conservatives (and neoconservatives), aimed at containing China, but at the same time they helped it surpass Great Britain and become by 2006 one of the world's top four economic powers—the kind of economic power that could be translated into military capability. This schizophrenic approach was, and is, a dangerous contradiction when set against Wolfowitz's claim, seconded by the Project for the New American Century, that China probably posed the greatest challenge to Americans. But having to deal with schizophrenia was the price to be paid when economic policy, backed by what became known as the highly potent New China Lobby of U.S. corporations, received greater priority than did the military containment of China.[10] During the Cold War, U.S. officials consistently had used both military buildups and economic denial to contain the Soviet Union. (A notable and instructive exception occurred when Nixon moved to buy off the Russians with economic lures in 1972–73. He was stopped by conservative Democrats, led by Senator Henry Jackson of Washington. Jackson was the godfather to influential neoconservatives, including Richard Perle, a widely known adviser to, and publicist for, the post-2001 Pentagon.)[11] But the consistent relationship between economic and military containment policies carried out toward the Soviets could never work toward China. The Russian Communist system was generally closed to foreign investors and, after the 1960s, stagnant, then declining. The Chinese Communist system was increasingly open to capitalists and booming. The Zelig of "China as Treasure," as Harries termed it, simply overwhelmed the Zelig of "China as Threat," regardless of how Wolfowitz, Vice President Richard Cheney, or others defined that threat.

This contradiction of U.S. policy framed the approach of the Bush administration's first eight months. Nothing was done to slow the economic drive. Indeed, China, with U.S. support, joined the World Trade Organization (WTO) in 2001. The WTO provided international rules, regulations, and frameworks for the rapidly spreading international trade and, in part, investment. Since their takeoffs in the 1960s and 1970s, these expanding economic trends had become known as globalization. This globalization, contrary to its nonspecific name, was not a project headed by the international community. It had been led by American corporations, which aimed at obtaining markets and production facilities, not least oil reserves. This business phalanx wanted to tear down tariff barriers and other forms of governmental obstruction so that trade and investment opportunities could be expanded and seized. Post-1960s globalization was the international counterpart of the post-1780s American frontier. International trade, and thus U.S. prosperity, leaped forward after the 1960s at a pace unrivaled in history.[12]

But the WTO demanded a high price for this capitalist advance, a price that punctured the possibility that the United States could discipline China through economic sanctions, as, indeed, Americans had tried to do from the 1950s through the 1970s. During the 1990s, Clinton had imposed tariffs to try to stop China's massive, illegal copying of popular American compact discs. After 2001, China's WTO membership restrained Bush from following Clinton's example. The WTO forced the Chinese to lower and then destroy many trade protectionist measures, but it also made illegal the unilateral imposition of economic sanctions against any of its membership, which now included China. The increasingly capitalist Chinese Zelig was helping protect the military Zelig against U.S. economic pressures.[13]

The economic realities limiting the power of U.S. officials to try to retaliate against China went further. The two economies had grown so close that any attempt to impose sanctions on Chinese production actually meant that the sanctions could hurt foreign-owned firms, especially the American, Taiwanese, and Japanese companies that spearheaded the investment drive into China. Japan and to a lesser extent Taiwan had been the most important U.S. allies in Asia since 1951. Sanctions would also harm American friends in other parts of Asia who sent mass shipments of parts (including those for communications technology) for final, cheap assembly in China. As one observer concluded, "That is why it's hard to conceive of a broad retaliation [against China] that doesn't ultimately come back to bite us."[14]

These new economic realities helped shape the U.S. response to the Bush administration's first crisis with China, in spring 2001. During the 2000 presidential campaign, Bush had termed China "a strategic competitor," a neoconservative phrase that indicated a much sharper anti-Chinese approach than Clinton's rhetoric and policies after 1996. The Project for a New American Century chimed in with the demand that the United States take a direct and unambiguous approach to protecting Taiwan. Throughout the 1980s and 1990s, U.S. officials had urged a peaceful settlement to the half-century-old question of whether China could once again annex Taiwan. (In 1894 a triumphant Japan had broken the link between the mainland and the island by taking over Taiwan, then known as Formosa, and had held it until 1945.) Since the time of Nixon, Washington had recognized "one China," as noted earlier, but had been deliberately vague about how the United States would respond if China tried to seize the island. Republicans, especially those from California, which had long been a source of strong pro-Taiwan feelings and investments, notably had pushed Bush to take an unambiguous anti-China position. During the early spring of 2001, the new president seemed to be following his policy.

In April 2001, a U.S. EP-3 reconnaissance plane, flying one of many American missions close to China's border, collided with a Chinese fighter plane that had been tailing it. The fighter crashed, and the pilot was never found. The EP-3 managed to land on China's Hainan Island and the twenty-four crew members were captured. A major crisis loomed as Chinese officials refused to pay attention to Washington's calls and demands, while conservative voices urged a get-tough policy. Led by Secretary of State Colin Powell, the Bush administration managed to work out wording about the United States being "very sorry" (not the full apology demanded by Beijing), and the crew was released. Conservatives and especially neoconservatives, led by William Kristol, blistered Powell and Bush for what they termed a "national humiliation." U.S.-China relations seemed well on the way to at least a mini–Cold War.[15]

Then came 9/11. As Bush embarked in October 2001 on a war in Afghanistan to destroy al-Qaeda terrorist bases, and then in March 2003 in Iraq to overthrow Saddam Hussein's regime, China slid down the U.S. priority list. This deemphasis of the Chinese did not mean, however, that they were ignored. To the contrary: as Bush's presidency moved well into its second term, the Chinese had become a major and unsettlingly effective opponent of the United States.

This growing opposition did not occur through military confrontations or even military threats. The intensified U.S.-China confrontation evolved because of Bush's determination to move into areas close to China, while the Chinese challenged (nonmilitarily) the United States directly in places peculiarly sensitive and important to Americans. Several brief case studies of Central Asia, China's creation of the Shanghai Cooperation Organization, the growing conflict over access to oil, and divisions over how to handle the growing nuclear power of Iran and Communist North Korea illustrated the differences between Washington and Beijing.

Most notable about this confrontation was how the old Zelig of China's military threat tended to fall out of sight, despite all the earlier neoconservative warnings about that military's intensifying danger. It was replaced by multiple Zeligs of China as a new center for Asian cooperation, as an economic danger to the United States (especially in all-important oil fields), and as a permanent member of the United Nations Security Council who could use its veto to stop U.S. initiatives.

In other words, as the Chinese threat became less military and more diplomatic/economic, the Bush administration grew less competent in dealing with the threat because the neoconservatives, who so largely shaped the administration's, and especially the president's, policy assumptions, had emphasized military power—not diplomatic or economic power—as the trump card in international politics. It so happened that this emphasis worked out nicely for Americans since their overwhelming military power supposedly gave them a firm grip on this trump card. The neoconservatives had developed it all neatly: since they assumed a nation's formal military power determined international affairs, and since the United States held by far the most formidable military power, it followed that Americans could control global affairs—if they only had the guts to commit that power. The neoconservatives would supply the guts and persuade less knowledgeable Americans to go along.

But the Chinese, and many others, refused to play such a game. Throughout the post-2001 years, while the United States initially displayed its military prowess in Afghanistan and Iraq (while making fun of "old Europe" for being too cowardly and politically paralyzed to join the supposedly slam-dunk, successful invasion of Iraq), China instead constructed a multifaceted diplomatic and economic offensive that had little to do with military strength. Since 1989, Americans, especially some conservatives and neoconservatives, had focused on Beijing's threat to Taiwan and (as Bush and his national security adviser, Condoleezza Rice, emphasized in 2000 and early 2001) the supreme importance of anti-missile defenses as a defense against Chinese nuclear weapons. Bush and his advisers failed to anticipate not only the extent of the non-state-based terrorism that changed their world on 9/11 but also, on quite another level, the range and success of the Chinese economic and diplomatic initiatives.[16]

Central Asia became a focal point for these initiatives, and not unnaturally, since it was geographically China's western neighbor. Politically, however, the Central Asian states had for nearly a century been part of the Soviet Union. As they declared independence during the 1990s, their oil wealth and access to pipelines needed to export that oil made three of the new nations—Kazakhstan, Uzbekistan, and Tajikistan—of special importance. U.S. petroleum companies had been active in staking claims to the reserves of the Caspian Sea area and Central Asia, and understandably so: the region supposedly held the world's second- or third-largest reserves of oil and natural gas. In 1999, Clinton quietly dispatched U.S. Green Beret special forces for the first time to the region. They camped in Uzbekistan, a dictatorship with a horrible human rights record, in part to track Islamic extremists, in part to plant an American presence near potential oil pipeline routes.[17]

For three years after 9/11, Uzbekistan became an all-important base for the U.S. invasion of neighboring Afghanistan. The American military presence proliferated throughout the region, and oil pipelines began to be built by U.S. interests to take the black gold out through Turkey or, indeed, any port other than those in Russia or Iran. The Chinese and Russians at first acquiesced in the American military buildup and its antiterrorism campaign. Involved with their terrorist threats (the Russians in their Islamic region of Chechnya, the Chinese against the Islamic Uighurs in the western reaches of the country), they wanted to run Islamic terrorists out of Afghanistan. By late 2002–3, however, the attitude of the Russians and Chinese changed. U.S. forces, it became clear, intended to establish permanent bases in the region. As Chinese oil consumption rocketed upward and petroleum grew valuable at twice the price of just several years before, American and European companies spread through the Caspian Sea region. With extensive control over Kazakhstan's oil riches, the Americans set up a pipeline into Turkey to export the liquid. Russia countered by renewing military ties, especially with Kazakhstan, the region's largest nation.

China conducted a multipronged response. Building on policies initiated in the 1990s, Beijing resolved border disputes with two neighbors, Kyrgyzstan and Tajikistan. This helped clear the way for massive Chinese investments, especially in Kazakhstan, the largest of the Central Asian nations, which, incidentally, also had the largest economy, with at least 1.7 billion barrels of oil reserves. The investments included Beijing's purchase of the leading Kazakh oil company, PetroKazakhstan, for nearly $5 billion. Another $700 million helped build a pipeline from the Kazakh oilfields to China. As the pipeline began to function in 2006, the Chinese became a major player for the region's huge oil reserves.[18] In 2004–5, the United States had protested Uzbekistan's increasing brutality against its own people, who went into the streets to protest corrupt electoral practices. This occurred as President Bush launched a major campaign to spread democracy through some highly non-democratic regions, especially in Central Asia and the Middle East. The Uzbek regime ordered the U.S. military base to close and expelled the Americans. Chinese officials quickly moved to cooperate economically and politically, including helping the Uzbeks develop their oil fields.

Beijing's moves in Central Asia were part of a larger offensive. On June 15, 2001, nearly three months before 9/11, China led in the creation of the Shanghai Cooperation Organization (SCO). The SCO was initially designed as a regional security group that would fight terrorism, religious extremism, and separatism. China, Russia, and four Central Asian nations (Kazakhstan, Kyrgyzstan, Tajikistan, and Uzbekistan) were the charter members. In its early years, the SCO indicated it had no plans to include new members. As the U.S. military and economic presence expanded in Central Asia and the Middle East, however, these plans changed. By 2005, India, Pakistan, Mongolia, and—of special significance—Iran had become "observer members." Iran joined as its differences with the United States, over both who was to control Iraq and whether the Iranians were to be allowed to develop a nuclear program, approached a crisis. The SCO, and especially China, carefully stated that the organization was not anti-American. But the SCO obviously worked against the U.S. military presence in Central Asia and tried to offset American oil interests while switching the movement of the region's petroleum riches eastward toward China. Indeed, in 2005, the SCO declared that "the anti-terrorist coalition" (that is, the United States) should set a schedule for pulling out all its military forces from Central Asia. On the economic side, SCO drafted a fifteen-year plan encompassing 127 joint projects, funded largely by China and aimed at integrating the SCO nations through highways, high-tech communications, and, of course, new pipelines.[19]

In the nineteenth century, one of the greatest of imperial stories was the ongoing conflict between Great Britain and Russia to see which would control Central Asia, coming to be prized for its oil potential as well for its strategic pathways leading to the British colonial jewel, India. The contest became known to fans of imperialism as "the Great Game." A century later, the game had resumed, only with the Americans taking the British role and the Chinese the Russian one. Given the rapidly growing value of oil, the stakes of the new game were considerably higher. And there was another, related confrontation developing. In 1949, Washington had led in the creation of the North Atlantic Treaty Organization (NATO), which brought in eleven European nations to ally with the United States against the Soviet Union. SCO was, at least in its first years, a nonmilitary version of NATO, only it included Russia and was aimed at the United States. By 2006, U.S.-led NATO forces operated in Afghanistan in an attempt to put down growing opposition to the post-invasion, Western-shaped government. The Chinese-led SCO was becoming an instrument to contain the presence and influence of NATO and its leader, the United States, in both Afghanistan and Central Asia.

Iran, the new SCO participant, became a flash point in U.S.-Chinese relations. The Americans and Iranians had no formal diplomatic relations after the 1979 revolution overthrew the pro-American shah. When the United States invaded Iraq in 2003, the Iranians (90 percent of whom are Shiite Muslims, as are 60 percent of Iraqis, with most of the remainder—like much of the Middle East—Sunni Muslim) became increasingly powerful in war-torn Iraq, especially as Iraq became not a proud American nation-building exercise but a bloody killing field. As Iranian-influenced Iraqi Shiites assumed leadership, the Iranians themselves began to move rapidly to develop nuclear energy—perhaps, Washington officials feared, nuclear weapons. When Bush indicated that economic sanctions should be imposed by the UN if Iran did not stop, China and Russia declared they would veto such a move. Both nations had extensive economic ties with Iran, and by 2004 neither was disturbed if the Iranian-supported Iraqi resistance bogged down the American military—an American military that once had been the lauded "unipolar power" but now was simply, and dangerously, far overstretched. China's leading Communist Party newspaper claimed that "the real intention" of U.S. policy aimed at "a regime change" in Iran. China (and Russia) was prepared to help the Iranians economically and in the UN.[20]

For a half century, and notably after the Soviet Union's collapse in 1991, the United States had been the dominant power in Asia, especially given the ongoing American-Japanese military alliance. During the late 1990s, the United States' hold began to slip as China moved to integrate Asian economies into its own. After 9/11, the pace quickened. By 2006, the Chinese had replaced the United States as the leading foreign economic power in Southeast and Northeast Asia, excluding Japan, and they were rapidly gaining on the Japanese economy. Americans began to appear militaristic, heavy-handed, and focused solely on anti-terrorism. "More and more, China is doing all the things the United States used to do: cooperating, pushing trade, offering help," declared an American-educated Thai businessman and former diplomat, Sarasin Viraphol. Washington "needs to do more than just talk about terrorism." Viraphol's home country had long been a friend of Americans. In late 2003, however, a poll revealed that 76 percent of Thais considered China their nation's closest friend, 9 percent chose the United States, and 8 percent Japan, still Thailand's number-one trading partner and source of foreign investment. In Indonesia, which once hated China so much that it banned Chinese writing, a Chinese firm became the nation's largest offshore oil producer. The company moved into an area once monopolized by Western oil companies.[21]

The Chinese economic offensive, including targeting access to oil, moved well beyond Asia into regions where the country's investors had seldom been seen, regions long dominated by American dollars. In 2004, China passed Japan to become the world's second-largest oil consumer, 6.5 million barrels a day. The United States consumed 20 million barrels daily. If the acceleration of automobile sales in China continued, by 2015 it could consume an estimated 14 million barrels each day. Since world oil production and refining capacity were already running at full tilt, it was not clear where those additional 7 million or so barrels of oil would come from each day. Saudi Arabia held the globe's largest oil reserves, and since at least 1945 it had worked closely with the United States. In early 2006, the king became the first Saudi ruler to visit China, in large part because after 2002 his nation's oil shipments to the United States had declined while they so increased to the Chinese that by 2005 Saudi Arabia was their leading source of oil. In regard to Iran, China signed a $100 billion contract to import 10 million tons of liquefied natural gas over twenty-five years, and in return took a 50 percent stake in a huge Iranian oil field—two reasons why Beijing demonstrated little interest in cooperating with Washington to sanction Iran's nuclear program.[22]

After 9/11, China sharply challenged U.S. power, both economic and military, in Asia and the Middle East. The challenge took its most surprising turn, however, in Latin America. Since at least the 1890s the United States considered Latin America to be its Monroe Doctrine–protected security zone, economic possession, oil provider, and backyard. During the 1980s, Washington had worked mightily, and militarily, to put down left-wing Central American revolts against oppressive military regimes. By the 1990s, the region turned toward U.S.-style globalization and freer trade, but the results were bitter: the rich grew richer and the poor poorer, and protests against Washington's pushing of democracy and more liberal trade grew louder. By 2005, a number of nations were choosing more nationalistic, anti-U.S. policies. Bush had entered office four years earlier pledging to open a new, better, and more cooperative era in U.S. relations with Latin America, but the terrorist attacks on New York and Washington seemed to push the southern continent into the memory hole of United States diplomacy. Populist governments—demonstrating little interest in the kind of freer-trade, easier-investment globalization urged by U.S. officials, business leaders, and writers—appeared in Venezuela and Bolivia, and sharply influenced the politics of other nations, including Ecuador, Peru, Brazil, and Mexico.

In 1999, former general Hugo Chávez assumed power in Venezuela, one of the world's leading oil producers. Following a populist line that attacked U.S. domination of Venezuelan oil exports, and which led him to become a friend of Cuba's Fidel Castro, by the post-9/11 years Chavez was looking to other Latin American leaders to help him map out a neutralist (that is, anti-Washington) set of policies. In 2004–5, top Chinese leaders visited Caracas and several other Latin American capitals to discuss a range of economic ventures, especially in oil. During 2004, President Hu Jintao pledged to invest over $100 billion in Latin America over ten years. He expressed special interest in oil, soybeans, and minerals. For a century, Chile's large copper exports had gone primarily to the United States, but now China replaced the United States as the top buyer. Similarly, Venezuelan oil pipelines and refineries had long been directed toward U.S. needs, and it would take years before the country's heavy crude could be redirected to Asian markets. But significant beginnings were made by the Chinese.[23]

In early 2006, U.S. officials sat down with their Chinese counterparts for the first time to have a secret, wide-ranging discussion of Latin American affairs. It was one of the more surprising events of the year. No U.S. leader before 2001 would have dreamed of negotiating with China (or, for that matter, nearly any other non–Western Hemisphere nation) about Latin America. Some of those earlier leaders, especially Theodore Roosevelt, had become highly popular as role models in the United States after 9/11 because of their belief in, and use of, unilateral U.S. military power, swaggering rhetoric, and expansion of American influence, notably into Latin America. At least eight major works on Roosevelt appeared between 2001 and 2006, and several approached or reached best-seller status. Roosevelt's popularity revealed the type of history many Americans repaired to in order to deal with their new crisis. But Roosevelt's career, especially as presented by most historians, was of little help in understanding developments in Chinese–Latin American relations—unless the readers understood that many people to the south were mobilizing to oppose Roosevelt's type of policies toward Latin America. Roosevelt had not thought the Chinese worthy of any serious diplomatic discussion. He considered them too weak militarily and too fixed upon the illusion of their own significance. As Roosevelt indicated in 1904 with his Roosevelt Corollary to the Monroe Doctrine, he viewed Latin America as largely a U.S. sphere. By President George W. Bush's second term, the Chinese, of all people, were invading that sphere.[24]

Another major reason for Americans and Chinese to enter into talks, in this case multiyear negotiations, was to deal with the growing threat of a North Korean nuclear weapon. In 1994, the United States and the North Korean Communist dictatorship had worked out a deal whereby the Koreans would stop working on the weapons and Americans would provide significant economic aid. By 2001, the arrangement had collapsed. The next year, President Bush famously included Kim Jong Il's dictatorship with the Iraqis and Iranians as the "axis of evil." Bush invaded Iraq a year later. Within months, the North Koreans indicated they would try to escape Iraq's fate by accelerating work on nuclear weapons. Kim declared he would stop only after the United States guaranteed not to threaten North Korea. Bush refused. Believing he was being blackmailed, and bogged down in Iraq, the president committed the United States to six-power talks whose key member was China, the nation closest to North Korea geographically and economically.

When negotiations broke down in 2005, Bush was prepared to impose sanctions against the North Koreas. The Chinese, backed by the Russians and South Koreans, objected; they blocked the president's move. North Korea's economy was one of the world's worst. China and South Korea feared a North Korean nuclear weapon, but more immediately they were terrified that the pressure of sanctions would cause a collapse of the country's economy and quickly lead to millions of North Koreans pouring across the Chinese and South Korean borders. In 2006, Kim tested rockets capable of carrying nuclear weapons, including one missile that theoretically could reach U.S. soil. But the world response was remarkably long on rhetoric and short on action. The Chinese success in not allowing Bush to pressure North Korea made Beijing, not Washington, the major player in the ongoing crisis.[25]

In none of these regions—Central Asia, the Middle East, Latin America, Northeast Asia, or Africa (where Chinese oil purchases and influence spread)—was Beijing's military a major player. The United States Defense Department issued its regular warnings about China's buildup, and indeed the Chinese navy was, finally, developing, but it was building on a small base, especially compared with the United States or even Japanese fleets, which dominated the seas around China. In any case, Beijing officials clearly stated after 2002–3, when the new Communist leadership of President Hu Jintao assumed power, that their primary goal was to stabilize China in the face of its soaring economy and the massive movement of its people from rural areas to cities. Chinese policies in Central Asia, the Middle East, and elsewhere moved from this determination to prevent massive protests, a move designed to short-circuit another type of Boxer Rebellion and its aftermath, which had brought down China's dynastic rulers. U.S. experts noted that Chinese economic policies consumed half the world's concrete production, a quarter of its steel production, and 40 percent of its coal output, while U.S. companies fought vastly higher oil and raw material prices, forced upward in large measure by China's demand. Hundreds of millions of Chinese laborers meanwhile drove down the price of the globe's finished goods and, by the end of President Bush's first term, played a major role in destroying more than an estimated 2 million U.S. manufacturing jobs.[26]

The Bush administration continued to focus on the Chinese military threat.[27] Not everyone agreed. In 2003, the prestigious New York Council on Foreign Relations created a distinguished task force, chaired by former secretary of defense Harold Brown, and charged it with examining the evolution of China's armed forces. The examination concluded that if the present rate of U.S. and Japanese resources continued to be devoted to their military establishments, "the balance between the United States and China, both globally and in Asia, is likely to remain decisively in America's favor beyond the next twenty years."[28] Meanwhile, as Washington officials concentrated on costly, intensifying wars in the Middle East and, increasingly, Afghanistan and Africa, they hoped world markets, globalization, and U.S. oil companies would somehow be able to work out the growing economic dilemmas largely on their own. As these officials simply hoped for the best, the Chinese Zelig continued to assume various forms for Americans, few of which the Americans seemed to understand.

12

Counterinsurgency, Now and Forever

MARILYN B. YOUNG

We weren't on the wrong side. We were *the wrong side.*
—Daniel Ellsberg, "Hearts and Minds," 1974

I am an American fighting man, and I have no
idea what the hell I'm shooting at. Or why.
—Christian Bauman, *The Ice Beneath You,* 2002

So you have a country that wants us out of there,
and we've become the enemy. We are the target.
—Representative John Murtha, *The NewsHour with Jim Lehrer,*
November 17, 2005

Over there, when we would do a patrol and have a car approach
us and we fired warning shots, that's a thrill, that's power.
Over there, everybody knew we were there. We were the king
of the road, and they either respected or hated us for it.
And now you're back here, and you ain't king of nothing.
—Ron Radaker, Alpha Company, 112th Regiment,
Pennsylvania National Guard[1]

The United States has had a long history of fighting small, dirty wars, though most Americans prefer to focus on the good war it fought in the middle of the last century, World War II. The suppression of the insurgency in the Philippines at the turn of the twentieth century was soon forgotten; pacification and counterinsurgency in the Korean War were rarely reported on at the time, and not much discussed by American historians thereafter; covert and overt subversion of governments in Latin America, the Middle East, and Africa were accomplished largely through the use of local military forces.[2]

Thus, the ambiguities of the Vietnam War came as a surprise.[3] The beginning, however one wishes to date it, was unproblematic for most Americans. Insofar as anyone noticed, the United States had come to the aid of an ally struggling against internal Communist subversion and external Communist aggression. Military advisers were dispatched; counterinsurgent special forces units were equipped, trained, named, and honored in song and film; and for a number of years public anxieties focused on the menace ninety miles off the coast of Florida. As Vietnam rose to public consciousness, there was an uneasiness about what exactly the United States was doing there. In a television documentary made a year before combat troops were officially dispatched to Vietnam, reporters worried that "in trying to kill a handful of Viet Cong in a village, why we've made at least a hundred recruits by indiscriminate bombing or strafing."[4] The point was made again in March 1965 when a CBS reporter, Morley Safer, witnessed the torching of the village of Cam Ne. "The day's operation, burned down 150 houses, wounded three women, killed one baby, wounded one marine and netted [pointing to them] these four prisoners. Four old men who could not answer questions put to them in English. Four old men who had no idea what an I.D. card was." Safer assured his audience that the United States could win a military victory in Vietnam—in 1965 few doubted it, but he went on, "to a Vietnamese peasant whose home is a—means a lifetime of backbreaking labor—it will take more than presidential promises to convince him that we are on his side."[5]

Convincing peasants that the United States was on their side was one aspect of counterinsurgency, and counterinsurgency greatly interested President Kennedy and his advisers. Proud of their knowledge of how the enemy operated—not necessarily the Vietnamese, but any enemy—they quoted Mao: the guerrilla is a fish swimming in the ocean of the people. Dry up the ocean and the problem is solved. No one paused for very long over the metaphor: what, after all, would it mean to dry up the ocean?

Over the course of the long war, there were many approaches to counterinsurgency: the strategic hamlet program (emptying villages into guarded encampments on the British colonial model in Malaya); poisoning the rice crop in areas in which the guerrillas were known to operate so as deny them food and transform farmers into refugees unable to plant new crops; eliminating, through assassination, the "infrastructure"—local village-level cadres; saturation bombing and the generation of more refugees; creating small, skilled special forces units that could move through the jungle, as silent and deadly as the guerrillas themselves; designated free-fire zones in which anything living was presumed hostile; training village-level troops for self-defense; "clear and hold" or the "oil-spot" strategy—establishing security and legitimacy one village at a time and slowly expanding the area of control; winning hearts and minds through countrywide land reform, rural medical clinics, and rural education.[6]

However contradictory, many of these approaches were employed simultaneously, though the more ambitious countrywide reform programs were initiated only in the ninth or tenth year of the war. In 1967, counterinsurgency programs were brought together under one unified command, a move strongly urged on the Bush administration by military and civilian devotees of counterinsurgency. Civilian Operations and Revolutionary Development Support (CORDS) was initially run by Robert "Blowtorch Bob" Komer, a man who cherished his reputation for volatility. Komer believed wholeheartedly in the importance of combining political and military warfare on the model of successful guerrillas everywhere. In the idiom of the twenty-first century, the United States had to learn not just to fight asymmetric wars but to fight them as if *it* were the weaker party. (This fantasy was played out after the Vietnam War in *Rambo* and other Hollywood movies in which the Americans fought as poorly armed guerrillas against Vietnamese with immense firepower at their command.)

Komer's goal was to contest the National Liberation Front (NLF) for control in every village and hamlet in South Vietnam through a flexible mix of welfare and security projects under the supervision of a revolutionary development team that would remain in place for up to six months. In addition, a vastly expanded number of trained and well-equipped rural paramilitary forces, drawn from the villages themselves, would provide overall security. Komer also insisted that deep intelligence would be necessary to root out the village-level cadres upon whose efforts the insurgency rested.

Thus, in 1967, the Phoenix (Phung Hoang) program developed out of earlier counterterrorist projects run by the Central Intelligence Agency. Mixed Vietnamese and American teams were set a quota of basic-level NLF cadres to be "neutralized" each month—and they delivered. The numbers were impressive: from 1968 to mid-1971, 28,000 "Viet Cong infrastructures" (VCIs) were captured, 20,000 were killed, and an additional 17,000 defected. Torture, corruption, and extortion marked the program from the outset, and it was never very clear exactly whom was being killed. Nevertheless, Komer was delighted. The figures on hamlet evaluation showed that the number of secure villages had improved markedly. At a Saigon dinner party, Komer told reporters "he had assured the President that the war would not be an election issue in 1968."[7] And then came Tet.

Throughout the war, the counterinsurgency experts were convinced that military security had to be established before any meaningful effort to win the allegiance of the population could take place. Rooting out the VCIs was a part of that effort. Obviously, there was a risk that establishing military security might involve alienating the population whose hearts and minds were waiting to be won; war is a risky business.

Later, long after the war was lost, some analysts insisted that had the United States fought a proper counterinsurgency war, rather than the war of attrition General Westmoreland pursued, it could have won.[8] Others argued that it had, in fact, fought such a war and won—only to be robbed of victory by Congress. As David Elliott explains elsewhere in this volume, these arguments deal with "the troubling Vietnam experience by historical revisionism, turning failure into remembered success." Vietnam is the negative example for almost everything connected to American war making, and this for pro- and antiwar people alike. On the other hand, many analysts consider counterinsurgency in El Salvador the positive example. There, it is said, an insurgency was defeated by a U.S.-trained and -equipped indigenous force with the help and support of a strictly limited number of American advisers. In El Salvador, the lessons of counterinsurgency, or what one of its students and practitioners has called "total war at the grassroots level," had at last been mastered. Not firepower but local knowledge and civic action was necessary—a combination of the political and military any revolutionary movement might envy.[9]

But the insurgency in El Salvador was not defeated, and the government did not win. Unlike Iraq, the insurgency in El Salvador was class-based. Unlike Vietnam, where the Saigon government refused to negotiate with the NLF to the bitter end, when the Salvadoran government realized it could not crush the insurgency outright, it negotiated its way out. According to Elisabeth Jean Wood's analysis of the Salvadoran settlement, "Once unyielding elites . . . conceded democracy because popular insurgency, although containable militarily, could not be ended, and the persisting mobilization eventually made compromise preferable to continued resistance."[10] In effect, a legitimate regime was constructed through negotiations between a coherent insurgency and a reasonably unified elite, negotiations in which the government as well as the insurgents made key concessions in return for peace. Nothing resembling this process appears likely in Iraq, where the insurgency has no known central leadership and such elite unity as exists has been steadily eroded by sectarian violence.

At the time of this writing, as the increasing violence of heavily armed police and militia units approximates open civil war in Iraq, the embrace of El Salvador as a model has virtually disappeared from the press.[11] But in 2005, the El Salvador model was hailed as the solution to Iraq's counterinsurgency problems. "The template for Iraq today is not Vietnam . . . but El Salvador," Peter Maass wrote in an essay with the rhetorical title "The Salvadorization of Iraq?" None of the people with whom Maass spoke, nor Maass himself, reflected on the differences between Iraq and El Salvador: one a country under occupation, where the United States is fighting an insurgency seeking to end that occupation, the other a country where a government fought a war against a rural revolution. What mattered instead was the form: how to train and equip an effective indigenous paramilitary force. "The strategic thought that we had," Douglas Feith explained, "is that we are going to get into very big trouble in Iraq if we are viewed as our enemies would have us viewed. As imperialists, as heavy-handed and stealing their resources." Iraqis must take on the burden of crushing resistance to the occupation.[12]

Civilian efforts to train an effective police force failed, though DynCorp, under contract to recruit police trainers, charged the government $50 million each month for its services; in the spring of 2004, the military took over. In the same period, the Iraqi minister of the interior under Ayad Allawi, Falah al-Naqib, in consultation with his senior U.S. adviser, Steve Casteel, organized a Special Police Commando unit that drew its manpower from Saddam Hussein's elite forces.[13] When the unit was in reasonably good shape, Casteel, a veteran of the U.S. drug wars in Latin America, together with James Steele, a veteran of the special forces in El Salvador, invited the general in charge of organizing the Iraqi police force, David Petraeus, to visit their headquarters. Petraeus tested the mettle of several of the commandos by challenging them to a push-up contest. Presumably satisfied with their prowess, he offered them "whatever arms, ammunition and supplies they required."[14] The force was largely Sunni, but Peter Maass, after spending a week with them, believed their "true loyalties . . . remain unclear." Steele and Casteel were indifferent to the fact that the commando unit was dominated by Sunnis trained, in another life, by Saddam Hussein. What had mattered in El Salvador, what Steele and Casteel believed would matter in Iraq, was a readiness to inflict maximum violence against the insurgency, anyone who might be associated with it, even remotely, and anyone who failed to inform against it.

The Sunni-dominated city of Samarra, Peter Maass reported, was to be the "proving ground" for the new El Salvador–model strategy. Maass visited the commandos there in March 2005. He watched as a hundred bound and blindfolded prisoners were slapped and kicked as they awaited interrogation. The interrogation room itself had a desk "with bloodstains running down its side." As the reporter was questioning a young Saudi prisoner about his treatment by his captors, he could hear the screams of a man being tortured next door. An American adviser with the commandos commented that he didn't think Iraqis "know the value of human life Americans have."[15]

In due course, the Special Police Commandos handed Samarra off to regular Iraqi police. By the summer of 2005, Major Patrick Walsh told a reporter, the city was once again becoming a "neutral-to-bad-news story." In August 2005 U.S. Army engineers built an earthen barricade over eight feet high and six and a half miles long around the city (Operation Great Wall). Three checkpoints controlled all traffic into and out of town, and the number of insurgent attacks subsided. To persuade Samarra's population of 200,000 to "cooperate or we'll clear the city," Walsh spread the rumor that a major offensive was about to begin. In response, over half the population fled, along with half the police force. There was a marked reduction in insurgent attacks—and in city life. As the U.S. troops withdrew, an American observer thought the remaining Iraqi police force, barricaded in their Green Zone and temporarily reinforced by the return of the Special Police Commandos, might be able to defend themselves, though over half of them rarely showed up for work.[16]

The Special Police Commando unit Maass visited was Sunni-led; other militias—the Mahdi Army, the Badr Corps—were affiliated with Shiite political parties. Naqib resigned as minister of defense in April 2005 and his successor, Bayan Jabr, at once moved to recruit a large number of Shiite police commandos. James Steele, though without regrets for his role in training the first commando units, worried about the growing sectarian violence: "That is more dangerous in terms of our strategic success than the insurgency," he told a reporter. "If this thing deteriorates into an all-out civil war our position becomes untenable. Who the hell are you fighting?"[17]

The problem, according to Colonel John Waghelstein, who served two tours in Vietnam and five in Central America, is that the military persisted in distinguishing between principles of "traditional war" and "those of counterinsurgency (COIN), as if conflicts on the lower end of the spectrum are aberrations" when history "clearly shows that most U.S. wars were at the spectrum's lower end."[18] A senior Pentagon official told Robert Kaplan: "After Iraq, we hope not to be invading a big country for a long time, so we'll be reduced to low profile raiding, which the military has a very long and venerable tradition of, from the 19th and early 20th centuries." These are the "savage wars of peace" Max Boot finds so attractive, and that Kaplan's "imperial grunts" look forward to fighting.[19]

There has been a chorus of complaints against the military for its reluctance to make counterinsurgency central to its mission, for dropping counterinsurgency courses and training from service academy curricula the instant a counterinsurgent conflict has concluded, for always taking "big war" as its central mission until the next time.[20] Bruce Hoffman, a Rand analyst, compared the military's experience of counterinsurgency to Bill Murray's eternal Groundhog Day. "But," Hoffman wrote, "whereas Murray eventually attains enlightenment, a similarly decisive epiphany has yet to occur with respect to American's historical ambivalence towards counterinsurgency."[21]

In response to the criticism, courses on counterinsurgency have returned to the service academies' curricula and there has been an increased emphasis on how to fight a guerrilla war. But the division between those who wish to hone the U.S. military for more wars like Vietnam and Iraq (or the subset of El Salvador and Guatemala) and those who prefer full-scale conventional warfare on the model of Gulf War I is significant. Buried in the discussion about tactics is a larger question: what sort of wars *should* the United States be fighting?

The simple principles of counterintersurgency have been summarized in a short essay for the *Military Review* by one senior political scientist and three lieutenant colonels, Eliot Cohen, Lieutenant Colonel Conrad Crane (Ret.), Lieutenant Colonel Jan Horvath, and Lieutenant Colonel John Nagl. The authors lay down a set of necessary conditions that must be fulfilled in order to defeat an insurgency. Many of these conditions would seem to be beyond the capacity of the U.S. military to implement.[22] Thus, the first principle is the establishment of a legitimate government. Legitimacy consists of free and fair "selection" of leaders, popular participation in politics, a "low level" of corruption, "a culturally acceptable level or rate of political, economic, and social development," and a "high level of regime support from major social institutions."[23] The authors do not tell us how a foreign power can confer legitimacy on another country's government. Indeed, the contradiction seems ab initio and insurmountable—unless you ignore it, as Cohen, Crane, Horvath, and Nagl do. The authors urge attention to politics, deep knowledge of the host country and its history and demographics, support for the rule of law, and a long-term commitment to the task. "The insurgent wins," they warn, "if he does not lose. The counterinsurgent loses if he does not win."[24]

Cohen and colleagues amplify the standard lessons of counterinsurgency. Americans, with their reputation for efficiency, must avoid promising more than they can deliver; expectations must be managed. "Managing expectations," they explain, "also involves showing economic and political progress as part of the campaign to show the populace how life is improving." But, one might wonder, if people's lives *are* improving, why is expectation management necessary? The authors recommend using the "minimum possible force" but add that at times, "to intimidate an opponent or to reassure the populace," "an overwhelming effort" may be required.[25]

Yet intimidating the enemy may not always reassure the population. While he was on duty in Iraq in December, 2003, Nagl's unit rushed to establish a perimeter around an Iraqi police station that had been blown up by insurgents, killing twenty-four policemen and two passersby. Rather than being reassured at this show of force, the mother of one of the dead policemen shouted imprecations not at the insurgents but at the American troops. Later that day, first one and then another procession passed by the station on their way to the cemetery. The second group, of over a thousand people, seemed especially angry, shouting at the troops and throwing rocks. Had they turned more actively threatening, Nagl would have ordered his troops to open fire.[26]

The authors go on to urge a more decentralized approach to fighting insurgencies: "higher commanders owe it to their subordinates to push as many capabilities as possible down to lower levels." Local commanders are likely to understand the immediate situation best and should have the necessary resources to act on their own. At the same time, American troops "must remember that they are conducing COIN operations to help a host government."[27]

They then list a set of "paradoxes of counterinsurgency," for example, "the more you protect your force, the less secure you are." Military forces that stay locked up in compounds "lose touch with the people." So U.S. troops "must conduct patrols, share risk, and maintain contact to obtain the intelligence to drive operations and to reinforce the connections with the people who establish legitimacy."[28] Perhaps.

The Marines in Kilo Company, for example, did not stay locked up in their compound outside of Haditha. Kilo's Lieutenant Colonel Nathan Sassaman got out and around among the people.[29] Sassaman, according to Dexter Filkins, had "distinguished himself as one of the nimblest, most aggressive officers in Iraq," embodying "not just the highly trained, highly educated officer corps . . . but also the promise of the American enterprise itself."[30] He is said to have had warm and friendly relations with the locals in the Shiite city of Balad, in which he was stationed. Although Sassaman had had no training in nation building or guerrilla war, "he had quickly figured out what he needed to do: remake the area's shattered institutions, jumpstart the economy and implant a democracy." Sassaman's power in Balad was absolute. "He could chart the future of a city, lock up anyone he wanted and, if trouble arose, call in an air strike." He was, in his own words, "the warrior king."[31]

While his relations with the Shiite community were good, his dealings with surrounding Sunni villages were less cordial.[32] In October 2003, as the insurgency gained strength, then Major General Raymond Odierno ordered the 4th Infantry Division to "increase lethality." Sassaman was apparently eager to comply: "When [he] spoke of sending his soldiers into Samarra, his eyes gleamed. 'We are going to inflict extreme violence.'"[33] As the insurgency intensified, so did Sassaman's reprisals. In November, after one of his men had been hit by a rocket-propelled grenade fired in the vicinity of the village of Abu Hishma, Sassaman, with the permission of his immediate superior, Colonel Frederick Rudesheim, wrapped the village in barbed wire, issued ID cards (in English), and threatened to kill anyone who tried to enter or leave without permission. In his own limited way, Sassaman used U.S. firepower as it had been used in Vietnam. In response to a single mortar round, Dexter Filkins reported, he fired "28 155-millimeter artillery shells and 42 mortar rounds. He called in two air strikes, one with a 500-pound bomb and the other with a 2,000-pound bomb." When his troops were fired on from a wheat field, Sassaman "routinely retaliated by firing phosphorus shells to burn the entire field down." Elsewhere in Iraq, the use of phosphorus shells was referred to as a "shake and bake" mission.[34]

The results of these efforts pleased Sassaman: "We just didn't get hit after that." He did not describe, and the reporter did not ask about, the effect on the human targets. Over and over again, Sassaman met resistance of any kind with massive force, and taught his men to do likewise. Like the Vietnamese, the Iraqis, according to Sassaman and the troops under his command, understood only the language of force. In any event, it was the only language any of the Americans spoke other than English.[35] Over the course of their tour, the men under Sassaman's command became increasingly punitive toward the Iraqis around them—any Iraqi, all Iraqis. When a shopkeeper gave passing troops the finger, they doubled back, searched his shop, drove him to a bridge over the Tigris, and threw him in. "The next time I went back, the guy is out there waving to us," a soldier told Dexter Filkins. "Everybody got a chuckle out of that."[36]

Sassaman's fall from grace followed his cover-up of the drowning of an Iraqi civilian by soldiers under his command. Two men whose truck had broken down as they raced to reach home before the 11 P.M. curfew had almost made it when they were stopped by American troops. They were searched, questioned, and waved on, only to be stopped again, handcuffed, driven to a point ten feet above the Tigris, uncuffed, and ordered to jump. The men begged not to be thrown into the river and indeed clung to the legs of the soldiers who, at gunpoint, pushed one of them in; the other jumped after him. Later, the soldiers claimed they had watched to make sure the men were okay—defined as "doing good treading water"—before taking off. One of the Iraqis, Marwan Fadhil, survived. His cousin Zaydoon did not. Their truck, Marwan reported, was where he'd left it—but the Americans had smashed it before going back to base.[37]

When Sassaman learned an investigation into the death would take place, he decided that "throwing Iraqis into the Tigris was wrong but not criminal" and that drawing attention to it would "whip up anti-American feeling." On these grounds he initially decided to cover the incident up entirely. Later, Sassaman testified forcefully in defense of the two men held directly responsible for Zaydoon's death. It had been a mistake, he insisted, a "bad call." The soldiers were sentenced to six months and forty-five days, respectively; Sassaman was reprimanded and shortly thereafter decided to retire from the military.

Filkins's account of Sassaman's fall from grace was, on the whole, sympathetic to the dilemmas the officer and his troops faced. After all, Filkins asked, "how much more serious was it to throw an Iraqi civilian into the Tigris, which was not approved, than it was to, say, fire an antitank missile into an Iraqi civilian's home, which was?" Where was the line between a justifiable use of nonlethal force and a criminal one? Like Andrew Krepinevich and Max Boot, Filkins stressed the lack of counterinsurgency training for both officers and the men they commanded. Toward the end of his essay, Filkins wrote that nearly "every major counterinsurgency in the 20th century [had] failed," leaving the armies that had fought them—the Americans in Vietnam, the French in Algeria, the Soviets in Afghanistan—utterly demoralized by the experience. But he took no direct issue with the current passion for counterinsurgency. Rather than question the advisability of entering into such conflicts, the response of the military—and of the media—has been an attempt to focus once more on counterinsurgency.

In their discussion of the principles and paradoxes of counterinsurgency, Cohen and his colleagues caution against the excessive use of force, which increases the possibility of "collateral damage" and the likelihood that enemy propaganda "will portray kinetic military activities as brutal." The problem, acknowledged but not addressed, is that "kinetic" military activities are inherently brutal. The remaining paradoxes discussed are predictable: the best counterinsurgent weapons are not guns but "gaining popular support and legitimacy for the host government," that it's better for the host government to do something poorly than for the United States to do it well, that insurgents constantly change tactics and counterinsurgents must adapt, and finally that "tactical success guarantees nothing."

The essay ends with the authors' own lesson from Vietnam. After that war, the military "responded to the threat of irregular warfare chiefly by saying 'never again.'" The result has been an army unprepared to fight insurgencies. "Our enemies are fighting us as insurgents because they think insurgency is their best chance for victory. We must prove them wrong." The authors ignore the possibility that insurgents fight the United States as insurgents because they have no other choice, rather than because they decide to leave behind their aircraft carriers, precision bombers, drones, B-52s, and attack helicopters.

On the ground in Iraq, the military is divided. In one part of the country, troops are being concentrated in huge bases far from contested urban or rural areas. The move will "force Iraqis to take up the burden of fighting the insurgency" and reduce the resentment caused by U.S. troop patrols.[38] Getting U.S. troops off the streets would seem like a good idea; having them sitting tight inside a number of Green Zones should make for easy total withdrawal when the day comes. Meanwhile, the enormous "enduring bases" will remain.

Those enamored of counterinsurgency obviously oppose such moves. "The key to counterinsurgency is presence among the population," said Kalev Sepp, a naval analyst of counterinsurgency. What's the good of hiding the troops on big bases? Instead, troops should move out into the villages of contested provinces such as Anbar. There aren't enough troops to move into every village. "But we'll continue to contest every town and village," Colonel W. Blake Crowe told a reporter. "We just need to contest them."[39] The approach is based on what supporters believe to have been the great success achieved by U.S. troops in 2005 in the village of Tall Afar. I have written elsewhere about the success story the Bush administration has constructed out of the uncertain state of this small town. It is enough to note here that the pacification of Tall Afar in 2005 began to come undone only a short time after its success was celebrated. Even if it means a longer period of Iraqi dependency, those committed to counterinsurgency, such as Conrad Crane, insist that U.S. troops must "immerse [themselves] in the lives of the people."[40] Although some officials believe—or hope—the two strategies can coexist, "critics consider it a choice between a smaller force and an effective one."

In July 2004, the Marines attacked the city of Ramadi. And again in February 2005. And again in June 2006. This last time, instead of a frontal assault, a "softer and more deliberate approach" was used. Instead of destroying the city wholesale, as in Fallujah in 2004, in Ramadi two years later American and Iraqi troops surrounded the city and moved through it, neighborhood by neighborhood. More American troops than Iraqi, however, as a very large number of Iraqis refused to leave their base, because, they said, "we don't want [to] fight our own people." It is, a reporter observes, a serious problem "to ask Iraqis to fight other Iraqis."[41]

The reporter's description of the city makes it hard to believe Ramadi represents a "softer" approach: "Whole city blocks here look like a scene from some post-apocaplyptic world: row after row of buildings shot up, boarded up, caved in, tumbled down." This time the Americans would not leave after the job was done, but would instead establish garrisons at various points in the city. This involved a certain degree of displacement of the local population. Some fifty civilians were told to "gather their things and go— where to was not clear." With the sort of deep knowledge of the country counterinsurgency experts hope to instill in all U.S. troops, they "assumed that the local Iraqis, in this land linked by bloodlines, would be able to flee to their relatives. They promised compensation."[42]

The city of Ramadi poses, in concentrated form, the problem of counterinsurgency in Iraq. Central Ramadi is being razed to the ground and in its place the Marines are erecting another Green Zone inside which the Americans and Iraqi government officials can be, relatively speaking, safe. The approach sounds like "clear and hold," the winning tactic that, according to Lewis Sorley, General Creighton Abrams initiated in Vietnam, replacing Westmoreland's disastrous "search and destroy" operations. The idea in Vietnam was that slowly but surely the areas cleared of guerrillas and held by the government would expand until the entire country was secure. Yet it is difficult to see how a Ramadi Green Zone can expand in any direction. Even the Green Zone in Baghdad has severe problems. A confidential memo from Ambassador Zalmay Khalilzad to Secretary of State Condoleezza Rice in early June 2006 suggested that the extraordinary pressure on Iraqis outside the zone had endangered the "objectivity, civility and logic that make for a functional workplace." No doubt remembering iconic photographs of the last days of the U.S. embassy in Saigon, the memo noted that some staff members had asked embassy staff "what provisions would we make for them if we evacuate."[43]

According to Dexter Filkins, the *New York Times* reporter accompanying the troops in Ramadi, the Marines "seem far less aggressive than they were during their earlier tours here, when the priority was killing insurgents. Now they seem much more interested in capturing the loyalty of the residents." Yet posters adorning the fortified Government Center in which the Marines are headquartered read: "Be polite, be professional and have a plan to kill everyone you meet." Suggestions for one company's T-shirts include: "Kilo Company: Killed more people than cancer."[44]

The return of counterinsurgency, the longing on the part of its devotees to do it right this time, and the insistence that counterinsurgency and only counterinsurgency can win the wars the U.S. needs and wants to fight in the future are disheartening. Nowhere did the authors whose reports I read question the mission itself. Nor, beyond the observation that insurgents gained when governments failed to attain legitimacy, did I find any serious discussion of why people joined a particular insurgency. Indeed, particularity did not seem to matter. Bruce Hoffman, the Rand expert, believes the "population will give its allegiance to the side that will best protect it." He quotes Charles Simpson, a former Green Beret in Vietnam, with approval: "Peasants will support [the guerrillas] . . . if they are convinced that the failure to do so will result in death or brutal punishment." Contemporary Rand studies showed, on the contrary, that in Vietnam the NLF had "easily won the psychological war for hearts and minds." The only option left to the United States was to turn the population into refugees with little choice and terrorize those who remained in the countryside.[45]

According to General John Abizaid, commander of U.S. Central Command, the insurgency in Iraq is a "classical guerrilla-type campaign." Some analysts have begun to examine the insurgency in Iraq as a particular case rather than a general one, and they disagree. Bruce Hoffman concludes his essay on counterinsurgency with the observation that in contrast to classic insurgencies, this one "has no clear leader (or leadership); no attempt to seize and actually hold territory; and no single, defined or unified ideology."[46] Instead, the insurgency consists of "small groups who communicate, coordinate, and conduct campaigns in an internetted manner, without a precise central command."[47] Hoffman suggests the conflict in Iraq "may represent a new form of warfare for a new, networked century," a kind of "postmodern insurgency." He has no suggestions as to how the United States should fight it.[48]

Stephen Biddle, a senior fellow in defense policy at the Council on Foreign Relations, is also convinced that the insurgency in Iraq bears little resemblance to past insurgencies. In an essay written in the spring of 2006, Biddle argues that in Iraq, the model is not a Maoist-style people's war but rather a Bosnia/Kosovo/Rwanda-style communal civil war. In such wars, the fight "is about group survival, not about the superiority of one party's ideology or one side's ability to deliver better governance."[49] Therefore the counterinsurgency tactics of Vietnam and El Salvador are equally irrelevant. Neither "hearts and minds" nor close cooperation with a national army have anything to offer the United States in Iraq. Indeed, unthinking strengthening of a "national army" that is in fact dominated by one sect can only make things worse.

Unlike Hoffman, Biddle offers an alternative: the United States must manipulate the military situation so as to force all sides to cooperate. Such manipulation might include, for example, threatening to arm the Shiite/Kurdish-dominated security forces with heavy firepower—tanks, attack helicopters, artillery. This would "increase dramatically—and very visibly" the capacity of the security forces to "commit mass violence against the Sunnis." Under threat of such dire punishment, the Sunni insurgency would be moved toward negotiation. Or if it's the Shiites and Kurds who aren't cooperating, the United States could threaten to withdraw its support and arm the Sunnis instead. These threats would be combined with a promise that U.S. troops would stay "as long as would be necessary to protect the parties who cooperate."[50] Biddle's confidence that U.S. military threats would bring compliance is puzzling. What if one side or the other called Biddle's bluff? Would the United States really supply either side with weapons that could make the war more violent?

Larry Diamond, who worked with Paul Bremer in the Coalition Provisional Authority in 2004, is the most trenchant of Biddle's critics. In a summer 2006 roundtable forum for *Foreign Affairs* that included Biddle, among others, Diamond agreed that Iraqification, on the model of Vietnamization, had been a disaster, exacerbating sectarian conflict at every turn. But he argued as well that for many Iraqis, the insurgency was a war of resistance against a foreign occupation and its quisling government. The military manipulations on which Biddle counted could be readily dealt with, and in the case of some Shiite groups, U.S. withdrawal would be welcomed rather than viewed as a threat. Most important, however, is what Biddle left out of his account. Diamond describes the efforts that have been made by a "significant portion of the Sunni insurgency" since the fall of 2003 to negotiate with the United States: peace in exchange for "an unambiguous statement from Washington that it will not seek permanent military bases in Iraq" and will set a definite timetable for withdrawal.[51] Indeed, according to Richard Dreyfuss, in response to a less-than-straightforward offer of amnesty to some insurgents by the current Iraqi government, "a majority bloc of the Iraqi resisistance" offered to stop all attacks against U.S. and Iraqi government forces for "a U.S. pledge to leave Iraq in two years."[52] The United States' refusal to negotiate anything except the other side's terms of surrender is a Vietnam analogy no one has yet drawn.

Biddle has been a minority voice. In the main, counterinsurgency in general, and the ongoing struggle to win hearts and minds in particular, remain central to the war in Iraq. The Marines, for example, have stepped up their "values" training in the wake of a series of incidents in which Iraqi hearts and minds were radically ignored. The study of counterinsurgency is now required at the Army's Command and General Staff College in Fort Leavenworth, and a text on counterinsurgency by a Tunisian-born French lieutenant colonel, David Galula, is a best-seller at the Fort Leavenworth bookstore.[53] Major Gregory Peterson has been persuaded by a course at Fort Leavenworth's School of Advanced Military Studies that the U.S. experience in Iraq can be usefully compared to that of the French in Algeria: "Both involved Western powers exercising sovereignty in Arab states, both powers were opposed by insurgencies contesting that sovereignty, and both wars were controversial back home." That the French wished to continue exercising a sovereignty they had established in the nineteenth century while the United States has declared that it does not now and never will wish to exercise sovereignty in Iraq does not seem to have been considered by Peterson or his instructors.

It is impossible at this point to predict the outcome of the push to ever-improved forms of counterinsurgency warfare in Iraq, as it is impossible to predict the outcome of the war itself. It is likely, however, that when it's all over, the call to master counterinsurgency, to get it right *this time*, will once again be heard.

13

Torture in the Crucible of Counterinsurgency

ALFRED W. MCCOY

After the attacks on September 11, 2001, the White House made torture its secret weapon in the war on terror. Although Washington mobilized its regular military forces for conventional attacks on Afghanistan and Iraq, the main challenge in this new kind of warfare was a covert campaign against "nonstate actors," terrorists who moved easily, elusively across the Muslim world from Morocco to Manila in "ad hoc networks that dissolve as soon as the mission is accomplished." With its countless Cold War victories, overthrowing enemies on four continents by coups and covert operations, the Central Intelligence Agency (CIA) had an aura of invincibility and soon became Washington's chosen instrument against al-Qaeda. Yet, in truth, the Agency's reputation for clandestine derring-do was grossly inflated and its qualifications for this new mission were few indeed.[1]

Though often brilliant against states or state agencies, the CIA remained, at base, a centralized Washington bureaucracy usually lacking the local knowledge, languages, or street smarts for effective intelligence gathering on nonstate actors. In its half-century history before September 2001, the CIA had fought only one covert war comparable to its new antiterror mission against al-Qaeda, and the results of its earlier counterterror campaign during the Vietnam War were decidedly mixed. Desperate for intelligence about its invisible enemy, an underground movement called the Vietcong, the agency soon descended into systematic torture of suspected Communists. Then, forty years later, confronted with a second, similar campaign against another nonstate actor, Islamic terrorists, the CIA soon found it had few, if any, assets inside al-Qaeda or militant Muslim circles, forcing the agency to revive the torture techniques it had once used in South Vietnam. With surprising speed, Washington's recourse to torture in Afghanistan and Iraq soon replicated the same patterns first seen during its "dirty war" in Vietnam—an uncontrolled proliferation of torture into a generalized brutality, anger among the local population, and alienation of the American people from the larger war effort.[2]

Once torture begins, its perpetrators—reaching into that remote terrain where pain and pleasure, procreation and destruction all converge—are often swept away by frenzies of power and potency, mastery and control. Just as interrogators are often drawn in by an empowering sense of dominance over victims, so their superiors, even at the highest level, can succumb to fantasies of torture as an all-powerful weapon. Thus, modern states that sanction torture, even in a limited way, run the risk of becoming increasingly indiscriminate in its application. When U.S. leaders have used torture to fight faceless adversaries, both communist and terrorist, its practice has spread almost uncontrollably. Only four years after the CIA compiled its 1963 manual for use against a few key Soviet counterintelligence targets, its agents were operating forty interrogation centers in South Vietnam that killed more than 20,000 suspects and tortured countless thousands more. Similarly, just a few months after the CIA used its techniques on a few "high target value" al-Qaeda suspects, the practice spread to the interrogation of hundreds of Afghans and thousands of Iraqis. In both cases, moreover, not only did torture spread, but the level of abuse escalated relentlessly beyond the scientific patina of the agency's formal psychological method to become pervasively, perversely brutal.

At the deepest level, the abuse at Abu Ghraib, Guantánamo, and Kabul are manifestations of a long history of a distinctive U.S. covert-warfare doctrine developed since World War II, in which psychological torture has emerged as a central albeit clandestine facet of American foreign policy. From 1950 to 1962, the CIA became involved in torture through a massive mind-control effort that reached a cost of a billion dollars annually—a veritable Manhattan Project of the mind.[3] After experiments with hallucinogenic drugs, electric shocks, and sensory deprivation, this work then produced a new approach to torture that was psychological, not physical, perhaps best described as "no-touch torture."

After a decade of this covert research, the CIA codified its new method in the curiously named "Kubark Counterintelligence Interrogation" manual in 1963 and then set about disseminating these torture techniques to anticommunist allies worldwide. In propagating its new interrogation doctrine from 1962 to 1991, the agency moved through two distinct phases, at first operating undercover through a U.S. police-training program active in Asia and Latin America and later collaborating with U.S. Army training teams that advised local counterinsurgency forces, largely in Central America. Throughout this thirty-year effort, the CIA's torture training grew increasingly brutal, moving by degrees beyond its original psychological techniques to harsh physical methods through its experience of pacification in Vietnam.

In sum, the development of the agency's techniques at the height of the Cold War, through a confused, even chaotic process, created a covert interrogation capacity that the White House could deploy at times of extraordinary crisis, whether in South Vietnam in 1968 or Iraq in 2003. Indeed, the pervasive, persistent influence of the Agency's torture paradigm can be seen in the recurrence of the same interrogation methods used by both American and allied security agencies in Vietnam during the 1960s, Central America in the 1980s, and Afghanistan and Iraq since 2001. Across the span of three continents and four decades, there is a striking similarity in U.S. torture techniques—from the CIA's 1963 Kubark interrogation manual to its 1983 Honduras training handbook and all the way to General Ricardo Sanchez's 2003 orders for interrogation in Iraq.

Office of Public Safety

From 1962 to 1974, the CIA worked through the Office of Public Safety (OPS), a division of the U.S. Agency for International Development (USAID) that posted American police advisers to developing nations.[4] Established by President John F. Kennedy in 1962, OPS grew, in just six years, into a global anticommunist operation with an annual budget of $35 million and more than 400 U.S. police advisers assigned worldwide. By 1971, the program had trained more than a million policemen in forty-seven nations, including 85,000 in South Vietnam and 100,000 in Brazil.[5] Concealed in the midst of this larger effort, CIA interrogation training soon proved controversial as police agencies across the Third World became synonymous with human rights abuses—particularly in South Vietnam, Uruguay, Iran, and the Philippines.

To launch this aggressive Cold War effort in the early 1960s, the Kennedy administration formed the interagency Special Group (Counter Insurgency) whose influential members could cut across bureaucratic boundaries to get the job done—General Maxwell Taylor, national security adviser McGeorge Bundy, CIA director John McCone, and undersecretary of state U. Alexis Johnson.[6] As a National Security Action Memorandum indicated in 1962, "the President desires that careful consideration be given to intensifying civil police programs in lieu of military assistance where such action will yield more fruitful results in terms of our internal security objective."[7] Although "the police program is even more important than Special Forces in our global C-I [counterinsurgency] effort," argued staff member Robert Komer in an April 1962 memo, finding a "congenial home" for this multiagency initiative proved difficult.[8] In sum, the problem was how to increase USAID's existing police program so that it would function as an instrument for a more aggressive CIA internal-security effort among Third World allies. The solution, apparently, was to expand the public safety program within USAID while simultaneously placing it under the control of CIA personnel— notably the program's head, Byron Engle.[9] During his decade as OPS chief, Engle recruited CIA personnel for the program and provided close coordination with the Agency's intelligence mission.[10]

The hybrid nature of OPS allowed CIA field operatives an ideal cover for dissemination of the agency's new interrogation techniques. In South Vietnam, for example, Public Safety trained national police in what the U.S. chief adviser called "stringent wartime measures designed to assist in defeating the enemy." At the provincial level, Vietnamese National Police Field Forces, trained by OPS, worked with CIA mercenaries in apprehending suspected communists for interrogation.[11] In Latin America, the CIA used Public Safety to recruit local police for training at a clandestine center in Washington, International Police Services, that operated behind a blind provided by USAID's International Police Academy (IPA). In its audit of OPS in 1976, the General Accounting Office reported that "there were allegations that the academy . . . taught or encouraged use of torture," but its investigation did not support a formal finding of that nature.[12]

Elsewhere in this worldwide effort, the CIA worked through public safety advisers in Brazil and Uruguay to provide local police with training and interrogation equipment. Through its field offices in Panama and Buenos Aires, the Agency's Technical Services Division (TSD), the unit responsible for this psychological research, shipped polygraph and electroshock machines in diplomatic pouches to Public Safety offices across Latin America.[13] For all its global reach, however, Public Safety's operations were, as the Vietnam War heated up during the 1960s, increasingly concentrated in South Vietnam.

Rise of Phoenix

From the start of the U.S. advisory effort in South Vietnam in 1961, the military concentrated on conventional combat, leaving operations against the communist underground government, or what the French called "dirty war," to the CIA. For nearly fifteen years, the agency waged a covert campaign against the communist infrastructure in South Vietnam that culminated in the formation of its most famous, or notorious, covert operation, the Phoenix Program. After experimenting with police training, psychological warfare, and rural reconstruction, the agency defaulted to a program of systematic torture and extrajudicial executions that killed, by its own count, more than 20,000 suspected communist cadres.

The first Public Safety advisers sent to South Vietnam tried to transform the National Police into an effective counterinsurgency force, but by 1963 the clear failure of this effort created pressures for a new approach. Arriving in Saigon in December of that year, the new CIA station chief, Peer DeSilva, soon decided that "the Vietcong were monstrous in their application of torture and murder." Inspired by a doctrine of counterterror, DeSilva began a campaign "to bring danger and death to the Vietcong functionaries themselves, especially in the areas where they felt secure."[14] It was this campaign of counterterror that would lead the agency, by degrees, to the development of extraordinary methods whose sum was formalized, after 1967, under the Phoenix Program.

The CIA thus embarked on a project of both expanding and centralizing South Vietnam's scattered intelligence operations, which all fell, at least nominally, under its counterpart agency, Saigon's Central Intelligence Organization (CIO). Four Agency advisers were assigned to give the Vietnamese hands-on training by interrogating the hundreds of prisoners locked up inside the concrete walls of the CIO's National Interrogation Center. After a year under DeSilva's leadership, each of the forty-plus provinces in South Vietnam had a Province Intelligence Coordination Committee and its own concrete prison compound, called the Provincial Interrogation Center (PIC). In these same years, the CIA sent many more "experts . . . most of whom had worked on Russian defectors" from its Technical Services Division to train or retrain the Vietnamese interrogators. Instead of the "old French methods" of crude physical torture, most evident in the Saigon police, the Vietnamese, in the words of one CIA trainer, "had to be re-taught with more sophisticated techniques," including the agency's new psychological paradigm. At the provincial centers, however, crude physical methods continued to prevail, including electrical shock, beatings, and rape.[15]

As the CIA brought this covert war to the countryside in 1965, its senior field operative William Colby launched the Counter Terror (CT) program. "CIA representatives," wrote Agency analyst Victor Marchetti, "recruited, organized, supplied, and directly paid CT teams, whose function was to use . . . techniques of terror—assassination, abuses, kidnappings and intimidation—against the Viet Cong leadership." A year later, the CIA "became wary of adverse publicity surrounding the use of the word 'terror' and changed the name of the CT teams to the Provincial Reconnaissance Units (PRUs)." Colby also supervised construction of the Provincial Interrogation Centers (PIC), where a CIA employee "directed each center's operations, much of which consisted of torture tactics against suspected Vietcong, such torture usually carried out by Vietnamese nationals."[16] By 1965–66, the CIA had thus developed a nationwide intelligence collection system that reached from the National Interrogation Center in Saigon down to the society's rice roots via the PIC operations and the PRU counterterror campaign.

The program expanded in 1967 when Washington established a centralized pacification bureaucracy, Civil Operations and Rural Development Support (CORDS). Under this umbrella, the CIA drew all the scattered U.S. counterinsurgency operations—Public Safety police training, military intelligence, the CIO, and its own interrogation units—into CORDS and then used this labyrinthine bureaucracy to conceal the covert assassination campaign that was later named the Phoenix Program. With limitless funding and unrestrained powers, Phoenix represented an application of the most advanced U.S. interrogation techniques to the task of destroying the Vietcong's revolutionary underground.

As conventional combat failed to defeat the enemy, the U.S. mission created Phoenix to correct a major contradiction in its complex, collaborative relationship with South Vietnam's weak government. The National Police, despite a doubling of their strength to 120,000 between 1966 and 1972, suffered poor leadership and "pervasive corruption" that blunted its effectiveness against the Vietcong's underground government. And the South Vietnamese army, as one of its officers explained, felt that "this unarmed enemy was not their proper adversary." With the police unable and the army unwilling to engage in effective counterinsurgency, the CIA felt the need for a new kind of clandestine operation to attack this invisible communist government that threatened to deny Saigon any control over its countryside and thus defeat the U.S. war effort.[17]

After two years of escalating military operations, the U.S. mission sensed, by mid-1966, that it had failed in its key mission of destroying the enemy's underground government, which it called the "Viet Cong infrastructure," or VCI. As Washington and its Saigon command began to realize the limitations of conventional combat, a search for solutions allowed this rare bureaucratic opening for a review of numerous smaller programs long obscured by main-force military operations—making the new pacification program the sum of diverse sources' superseded efforts.[18]

In the Mekong Delta's IV Corps, for example, the chief of U.S. Army intelligence, General Joseph McChristian, found himself in conflict with the CIA and so allied with the head of the National Police, General Nguyen Ngoc Loan, to launch Operation Cong Tac IV in mid-1966 with the aim of gathering "intelligence on the identification and location of Viet Cong." As this program expanded, General Loan in turn delegated its supervision to his CIA-trained Branch chief, Colonel Dang Van Minh, who proposed to transform it into a supple program he called Phung Hoan, or Phoenix, reflecting his view that VC cadres were "to be monitored, not killed."[19]

In the far north of I Corps, by contrast, the U.S. Marines and the CIA collaborated effectively in pacification. To help the Marines cut casualties from entrenched Vietcong units, the regional CIA paramilitary chief, Robert Wall, developed a localized counterguerrilla net, the District Intelligence and Operations Coordination Center (DIOCC), that became "the model on which Phoenix facilities were later built throughout Vietnam."[20]

This long-gestating bureaucratic process began to crystallize in November 1966 when Nelson H. Brickham, a senior CIA analyst generally credited with "the organizational reforms that paved the way for Phoenix," briefed the U.S. commander, General William Westmoreland, on his proposal for an "Attack Against the Viet Cong Infrastructure." Viewing the Vietcong as a "mafia" that controlled the countryside through terror, Brickham proposed a multifaceted assault on the communist underground through a mix of penetration, arrest, and assassination by an array of nonmilitary forces, including the National Police Special Branch, the CIA's Provincial Reconnaissance Units (PRUs), and regional militia. "Without an infrastructure," Brickham later explained, "there is only a headless body. Destroy the infrastructure, you destroy the insurgency."[21]

Reflecting these new priorities, in May 1967 President Lyndon Johnson dispatched Robert W. Komer, a tough CIA bureaucratic infighter known as the "blowtorch," to head CORDS as his new hand-picked pacification czar. To liaise with this additional layer of bureaucracy, the agency's Saigon station chief assigned Brickham to draft "a general plan for pacification," and he in turn sent Komer his "Personal Observations" with proposals for an intensified attack on the Vietcong. "The war is a run on a treadmill," Brickham warned, "as long as existing and totally inadequate process and facilities for detention and neutralization of captured VC remains unchanged." More broadly, the ephemeral rural presence of U.S. representatives, military and civil, meant that the massive American commitment to Vietnam was having surprisingly little impact. In most rural districts, a refugee officer "kicks bags of rice off of his helicopter and then disappears"; a Public Safety officer assigned to open a detention camp "looks around for fifteen minutes and disappears, never to be seen again"; and a Popular Forces company receives "an occasional visit by a so-called adviser." Instead of focusing on the battle for the countryside, most agencies, Vietnamese and American, devoted themselves to "private wars" against bureaucratic rivals in Saigon. ARVN, for example, "will have nothing but contempt for Police Intelligence," while combat units "ignore 'infrastructure' and go around looking for big main force enemy which they never or rarely find." Not surprisingly, "all agencies betray an abysmal ignorance of programs of their colleagues." This babel of autonomous information systems—including the Police Special Branch, the Provincial Interrogation Centers, and "various military intelligence sub-systems"—meant "no effective attack has yet been devised for . . . degradation of VC infrastructure."[22]

To correct these "numerous grave weaknesses,' Brickham recommended a "centrally designed and controlled reporting and information system" using "automated data processing systems which have a greatly expanded capacity for storing, manipulating and reproducing information." With a management model borrowed from the Ford Motor Company, he proposed formation of a centralized pacification committee in Saigon with Robert Komer as chair and a "board of directors" drawn from all U.S. intelligence organizations, civil and military.[23]

Ambassador Komer found the proposal persuasive, and in June 1967 his CORDS office convened a whirlwind round of meetings among top American and Vietnamese officials to build support for a fundamental reorganization of allied intelligence. Under the rubric of the ICEX program, bureaucratic shorthand for Infrastructure Intelligence Coordination and Exploitation, he proposed nothing less than an all-out attack on the Vietcong. At one of these early briefings in Saigon, CORDS explained that until now the Vietnamese National Police had compiled most of the intelligence on the Vietcong's 80,000 members, but much of this data had been "buried in files, and little effort has been directed toward properly exploiting this information." To correct this failing and facilitate "the identification and destruction of the infrastructure," ICEX, a direct predecessor of the Phoenix program, would operate at four closely coordinated levels: a centralized command in Saigon of top civil and military representatives, chaired by Komer himself and managed by a senior CIA paramilitary specialist, Evan Parker; regional committees in the country's four corps areas, headed by "the CIA Regional Officer in Charge"; provincial committees, led by the senior American adviser in each province, who "will be provided a Province ICEX Advisor by CIA"; and, in each of some hundred selected localities where the Vietcong were strong, a District Operations Intelligence Coordinating Center (DIOCC) supported by the local Provincial Reconnaissance (PRU) and Provincial Interrogation Center (PIC). Though this ICEX structure was still new, there had already been, CORDS reported, some promising signs—notably, the identification of "9,000 VC personalities," the insertion of "21,000 additional names . . . in the base data," and the recent capture of 160 VC cadres in the capital, Saigon.[24]

Within days, both the U.S. embassy and the U.S. military command endorsed "the proposed concept for mounting a stepped-up, coordinated attack on the VC infrastructure." In internal memos, CORDS reported that the U.S. military had committed 126 additional officers to "a joint civil-military management structure." By centralizing all existing intelligence operations under ICEX, this new effort would, CORDS promised, produce a "timely exploration of operational intelligence" for a "more sharply focused attack."[25]

From the outset, however, the Saigon regime's bureaucratic inertia, corruption, and incapacity threatened the program's success. Most fundamentally, the country's judicial system proved problematic. As ICEX generated a tide of arrests, CORDS soon discovered what it called "the total inadequacy of physical facilities . . . for either processing, holding or imprisoning civil detainees."[26] In December, a top CORDS official, John G. Lybrand, reported that civil court system "does not handle VC defendants," making "judicial processing . . . the responsibility of various military tribunals." After capture by police or military, VC suspects were subjected to tactical interrogation before transfer to "higher headquarters for further interrogation," where the "processing . . . loses all coherence." Since the country's forty-four civil and military prisons were filled to bursting, most detainees rounded up in these early sweeps were soon released. For example, searches by the U.S. 4th Infantry Division in Pleiku province in early 1967 had netted some

165 Vietcong suspects, but 158 of these were soon released, including senior cadres "with the means to effect reprisals or the means to buy release." The seven detained "appeared to be those who had neither the money to bribe their way free nor sufficient importance to the VC organization to warrant an outlay of money for their release." In general, CORDS concluded, "any individual possessing a sufficient amount of cash can purchase his freedom at any level of the penal system in Vietnam."[27]

More critically, the ICEX program, as CORDS noted in an internal memo, "cannot succeed without acceptance and energetic support by the Director General of National Police," the all-powerful General Nguyen Ngoc Loan. As the trusted ally of Premier Nguyen Cao Ky and the head of every major Saigon security agency, General Loan was the dominant force in Saigon's security effort. When CORDS presented the program to Loan, he "turned it down flat" in part because he thought it would promote his rival Nguyen Van Thieu and in part because, as Brickham put it, he "looked upon it as an infringement of their sovereignty."[28] It was not until November that General Loan's "earlier misgivings" were overcome after assurances "that police intelligence sources and operations need not be revealed, and that police participation . . . will be to their advantage." Despite this "disheartening . . . initial reluctance of the National Police," CORDS had already established some 115 of the local coordinating committees, the critical DIOCCs, which were preparing "blacklists and most-wanted lists . . . to good effect." By late 1967, however, it was still not clear whether Saigon officials would "really be willing to go all out and apprehend, try, and imprison, or destroy identified and identifiable VC infrastructure."[29]

In December, the prime minister's office finally backed the ICEX program by issuing a "Directive on the Neutralization of the VCI" instructing all relevant South Vietnamese agencies to "take full note of the importance of the matter." By ordering that the "committees in charge of VCI are called Phung Hoang Committees," this order gave the program both its distinctive name, Phung Hoang or Phoenix, and its basic organizational character as a collaborative, Vietnamese-American pacification effort.[30] Six months later, in July 1968, President Nguyen Van Thieu issued a supplementary directive establishing Phoenix in its final form as "a program, not an organization, to bring about collaboration . . . among all government agencies which could contribute to the identification and neutralization of the VCI." Within a year, as Vietnamese took control, U.S. officials withdrew from "direct responsibility for the program," though they remained involved as advisers to the Vietnamese Special Police and coordinators for intelligence gathering "on the American side."[31]

In Saigon, the fully evolved Phoenix program used sophisticated computer information banks, located at the Combined Intelligence Center Vietnam (CICV), to centralize all data on the Vietcong infrastructure, identifying key Communist cadres for interrogation or elimination. In the countryside,

Phoenix made use of this intelligence through specially trained counter-guerrilla teams, the PRUs, attached to one of the CIA's forty-plus Provincial Interrogation Centers or PICs. Miming the clandestine cell structure of the Vietcong units, each PRU was a six-man team that elaborated, through a pyramid structure, into a provincial unit of 146 men.[32]

After three years of operations, from 1967 to 1969, the CIA transferred Phoenix operations to the U.S. Army's military intelligence, and the U.S. command, in turn, conceded control to the Vietnamese police. Upon arrival in Saigon in November 1969, the new CIA station chief, Ted Shackley, decided that "the pacification programs had come of age . . . that the agency contribution was no longer required," launching a six-month phase-out that would "free up CIA resources to improve the quality of the intelligence product, to penetrate the Vietcong." In this transition, the CIA conducted an internal review of Phoenix that summarized the program's fitful three-year progress to the point where the situation in the countryside could be described as a "race" between the Vietcong, whose infrastructure had declined to 63,000 members, and the Saigon government, which "has also been slowing in developing its tools for this new nature of the war, Phoenix and the National Police." Despite promising growth since its inception in mid-1967, Phoenix was still troubled by "its poor press image, highlighted by charges that it was a program of assassination." Indeed, through what the mission called an "intensive effort at computer mechanization," the program had developed "a successive hardening of the quota system . . . to obtain maximum incentive toward elimination of higher level VCI," raising the monthly total of those "captured, rallied, killed" from 1,200 in 1968 to 1,800 in 1969. By October 1970, Phoenix accounted for "82.9 percent of VCI killed or captured" by all allied forces, U.S. and South Vietnamese. Simultaneously, a "series of actions were launched to . . . make more effective the overall Phoenix program"—including the creation of "operations centers . . . at the national, regional, provincial, and district level"; an acceptance among Saigon officials that it was, in fact, their program, culminating in a "marked rise in command attention to Phoenix"; and, in May 1970, a Saigon government decision to place the entire program under the Directorate General of National Police.[33]

The sum of these changes was, the CIA reported, a significant increase in the Saigon government's presence in the countryside. Long the "stepchild" of the Saigon government, the National Police was finally moving beyond its "strong colonial tradition" as a highly bureaucratic capital security force "in the best French tradition." Starting in 1969, the National Police shifted its focus from capital to countryside, placing 50 percent of its forces at the district level and establishing 1,800 village police stations. This latter move had produced promising results by "permitting direct . . . report through Police channels to Phoenix." In Quang Tin province, for example, local officials "conducted several massive . . . offensives against many targets" and created "a Phoenix operations unit, consisting of the National Police Field Force (NPFF), Provincial Reconnaissance Unit (PRU), and Armed Propaganda Team (APT)." From a low of 16,890 officers in 1963, the National Police had grown rapidly, through transfer of 25,000 military personnel, to a projected strength of 122,000 by late 1971. Centralization of Saigon's effort under the National Police had, moreover, facilitated the ongoing U.S. advisory support for Phoenix by CORDS, Public Safety, military intelligence, and the CIA. Through its lead role in rural pacification, the National Police were overcoming their low status "behind the power curve in this military society" and "slowly rising (albeit from the cellar) in public . . . esteem."[34]

Simultaneously, the detention system, the CIA reported, had shown a marked improvement in operation and capacity. Instead of the wholesale corruption evident in 1967, legal handling of captured VCI had improved "to provide a greater component of justice in the proceedings." Between 1966 and 1970, some 193,000 prisoners, including 100,725 "communist criminals," had been released from Correction Centers after serving their sentences. But there was still little effort "on a consistent basis in Vietnam to rehabilitate detainees." Nonetheless, the sum of these changes allowed the Saigon government, in October 1969, to launch the "Phoenix Public Information program" in an attempt to "surface Phoenix publicly, under the rationale of protecting the people from terrorism."[35]

Even so, the program preserved much of the covert and coercive facets built into its institutional DNA. In 1970, the first year of Vietnamese control, Phoenix assassinations reached their all-time peak of 8,191. Vietnamese police officers selected for training in advanced interrogation techniques at the International Police Academy (IPA) in Washington, a front for covert CIA torture training, readily accepted such brutality as essential for national security. After devoting four pages of his fourteen-page thesis to a history of European torture, Luu Van Huu of the National Police summarized lessons learned: "We have 4 sorts of torture: use of force as such; threats; physical suffering, imposed indirectly; and mental or psychological torture."[36] Similarly, in his 1971 paper for the IPA, Le Van An of Vietnam's National Police defended torture, saying: "Despite the fact that brutal interrogation is strongly criticized by moralists, its importance must not be denied if we want to have order and security in daily life."[37]

Despite later CIA rhetoric designed to give Phoenix a sanitized, technical patina, it soon devolved into a brutality that produced many casualties but few verifiable results. For all its management gloss, the program's strategy remained grounded in DeSilva's original vision of physical and psychological counterterror. After a PRU brought in suspected Communists, PIC interrogators, often under CIA supervision, tortured these prisoners and summarily executed many without trial or due process. Often these PRUs degenerated into petty protection rackets, extracting bribes from accused communists and eliminating suspects on the basis of unsubstantiated gossip. Although early recruits were often well motivated, the PRUs began to attract social outcasts, including convicted criminals, who embraced their basic task, murder, by tattooing themselves "Sat Cong" (Kill Communists). According to a 1970 report in the *New York Times*, each PRU "consists of a dozen or more South Vietnamese mercenaries, originally recruited and paid handsomely by the CIA," who were usually "local hoodlums, soldiers of fortune, draft-dodgers, defectors."[38]

In their memoirs, former CIA operatives confirmed this dismal assessment of Phoenix's operations. During a tour of the program's provincial interrogation centers near Saigon in 1969, a CIA regional chief, Orrin DeForest, was "disgusted" to find them "irretrievable, just a horrible mess . . . commonly considered the sites of the worst tortures—in particular the water treatment, where they forced water down prisoners' throats until their stomachs swelled up, or the torture in which they applied electric shock to the genitals and nipples."[39] Assigned to this same region as CIA chief for Gia Dinh province in 1968, Ralph W. McGehee found himself in "the middle of an insane war" that defied rationality and mocked the statistical indices of progress amassed by the vast CORDS counterinsurgency program. "The CORDS meetings," he recalled, "the killings by the CIA's assassination teams—the Provincial Reconnaissance Units—and the absurd intelligence-collection activities progressed as in a Greek tragedy."[40] As he left Saigon in 1970, the Phoenix program's founder, Robert Komer, described it as "a small, poorly managed, and largely ineffective effort." Indeed, one Pentagon contract study of Phoenix's operations found that in 1970–71, only 3 percent of the Vietcong "killed, captured, or rallied were full or probationary Party members above the district level." Over half the supposed Vietcong captured or killed "were not even Party members."[41] CIA veteran McGehee was even blunter, stating: "The truth is that never in the history of our work in Vietnam did we get one clear-cut, high-ranking Viet Cong agent."[42] Not surprisingly, a pacification effort based on this problematic program failed to either crush the Vietcong or win the support of Vietnamese villagers, contributing to the ultimate U.S. defeat in the Vietnam War.[43]

Investigating Phoenix

The character of CIA pacification in Vietnam first emerged, albeit obliquely, in 1969 during the investigation of Colonel Robert B. Rheault, a West Point graduate and Special Forces commander, for the summary execution of a suspected Vietcong spy named Thai Khac Chuyen. After the Green Berets captured a roll of film revealing that their Vietnamese operative was a double agent working for the enemy, they used sodium pentathol ("truth serum") and lie-detector tests, probably with CIA assistance, for an interrogation that supposedly confirmed his treason. Thinking the agency had ordered his "elimination," the Special Forces unit at Nha Trang drugged

Chuyen with morphine, shot him with a .22 caliber pistol, and dumped his body at sea. Furious, the U.S. commander in Vietnam, General Creighton Abrams, ordered a "no-holds-barred" investigation that culminated in murder charges against Colonel Rheault; the alleged trigger man, Captain Robert F. Marasco; and five other Green Beret officers. But the CIA, at the behest of the Nixon White House, refused to allow its agents to testify, ultimately forcing the Army to back down and dismiss charges against Colonel Rheault and his five co-accused. In its analysis of the case, the *New York Times* argued the killing was a product of confused intelligence operations that had been the impetus, two years earlier, for formation of the CIA's Phoenix Program to train Vietnamese assets "in the fine art of silent killing." Indeed, two years later Captain Marasco admitted that he had shot the double agent on "very, very clear orders from the CIA," and claimed there had been "hundreds" of similar summary executions in South Vietnam. Despite the case's dismissal, the investigation thus alerted the U.S. Congress and the public to the covert war against the Vietcong, one that apparently included summary executions of "suspected" VC agents.[44]

After nearly four years of these murky operations, Congress and the press finally exposed the Phoenix Program in 1970. William Colby, a career CIA officer and chief of pacification in Vietnam, testified before the Senate Foreign Relations Committee that in 1969 alone, Phoenix had killed 6,187 members of the 75,000-strong Vietcong infrastructure. Although admitting some "illegal killings," Colby rejected a suggestion by Senator J. William Fulbright (D.-Ark.) that it was "a program for the assassination of civilian leaders."[45]

In the wake of this press exposé, the House Operations Subcommittee conducted the first wide-ranging congressional probe of CIA pacification operations, finding that Phoenix had killed 9,820 Vietcong suspects in the past fourteen months. "I am shocked and dismayed," said Representative Ogden R. Reid (R.-N.Y.). "Assassination and terror by the Viet Cong or Hanoi should not, and must not, call forth the same methods by Saigon, let alone the United States, directly or indirectly."[46]

Several days later, William Colby told the committee that Phoenix had killed 20,587 Vietcong suspects since 1968. The Saigon government provided figures attributing 40,994 Vietcong kills to the Phoenix Program.[47] When Representative Reid charged that Phoenix was responsible for "indiscriminate killings," Colby defended his program as "an essential part of the war effort" that was "designed to protect the Vietnamese people from terrorism."[48]

In these same hearings, K. Barton Osborn, a Military Intelligence veteran who had worked with the CIA's Phoenix program in 1967–68, described "the insertion of the six-inch dowel into the ear canal of one of my detainee's ears and the tapping through the brain until he died; and the starving to death of a Vietnamese woman who was suspected of being part of the local [Vietcong] political education cadre." He also recalled "the use of electronic gear such as sealed telephones attached to the . . . women's vagina and the men's testicles . . . [to] shock them into submission." During his eighteen months with the Phoenix program, not a single VC suspect had survived CIA interrogation. All these "extralegal, illegal, and covert" procedures were, Osborn testified, found in the "Defense Collection Intelligence Manual," issued to him during his intelligence training at Ft. Holabird, Maryland. Adding to this lethal aura, by 1972 the Phoenix total for enemy "neutralization" had risen to 81,740 Vietcong eliminated and 26,369 prisoners killed.[49]

To discredit such damaging testimony, the U.S. Army Intelligence Command conducted a thorough investigation of Osborn's charges, which William Colby released, in a declassified summary, during his 1973 confirmation hearings as CIA director. Though the Army's classified report nitpicked many of his secondary details, it did not challenge Osborne's overall sense of Phoenix's systematic brutality—a negative assessment confirmed by both eyewitness accounts and official studies.[50]

In early 1968, for example, two CORDS evaluators, John G. Lybrand and L. Craig Johnstone, conducted an official review of the program in II Corps (Central Vietnam), finding that "the truncheon and electric shock method of interrogation were in widespread use, with almost all [U.S.] advisers admitting to have witnessed instances of the use of these methods." As their Saigon counterparts started these cruel interrogations, the study found that "most advisers claimed they did not personally take part in [tortures] but 'turned their backs on them.'" Similarly, an American who advised PRU irregulars in Binh Thuan province during 1968–69, Richard Welcome, indicates that Americans allowed their Phoenix allies wide latitude: "Prisoners were abused. Were they tortured? It depends on what you call torture. Electricity was used by the Vietnamese, water was used, occasionally some of the prisoners got beat up. Were any of them put on the rack, eyes gouged out, bones broken? No, I never saw any evidence of that at all." Even Colby himself, the program's founder, admitted "various of the things that Mr. Osborn alleges might have happened." In the wink-nudge approach that Phoenix advisers adopted to abuses by their Saigon allies, Colby added that "Phoenix . . . was not to be a program of assassination and we issued instructions . . . that not only were Americans not to participate . . . but they were to make their objections known. . . . I did receive some reports of this nature . . . and took them up with the government of South Vietnam. . . . I knew there were people killed, there is no question about it, . . . but I certainly reject the idea that it was a systematic program of assassination." Reviewing this evidence, one recent conservative history of Phoenix concluded that "the large majority of South Vietnamese interrogators tortured some or all of the Communist prisoners in their care" and "a smaller number tortured villagers suspected of collaborating with the Communists."[51]

Even in the aftermath of revelations about Phoenix, there was still a deep, almost inexplicable silence over the issue of torture. In 1977, for example, former CIA agent Frank Snepp published a bestselling memoir of his Vietnam experience. With graphic detail reminiscent of George Orwell's *1984*, Snepp's first chapter described the months he spent torturing a captured North Vietnamese cadre, Nguyen Van Tai. Just as Orwell's fictional interrogator broke the antihero Wilson by discovering his greatest fear, rats, so CIA and Vietnamese interrogators found that this dedicated communist cadre had one "psychic-physical flaw"—a deep fear of cold. For over four years, the CIA, using its torture technique of sensory deprivation, kept Tai in solitary confinement inside an all-white, windowless room with just one feature—"heavy-duty air conditioners." Even so, the Vietnamese interrogators failed. Next, an "American specialist" made little progress. Finally, Snepp himself, assigned to the case as lead interrogator, maintained the endless, painfully cold air-conditioning and probed, through two or three interrogations daily, to discover "only two discernibly exploitable flaws" in Tai's personality—most importantly, a deep longing to return to his wife and child. Playing upon this weakness "to drive the wedge deeper," Snepp varied Tai's interview times "so as to throw off his internal clock" and tantalized him with the hope of reunion with his family. These CIA textbook techniques finally worked and the dossier began to grow as Tai, enticed by Snepp's hints of release, began talking. Just before Saigon fell, however, a "senior CIA official" suggested that Tai should be "disappeared," and he was "loaded onto an airplane and thrown out over the South China Sea."[52]

By his references to an "American specialist" in interrogation, the elaborate sensory deprivation, and psychological probing to produce personality regression, Snepp provided unmistakable clues that the CIA was, by this point, applying sophisticated torture techniques. But the press focused on his tales of political intrigue and ignored these revelations that the Agency was engaged in torture.[53] In retrospect, all the sensational revelations about the Phoenix Program's extraordinary toll of extrajudicial executions and CIA drug experimentation failed to expose anything approaching the full extent of the agency's torture training and thus produced little lasting reform.

Lessons for Latin America

In retrospect, Phoenix proved a seminal experience for the U.S. intelligence community, combining both physical and psychological techniques in an extreme method that would serve as a model for later U.S. counterinsurgency training in Latin America. At a deeper level, moreover, the year 1975 is doubly significant, marking not only the defeat of the United States in Vietnam but also the dissolution of the Office of Public Safety, a longtime cover for CIA torture training.

Amidst these traumatic transitions, the CIA, in collaboration with the Defense Department, intensified its efforts in Latin America, where Washington was determined to hold the line against Communism. Denied access to Latin American police after the abolition of OPS in 1975, the CIA would work primarily through U.S. military advisers to train allied armies. We can track this paper trail through once-secret Pentagon memos about Project X, the Army's program for transmitting Vietnam's lessons to South and Central America.[54]

In 1965–66, U.S. Army intelligence launched Project X, designed, according to a confidential Pentagon memo, "to develop an exportable foreign intelligence package to provide counterinsurgency techniques learned in Vietnam to Latin American countries."[55] According to a Pentagon counterintelligence staffer, Linda Matthews, the team of U.S. Army officers drafting one of the project's training manuals, "Intelligence for Stability Operations," in 1967–68 was in contact with "a resident instruction course . . . in the Phoenix program" at the Army Intelligence School, and thus "some offending material from the Phoenix program may have found its way into the Project X materials."[56] One of these manuals, in the Pentagon's words, "provided training regarding use of sodiopentathol compound in interrogation, abduction of adversary family members to influence the adversary, prioritization of adversary personalities for abduction, exile, physical beatings and execution"—in short, all the trademark Phoenix techniques.[57] For the next quarter century, the U.S. Army would transmit these extreme tactics, by both direct training and mailing manuals, to the armies of ten Latin American nations. By the mid-1980s, counterguerrilla operations in Colombia and Central America would thus bear an eerie but explicable resemblance to South Vietnam.

Eventually, Project X developed a complete counterinsurgency curriculum based on seven training manuals, all in Spanish, that addressed key tactical problems—including, "Handling of Sources," "Interrogation," "Combat Intelligence," and "Terrorism and the Urban Guerrilla." Among these seven handbooks, at least five contained violent counterterror tactics far beyond anything in the CIA's 1963 Kubark manual. For example, the agency's handbook "Handling of Sources" refers, in the words of a Pentagon content analysis, "to motivation by fear, payment of bounties for enemy dead, beatings, false imprisonment, executions and the use of truth serum."[58]

Upon closer reading, the 1989 edition of "Handling of Sources" has chilling lessons about control of assets in counterinsurgency, applying past examples from the Philippines and Malaysia to current Latin American operations. By appealing to "mercenary motivations" or using "fear as a weapon," the counterintelligence agent recruits an "employee" for infiltration into a guerrilla zone, taking care to psychologically manipulate the employee's every emotion and thus "maintain the necessary control." To establish his asset's credibility as a "guerrilla recruit," the agent, the manual says, "could cause the arrest or detention of the employee's parents, imprison the employee or give him a beating." And if regular scrutiny of this employee's reports reveals "possible deception," then the agent begins with "friendly character interrogations," checking all answers against an operational archive and preparing a "new Declaration of Personal History." If this friendly approach fails to produce a similar breakthrough, then the agent should escalate to the "mental test," waking the employee from a deep sleep for questioning, and then to the "mechanical test," with hypnotism and injection of sodiopentathol ("truth serum"). If the employee turns out to be an "information trafficker" or a guerrilla "penetration agent," then our operative should "initiate termination proceedings" on "bad terms" through means "which are only limited by the agent's imagination." Although "threats of physical violence or true physical abuse" should be avoided if possible, the agent can effect an erring employee's "removal by means of imprisonment" after setting him up "to commit an illegal act." Or, in the ultimate twist, the agent can send "him in a specially dangerous mission for which he has been inadequately prepared . . . [and] pass information to guerrilla security elements"—thus saving his government the cost of the bullet.[59] Apart from these cold-blooded tactics of kidnap, murder, beatings, and betrayal, the manual evidences throughout its 144 single-spaced pages an amorality, a studied willingness to exploit an ally without restraint or compunction, hardened on the anvil of the Vietnam conflict.

For over twenty years, Project X was energetic, even determined, in its dissemination of these ruthless techniques. From 1966 to 1976, the U.S. Army's School of the Americas, then based in Panama, taught these methods to hundreds of Latin American officers at its military intelligence course. After a four-year hiatus in this training caused by President Jimmy Carter's human rights concerns, the U.S. Army's Southern Command resumed distribution of revised editions of these manuals during the 1980s, using them as handouts for its training programs in Colombia, Peru, Ecuador, El Salvador, and Guatemala.[60] Between 1989 and 1991, moreover, the School of the Americas, now relocated to Georgia, issued 693 copies of these handbooks as texts in intelligence courses for students from ten nations, including Bolivia, Colombia, Peru, Venezuela, Guatemala, and Honduras.[61]

Human Resources Manual

Though the U.S. intelligence community operated in this way across the continent, our detailed knowledge of the actual torture training in Latin America comes from a single surviving document, the Agency's Honduras "Human Resources Exploitation Manual—1983." In comparison with the Army's Project X handbooks, with their lurid, post-Phoenix methods of kidnapping and murder, this CIA manual emphasizes the nonviolent psychological techniques defined in the original Kubark interrogation doctrine—a reason, perhaps, that it survived the Pentagon's later systematic destruction of almost all Project X documents. After completing a training session for Honduran military interrogators in early 1983, an anonymous CIA instructor evidently combined this field experience with the Agency's psychological doctrine to produce a full statement of its methods.[62]

At the outset of the Honduran training session, this anonymous instructor emphasizes that he will explain two types of "psychological techniques," the coercive and the noncoercive. "While we do not stress the use of coercive techniques," the agent tells his students, "we do want to make you aware of them and the proper way to use them."[63] In his review of noncoercive techniques, the agent explains that they "are based on the principle of generating pressure inside the subject without application of outside force. This is accomplished by manipulating the victim psychologically until resistance is broken and an urge to yield is fortified."[64]

To establish control from the start the questioner should, the CIA instructor said, "manipulate the subject's environment, to create unpleasant or intolerable situations, to disrupt patterns of time, space, and sensory perception. The subject is very much aware that the 'questioner' controls his ultimate disposition."[65] Among many possible techniques, the subject can be arrested at a time selected to "achieve surprise and the maximum amount of mental discomfort," particularly early morning, when "most subjects experience intense feelings of shock, insecurity, and psychological stress."[66] Once in custody, a subject should be immediately placed in "isolation, both physical and psychological," "completely stripped and told to take a shower" while blindfolded before a guard, and "provided with ill-fitting clothing (familiar clothing reinforces identity and thus the capacity for resistance)."[67] If the subject proves resistant, then an interrogator can employ a "few non-coercive techniques which can be used to induce regression"—techniques that would be repeated twenty years later at Abu Ghraib and Guantánamo Bay:[68]

A. Persistent manipulation of time
B. Retarding and advancing clocks
C. Serving meals at odd times
D. Disrupting sleep schedules
E. Disorientation regarding day and night

Though the manual's overall approach is psychological, the CIA trainer points out that coercion still plays an important role in effective interrogation. "The purpose of all coercive techniques," the CIA trainer explains, "is to induce psychological regression in the subject by bringing a superior outside force to bear on his will to resist." As coercion is applied, the subject suffers "a loss of autonomy, a reversion to an earlier behavioral level."[69]

There are, the manual states, three basic coercive techniques—debility, disorientation, and dread. "For centuries," the CIA trainer explains, "'questioners' have employed various methods of inducing physical weakness . . . [on the] assumption that lowering the subject's physiological resistance will lower his psychological capacity for resistance."[70] While disorientation can "destroy his capacity to resist," sustained dread also "induces regression."[71] Thus, the trainer explains, in words that emphasize the primacy of the psychological over the physical, "the threat of coercion usually weakens or destroys resistance more effectively than coercion itself. For example, the threat to inflict pain can trigger fears more damaging than the immediate sensation of pain."[72]

But even within the CIA's psychological paradigm, there are times when threats of physical pain are necessary. "Threat is basically a means for establishing a bargaining position by inducing fear in the subject," the trainer explains. "A threat should never be made unless it is part of the plan and the 'questioner' has the approval to carry out the threat."[73] In his conclusion, however, the trainer reiterates his emphasis on the psychological. "The torture situation is an external conflict, a contest between the subject and his tormentor," he explains. Pain inflicted on the victim "from outside himself may actually . . . intensify his will to resist," but pain that "he feels he is inflicting upon himself is more likely to sap his resistance."[74] Restating the defining tenet of the Agency's interrogation doctrine, the manual warned that crude physical torture weakens the "moral caliber of the [security] organization and corrupts those that rely on it."[75]

Comparing this 1983 Honduran handbook with the CIA's original 1963 Kubark manual reveals, in ten key passages, almost verbatim similarities in language for both conceptual design and technical detail. After psychological techniques to induce "regression" in the subject, both documents emphasize elimination of "sensory stimuli" through "solitary confinement to induce sensory disorientation." In their emphasis on the use of self-inflicted pain, both manuals warn that pain inflicted externally, by an interrogator, can actually strengthen a subject's resistance. Having articulated these two central elements, both documents then itemize the particular methods whose sum will effect a devastating psychological assault on individual identity—disorienting arrest, isolation, manipulation of time, threats of physical pain or drug injection, and careful staging of the interrogation room. Between 1963 and 1983, enemies, continents, and interrogators may have changed, but the two essential elements of this interrogation method remained constant—sensory disorientation and self-inflicted pain.

OPS in Latin America

Although the Phoenix Program was the largest and bloodiest CIA interrogation effort, it was the OPS police training in Latin America that prompted a Senate attempt to end U.S. torture training altogether. Ironically, it was the murder of an American police adviser in Uruguay that exposed Public Safety's involvement in torture and precipitated the program's abolition.

This story broke in August 1970 when the *New York Times* reported that an American police adviser, Dan A. Mitrione, had been kidnapped by Tupamaro guerrillas in Montevideo. The first reports described him as an ordinary family man from Indiana who was heading the U.S. Public Safety program in Uruguay to encourage "responsible and humane police administration." In an inadvertent hint of Mitrione's actual mission, the report added that he "unquestionably knew more about the Tupamaro operations than any other United States official."[76] Ten days later, in its report of his point-blank execution, the *Times* noted he "was considered to have contributed materially to the Government's antiguerrilla campaign." Nonetheless, an accompanying editorial expressed the paper's "shock and horror," saying: "Only diseased minds could see in the gunning down of this father of nine from Indiana the weakening of the capitalist system or the advancement of social revolution in the Americas."[77]

Only days after an emotional funeral in his hometown of Richmond, Indiana, the story of Mitrione's role began to emerge. A senior Uruguayan police official, Alejandro Otero, told the *Jornal do Brasil* that Mitrione had used "violent techniques of torture and repression." On August 15, a U.S. embassy spokesman in Montevideo called the charge "absolutely false."[78] Eight years later, however, a Cuban double agent, Manuel Hevia Cosculluela, who had joined the CIA and worked with Mitrione in Montevideo, published a book with a very different picture of this American hero. In the Cuban's account, Mitrione had tortured four beggars to death with electrical shocks at a 1970 seminar to demonstrate his techniques for Uruguayan police trainees. "The special horror of the course," Hevia added, "was its academic, almost clinical atmosphere. Mitrione's motto was: 'The right pain in the right place at the right time.' A premature death, he would say, meant that the technique had failed." Significantly, the Cuban charged that Mitrione's deputy in the Public Safety office was William Cantrell, a CIA agent.[79]

Only three months before Mitrione's death in Uruguay, the unsettling coincidence of U.S. police training in Brazil and evidence of police torture finally raised questions in the U.S. Congress about torture training. In May 1971, the Senate Foreign Relations Committee summoned the chief U.S. Public Safety adviser for Brazil, Theodore D. Brown, and scrutinized his program. Brown's statement that OPS taught "minimum use of force, humane methods" sparked a dialogue that led to an affirmation by all, senators and police adviser alike, that America would not, could not train torturers. In his questioning of Brown, Senator Claiborne Pell (D.-R.I.) had the uncommon insight to recognize the delegitimizing impact of torture on the regimes it was designed to defend, asking, "Why is it the Brazilians . . . use torture as a police method when it will alienate their friends and allies around the world?" Yet Senator Pell also followed up with a question revealing the mistaken assumption that psychological torture was not really torture, asking: "But from a police viewpoint, you would agree that psychological, nonphysical methods of interrogation can be just as effective as the physical, as torture?"[80]

It took another four years for Congress to curtail the Public Safety program's operations. Led by Senator James Abourezk (D.-S.D.), congressional investigators found widespread allegations that the program was training torturers in the Latin American police.[81] Concerned about these persistent allegations, Congress finally cut all funds effective July 1975 for "training or advice to police, prisons, or other law enforcement"—in effect, abolishing the Office of Public Safety. Many of the USAID Public Safety officers soon found themselves disavowed, discredited, and unemployed.[82]

Though these reforms were well-intentioned, Congress had failed to probe for the source of this torture. And although these investigations had exposed some elements of the CIA's mind-control project, there was no public pressure to restrain the Agency's propagation of psychological torture. Furthermore, by the time Congress began investigating the Office of Public Safety, the CIA had already stopped using it as a cover for its foreign operations, shifting its torture training to the U.S. Army's Military Adviser Program (MAP).[83]

During the last decade of the Cold War in the 1980s, media probes and congressional pressure led to surprising revelations about the extent of CIA torture training in Latin America. While congressional inquiries in the 1970s had been inconclusive, these later investigations established unequivocally that the Agency coached military interrogators throughout the region, promoting the systematic tortures that became the hallmark of its military dictatorships.

In 1988, reporter James LeMoyne, writing in the *New York Times Magazine*, uncovered the CIA's role in Honduras' brutal counterinsurgency, producing another cycle of public shock and official indifference. Most importantly, the *Times* revealed both the extent of Agency torture training and its impact on actual military operations. As civil war had intensified in Honduras during the late 1970s, the CIA imported Argentine officers, veterans of that nation's "dirty war," to train local army interrogators and also sent Honduran soldiers to the United States for instruction by its own experts. "I was taken to Texas with 24 others for six months between 1979 and 1980," Sergeant Florencio Caballero told the *Times* reporter. "There was an American Army captain there and men from the CIA." The sergeant knew the chief Agency instructor only as a "Mr. Bill" who had served in Vietnam. Sergeant Caballero said the American officers "taught me interrogation in order to end physical torture in Honduras. They taught us psychological methods—to study the fears and weaknesses of a prisoner. Make him stand up, don't let him sleep, keep him naked and isolated, put rats and cockroaches in his cell, give him bad food, serve him dead animals, throw cold water on him, change the temperature."[84]

After their training, these soldiers joined Battalion 316, a special army intelligence unit supported by the CIA and organized by Colonel Gustavo Álvarez Martínez, a "vitriolic, anti-communist . . . trained in Argentina" who commanded both the national police and a private death squad. One of those tortured by Sergeant Caballero's unit, a young Marxist named Inés Murillo, recalled her eighty days of torture in an interview with the *Times* from exile in Mexico. Following her capture in 1983, she was taken to a secret army safe house in the town of San Pedro Sula, where she was stripped naked and subjected to electrical shock for thirty-five days. Then she was moved to a secret prison near Tegucigalpa where her questioners, following the CIA's more refined psychological methods, "gave her raw dead birds and rats for dinner, threw freezing water on her naked body every half hour for extended periods and made her stand for hours without sleep and without being allowed to urinate." Although American CIA agents visited both prisons and interrogated the prisoners, it is not clear whether they knew of these abusive practices and tolerated them as an acceptable level of coercion. Sergeant Caballero said the "Americans didn't accept physical torture," but the CIA nonetheless backed the rise of Colonel Álvarez to command the army even though another local colonel had denounced him as a killer at a press conference in 1982. Indeed, U.S. ambassador John D. Negroponte told the *Times* that Colonel Álvarez was "a hard man but an effective officer" needed in a country where "Marxist guerillas are organizing." And one U.S. official added about the torture: "The C.I.A. knew what was going on, and the Ambassador complained sometimes. But most of the time they'd look the other way."[85]

This *New York Times* exposé of the CIA's role in Honduras prompted a congressional inquiry that, though somewhat cursory, did reveal, for the first time, the existence of the Agency's torture training manuals. When the U.S. Senate's Select Committee on Intelligence, responsible for legislative oversight of the CIA, met in closed session to review the *Times*'s allegations, its chair, Senator David Boren (D.-Okla.), stated that in the course of the Agency's internal review of these allegations "several interrogation training manuals, including one used to train the Hondurans, had been uncovered." The techniques in these manuals were, in Boren's view, "completely contrary to the principles and policies of the United States."[86]

Significantly, a fact sheet prepared for the committee showed that U.S. Army Special Forces had conducted at least seven "human resources exploitation" courses in Latin America between 1982 and 1987—a frequency confirming that the CIA had indeed shifted its interrogation training from police advisers to U.S. Army instructors after Congress abolished OPS in 1975.[87]

Cold War Aftermath

With the end of the Cold War, the United States resumed its active participation in the global human rights movement through both diplomacy and domestic legislation. In 1991, Congress passed the U.S. Protection for Victims of Torture Act to allow civil suits in U.S. courts against foreign perpetrators who enter American jurisdiction—using the same narrow definition of "mental pain" that the State and Justice Departments had drafted for the Reagan administration back in 1988.[88] And at the 1993 Vienna Human Rights conference, Washington revived its vigorous advocacy of a universal humanitarian standard, opposing the idea of exceptions for "regional peculiarities" advocated by dictatorships of the left and right, China and Indonesia.[89] A year later, when Congress, at President Clinton's behest, ratified the UN Torture Convention, it also amended the U.S. criminal code to make torture, as narrowly redefined by the Reagan administration in 1988, a crime punishable by twenty years' imprisonment.[90]

While civil authorities had ratified the UN anti-torture convention in ways that legitimated psychological torture within U.S. criminal law, the Army was complying fully with the Geneva Conventions by making all torture, physical and psychological, crimes under the U.S. Uniform Code of Military Justice.[91] The sum of these reforms, civil and military, amounted to a contradictory conclusion of the Cold War. In effect, Washington had by the late 1990s buried this contradiction between its anti-torture principles and its continuing practice of torture, only to see it erupt with phenomenal force just a few years later in the Abu Ghraib controversy.

Global War on Terror

Right after his public address to a shaken nation on September 11, 2001, President Bush gave his White House staff wide secret orders, saying, "I don't care what the international lawyers say, we are going to kick some ass." Within weeks, the White House began issuing formal, albeit top-secret, orders for extreme interrogation by both the military and CIA.[92]

In the months that followed, administration attorneys devised three controversial legal doctrines to translate their president's otherwise unlawful orders into U.S. policy. From the start, these controversial directives were carefully cloaked in three legal arguments derived, at base, from a neoconservative doctrine of overarching presidential power called the "New Paradigm." Arguing, most fundamentally, that the president is above the law, administration lawyers such as Alberto Gonzales, then White House counsel, and David S. Addington, the vice president's chief of staff, said the president could override laws and treaties as commander in chief to order torture or ignore the Geneva Conventions.[93] Next, in a search for legal loopholes to justify such orders, Assistant Attorney General Jay Bybee found grounds, in his now notorious August 2002 memo, for exculpating any CIA interrogators who would torture but later claimed their intention was not to inflict pain but to gain information. Moreover, by parsing the UN and U.S. definitions of torture as "severe" physical or mental pain, Bybee concluded that suffering equivalent to "organ failure" was legal—effectively allowing torture up to the point of death. Finally, as the administration began confining terror suspects at Guantánamo Bay in January 2002, Justice Department lawyer John Yoo argued that this U.S. Navy base was not U.S. territory and was thus beyond the writ of U.S. courts.

Throughout 2002–3, the CIA controlled a clandestine network of allied security services—a veritable "spider's web spun across the globe" of prisons, planes, and operatives—that allowed it to seize and torture suspects, successfully and secretly, anywhere in the world. In February 2002, the CIA asked for assurances that the Bush administration's public pledge to abide by the Geneva Conventions did not apply to its operatives, and it was allowed ten "enhanced" interrogation methods designed by "agency psychologists," including "water boarding." In a departure from past practice, the White House allowed the agency to hold suspects in its own prisons, and soon the CIA opened some eight "black sites" stretching from Poland to Thailand. Inside these secret prisons, the CIA used enhanced psychological torture techniques, minimizing fatalities or crude brutality that might spark dissent within the Agency or the military. When blatant physical techniques were needed, the CIA dispatched detainees to nations notorious for torture—including, Morocco, Egypt, Syria, and, most brutal of all, Uzbekistan. To maintain the secrecy of these movements, the agency operated two dozen charter jets, veiled by front companies, that made some 2,600 secret flights between 2001 and late 2005. Through this network of allied secret services, the CIA transcended the territorial controls of any nation or international body, plucking individuals from sovereign states and levitating them into a secret, supranational gulag.[94]

Under the escalating pressures of the war on terror, the expanded interrogation techniques originally intended for a few top al-Qaeda targets would migrate from Guantánamo to Bagram and Abu Ghraib, becoming more brutal with each stage in this clandestine progress.

In late 2002, Defense Secretary Rumsfeld appointed General Geoffrey Miller to command Guantánamo, giving him wide latitude for interrogation and allowing him to make this prison an ad hoc behavioral laboratory for the perfection of the CIA's psychological paradigm. Moving beyond the original attack on sensory receptors universal to all humans, Guantánamo's interrogators stiffened the psychological assault by exploring Arab "cultural sensitivity" to sexuality, gender identity, and fear of dogs. General Miller also formed Behavioral Science Consultation teams of military psychologists who probed each detainee for individual phobias, such as fear of the dark or attachment to mother.[95] Through this total three-phase attack on sensory receptors, cultural identity, and individual psyche, Guantánamo perfected the CIA's psychological paradigm. Significantly, after visits to Guantánamo between January 2002 and June 2004, the International Red Cross, in uncharacteristically blunt language, concluded: "The construction of such a system . . . cannot be considered other than an intentional system of cruel, unusual and degrading treatment and a form of torture."[96]

Under the pressure of the Iraq occupation, these brutal interrogation policies quickly proliferated to involve thousands of ordinary Iraqis. In August 2003, Iraq suffered a wave of terror bombings that rocked the Jordanian embassy, causing nineteen deaths, and blasted UN headquarters, leaving twenty-three dead, including its head, Sérgio Vieria de Mello. One U.S. military study soon found that the lethal roadside bombings were "the result of painstaking surveillance and reconnaissance" and that rebels drew their intelligence from sympathizers in both the Iraqi police and the secure U.S. Green Zone in downtown Baghdad. In striking contrast to the rebels, the U.S. command realized, in this study's words, that its own "human intelligence is poor or lacking . . . due to the dearth of competence and expertise." As American casualties surged and violence spread, U.S. headquarters in Baghdad ordered sweeps of civilian neighborhoods, rounding up suspects and filling up military prisons, whose populations soon swelled from 3,500 to 18,000. "The gloves are coming off gentlemen regarding these detainees," a captain e-mailed his Military Intelligence (MI) comrades in mid-August. "Casualties are mounting and we need to start gathering info to help protect our fellow soldiers from any further attacks. I thank you for your hard work and dedication. MI ALWAYS OUT FRONT!"[97]

These CIA torture techniques reached Abu Ghraib from Guantánamo by two routes—indirectly from Afghanistan and directly through General Miller's personal mission to Iraq. As the insurgency erupted in August, Defense Secretary Donald Rumsfeld reportedly acted with characteristic decisiveness by ordering his "special-access program" operatives into Iraq, inserting them into U.S. military prisons with authority for harsh interrogation beyond U.S. Army regulations.[98] That summer, at a Pentagon briefing about the growing Iraq insurgency, Secretary Rumsfeld "complained loudly" about poor intelligence from Iraq, contrasting it with the yield from his new "extreme" interrogation practices at Guantánamo. Voicing "anger and frustration" over the application of the Geneva Conventions in Iraq, Rumsfeld gave oral orders for his Guantánamo commander, General Miller, to "Gitmo-ize" Iraqi intelligence. Consequently, in early September 2003, the general, who had spent the past nine months developing Guantánamo's regimen, inspected Iraqi prisons with "a team of personnel experienced in strategic interrogation," recommending, in a classified report for army headquarters in Baghdad, that "it is essential that the guard force be actively engaged in setting the conditions for successful exploitation of internees." General Miller also urged a radical restructuring in detainee policy to make

Iraq's prisons the front line for information warfare, saying: "Detention operations must act as an enabler for interrogation . . . to provide a safe, secure and humane environment that supports the expeditious collection of intelligence." In expansive, almost visionary rhetoric, General Miller wrote that his program would allow Abu Ghraib to "drive the rapid exploitation of internees to answer . . . theater and national level counter terrorism requirements," thus meeting the "needs of the global war on terrorism." If implemented immediately, his plan would, he said, produce "a significant improvement in actionable intelligence . . . within thirty days."[99]

Explaining his plan to "Gitmo-ize" Abu Ghraib, General Miller added, "We're going to select the MPs [Military Police] who can do this, and they're going to work specifically with the interrogation team." General Miller left an interrogation manual and compact disc with what he called "training information" to facilitate integration of the MPs into his new procedure. In one of his internal reports that September, Miller also advised that "teams, comprised of operational behavioral psychologists and psychiatrists, are essential in developing integrated interrogation strategies and assessing interrogation intelligence."[100]

Indeed, on September 14, just five days after General Miller's departure, the U.S. commander for Iraq, Lieutenant General Ricardo S. Sanchez, signed a remarkable memo authorizing, in the words of a later inquiry, "a dozen interrogation techniques beyond [Army] Field Manual 34–52—[and] five beyond those applied at Guantanamo."[101] In his instructions, Sanchez explained that his "Interrogation and Counter-Resistance Policy" was "modeled on the one . . . for interrogations conducted at Guantanamo Bay, but modified for applicability to a theater of war in which the Geneva Conventions apply." In a very restricted distribution, Sanchez provided copies of his guidelines only to Military Intelligence, denying knowledge of these extreme measures to his Military Police chief, General Janis Karpinski, or her officers. In this memo, which remained in effect for a month until modified in October, the general ordered sophisticated psychological torture, derived from the CIA's basic methods of sensory disorientation and self-inflicted pain:

T. Dietary Manipulation: Changing the diet of a detainee . . .

U. Environmental Manipulation: Altering the environment to create moderate discomfort (e.g. adjusting temperatures or introducing an unpleasant smell) . . .

V. Sleep Adjustment: Adjusting the sleeping times of the detainee (e.g. reversing the sleeping cycles from night to day) . . .

X. Isolation: Isolating the detainee from other detainees while still complying with basic standards of treatment . . . Use of this technique for more than 30 days . . . must be briefed to 205th MI BDE Commander prior to implementation.

Y. Presence of Military Working Dogs: Exploits Arab fear of dogs while maintaining security during interrogations . . .

Z. Sleep Management: Detainee provided minimum 4 hours of sleep per 24 hour period, not to exceed 72 continuous hours.

AA. Yelling, Loud Music, and Light Control: Used to create fear, disorient detainee and prolong capture shock. Volume controlled to prevent injury . . .

CC. Stress Positions: Use of physical posturing (sitting, standing, kneeling, prone, etc.) . . . Use of technique(s) will not exceed 4 hours.

So extreme was the sum of these methods that military lawyers objected and, a month later, Sanchez rescinded some of the "harshest techniques." Nonetheless, the force of these memos was soon felt at remote Army outposts and inside Abu Ghraib prison. "On 15 Oct 2003," one prisoner told investigators, "they started punishing me in all sorts of ways . . . and they cuffed me high for 7 or 8 hours. And that caused a rupture to my right hand . . . And in the following days, they also put a bag over my head, and of course, this whole time I was without clothes and without anything to sleep on." That September as well, the 82nd Airborne Division started torturing Iraqi captives with "beatings, exposure to extremes of heat and cold . . . and sleep deprivation." Of particular note, the *New York Times* reported the soldiers had learned these "stress techniques" in Afghanistan "watching Central Intelligence Agency operatives interrogating prisoners."[102]

Significantly, General Sanchez, though trained as an ordinary combat commander, had issued orders for a multifaceted assault on the human psyche. The synergy of these specific interrogation techniques was a systematic attack on all human stimuli, psychological and biological, quite similar to the CIA's 1963 Kubark manual and its 1983 Honduran handbook.

Indeed, a close comparison of Sanchez's memo with the CIA's 1983 manual for training Honduran military interrogators reveals six key points of similarity, in both broad principles and particular methods. As the Honduran handbook explains, "successful questioning is based upon . . . psychological techniques." In very similar language, General Sanchez advises that "interrogation approaches are designed to manipulate the detainee's emotions and weaknesses to gain his willing cooperation." Just as the CIA's 1963 Kubark manual and 1983 Honduran handbook emphasize "isolation, both physical and psychological, must be maintained" to effect sensory disorientation, so in 2003 Sanchez orders "isolating the detainee from other detainees," "reversing sleep cycles from night to day," and "dietary manipulation." Emphasizing the importance of self-inflicted pain, the CIA's Honduran handbook teaches that "pain which he [the subject] feels he is inflicting upon himself is more likely to sap his resistance," while the general achieves the same effect by authorizing "stress positions: use of physical postures (sitting, standing, kneeling, prone, etc.)." In their lists of more specific techniques, all three documents try to create an environment that elevates the interrogator, by making him, as Sanchez puts it, "appear to be the one who controls all aspects of the interrogation," while simultaneously breaking down the detainee by "significantly increasing the fear level." This specific sequence of psychological techniques indicates the Agency's methods had, in fact, spread to become the conceptual foundation for standard U.S. interrogation doctrine, even within the regular military. Clearly, in both its design and detail, General Sanchez's memo was influenced by past CIA interrogation research.[103]

The impact of these command initiatives was soon manifest in harsher interrogation at Abu Ghraib. To improve the intelligence yield, in July 2003 veteran army interrogators from the 519th Military Intelligence Battalion, led by Captain Carolyn A. Wood, had arrived from the CIA's Bagram center near Kabul. As the insurgency intensified, these interrogators were already working to introduce harsh methods to Abu Ghraib—including some that had already produced several Afghan fatalities. From October to December, moreover, a six-person team traveled from Cuba to Iraq bringing the "lessons learned" at Guantánamo Bay, notably the use of military dogs. One team member, Staff Sergeant James Vincent Lucas, later testified that they introduced Abu Ghraib interrogators to Guantánamo's aggressive, innovative techniques including "short chaining" and "clothing removal." Apparently building upon these procedures, as well as orders from Miller and Sanchez, Military Police in the security blocks at Abu Ghraib began to soften up detainees for CIA and MI interrogation with techniques documented, in the words of a later Army report, by "numerous photos and videos portraying in graphic detail detainee abuse by Military Police." One of the MPs later convicted of abuse, Private Ivan L. Frederick, recalled that an interrogator gave him lists of prisoners he wanted dog handlers to visit, and guards then used the animals to "intimidate inmates." Significantly, cell blocks 1-A and 1-B, the sites of the notorious Abu Ghraib photographs, had been informally removed from General Karpinski's command and were now controlled by two intelligence officers who reported directly to General Sanchez's headquarters in Baghdad—Colonel Thomas M. Pappas and Lieutenant Colonel Steve Jordan.[104]

Then, on November 19, 2003, General Sanchez issued orders removing all of Abu Ghraib prison from General Karpinski's command and assigning it, along with the top-secret facility near Baghdad airport known as Camp Cropper, to the 205th Military Intelligence Brigade under Colonel Pappas— a division of authority that army investigators later called "not doctrinally sound" since it exacerbated an already "ambiguous command relationship." In the months of most intense abuse in late 2003, General Sanchez summoned Colonel Pappas for periodic grillings and pressed him hard to deliver more intelligence.[105]

Under Colonel Pappas, MPs at Abu Ghraib were responsible for an initial phase of intensive disorientation to prepare detainees for later interrogation by CIA, MI, and private contractors, producing what the Army's investigation later called "numerous incidents of sadistic, blatant, and wanton criminal abuses . . . on several detainees." In the words of Major General Antonio Taguba's investigation, this abuse involved "punching, slapping, and kicking detainees" and "keeping them naked for several days at a time." In the escalation that often comes with psychological torture, this treatment soon moved beyond sleep and sensory deprivation to sexual humiliation marked by "photographing naked male and female detainees; forcibly arranging detainees in various sexually explicit positions . . . ; forcing groups of male detainees to masturbate while being photographed." Dismissing the idea of such behavior as simply aberrant, General Taguba's inquiry found that "Military Intelligence (MI) interrogators and Other U.S. Government Agency's (OGA) [CIA] actively requested that MP guards set physical and mental conditions for favorable interrogation."[106]

In making this latter charge, General Taguba cited a revealing statement by one of the MPs later accused of abuse, Sabrina Harman. She was, she said, ordered to stop prisoners from sleeping, including one famously photographed on a box with wires attached to his hands and feet. "MI wanted them to talk," she said, and then implicated two of her fellow MPs. "It is Graner and Frederick's job to do things for MI and OGA [CIA] to get these people to talk."[107]

As part of General Taguba's investigation, the MI chief at Abu Ghraib, Colonel Pappas, drew up a memo on "Interrogation and Counter-Resistance Policy" in January 2004 outlining the procedures he had been using in cell blocks 1-A and 1-B. Significantly, his orders required MI interrogators, in cooperation with physicians and MPs, to apply a method whose larger design seems derived from the CIA's trademark fusion of sensory deprivation and self-inflicted pain. "Typically," Pappas wrote, MI interrogators give MP guards "a copy of the interrogation plan and a written note as to how to execute [it] . . . The doctor and psychiatrist also look at the files to see what the interrogation plan recommends." This policy, Pappas contends, followed innovations at Guantanamo Bay where teams of psychologists and psychiatrists helped tailor harsh techniques to break individual prisoners. At Abu Ghraib, Colonel Pappas's interrogators used seven sensory-disorientation techniques to soften up prisoners, including:

1. "dietary manipulation—minimum bread and water, monitored by medics"
2. "environmental manipulation—i.e. reducing A.C. [air-conditioning] in summer, lower[ing] heat in winter"
3. "sleep management—for 72-hour time period maximum, monitored by medics"

4. "sensory deprivation—for 72-hour time period maximum, monitored by medics"
5. "isolation—for longer than 30 days"
6. "stress positions"
7. "presence of working dogs"[108]

Then, in the second phase of Colonel Pappas's program, trained MI and CIA operatives administered the requisite mix of interrogation and self-inflicted pain—a process that evidently took place outside the frame of the now famous photographs. Under the 205th Military Intelligence Battalion, forced nudity became a standard interrogation procedure to humiliate and break prisoners at Abu Ghraib, seeking answers to seven key questions—notably, "who and where are the mid-level Ba'athists," "which organizations or groups . . . will conduct high payoff attacks," "what organizations are Ba'athist surrogates," and "who are the saboteurs against infrastructure?" Amidst this harsh regimen, there were, moreover, increasing incidents of capricious cruelty. In November 2003, for example, five Iraqi generals suspected of instigating a small prison riot were manacled, blindfolded, and beaten by guards "until they were covered in blood." Although the prison's Detainee Assessment Branch filed at least twenty reports of serious abuse with General Sanchez and General Fast, headquarters did not intervene. Significantly, General Taguba later found that Colonel Pappas and his deputy, Lieutenant Colonel Steven L. Jordan, chief of the Joint Interrogation and Debriefing Center, were "directly or indirectly responsible" for the prisoner abuse at Abu Ghraib.[109]

In contrast to General Taguba's succinct, dispassionate descriptions, a February 2004 Red Cross report offers explicit, even chilling details of U.S. interrogation techniques. Through late 2003, the International Committee of the Red Cross (ICRC) made twenty-nine visits to U.S. detention facilities across Iraq, exercising their right to arrive unannounced for unrestricted inspections. While conditions for most detainees were, the Red Cross found, satisfactory, those "under supervision of Military Intelligence were at high risk of being subjected to a variety of harsh treatments ranging from insults, threats and humiliation to both physical and psychological coercion, which in some cases was tantamount to torture." Some coalition military intelligence officers told the ICRC that "between 70 percent and 90 percent" of detainees in Iraq, totaling over 41,000 by mid 2004, "had been arrested by mistake." In their visits to Abu Ghraib's military intelligence section, several U.S. officers told the ICRC that "it was part of the military intelligence process to hold a person . . . naked in a completely dark and empty cell for a prolonged period [and] to use inhumane and degrading treatment, including physical and psychological coercion." In words that could have been lifted almost verbatim from past CIA interrogation manuals, the ICRC detailed the forms of "ill treatment" that U.S. Military Intelligence used "in a systematic way to . . . extract information" from Iraqi detainees:

—Hooding, used to prevent people from seeing and to disorient them, and also to prevent them from breathing freely . . . ;

—Beatings with hard objects (including pistols and rifles) . . . ;

—Threats (of ill-treatment, reprisals against family members, imminent execution . . .);

—Being stripped naked for several days while held in solitary confinement . . . ;

—Being paraded naked outside their cells in front of other persons . . . ;

—Being attached repeatedly over several days, for several hours each time, with handcuffs to the bars of their cells door in humiliating (i.e. naked or in underwear) and/or uncomfortable position causing physical pain;

—Being forced to remain for prolonged periods in stress positions such as squatting or standing with or without the arms lifted.[110]

During a visit to Abu Ghraib in October 2003, the height of General Sanchez's extreme regimen, the ICRC discovered detainees "completely naked in totally empty concrete cells and in total darkness, allegedly for several days." The Red Cross medical staff determined that prisoners so treated were suffering from "memory problems, verbal expression difficulties, incoherent speech, acute anxiety reactions, . . . and suicidal tendencies." In sum, the ICRC concluded that U.S. Military Intelligence was engaged in practices that "are prohibited under International Humanitarian Law."[111]

In the aftermath of the Abu Ghraib scandal, the national press pursued stories confirming that the abuse shown in those photos was not, as the White House would have it, the work of a few bad apples but was instead both widespread and systematic. In September 2005, for example, the *New York Times* reported allegations by Captain Ian Fishback, a West Point graduate, that the 82nd Airborne Division had engaged in routine torture of Iraqi captives that included "beatings, exposure to extremes of hot and cold, stacking in human pyramids and sleep deprivation." Indicating the covert source of such methods, soldiers had "learned the stress techniques from watching Central Intelligence Agency operatives interrogating prisoners" in Afghanistan.[112] Similarly, in April 2006, the *Times* reported that a special Military Intelligence unit called Task Force 6–26, operating out of a secret base near Baghdad in 2003–4, had used a mix of elaborate psychological and crude physical tortures in its search for al-Qaeda leaders, becoming capriciously, even playfully cruel in their treatment of detainees.[113] A later Pentagon inquiry found that Special Operations forces had, during a four-month period in 2004, subjected Iraqi detainees to an extreme form of psychological torture involving starvation, stress positions, extreme cold, blaring music, and confinement in cells so small they could neither stand nor sit.[114] Reflecting on these incidents in Abu Ghraib prison and beyond, it seems that torture was systematic, not aberrant, and its widespread proliferation may be symptomatic of both command decisions and a crisis over a failing pacification effort.

Conclusion

If a Vietnam/Iraq analogy has relevance beyond a few obvious similarities such as the use of torture, then other aspects of Phoenix should prove predictive of future revelations about the underside of the Iraq war. Though it is difficult to document, torture's dual psychopathology of fear and empowerment makes it possible that this policy was adopted not just to extract information but to pacify a recalcitrant population with something akin to the counterterror used in South Vietnam. For hints of these revelations, we can, over the next half century, look beyond the specifics of torture techniques to the full Phoenix Program for other aspects of this counterterror campaign, for other dimensions of this dirty war, this *guerre sale.*

Apart from torture per se, CIA black lists, death squads, and deep-penetration agents were key facets of Phoenix that might be operating, beyond the ken of a press cosseted inside Baghdad's Green Zone, in the cities and villages of Iraq. It took thirty-five years for the most serious of Vietnam-era atrocities to emerge—notably, a systematic counterterror campaign by the 101st Airborne's elite Tiger Force that murdered hundreds of unarmed civilians, with command approval, over a period of six months.[115]

To date, just a few hints of similar covert operations have escaped the strict classification procedures the Bush administration has imposed over combat in Iraq. The first revelations about the CIA use of Iraq mercenaries, for example, emerged when the *Denver Post* won a court order breaking the national-security seal on pretrial hearings for soldiers charged with the murder of Major General Abed Hamed Mowhoush, the former Iraqi air defense chief. According to court records, General Mowhoush had walked into Forward Base "Tiger" at al-Qaim in the Iraqi desert on November 10, 2003, asking to see U.S. officers about the release of his son. At first the general cooperated, telling interrogators he was "commander of the al Quds Golden Division," a network of Saddam loyalists supplying the insurgents. When tough tactics backfired and the general grew silent, soldiers transferred him to the nearby "Blacksmith Hotel," a ramshackle desert prison where CIA and Special Forces were doing tactical interrogation. There he was worked over by an Agency operative named "Brian," a Special Forces veteran, and his four-man squad of "Scorpions," Iraqi mercenaries the CIA had first recruited for sabotage but were now using for counterguerrilla operations—just as the Phoenix Program had once used similar units, the PRUs, in South Vietnam. "When he didn't answer or provided an answer they didn't like, at first [redacted] would slap Mowhoush, and then after a few slaps, it turned into punches," Army investigator Curtis Ryan told the military court. "And then from punches, it turned into [redacted] using a piece of hose."[116]

Subsequent research indicates that the scope of the Scorpion operation was larger and more lurid than it had appeared from these first, fragmentary revelations. A year after the *Denver Post* exposé, the *Washington Post* reported that the CIA, acting on presidential finding signed in early 2002, had formed the Scorpions for an elaborate destabilization operation before the Iraq invasion and later, after Baghdad's fall, used them to penetrate the insurgency, doing what one agent called the "dirty work." At some point in this process, the CIA began using the Scorpions in interrogation and to snatch informants from dangerous areas outside the Green Zone. Most recently, *Newsweek* reporter Michael Isikoff reveals from interviews with the agency official who ran the program that about eighty Scorpions were trained in Nevada and were used for sabotage in western Iraq. During the invasion, however, they were preempted by another CIA squad of Kurdish paramilitary that "conducted a deadly series of drive-by shootings and ambushes of Iraqi military and Baath Party security officials. These were in effect targeted assassinations against identified regime figures."[117] At this rather preliminary point in our knowledge, it seems that the CIA has revived at least three key attributes of the Vietnam-era Phoenix Program—torture, assassination, and native mercenaries—for its covert war in Iraq.

In the future, we can expect more such revelations whose sum will portray the full scope of the covert pacification operations in Iraq and allow new comparisons with other similarities and differences, continuities and discontinuities with earlier U.S. efforts in South Vietnam.

Notes

Introduction by Lloyd C. Gardner and Marilyn B. Young

1. Editorial, "The Sound of One Domino Falling," *New York Times*, August 4, 2006.

2. Mark Silva, "No 'Amen Chorus' for Bush," *Chicago Tribune*, August 14, 2006, http://newsblogs.chicagotribune.com/news_theswamp/2006/08/no_amen_chorus_.html.

3. Friedman, "Big Talk, Little Will," *New York Times*, August 16, 2006.

4. Josef Joffe, *Uberpower: The Imperial Temptation of America* (New York: W.W. Norton, 2006), p. 100.

5. Henry Kissinger, *White House Years* (Boston: Little, Brown, 1979), pp. 56–57.

6. Paul Johnson, "America's New Empire for Liberty," *Hoover Digest*, fall 2003, http://www.hooverdigest.org/034/johnson.html.

7. Jim Rutenberg and Megan C. Thee, "Poll Shows Growing Skepticism in U.S. over Peace in the Middle East," *New York Times*, July 27, 2006.

8. "Notes on an Interview with Walter Lippman," Henry Brandon Papers, Library of Congress, box 59, folder 3.

9. Karl E. Meyer, *The Dust of Empire: The Race for Mastery in the Asian Heartland* (New York: Public Affairs, 2003), p. 21.

10. Memorandum, "Implications of an Unfavorable Outcome in Vietnam," September 11, 1967, p. 33, in Robert S. McNamara with Brian VanDeMark, *In Retrospect: The Tragedy and Lessons of Vietnam* (New York: Vintage, 1996), pp. 292–93.

11. Marilyn Young, *The Vietnam Wars, 1945–1990* (New York: Harper Collins, 1991), p. 135.

12. Michael Hirsh, "End of Days?" *Newsweek*, Web-exclusive commentary, July 31, 2006, MSNBC.com.

13. Kevin Phillips, "American Petrocracy," *American Conservative*, July 17, 2006.

14. John M. Broder, "Bush Calls Attack on Qana 'Awful,' but Refrains from Calling for Immediate Cease-Fire," *New York Times*, August 1, 2006. Emphasis added.

15. It is interesting to note, nevertheless, that the media still occasionally call American soldiers "GIs," short for "general inductees," thereby helping a very needy administration perpetuate the myth of the Iraq War as simply another phase of the World War II struggle in Europe and Asia.

16. David S. Cloud, "Rumsfeld, in Tajikistan, Urges Tough Stand Against Taliban," *New York Times*, July 11, 2006.

17. Paul von Zielbauer and David S. Cloud, "General Sees Need for More U.S. Forces in Baghdad," *New York Times*, July 12, 2006; Associated Press, "Iraqi Gunmen Kill 41 in Attack on Market," *International Herald Tribune*, July 17, 2006.

18. "Press Availability with Secretary Rumsfeld at the Pentagon," July 25, 2006, http://155.7.40.210/Transcripts/Transcript.aspx?TranscriptID=3054.

19. Edward Wong and Damien Cave, "July Deadliest Month in Iraq," *New York Times*, August 15, 2006.

20. "Putin Rejects Bush's Iraq Democracy Model," CNN.com, July 15, 2006.

1. *Parallel Wars?* by David Elliott

A version of this essay was initially given as a talk at the Shorenstein Asia Pacific Research Center, Stanford University, on May 15, 2006.

1. Bob Woodward, *Plan of Attack* (New York: Simon & Schuster, 2004), p. 37.

2. "Iraq No Quagmire for U.S.: Defense Secretary Says Fighting Likely Will 'Go On for Some Time,'" Associated Press and Reuters, July 1, 2003.

3. Melvin Laird, "Learning the Lessons of Vietnam," *Foreign Affairs*, November/December 2005.

4. Robert Taylor review of Yuen Foong Khong, *Analogies at War: Korea, Munich, Dien Bien Phu, and the Vietnam Decisions of 1965* (Princeton, NJ: Princeton University Press, 1992) in the *American Historical Review*, April 1993, pp. 786–87.

5. Mike Allen and Charles Lane, "Resolution Likened to '64 Vietnam Measure," *Washington Post*, September 20, 2002.

6. Warren Stroebel, "Bush Alters Plan to Stabilize Iraq: Administration Makes Sharp Policy Reversal," *Pittsburgh Post-Gazette*, May 1, 2004.

7. H.D.S. Greenway, "Vietnam's Lessons Forgotten in Iraq," *Boston Globe*, April 4, 2003.

8. Jules Crittenden, "Experts: Iraq War no Vietnam," *Boston Herald*, July 21, 2003.

9. John Hughes, "Why Iraq Is Not Like Vietnam," editorial, *Christian Science Monitor*, August 29, 2003.

10. "Iraq Is No Vietnam: The Flora and Fauna Are Different; So Is U.S. Strategy," *Pittsburgh Post-Gazette*, August 3, 2003.

11. John O'Sullivan, "Signs of Revived Order and Economic Recovery Are Real and Impressive," *Chicago Sun-Times*, July 29, 2003. For a critical view of the contention that Tet was really a disguised victory for the United States, see David W.P. Elliott, "Hanoi's Strategy in the Second Indochina War," in *The Vietnam War: Vietnamese and American Perspectives*, ed. Jayne S. Werner and Luu Doan Huynh (Armonk, NY: M.E. Sharpe, 1993).

12. Craig R. Whitney, "Tunnel Vision: Watching Iraq, Seeing Vietnam," *New York Times*, November 9, 2003.

13. *USA Today*, "Facts Fail to Support Popular Iraq-Vietnam Comparisons . . . Our View: History Shows Parallels Are Flawed. Repeat of Mistakes Can Be Avoided," November 7, 2003.

14. Bradley Graham, "Is Iraq Another Vietnam Quagmire? No and Yes," *Washington Post*, October 5, 2003.

15. Richard Cohen, "Vietnam It Isn't," editorial, *Washington Post*, October 30, 2003.

16. Thomas E. Ricks, *Fiasco: The American Military Adventure in Iraq* (New York: Penguin, 2006), p. 49.

17. Ibid., p. 321.

18. Ibid, p. 380.

19. Ibid.

20. Ibid, p. 380.

21. Richard Cohen, "Blind in Bangkok," *Washington Post*, April 13, 2004.

22. Michael Oreskes, "What's the Presidential Tipping Point?" *New York Times*, July 25, 2004.

23. Fung Yu-lan, *A Short History of Chinese Philosophy*, ed. Dirk Bodde (New York: Macmillan, 1948), p. 152.

24. Christine Hauser, "White House Disputes Iraq Is Sinking into Civil War," *New York Times*, March 19, 2006.

25. Jeet Heer, "Revisionists Argue that Counterinsurgency Won the Battle Against Guerrillas in Vietnam, but Lost the Larger War. Can It Do Better in Iraq?" *Boston Globe*, January 4, 2004.

26. Tom Donnelly and Gary Schmitt, "Counterinsurgency, Not Caution, Is the Answer in Iraq," *Washington Post*, October 26, 2003.

27. David Galula, the French advocate of using "revolutionary warfare" to retain control of Algeria, "was hardly an outrider in counterinsurgency theory. Rather, his work amounts to an updating and refinement of methods British officers had developed during many decades of operations in India, Africa, China, and the Middle East." Ricks, *Fiasco*, p. 266.

28. See, for example, the remarkable book by Janet Wallach, *Desert Queen: The Extraordinary Life of Gertrude Bell: Adventurer, Adviser to Kings, Ally of Lawrence of Arabia* (New York: Anchor Books, 1996).

29. Ricks, *Fiasco*, p. 267.

30. See Ricks's interesting discussion of this effort in the summer of 2004 in *Fiasco*, pp. 392–94.

31. Heer, "Counterpunch Revisionists."

32. Gregory Vistica, "Military Split on How to Use Special Forces in Terror War," *Washington Post*, January 5, 2004.

33. James Risen and John Burns, "Account of Broad Shiite Revolt Contradicts White House Stand," *New York Times*, April 8, 2004.

34. Lawrence Kaplan, "Clear and Fold: Forgetting the Lessons of Vietnam," *New Republic*, December 19, 2005.

35. Douglas Jehl and Thom Shanker, "For the First Time Since Vietnam, the Army Prints a Guide to Fighting Insurgents," *New York Times*, November 13, 2004.

36. Peter Maass, "Professor Nagl's War," *New York Times Magazine*, January 11, 2004.

37. David Galula, "From Algeria to Iraq: All but Forgotten Lessons from Nearly 50 Years Ago," *Rand Review*, summer 2006.

38. Ricks, *Fiasco*, p. 250.

39. D. Michael Shafer, *Deadly Paradigms: The Failure of U.S. Counterinsurgency Policy* (Princeton, NJ: Princeton University Press, 1988), p. 152.

40. Ibid.

41. Ricks, *Fiasco*, p. 267.

42. Matt Steinglass, "Vietnam and Victory," *Boston Globe*, December 18, 2005.

43. Ibid.

44. David W.P. Elliott, *The Vietnamese War: Revolution and Social Change in the Mekong Delta 1930–1975*, 2 vols. (Armonk, NY: M.E. Sharpe, 2002).

45. Maass, "Professor Nagl's War."

46. Ricks, *Fiasco*, p. 187.

47. Ibid., p. 188.

48. See, for example, Jonathan Finer, "In Iraqi Town, Trainees Are Also Suspects: U.S. Troops Wary After Incidents Suggest Betrayal," *Washington Post*, April 29, 2006.

49. Laird, "Learning the Lessons of Vietnam."

50. Jonathan Weisman, "Projected Iraq War Costs Soar," *Washington Post*, April 27, 2006.

51. Laird, "Learning the Lessons of Vietnam."

52. Marilyn B. Young, *The Vietnam Wars: 1954–1990* (New York: HarperCollins, 1991), p. 135.

53. Laird, "Learning the Lessons of Vietnam."

54. Ray Takeyh and Nikolas Gvosdev, "Flagging Winds of American Idealism Across the Middle East," *Christian Science Monitor*, December 15, 2004.

55. Warren Strobel, "Bush Alters Plan to Stabilize Iraq: Administration Makes Sharp Policy Reversals," *Pittsburgh Post-Gazette*, May 1, 2004.

56. Robin Wright and Ellen Knickmeyer, "US Lowers Sights on What Can Be Achieved in Iraq," *Washington Post*, August 14, 2005.

57. Maura Reynolds and Mark Mazzetti, "Senate Overwhelmingly Backs Resolution to Ease Out of Iraq," *Los Angeles Times*, November 16, 2005.

58. The most authoritative research on this subject has been done by Jeffrey Kimball. See "The Case of the 'Decent Interval': Do We Now Have a Smoking Gun?," http://www.ohiou.edu/shafr/NEWS/2001/SEP/INTERNAL.HTM.

59. Mark Mazzetti, "U.S. Generals Now See Virtues of a Smaller Troop Presence in Iraq," *Los Angeles Times*, October 1, 2005.

60. Ibid.

61. Lloyd C. Gardner, *Pay Any Price: Lyndon Johnson and the Wars for Vietnam* (Chicago: Ivan R. Dee, 1995), p. 446.

62. Mazzetti, "U.S. Generals Now See Virtue."

63. Borzou Daragahi, "Envoy to Iraq Sees Threat of Wider War," *Los Angeles Times*, March 7, 2006.

64. "President Bush and his aides are annoyed that people keep misinterpreting his Iraq policy as 'stay the course.' A complete distortion, they say. 'That is not a stay-the-course policy,' White House press secretary Tony Snow declared yesterday. Where would anyone have gotten that idea? Well, maybe from Bush." Peter Baker, "Bush's New Tack Steers Clear of 'Stay the Course,'" *Washington Post*, October 24, 2006.

65. Michael Abramowitz, "Called from Diplomatic Reserve: Former Secretary of State Leads Attempt to Salvage Iraq Mission," *Washington Post*, September 17, 2006.

66. Scott Shane, "Bush's Speech on Iraq War Echoes Voice of an Analyst," *New York Times*, December 4, 2005.

67. Robin Wright, "President's 'Strategy for Victory' Does Not Address Problems," *Washington Post*, December 1, 2005.

68. Ibid.

69. David Sanger, "Bush's Shift of Tone on Iraq: The Grim Cost of Losing," *New York Times*, September 2, 2006.

70. Ibid.

71. Nick Clooney, "Dust Off 'Enclave' Strategy for Iraq," *Cincinnati Post*, November 18, 2005.

72. Senator John McCain, "Senator McCain's Remarks on 'Winning the War in Iraq,'" speech at the American Enterprise Institute, November 10, 2005, http://www.friendsofmccain.com/news/dspnews.cfm?id=311 (accessed October 20, 2006).

73. Solomon Moore and Peter Spiegel, "U.S. Military Is Split on Insurgency Strategy," *Los Angeles Times*, May 13, 2006.

74. Fred Kaplan, "Hunkering Down," *Atlantic Monthly*, June 2006.

75. Stanley Karnow, *Vietnam: A History* (New York: Penguin, 1984), p. 19.

76. Stephen T. Hosmer, Brian M. Jenkins, and Konrad Kellen, *The Fall of South Vietnam* (New York: Crane, Russak, 1980).

77. Mark Mazzetti, "Pentagon Planning Document Leaves Iraq Out of the Equation," *Los Angeles Times*, January 24, 2006.

78. For a brilliant analysis of these and other historical traditions that have influenced U.S. foreign policy, see Walter A. McDougall, *Promised Land, Crusader State: The American Encounter with the World Since 1776* (Boston: Houghton Mifflin, 1998).

79. Ron Suskind, "Without a Doubt," *New York Times Magazine*, October 17, 2004.

80. Robert Jervis, *Perception and Misperception in International Politics* (Princeton, NJ: Princeton University Press, 1976).

81. Adam Gopnik, "The Big One," *New Yorker*, August 23, 2004.

2. *"I'm with You"* by Alex Danchev

1. Aristotle, *Ethics*, trans. J.A.K. Thomson (London: Penguin, 1976), p. 262 [1156a16–b2].

2. Ibid., pp. 263–64 [1156b2–1157a9].

3. On Nietzsche and the storied past, see Alex Danchev, "The Cold War 'Special Relationship' Revisited," *Diplomacy and Statecraft*, forthcoming.

4. Toast at the White House, February 5, 1998, www.number-10.gov.uk. The story was originally recorded by Churchill's doctor, who was there; Moran diary, January 1941, in Lord Moran, *Churchill: The Struggle for Survival* (London: Constable, 1966), p. 6. Blair came across it, he said, in Martin Gilbert's authorized biography. For Clinton's reaction, and the scandal-soaked atmosphere in Washington, see John Kampfner, *Blair's Wars* (London: Free Press, 2004), p. 89; Anthony Seldon, *Blair* (London: Free Press, 2005), pp. 372–73.

5. Oliver Franks, *Britain and the Tide of World Affairs* (Oxford: Oxford University Press, 1955), p. 35.

6. Speech at British Residence, Washington, February 20, 1985, www.margaret thatcher.org. There is a telling imbalance. Such speeches are more often delivered by prime ministers than presidents. Compare the irrepressible Bill Clinton, reminded of his obligation to mention the special relationship on the occasion of his first meeting with John Major, in 1993. "'Oh yes,' said Clinton. 'How could I forget. The "special relationship"!' And he threw back his head and laughed." Raymond Seitz, *Over Here* (London: Weidenfeld & Nicolson, 1998), p. 322. On the other hand, that was in private. In public, many gave as good as they got. See, e.g., Ronald Reagan's response to Thatcher, above.

7. Speech at Foreign Office Conference, London, January 7, 2003, www.number-10 .gov.uk.

8. Stephen Potter, "Hands-Across-the-Seamanship," in *One Upmanship* (1952), reprinted in *The Complete Upmanship* (London: Hart-Davis, 1970), p. 263.

9. See the Defence White Paper, *Delivering Security in a Changing World* (London: TSO, 2003). "The Defence Vision" in this document is a three-pronged affair: "defending the UK and its interests; strengthening international peace and security; a force for good in the world."

10. Bennett diary, May 29, 2003, in Alan Bennett, *Untold Stories* (London: Faber, 2005), p. 331; Jeff Chu, "Winning the Battle, Losing the War," *Time*, September 8, 2003.

11. John Lanchester, "Unbelievable Blair," *London Review of Books*, July 10, 2003. On the authenticity project, see Alex Danchev, "Provenance," *Journal for Cultural Research* 10 (January 2006), pp. 23–33.

12. Speech to Congress, July 18, 2003, www.number-10.gov.uk.

13. Speech at Bush Presidential Library, April 7, 2002, www.number-10.gov.uk.

14. Ibid.; speech to Congress, July 18, 2003; speech to Labour Party Conference, September 30, 2003, www.number-10.gov.uk. See Seldon, *Blair*, p. 616, drawing on an interview with Sir Peter Stothard, April 2, 2004. Stothard's fly-on-the-wall diary is *30 Days* (London: HarperCollins, 2003). He records as axiomatic in Blair's circle by September 2002 that "it would be more damaging to long-term peace and security if the Americans alone defeated Saddam Hussein than if they had international support to do so" (p. 87).

15. "Iraq: Prime Minister's Meeting," July 23, 2002, in Mark Danner, *The Secret Way to War* (New York: New York Review Books, 2006), p. 91. The memo was first published in the *Sunday Times*, May 1, 2005. At the meeting the attorney general listed three possible legal grounds for military action: self-defense, humanitarian intervention, and UN Security Council authorization. He discounted the first two, and considered the third "difficult" on the basis of preexisting resolutions. Blair's subsequent public pronouncements take their cue from this. "Regime change alone could not be and was not our justification for war. Our primary purpose was to enforce UN resolutions over Iraq and WMD." Speech in Sedgefield Constituency, March 5, 2004, www.number-10 .gov.uk.

16. Meeting of July 23, 2002, in Danner, *Secret Way*, p. 89 (emphasis added).

17. This memorandum, of a meeting on January 31, 2003, was disclosed in Philippe Sands, *Lawless World* (London: Penguin, 2006). Its contents are summarized in *The Guardian*, February 3, 2006, and the *New York Times*, March 27, 2006. A very similar

formulation was used by the CIA's former head of covert operations in Europe, Tyler Drumheller, in an April 23, 2006, interview with CBS News, at www.cbsnews.com/stories/2006/04/21/60minutes/main1527749.shtml.

18. Donald Rumsfeld was asked at a press conference on March 11, 2003, whether the United States would go to war without Britain. His answer is printed and discussed in Kampfner, *Blair's Wars*, pp. 290–91.

19. Hunter S. Thompson interviewed by Robert Chalmers, *Independent on Sunday*, October 31, 2004. "I almost felt sorry for Bush, until I heard someone call him 'Mr President,' and then I felt ashamed. Every nation in the world despises us, except for a handful of corrupt Brits, like that simpering little whore, Tony Blair."

20. Meeting of January 31, 2003. At this meeting Blair was still talking about a second UN resolution, though in purely instrumental (and somewhat debased) terms: as "insurance policy," providing "international cover," in case anything went wrong with the military campaign or Saddam raised the stakes (burning oil wells, killing children). Whether these were the terms he thought best calculated to appeal to the president is a matter for speculation, but they do not sit well with the public presentation of "offering Saddam the prospect of voluntary disarmament through the UN."

21. He is still proud of it, or at least determined to justify it. See his speech to the Foreign Policy Centre in London, March 21, 2006, at www.number10.gov.uk.

22. Bob Woodward, *Bush at War* (London: Pocket, 2003), p. 107, quoting an unnamed British official, apropos of Blair's visit to Washington in September 2001; speech to Labour Party Conference, September 30, 2003; speech at Foreign Office Conference, January 7, 2003.

23. James Naughtie, *The Accidental American* (London: Pan, 2005), quoting an unnamed British minister. In the 2003 film, the make-believe prime minister (the winsome Hugh Grant) finally repudiates the terms of the relationship: "A friend who bullies us is no longer a friend."

24. "Blair Might Be a Poodle, but at Least He Should Bark," "Blair the Intervener," and "Under Blair, Britain Has Ceased to Be a Sovereign State," *The Guardian*, February 22, 2001, April 30, 2002, and September 16, 2003. The latter two are collected in Hugo Young, *Supping with the Devils* (London: Atlantic, 2004), pp. 141–44 and 319–22. Young died a few days after the final column appeared. Blair paid him fulsome tribute.

25. John le Carré, *Absolute Friends* (London: Hodder, 2003), p. 257 (emphases in original). See also the interview with le Carré in Naughtie, *Accidental American*, p. 122.

26. Speech at the Economic Club, Chicago, April 24, 1999, www.number-10.gov.uk. The speech identified two dictators directly: "Many of our problems have been caused by two dangerous and ruthless men—Saddam Hussein and Slobodan Milosevic."

27. Kampfner, *Blair's Wars*, pp. 50–53; Seldon, *Blair*, p. 398. The invitees included the former diplomats Sir Rodric Braithwaite, Sir Michael Butler, Sir David Hannay, Sir Nicholas Henderson, Sir Robin Renwick, and Raymond Seitz, a transplanted American, together with Freedman and Timothy Garton Ash, of St Antony's College, Oxford. Freedman himself reflects briefly on the Blair and Weinberger doctrines in "The Transformation of Strategic Affairs," *Adelphi Paper* 379 (2006), pp. 43–44.

28. Caspar Weinberger, "The Uses of Military Power," *Defense '85* (January 1985), p. 10. The author was then secretary of defense. The Weinberger Doctrine was later supplemented by Colin Powell, as chairman of the Joint Chiefs of Staff, whose criteria centered on the clarity of the military objective and the ability to gauge when it has been achieved. For a recapitulation of U.S. doctrine, see Edwin J. Arnold, "The Use of Military Power in Pursuit of National Interests," *Parameters* XXIV (spring 1994), pp. 4–12.

29. Bin Laden's acute historical memory is a pronounced feature of his *Messages to the World*, ed. Bruce Lawrence, trans. James Howarth (New York: Verso, 2006).

30. Kampfner, *Blair's Wars*, p. 48; John Rentoul, *Tony Blair* (London: Time Warner, 2001), extracted at www.pbs.org/wgbh/pages/frontline/shows/blair/prime/better.html. Did Blair's advisers also come across Gideon Rose, "The Exit Strategy Delusion," *Foreign Affairs* 77 (January/February 1998), conveniently available on the Internet?

31. Kampfner, *Blair's Wars*, p. 49; Seldon, *Blair*, p. 395. See, e.g., the interview with Jack Straw in the *Times* (London), January 1, 2002, quoted in Peter Riddell, *Hug Them Close* (London: Politico's, 2004), p. 141.

32. Admiral Lord Lewin interviewed in Michael Charlton, *The Little Platoon* (Oxford: Blackwell, 1989), p. 203.

33. See Margaret Thatcher, *The Path to Power* (London: HarperCollins, 1995), pp. 87–91.

34. Nicholas Henderson interviewed in Charlton, *Little Platoon*, p. 195; *Mandarin* (London: Weidenfeld & Nicolson, 1994), p. 444. Henderson was British ambassador in Washington at the time. *The Official History of the Falklands Campaign* (London: Routledge, 2005) reveals an interesting strain of calculation and lack of wholeheartedness in Washington, mirrored by irritation and a sense of grievance in London. See Alex Danchev, "England Your England," *International Relations* 20, no. 3 (2006), pp. 364–69.

35. Kampfner, *Blair's Wars*, p. 6.

36. Meeting of July 23, 2002. Typically, this was an informal meeting, not a calendared meeting of the cabinet or a cabinet committee. Those present were the defense secretary (Geoff Hoon), the foreign secretary (Jack Straw), the attorney general (Lord Goldsmith), the cabinet secretary (Sir Richard Wilson), the chairman of the Joint Intelligence Committee (John Scarlett), the director of GCHQ (Francis Richards), the chief of the Secret Intelligence Service (Sir Richard Dearlove), the chief of the Defence Staff (Admiral Sir Michael Boyce), the prime minister's chief of staff (Jonathan Powell), and foreign policy adviser (David Manning), the director of policy and government relations (Sally Morgan), the director of government communications and strategy (Alastair Campbell), and an aide to David Manning (Matthew Rycroft). These last were truly the prime minister's people.

37. Kampfner, *Blair's Wars*, p. 117.

38. See Robin Cook, *The Point of Departure* (London: Pocket, 2004), p. 104; Kampfner, *Blair's Wars*, p. 161.

39. Woodward, *Plan of Attack*, p. 297, apparently on the evidence of Bush himself.

40. Blair interviewed by Michael Cockerell in *Hotline to the President*, BBC2, September 8, 2002. The interview was conducted on July 31, 2002. Parts of it are in Naughtie, *Accidental American*, pp. 135–36.

41. Ron Suskind, "Without a Doubt," *New York Times Magazine*, October 17, 2004.

42. Woodward, *Plan of Attack*, p. 178; Riddell, *Hug Them Close*, p. 199.

43. For the tiger-shooting test in Anglo-American relations, see Alex Danchev, "Tiger Shooting Together," *Reviews in American History* 18 (spring 1990), pp. 112–17.

44. Cockerell, *Hotline*, extracted in BBC News, "Britain Will Pay 'Blood Price'—Blair," September 6, 2002, http://news.bbc.co.uk/1/low/uk_politics/2239887.stm.

45. See Alex Danchev, *Oliver Franks* (Oxford: Clarendon, 1993), pp. 124ff.

46. By Margaret Thatcher and John Major during the Gulf conflict of 1990–91, for example, as Tony Blair must have known.

47. Wilson-Johnson telephone conversation, February 11, 1965, PREM 13/692, National Archives (UK); Harold Wilson, *The Labour Government* (London: Weidenfeld & Nicolson, 1971), pp. 80, 116. For Britain's miscellaneous contributions, overt and covert, and a judicious overall assessment, see John W. Young, "Britain and 'LBJ's War,' 1964–68," *Cold War History* 2 (April 2002), pp. 63–92.

48. Wilson, *Labour Government*, p. 264; Louis Heren, *No Hail, No Farewell* (London: Harper and Row, 1970), p. 231.

49. Bruce diary, March 22, 1965, quoted in John Dumbrell and Sylvia Ellis, "British Involvement in Vietnam Peace Initiatives, 1966–67," *Diplomatic History* 27 (January 2003), p. 117.

50. Jonathan Coleman, "Harold Wilson, Lyndon Johnson and the Vietnam War, 1964–68," *American Studies Today Online*, p. 3, www.americansc.org.uk; Wilson-Johnson telephone conversation, February 11, 1965.

51. Bundy to Johnson, July 28, 1965, in Coleman, "Harold Wilson," p. 3.

52. Coleman, "Harold Wilson," p. 4.

53. Bruce and Cooper to Rusk, February 11, 1967, in Dumbrell and Ellis, "Peace Initiatives," p. 140.

54. Cabinet meeting of November 15, 1967, in John Dumbrell, *A Special Relationship* (London: Macmillan, 2001), p. 150.

55. Cabinet meeting of March 7, 2002, in Cook, *Point of Departure*, p. 116.

56. Wilson preferred "close" to "special," and made some rhetorical play with the difference. See, e.g., speech of the University of Texas, April 30, 1971, in Ian S. McDonald, *Anglo-American Relations Since the Second World War* (London: David & Charles, 1974), pp. 219–22.

57. Cf. David Runciman, *The Politics of Good Intentions* (Princeton, NJ: Princeton University Press, 2006).

58. Seldon, *Blair*, p. 76; Woodward, *Plan of Attack*, pp. 178, 338.

59. Meeting of July 23, 2002, in Danner, *Secret Way*, p. 92. The foreign secretary, for his part, had ample cause for suspicion: he was removed from his post in May 2006. Allegedly the White House had conveyed its displeasure over his expressed views on the "military option" in the case of Iran.

60. Castle diary, July 18, 1966, in Barbara Castle, *The Castle Diaries 1964–70* (London: Weidenfeld and Nicolson, 1974), p. 148.

61. Noted (and contested) by Tony Blair himself, in an obituary appreciation, "Lessons of the Wilson Years," *Independent*, May 25, 1995. Cf. R.W. Johnson, "So Much Was Expected," *London Review of Books*, December 3, 1992; Hugo Young, "Architect of Labour's Ruined Inheritance," *Guardian*, May 25, 1995.

3. *Forlorn Superpower* by Wilfried Mausbach

1. Ivo H. Daalder, "The End of Atlanticism," in *Beyond Paradise and Power: Europe, America and the Future of a Troubled Partnership*, ed. Tod Lindberg (New York and London: Routledge, 2005), pp. 39–59.

2. See Jennifer Lee, "Critical Mass," *New York Times*, February 23, 2003.

3. Timothy Garton Ash, "The New Anti-Europeanism in America," in *Beyond Paradise and Power*, pp. 121–33, 130.

4. See, e.g., Martin Kettle, "Bush Blows In on a Chill Wind of Change," *The Guardian*, January 20, 2001; Michael Remke, "Er bleibt ein Cowboy," *Welt am Sonntag*, January 21, 2001.

5. President's Remarks at the 2004 Republican National Convention, Madison Square Garden, New York, September 2, 2004, http://www.whitehouse.gov/news/releases/2004/09/20040902-2.html.

6. Quoted in David E. Sanger, "To Some in Europe, Bush the Cowboy Is the Major Problem," *International Herald Tribune*, January 25, 2003.

7. Carlos Widmann, "Leichtgewicht, fest im Sattel," *Der Spiegel*, April 23, 2001, pp. 137–50; Andrew Gumbel, "President George W. Bush, Polluter of the Free World," *The Independent*, March 30, 2001.

8. Nobody has shaped George W. Bush's image in Europe more, of course, than author and director Michael Moore. His *Stupid White Men—and Other Sorry Excuses for the State of the Nation!* (New York: Regan Books, 2001) was quickly translated into major European languages, going through more than fifty printings with sales close to 1 million copies in Germany alone, where it also topped the nonfiction bestseller lists for more than a dozen weeks. In England, the book outsold soccer star David Beckham's biography and was named book of the year at the British Book Awards. Several hundred thousand copies were sold as well in Italy and France, where, moreover, Moore's anti-Bush film *Fahrenheit 9/11* won the top prize at the Cannes Film Festival in 2004.

9. USIA M-171-64: "West European Press Views President's '100 Days,'" January 13,

1964, Box 2, Record Group (hereafter RG) 306, Office of Research, Research Memoranda, 1963–1982, National Archives, College Park, MD (hereafter NA); Heinz Paechter, "Weisheit oder Ratlosigkeit? Johnsons Außenpolitik," *Der Monat* 16 (April 1964), pp. 27–31; Thomas Alan Schwartz, *Lyndon Johnson and Europe: In the Shadow of Vietnam* (Cambridge, MA: Harvard University Press, 2003), pp. 28–29.

    10. Robert Dallek, *Flawed Giant: Lyndon Johnson and His Times 1961–1973* (New York: Oxford University Press, 1998), pp. 84–90; *Parade*, May 31, 1964, p. 10; Schwartz, *Lyndon Johnson and Europe*, pp. 1–8.

    11. Kurt Birrenbach to Robert Strausz-Hupé, February 15, 1965, Box 015, I-433, Archiv für Christlich-Demokratische Politik, St. Augustin; Frank Costigliola, "Lyndon B. Johnson, Germany, and 'the End of the Cold War,' " in *Lyndon Johnson Confronts the World: American Foreign Policy 1963–1968*, ed. Warren I. Cohen and Nancy Bernkopf Tucker (New York: Cambridge University Press, 1994), pp. 173–210; Frank Costigliola, *France and the United States: The Cold Alliance since World War II* (New York: Twayne, 1992), p. 146; Richard N. Goodwin, *Remembering America: A Voice from the Sixties* (Boston: Little, Brown, 1988), p. 283.

    12. George Reedy, *Lyndon B. Johnson: A Memoir* (New York: Andrews and McMeel, 1982), p. 157; William H. Sullivan, *Obbligato 1939–1979: Notes on a Foreign Service Career* (New York: W.W. Norton, 1984), p. 234.

    13. Niels Werber, "Der Sheriff ist ohne Colt," *Taz*, October 2, 2001, p. 15; Gerald Kaufman, "Why I Oppose an Attack on Iraq," *Spectator*, August 17, 2002, pp. 12–13; Pew Global Attitudes Project, *America's Image Further Erodes, Europeans Want Weaker Ties: A Nine-Country Survey*, March 18, 2003, p. 1; Forschungsgruppe Wahlen, *Politbarometer*, February 2003; Trudy Rubin, "Bush: Disliked Cowboy?" *Philadelphia Inquirer*, February 21, 2003, p. A23.

    14. James Kitfield, "Daring and Costly," *National Journal*, July 10, 2004; Solana quoted in James Kitfield, "Pox Americana," *National Journal*, April 6, 2002. See also Michael Hirsh, "Bush and the World," *Foreign Affairs* 82 (September–October 2002), pp. 18–43; Elizabeth Pond, *Friendly Fire: The Near-Death of the Transatlantic Alliance* (Washington, DC: Brookings Institution Press, 2004), pp. 1–20.

    15. Philip H. Gordon and Jeremy Shapiro, *Allies at War: America, Europe, and the Crisis over Iraq* (New York: McGraw-Hill, 2004), pp. 49–55.

    16. Secretary Rumsfeld at Camp Pendleton Town Hall Meeting, August 27, 2002, www.dod.mil/transcripts/2002/t08282002_to827thm.html; Bob Woodward, *Bush at War* (New York: Simon & Schuster, 2002), p. 81.

    17. Memorandum for the President, Subject: A High Noon Stance on Berlin, July 22, 1961, box 117, President's Office Files: Countries, John F. Kennedy Library, Boston, MA; Frank Costigliola, "Kennedy, the European Allies, and the Failure to Consult," *Political Science Quarterly* 101 (1995), pp. 105–23; German Foreign Office Memorandum quoted in Knut Linsel, *Charles de Gaulle und Deutschland 1914–1969* (Sigmaringen: Jan Thorbecke Verlag, 1998), p. 174; Colin Powell Press Briefing on the President's Trip to Europe, May 28, 2002, www.state.gov/secretary/rm/2002/10516.htm.

    18. James Kitfield, "Divided We Fall," *National Journal*, April 8, 2006; Ball to Rusk, December 13, 1964, folder: NATO Mtg.—vol. II, box 365, Executive Secretariat—Conference Files 1949–1972, RG 59, NA; Atlantic Affairs Conference in Bonn, May 15–16, 1964, box 2, Bureau of European Affairs—Subject Files (J. Robert Schaetzel), RG 59, NA.

    19. Summary Record of the 528th Meeting of the National Security Council, April 22, 1964, Department of State, ed., *Foreign Relations of the United States* (henceforth *FRUS*) 1964–1968, vol. 1, p. 258; Fredrik Logevall, *Choosing War: The Lost Chance for Peace and the Escalation of War in Vietnam* (Berkeley: University of California Press, 1999), pp. 134–53; Rusk to U.S. ambassadors (circular), May 1, 1964, box 4, National Security File (NSF)—Vietnam, Lyndon B. Johnson Library (henceforth LBJL), Austin, TX.

    20. Aufzeichnung des Vortragenden Legationsrats I. Klasse Graf von Hardenberg, May 11, 1964, *Akten zur Auswärtigen Politik der Bundesrepublik Deutschland* (hence-

forth *AAPD) 1964*, ed. Institut für Zeitgeschichte (Munich: Oldenbourg, 1995), vol. 1, pp. 526–27, n. 7; Vermerk des Staatssekretärs Carstens, May 14, 1964, ibid., p. 540; George McGhee, *At the Creation of a New Germany: From Adenauer to Brandt. An Ambassador's Account* (New Haven and London: Yale University Press, 1989), pp. 143–45.

21. Lodge to Rusk, April 29, 1964, box 3, NSF—Vietnam, LBJL; Logevall, *Choosing War*, pp. 182–83; Ball to AmEmbassy Saigon, May 30, 1964, POL 27 VIET S, box 2943, Central Foreign Policy Files 1964–1966, RG 59, NA.

22. LBJ to U.S. ambassadors in Athens, Bangkok, Bonn, Brussels, Copenhagen, Karachi, London, Ottawa, Rome, Taipei, and Tokyo, July 2, 1964, box 6, NSF—Vietnam, LBJL.

23. Logevall, *Choosing War*, pp. 206–7; Lodge to LBJ, Visit to Western European Capitals as Your Special Representative, August 16 to September 2, 1964, September 9, 1964, box 484, W. Averell Harriman Papers, Library of Congress, Washington, DC; Hughes to Rusk, Research Memorandum INR-33: Third Country Assistance to South Vietnam, August 28, 1964, box 7, NSF—Vietnam, LBJL; CIA, The Situation in South Vietnam (15–21 October 1964), n.d., box 9, ibid.; Chester L. Cooper Memorandum for Mr. Bundy, Subject: Free World Assistance to Vietnam, April 29, 1965, box 18, NSF—Bundy File, LBJL; Michael Forrestal, Memorandum for the President, Third Country Assistance to Viet-Nam, December 11, 1964, box 11, NSF—Vietnam, LBJL.

24. Jansen to Lahr, Die Haltung der Bundesregierung zur Südvietnam-Frage, August 24, 1964, B 37/62, Politisches Archiv des Auswärtigen Amtes, Berlin (henceforth PAAA); Logevall, *Choosing War*, pp. 150–51, 222–26.

25. Logevall, *Choosing War*, pp. 152, 338–40; Dallek, *Flawed Giant*, pp. 258–60; Congressional Reception, February 12, 1965, box 1, Congressional Briefings, LBJL; Summary Record of National Security Council Meeting No. 532, May 15, 1964, *FRUS 1964–1968*, vol. 1, pp. 328–32.

26. Cooper to McGeorge Bundy, Subject: The British and Vietnam, December 4, 1964 [sanitized], box 214, NSF—United Kingdom, LBJL; TELCON Fowler-Ball, July 29, 1965, box 4, George W. Ball Papers, LBJL; John Dumbrell, "The Johnson Administration and the British Labour Government: Vietnam, the Pound and East of Suez," *Journal of American Studies* 30 (1996), pp. 211–31.

27. Von Jena to the German Defense Minister, May 5, 1965, B 37/161, PAAA; Institut für Demoskopie Allensbach, *Jahrbuch der öffentlichen Meinung 1965–1967* (Bonn: Verlag für Demoskopie, 1967), p. 478; "No Sir!," *Bild-Zeitung*, March 10, 1965.

28. McNaughton to McGeorge Bundy, December 4, 1965, box 17, NSF—Bundy File, LBJL; Rusk to the President and Acting Secretary, December 15, 1965, box 396, Executive Secretariat—Conference Files, RG 59, NA; Aufzeichnung über das Vier-Augen-Gespräch mit dem amerikanischen Verteidigungsminister McNamara am 20. Dezember 1965, January 11, 1966, Kai-Uwe von Hassel Papers, I-157–011/1, ACDP; Meeting in the West Hall, the White House, 10:45 p.m., Monday, December 20, 1965, box 26, NSF—President's Appointment File (Diary Backup), LBJL; McGhee, *At the Creation of a New Germany*, pp. 184–85.

29. Vorlage Dr. Lamby für Herrn Minister, Sitzung des Auswärtigen Ausschusses des Bundestages am 19.1.1966, January 17, 1966, Friedrich Karl Vialon Papers, I-475-016/4, ACDP; Schaefer to Lücke, Deutsche Hilfe für die Opfer des Krieges in Süd-Vietnam; Sitzung des Arbeitsausschusses am 4. März 1966 im BMI, March 3, 1966, B 106/41430, Bundesarchiv Koblenz (henceforth BAK); Press Conference von Hase, January 12, 1966, B 136/3656, BAK; Aufzeichnung für die Chefbesprechung am 24. Juni 1966 im Bundeskanzleramt für die weitere Finanzierung von Südvietnam-Hilfsprojekten, June 23, 1966, B 136/3657/1, BAK; Blumenfeld to Erhard, June 24, 1966, ibid.; Westrick to Blumenfeld, July 18, 1966, ibid.; Memorandum of Conversation (Lilienfeld—William Bundy), German Assistance to Southeast Asia, March 18, 1966, box 506, AID (GER W) ASIA SE, CFPF 1964–1966, RG 59, NA; Rüdt to Auswärtiges Amt, Subject: Deutsche Humanitäre Hilfe für Südvietnam, December 21, 1966, B 136/3657/1, BAK; Ergebnisvermerk über die Ressortbesprechung am 15. Februar 1967 im Bundesministerium des Innern, n.d., B 106/41432, BAK.

30. Dumbrell, "The Johnson Administration and the British Labour Government," p. 221; Hillenbrand to SecState, Kissinger Press Conference, August 23, 1967, box 194, NSF–Germany, LBJL; Nenni quoted in Leopoldo Nuti, "The Center-Left Government in Italy and the Escalation of the Vietnam War," in *America, the Vietnam War, and the World: Comparative and International Perspectives*, ed. Andreas W. Daum, Lloyd C. Gardner, and Wilfried Mausbach (New York: Cambridge University Press, 2003), pp. 259–78, 267; Cleveland to SecState, NATO Checklist for the New Administration, January 24, 1969, DEF 4 NATO box 1589, CFPF 1967–1969, RG 59, NA.

31. Carl T. Rowan, Memorandum for Heads of Elements/Country PAOs, Assignment of Priority Project: Viet-Nam, July 17, 1964, box 1, Administrative History—USIA, LBJL; Rowan Memorandum for the President, Information Support for Ambassador Lodge's European Mission, August 24, 1964, box 7, NSF—Vietnam, LBJL.

32. U.S. House of Representatives, 88th Congress, 2nd Session, *Hearings before a Subcommittee of the Committee on Appropriations. Departments of State, Justice, Commerce, the Judiciary, and Related Agencies Appropriations for 1967* (Washington, DC: GPO, 1966), p. 583; USIA, 24th Report to Congress, January 1–June 30, 1965, pp. 20–24; USIA, 25th Report to Congress, July 1–December 31, 1965, p. 6; Memorandum of Discussion, United States—Federal Republic of Germany Information Talks, Washington, May 6–7, 1965, box 2, Records of the Special Assistant to the Under Secretary for Political Affairs, 1963–1965, RG 59, NA; United States Senate, 89th Congress, 2nd Session, *Hearings Before the Committee on Foreign Relations: News Policies in Vietnam* (Washington, DC: GPO, 1966), p. 48.

33. Francis Fukuyama, "U.S. vs. Them," *Washington Post*, September 11, 2002, p. A17; Bush quoted in David S. Broder and Dan Balz, "How Common Ground of 9/11 Gave Way to Partisan Split," *Washington Post*, July 16, 2006, p. A1.

34. Address to a Joint Session of Congress and the American People, September 20, 2001, http://www.whitehouse.gov/news/releases/2001/09/print/20010920-8.html.

35. T.R. Reid and William Drozdiak, "Allies Express Support, Caution," *Washington Post*, September 23, 2001, p. A18; Stefan Kornelius, "Bushs Versprechen," *Süddeutsche Zeitung*, September 22, 2002, p. 4.

36. *Economist*, September 22, 2001; John Vinocur, "EU Solidarity Declaration Gives Both Sides a Victory," *International Herald Tribune*, September 24, 2001, p. 1; Simon Serfaty, "Cooperation or Failure," in *Beyond Paradise and Power*, pp. 181–97, 186.

37. James Kitfield, "A Suddenly Untethered Germany," *National Journal*, September 28, 2002; Kitfield, "Pox Americana."

38. Melvin R. Laird, "Iraq: Learning the Lessons of Vietnam," *Foreign Affairs*, November/December 2005; Ann Scott Tyson, "Rumsfeld Assails Critics of War Policy," *Washington Post*, August 30, 2006, p. A6; Preliminary Report of the Council on Global Terrorism, State of the Struggle Against Global Terrorism, September 2006, pp. 56–57; Mark Mazzetti, "Spy Agencies Say Iraq War Worsens Terror Threat," *New York Times*, September 24, 2006, p. A1.

39. U.S. Department of State, Aggression from the North: The Record of North Viet-Nam's Campaign to Conquer the South, Washington, DC, February 27, 1965; USIA, 24th Report to Congress, January 1–June 30, 1965, pp. 22–23; George Ball, Draft Presentation on Viet-Nam, NAC, Paris, July 12–13, 1965, box 380, Executive Secretariat—Conference Files, RG 59, NA; Rusk to SecState, May 12, 1965 and Rusk to SecState, NATO MinMtg Restricted Session May 12 on Viet-Nam and Dominican Republic, May 13, 1965, box 376, ibid.; USIA Office of Research, R-19-67: Trends in West European Public Opinion on Current International Issues, May 1967, box 14, RG 306, NA; USIA Office of Research, Special Report: Foreign Attitudes on the Viet-Nam Conflict, July 1970, box 8, ibid.

40. Asked in October 2003 whether military intervention in Iraq had been justified, majorities in all but two of the EU's fifteen member states answered in the negative. Only in Denmark did the majority (57 percent) think it was justified, while public opinion in the Netherlands was split down the middle (50–49). In all other countries, majorities ranging from 96 percent in Greece and 86 percent in Austria to 59 percent in Ireland and

Sweden felt that the war was unjustified. Even in Spain and the United Kingdom—U.S. allies in the endeavor—majorities of 79 and 51 percent, respectively, thought that military intervention was not justified. See Flash Eurobarometer, "Iraq and Peace in the World," November 2003, pp. 4–7.

41. See James Chace and Elizabeth Malkin, "The Mischief-Maker: The American Media and de Gaulle, 1964–68," in *De Gaulle and the United States: A Centennial Appraisal*, ed. Robert O. Paxton and Nicholas Wahl (Oxford and Providence, RI: Berg, 1994), pp. 359–76, and Robert Paxton's comment, 418; Elizabeth Pond, "The Dynamics of the Feud over Iraq," in *The Atlantic Alliance Under Stress: US-European Relations After Iraq*, ed. David M. Andrews (New York: Cambridge University Press, 2005), pp. 30–55, especially pp. 42–45; Gordon and Shapiro, *Allies at War*, 120–28; Wilfried Mausbach, "Triangle of Discord: The United States, Germany, and French Peace Initiatives for Vietnam," in *The Search for Peace in Vietnam, 1964–1968*, ed. Lloyd C. Gardner and Ted Gittinger (College Station: Texas A&M University Press, 2004), pp. 166–82.

42. Gary Younge and Jon Henley, "Wimps, Weasels and Monkeys: The US Media View of Perfidious France," *The Guardian*, February 11, 2003, p. 3; Christopher Hitchens, "The Rat that Roared," *Wall Street Journal*, February 6, 2003, p. A18; Felicia R. Lee, "Americans Turn Eagerly to Gibes at the French," *New York Times*, February 15, 2003; Justin Vaïsse, "Bringing Out the Animal in Us," *Financial Times*, March 15, 2003, p. 2; Jean-David Levitte, "A Warning on Iraq, from a Friend," *New York Times*, February 14, 2003, p. A31.

43. Viola Herms Drath, "Coalition of the Unwilling," *Washington Times*, March 28, 2003, p. A21; Anne Applebaum, "'Old Europe' versus 'New Europe,'" in *Beyond Paradise and Power*, pp. 25–37; Peter Berkowitz, "Liberalism and Power," in *Beyond Paradise and Power*, pp. 199–213; William Shawcross, *Allies: The U.S., Britain, Europe, and the War in Iraq* (New York: Public Affairs, 2004), pp. 96–98. Gordon and Shapiro, *Allies at War*, pp. 77–78, convincingly refute these imputations.

44. Carolin Emcke, Erich Follath, and Bernhard Zand, "Der Treibstoff des Krieges," *Der Spiegel*, January 13, 2003; Editorial, "The Iraq Oil Questions," *Los Angeles Times*, January 31, 2003, 14; Walter Russell Mead, *Special Providence: American Foreign Policy and How It Changed the World* (New York: Alfred A. Knopf, 2001); Pew Global Attitudes Project, *What the World Thinks in 2002*, December 4, 2002, p. 3; Andreas Oldag, "Öl taugt nicht als Kriegsgrund," *Süddeutsche Zeitung*, March 31, 2003, p. 4; Michael Hirsh, "Blood, Oil & Iraq," *Newsweek*, March 10, 2003, p. 37.

45. Deputy Secretary Wolfowitz interview with Sam Tanenhaus, *Vanity Fair*, May 9, 2003, http://www.defenselink.mil/Transcripts/Transcript.aspx?TranscriptID=2594; Remarks by Jean-David Levitte, French Ambassador to the U.S. to the United States Institute of Peace, Washington, DC, Federal News Service, February 7, 2003.

46. U.S. Senate, 109th Congress, 2d Session, Report of the Select Committee on Intelligence on Postwar Findings about Iraq's WMD Programs and Links to Terrorism and How They Compare with Prewar Assessments, September 8, 2006; Guy Dinmore, James Harding, and Cathy Newman, "Iraqi Arms Finds Not Likely, Says US Official," *Financial Times*, May 3, 2003; Noam Chomsky, "One Man's World," *New Statesman*, November 17, 2003; Gordon and Shapiro, *Allies at War*, p. 170; Henry A. Kissinger, "American Strategy and Pre-emptive War," *International Herald Tribune*, April 13, 2006; Philip Stephens, "Bush and Blair's Differing Designs for a Secure World," *Financial Times*, March 21, 2003, p. 23; Aillot-Marie quoted in Ralf Beste, "Gewaltiger Sturm," *Der Spiegel*, January 27, 2003, p. 83.

47. Bohlen Memorandum for the Secretary, December 12, 1966, folder Research Material, box 11, Records of Ambassador Charles E. Bohlen, Special Assistant to the Secretary, 1952–1963, RG 59, NA; Frank Costigliola, *France and the United States: The Cold Alliance since World War II* (New York: Twayne, 1992), pp. 136–46; Lloyd Gardner, "Lyndon Johnson and de Gaulle," in *De Gaulle and the United States*, pp. 257–78; Schwartz, *Lyndon Johnson and Europe*, pp. 104–5, 229–30; Tony Judt, "The Way We Live Now," *New York Review of Books*, March 27, 2003.

48. McLellan to Ryan, European Rider Survey No. 2, June 23, 1967, folder ZQ 6401, box 21, Office of Research, Records of Research Projects, Western Europe, 1964–1973, RG 306, NA; Wilfried Mausbach, "Auschwitz and Vietnam: West German Protest Against America's War During the 1960s," in *America, the Vietnam War, and the World*, pp. 279–98; Rush to Department of State, German Reactions to the Pinkville Issue, December 5, 1969, POL 27 VIET S, box 2823, CFPF 1967–1969, RG 59, NA; Helmut Sonnenfeldt, Memorandum for Mr. Kissinger: Schmidt, Brandt, and Heinemann on Vietnam, January 19, 1973, box 687, NSC—Country Files Europe, Nixon Presidential Materials Staff, NA.

49. Editorial, "Iraq: My Lai on the Euphrates?" *The Guardian*, June 1, 2006, p. 32; Thomas E. Ricks, "Officer Called Haditha Routine," *Washington Post*, August 19, 2006, p. A1; "My Lai Colonel Says All Big Units Are Guilty of Atrocities," *Los Angeles Times*, May 25, 1971, p. 1.

50. Seymour M. Hersh, *Chain of Command: The Road from 9/11 to Abu Ghraib* (New York: HarperCollins, 2004). The book was quickly translated into several European languages and published in inexpensive paperback editions. See Seymour M. Hersh, *Die Befehlskette: Vom 11. September bis Abu Ghraib* (Reinbek bei Hamburg: Rowohlt, 2004); *Dommages Collatéraux: La Face Obscure de la Guerre Contre le Terrorisme* (Paris: Denoël, 2005); *Catena di Comando: Dall'11 Settembre allo Scandalo di Abu Ghraib* (Milan: Rizzoli, 2004); *Obediencia Debida: Del 11-S a las Torturas de Abu Ghraib* (Madrid: Aguilar, 2004); *Bevel van Hogerhand: De Weg van 11 September tot het Abu Ghraib-Schandaal* (Amsterdam: De Bezige Bij, 2004). See also Mark Danner, *Torture and Truth: America, Abu Ghraib, and the War on Terror* (New York: New York Review Books, 2004); Karen J. Greenberg and Joshua L. Dratel, eds., *The Torture Papers: The Road to Abu Ghraib* (New York: Cambridge University Press, 2005).

51. "European Press Blast Rumsfeld Over Iraqi Prisoner Abuse," ONASA News Agency, May 8, 2004; editorial, "Resign, Rumsfeld," *The Economist*, May 8, 2004.

52. Hugo Young, "We Will Not Tolerate the Abuse of War Prisoners: Guantanamo Could Be Where America and Europe Part Company," *The Guardian*, January 17, 2002, p. 18; editorial, "The Mark of Civilisation," *Daily Telegraph*, January 16, 2002, p. 25; editorial, "The Guantanamo Story," *Washington Post*, January 25, 2002, p. A24.

53. Memorandum for the Vice President [et al.], Humane Treatment of al Qaeda and Taliban Detainees, February 7, 2002, in *Torture Papers*, pp. 134–35; Jay S. Bybee Memorandum for Alberto R. Gonzales, August 1, 2002, in *Torture Papers*, pp. 172–217, 172; William J. Haynes II Action Memo for the Secretary of Defense, Counter-Resistance Techniques, November 27, 2002 (approved by Secretary Rumsfeld December 2, 2002), in *Torture Papers*, pp. 236–37; Working Group Report on Detainee Interrogations in the Global War on Terrorism: Assessment of Legal, Historical, Policy, and Operational Considerations, April 4, 2003, in *Torture Papers*, pp. 286–359, especially pp. 302–7; Jennifer K. Elsea, "Presidential Authority to Detain 'Enemy Combatants,'" *Presidential Studies Quarterly* 33 (September 2003), pp. 568–601.

54. Thomas Kielinger, "Ein Volk hadert mit dem tiefen Sturz aus der Höhe des Idealismus," *Die Welt*, May 10, 2004; David Rose, *Guantánamo: America's War on Human Rights* (London: Faber and Faber, 2004), German edition: *Guantánamo Bay: Amerikas Krieg gegen die Menschenrechte* (Frankfurt am Main: S. Fischer, 2004).

55. Rumsfeld Memorandum for Commander USSouthCom, Counter-Resistance Techniques (U), January 15, 2003, in *Torture Papers*, p. 239; Sheryl Gay Stolberg, "President Signs New Rules to Prosecute Terror Suspects," *New York Times*, October 18, 2006, p. A20; Scott Shane and Adam Liptak, "Shifting Power to a President," *New York Times*, September 30, 2006, p. A1; Walter Pincus, "Waterboarding Historically Controversial," *Washington Post*, October 5, 2006, p. A17; Heisbourg quoted in John Ward Anderson, "Confirmation of CIA Prisons Leaves Europeans Mistrustful," *Washington Post*, September 8, 2006, p. A8; Andrew Moravcsik, "The Human Rights Blame Game," *Newsweek*, April 22, 2002, p. 26.

56. Jürgen Habermas and Jacques Derrida, "February 15, or, What Binds Europeans

Together," in *Old Europe, New Europe, Core Europe: Transatlantic Relations After the Iraq War*, ed. Daniel Levy, Max Pensky, and John Torpey (New York and London: Verso, 2005), pp. 3–13.

57. See Wilfried Mausbach, "European Perspectives on the War in Vietnam," *German Historical Institute Bulletin*, no. 30 (Spring 2002), pp. 71–86.

58. Craig Whitlock, "French Push Limits in Fight on Terrorism," *Washington Post*, November 2, 2004, p. A1; Craig Whitlock, "U.S. Faces Obstacles to Freeing Detainees," *Washington Post*, October 17, 2006, p. A1; "German Special Forces Admit Encounter with Kurnaz," *Spiegel Online*, October 19, 2006, http://www.spiegel.de/international/0,1518,443493,00.html.

4. *Manufacturing the Threat to Justify Aggressive War in Vietnam and Iraq* by Gareth Porter

1. Walter S. Robertson, the assistant secretary of state for Far Eastern affairs in the Eisenhower administration (and the father of televangelist and extreme right-wing political figure Pat Robertson), articulated this strategy in testimony for a congressional Committee in early 1954: "The heart of the present policy toward China and Formosa [Taiwan] is that there is to be kept alive a constant threat of military action vis-à-vis Red China in the hope that at some point there will be an internal breakdown. . . . In other words, a cold war waged under the leadership of the U.S. with constant threat of attack against Red China, led by Formosa and other Far Eastern groups and militarily supported by the United States." *Hearing before the Subcommittee on Appropriation*, House of Representatives, U.S. Cong., 2nd Sess. 1954, pp. 124–25.

2. Shu Guang Zhang, *Deterrence and Strategic Culture: Chinese American Confrontation, 1949–1958* (Ithaca, NY: Cornell University Press, 1992), p. 227; Wu Longxi, "Memoir: Inside Story of the Decision-making During the Shelling of Jinmen,'" *CWIHP Bulletin* 6–7 (winter 1995–96), p. 209.

3. Jay Taylor, *China and Southeast Asia: Peking's Relations with Revolutionary Movements* (New York: Praeger, 1976), pp. 195–203, 276–80; Melvin Gurtov, *China and Southeast Asia—the Politics of Survival* (Baltimore: Johns Hopkins University Press, 1971), pp. 11–12, 102–3; J.H. Brimmel, *Communism in Southeast Asia* (London: Oxford University Press, 1959), p. 318; Stanley S. Bedlington, *Malaysia and Singapore: The Building of New States* (Ithaca, NY: Cornell University Press, 1978), pp. 82, 83.

4. Gareth Porter, *Perils of Dominance: Imbalance of Power and the Road to War in Vietnam* (Berkeley: University of California Press, 2004), pp. 40–49, 108–19, 236–39.

5. Ibid., pp. 86–107, 255–56; Len E. Ackland, "No Place for Neutralism: The Eisenhower Administration and Laos," in *Laos: War and Revolution*, ed. Nina S. Adams and Alfred W. McCoy (New York: Harper and Row, 1970), pp. 139–55.

6. NSC 5612/1 and NSC 5809, "Statement of Policy on U.S. Policy in Mainland Southeast Asia," September 5, 1956, and April 2, 1958, *United States-Vietnam Relations, 1945–1967*, study prepared by the Department of Defense (Washington, DC: Government Printing Office, 1971), book 10, pp. 1094, 1133.

7. Testimony by Secretary of State Dean Rusk, January 15, 1962, in U.S. Congress, Senate, *Executive Sessions of the Senate Foreign Relations Committee Together with the Senate Armed Services Committee*, 87th Cong., 2d sess., 1962, Historical Series (Washington, DC: Government Printing Office, 1986), vol. 14, pt. 1, p. 68; memorandum from Assistant Secretary of State for Far Eastern Affairs Averell Harriman to Rusk, April 13, 1962, *Foreign Relations of the United States* [henceforth *FRUS*], *1961–1963*, vol. 12, pp. 216–17; memorandum from Deputy Assistant Secretary of State Edward Rice to Harriman, March 28, 1962, ibid., p. 199; Roger Hilsman, *To Move a Nation: The Politics of Foreign Policy in the Administration of John F. Kennedy* (New York: Dell, 1967), p. 317; "U.S. Policy toward Communist China," November 30, 1962, *FRUS, 1961–1963*, vol. 22, p. 273.

8. "SNIE 50–61: Outlook in Mainland Southeast Asia," March 28, 1961, *FRUS, 1961–1963*, vol. 23, pp. 59–60.

9. Daniel Fineman, *A Special Relationship: The United States and the Military Government in Thailand, 1947–1958* (Honolulu: University of Hawaii Press, 1997), 209–57; "Progress Report on U.S. Policy in Mainland Southeast Asia (NSC 5612/1)," November 26, 1957, in *United States-Vietnam Relations*, book 10, p. 1109.

10. Joseph B. Smith, *Portrait of a Cold Warrior* (New York: Ballantine, 1976), pp. 246–47, 271–72.

11. David Kaiser, *American Tragedy: Kennedy, Johnson and the Origins of the Vietnam War* (Cambridge, MA: Belknap Press of Harvard University Press, 2000), p. 101.

12. Ironically, Kennedy himself publicly embraced the domino theory in an interview with NBC on September 30, 1963. See *The Pentagon Papers*, Gravel edition (Boston: Beacon Press, 1972), vol. II, p. 828. But at that moment, Kennedy was planning secretly with his two leading national security advisers, McNamara and Taylor (then chairman of the Joint Chiefs of Staff), to get an official recommendation from them for withdrawal of all U.S. forces from South Vietnam by the end of 1965 accepted by the National Security Council as U.S. policy. With the 1964 election in mind, he was endorsing the domino theory to establish his strong anticommunist credentials with the public. See Porter, *Perils of Dominance*, pp. 165–79.

13. SNIE 50–64, "Short Term Prospects in Southeast Asia," February 12, 1964, quoted in Porter, *Perils of Dominance*, p. 245.

14. William Bundy, draft memo for LBJ, March 1, 1964, quoted in Porter, *Perils of Dominance*, pp. 245–46.

15. On State Department reporting and intelligence analysis on Malaysia and Indonesia in late 1963 and early 1964, see Porter, *Perils of Dominance*, p. 247.

16. William Bundy, memo to LBJ, January 7, 1964, quoted in Porter, *Perils of Dominance*, pp. 243–44.

17. Porter, *Perils of Dominance*; telephone conversation with Russell, May 27, 1964, in *Taking Charge: The Johnson White House Tapes, 1963–1964*, ed. Michael Beschloss (New York: Simon & Schuster, 1997), pp. 364–65.

18. Memorandum from Director of the Board of Estimates (Sherman Kent) to John McCone, June 9, 1964, *FRUS, 1964–1968*, vol. 1, p. 484.

19. Kai Bird, *The Color of Truth: McGeorge Bundy and Bill Bundy: Brothers in Arms* (New York: Touchstone, 1998), p. 285.

20. William Bundy, "Questions and Answers on a Congressional Resolution," June 15, 1964, quoted in Porter, *Perils of Dominance*, p. 251.

21. H.R. McMaster, *Dereliction of Duty: Lyndon Johnson, Robert McNamara, the Joint Chiefs of Staff and the Lies that Led to Vietnam* (New York: HarperCollins 1997), pp. 117–18.

22. Notes of a White House meeting, September 9, 1964, *FRUS, 1964–1968*, vol. 1, pp. 752–53.

23. William Bundy, "The Choices We Face in Southeast Asia," attachment to memorandum for Rusk, McNamara, Ball, and McGeorge Bundy (marked "First Draft"), October 15, 1964, and William Bundy, "II. U.S. Objectives and Stakes in South Viet-Nam and Southeast Asia," November 8, 1964, p. 2, both in the Kai Bird Collection of declassified documents, quoted in Porter, *Perils of Dominance*, pp. 252–53.

24. William Bundy, memorandum of Executive Committee meeting, November 24, 1964, Kai Bird Collection, cited in Porter, *Perils of Dominance*, p. 255; William P. Bundy and John P. McNaughton, "Courses of Action in Southeast Asia," revised draft, November 21, 1964, revised page, November 26, 1964, *Pentagon Papers*, Gravel ed., vol. 3, p. 658.

25. For profiles of the neoconservatives, see James Mann, *Rise of the Vulcans: The History of Bush's War Cabinet* (New York: Viking, 2004); Elizabeth Drew, "The Neocons in Power," *New York Review of Books*, June 12, 2003.

26. Statement of Russell E. Travers, DIA officer for general purpose forces, *An Assessment of the Bottom Up Review, Hearings Before the Military Forces and Personnel*

Subcommittee of the Committee on Armed Services, House of Representatives, 103rd Cong., 2nd Sess., March 1 and 22, 1994, pp. 7–8; Anthony Cordesman, *Iraqi Military Forces Ten Years after the Gulf War* (Washington, DC: CSIS, 2002).

27. Letter to Clinton, January 26, 1998, online at Project for the New American Century, http://www.newamericancentury.org/iraqclintonletter.htm.

28. Thomas Donnelly, *Rebuilding America's Defenses: Strategy, Forces and Resources for a New Century*, September 2000, online at Project for the New American Century, http://www.newamericancentury.org/RebuildingAmericasDefenses.pdf.

29. Ron Suskind, *The Price of Loyalty: George W. Bush, The White House, and the Education of Paul O'Neill* (New York: Simon & Schuster, 2004), p. 85.

30. Michael R. Gordon and General Bernard E. Trainor, *Cobra II: The Inside Story of the Invasion and Occupation of Iraq* (New York: Pantheon, 2006), p. 15.

31. Wesley K. Clark, *Winning Modern Wars: Iraq, Terrorism and American Empire* (New York: Public Affairs, 2003), pp. 120, 130.

32. Connie Bruck, "How Iran's Expatriates Are Gaming the Nuclear Threat," *New Yorker*, March 6, 2006, p. 51.

33. Jim Lobe, "How Neo-cons Influence the Pentagon," *Asia Times*, August 8, 2003.

34. Murray Waas, "Key Bush Intelligence Briefing Kept from Hill Panel," *National Journal*, November 22, 2005. Waas reported that the Senate Intelligence Committee later requested a copy of the "President's Daily Brief" for September 21 as part of its investigation of possible misrepresentation of prewar intelligence information about Iraq, but the Bush administration refused to make it available.

35. Ibid.; Robert Dreyfuss, "The Pentagon Muzzles the CIA," *American Prospect*, December 16, 2002; James Bamford, *A Pretext for War: 9/11, Iraq and the Abuse of America's Intelligence Agencies* (New York: Doubleday, 2004), pp. 289–90.

36. Bamford, *Pretext for War*, pp. 287–90; Waas, "Key Bush Intelligence Briefing"; Jeffrey Goldberg, "A Little Learning," *New Yorker*, June 9, 2005; Select Committee on Intelligence, U.S. Senate, 104th Cong., *Report on the U.S. Intelligence Community's Prewar Intelligence Assessments on Iraq*, July 9, 2004, p. 308; Robert Dreyfuss and Jason Vest, "The Lie Factory," *Mother Jones*, January–February 2004.

37. Paul Pillar, "Intelligence, Policy and the War in Iraq," *Foreign Affairs*, March–April 2006, pp. 20–21.

38. Drew, "The Neoconservatives in Power"; Bamford, *Pretext for War*, p. 313; David Rieff, "Blueprint for a Mess," *New York Times Magazine*, November 2, 2003; Gordon and Trainor, *Cobra II*, p. 18. In February 2003, the Wolfowitz plan for the establishment of Chalabi as head of the provisional government was rejected by the White House in favor of a U.S military government. Gordon and Trainor, *Cobra II*, p. 107.

39. Jane Mayer, "The Manipulator," *New Yorker*, June 7, 2004.

40. Bamford, *Pretext for War*, pp. 313–14, 297.

41. Douglas McCollam, "The List: How Chalabi Played the Press," *Columbia Journalism Review*, July–August 2004, p. 32.

42. Ibid., p. 34; Evan Thomas and Mark Hosenball, "The Rise and Fall of Chalabi: Bush's Mr. Wrong," *Newsweek*, May 31, 2004.

43. James Risen, "How Pair's Finding on Terror Led to Clash on Shaping Intelligence," *New York Times*, April 28, 2004.

44. John B. Judis and Spencer Ackerman, "The Selling of the Iraq War: The First Casualty," *New Republic*, June 30, 2003.

45. *Report on the U.S. Intelligence Community's Prewar Intelligence Assessments on Iraq*, p. 360.

46. Richard Kerr, Thomas Wolfe, Rebecca Donegan, and Aris Pappas, "Intelligence and Analysts on Iraq: Issues for the Intelligence Community," July 29, 2004, released to the public in August 2005.

47. Waas, "Key Bush Intelligence Briefing Kept from Hill Panel"; Michael Issikoff, "A Spy Story Tying Saddam to 9–11 Is Looking Very Flimsy," *Newsweek*, May 6, 2002; David Corn, *The Lies of George W. Bush* (New York: Crown Books, 2003), pp. 216–17.

48. *Report on the U.S. Intelligence Community's Prewar Intelligence Assessments on Iraq*, p. 309.

49. For the most detailed account of the 1976 "Team B" exercise, in which a panel of hardliners was allowed to critique the CIA's estimate of Soviet strategic forces, see Anne Hessing Cahn, *Killing Détente: The Right Attacks the CIA* (University Park, PA: Pennsylvania State University Press, 1998), especially pp. 121–84. In both the Team B and Iraq episodes not only were the Rumsfeld-Cheney duo pulling strings but Paul Wolfowitz was a key player.

50. *Report on the U.S. Intelligence Community's Prewar Intelligence Assessments on Iraq*, pp. 309–10.

51. Norman Solomon, "Media Beat: Branding New and Improved Wars," *FAIR*, October 29, 2002.

52. Bamford, *Pretext for War*, pp. 318–19.

53. Judith Miller and Michael R. Gordon, "U.S. Says Hussein Intensifies Quest for A-Bomb Parts," *New York Times*, September 8, 2002.

54. "Top Bush Officials Push Case against Saddam," CNN, September 8, 2002, http://archives.cnn.com/2002/ALLPOLITICS/09/08/iraq.debate/.

55. Transcript of interview with Vice President Dick Cheney on *Meet the Press*, September 8, 2002.

56. Bob Graham, "What I Knew Before the Invasion," *Washington Post*, November 20, 2005.

57. Jonathan S. Landay, "Intelligence Officials Warned That Iraq WMD Information Was Iffy," Knight Ridder, February 6, 2004; Bob Drogin and Greg Miller, "Iraqi Defector's Tales Bolstered U.S. Case for War," *Los Angeles Times*, March 28, 2004; Bob Drogin and Greg Miller, "Curveball the Source of Fresh CIA Rancor," *Los Angeles Times*, April 2, 2005; Bob Drogin and John Goetz, "Germans Say Informant US Used to Justify War Was Unreliable," *Los Angeles Times*, November 20, 2005; Joby Warrick, "Warnings on WMD 'Fabricator' Were Ignored, Ex-CIA Aide Says," *Washington Post*, June 25, 2006.

58. Pillar, "Intelligence, Policy and the War in Iraq," pp. 19–20.

59. Bamford, *Pretext for War*, p. 370.

60. Telephone interview with Tom Hughes, July 11, 2006.

5. *Wise Guys, Rough Business* by John Prados

1. David Halberstam, *The Best and the Brightest* (New York: Fawcett Books, 1972).

2. Colin L. Powell with Joseph E. Persico, *My American Journey* (New York: Random House, 1995), p. 434. Powell describes his views as hardened by experience as Joint Chiefs chairman during President George H.W. Bush's 1989 intervention in Panama. In actuality, similar strictures on military intervention had earlier been advanced by Secretary of Defense Caspar Weinberger, to whom Powell had been senior military aide, in the mid-1980s. See Caspar W. Weinberger, *Fighting for Peace* (New York: Warner Books, 1990), pp. 433–45. The doctrine has since become identified far more with Colin Powell than with Weinberger.

3. David Rothkopf, *Running the World: The Inside Story of the National Security Council and the Architects of American Power* (New York: Public Affairs Press, 2005), quoted on p. 409. Also see John Prados, "The Pros from Dover," in *American Foreign Policy, 2005–2006*, ed. Glenn P. Hastedt (New York: McGraw-Hill Annual Editions, 2005).

4. PNAC letter to President William J. Clinton, January 26, 1998, http://www.newamericancentury.org/iraqclintonletter.htm.

5. 9/11 Commission staff reports; also *Report of the 9/11 Commission* (New York: W.W. Norton, 2004), p. 335.

6. Tommy Franks, *An American Soldier* (New York: HarperCollins, 2004), quoted on p. 268.

7. The account of Iraq military planning here is constructed from several sources,

starting with the Franks memoir. Of key importance is the Bush-commissioned account by Bob Woodward, *Plan of Attack* (New York: Simon & Schuster, 2004). Also important is Michael R. Gordon and Bernard E. Trainor, *Cobra II: The Inside Story of the Invasion and Occupation of Iraq* (New York: Pantheon Books, 2006). For an Army perspective, see Gregory Fontenot, E.J. Degen, and David Tohn, *On Point* (Fort Leavenworth, KS: Center for Army Lessons Learned, 2004).

8. Hans Blix, *Disarming Iraq* (New York: Pantheon Books, 2004), p. 61.

9. Karen Kwiatkowski, "The New Pentagon Papers," *Salon.com*, March 10, 2004, http://www.salon.com/opinion/feature/2004/03/100sp_mpveon/print.html.

10. Blix, *Disarming Iraq*, p. 58.

11. President George W. Bush press conference, February 13, 2002, White House text.

12. Bob Woodward, *Plan of Attack*, quoted on pp. 119–20.

13. National Security Council, National Security Strategy of the United States, June 2002, passim.

14. Brent Scowcroft, "Don't Attack Saddam, It Would Undermine Our Antiterror Efforts," *Wall Street Journal*, August 15, 2002.

15. John Prados, *Hoodwinked: The Documents That Reveal How Bush Sold Us a War* (New York: The New Press, 2004), quoted on p. 25.

16. Ibid., quoted on p. 26. See that book throughout for many examples of the tactics summarized in this paragraph, as well as for analysis of the specific statements and why they were misleading.

17. See Commission on the Intelligence Capabilities of the United States Regarding Weapons of Mass Destruction, *Report*, Washington, March, 2005; and also United States Senate (108th Congress), Select Committee on Intelligence, *Report on the U.S. Intelligence Community's Prewar Intelligence Assessments on Iraq*, Washington, July 7, 2004. Both these official investigations, it may be noted, confirm the technical analysis presented in *Hoodwinked* in *every* particular, save that both investigations were specifically prevented from looking into the political use of intelligence by the Bush administration.

18. Text of the resolution was printed in the *New York Times*, October 12, 2002, p. A10.

19. See Edwin E. Moise, *Tonkin Gulf and the Escalation of the Vietnam War* (Chapel Hill: University of North Carolina Press, 1996); also John Prados, "Tonkin Gulf, 40th Anniversary," National Security Archive Electronic Briefing Book, Archive Web site, http://www.gwu.edu/~nsarchiv/NSAEBB/NSAEBB/132/index.htm.

20. See National Security Agency, Website, Declassification Initiatives: Tonkin Gulf Release 1 (2005) and Release 2 (2006), http://www.nsa.gov/vietnam/.

21. Lloyd Gardner, *Pay Any Price: Lyndon Johnson and the Wars for Vietnam* (Chicago: Ivan R. Dee, 1995), p. 129.

22. Ibid., quoted on p. 131.

23. George C. Herring, *America's Longest War: The United States and Vietnam, 1950–1975*, 3rd ed. (New York: McGraw-Hill, 1996), p. 130.

24. Summary Record of the 524th Meeting of the National Security Council, Washington, March 17, 1964, Noon. Reprinted in *Foreign Relations of the United States, 1964–1968*, vol. 1: *Vietnam 1964* (Washington: U.S. Government Printing Office, 1992), pp. 170–72 (hereafter cited as *FRUS 1964*, with page numbers: Note that where some scholars cite the FRUS series documents by item number in the books, this text will use pages, which seem less cumbersome).

25. NSC, Memorandum, Michael Forrestal–McGeorge Bundy, "Vietnam," March 18, 1964, *FRUS 1964*, p. 174.

26. State (Saigon) Cable 1776, Lodge–Lyndon Johnson, March 19, 1964. *FRUS 1964*, p. 183.

27. NSC, Memorandum, Michael Forrestal–McGeorge Bundy, March 31, 1964. *FRUS 1964*, p. 206.

28. NSC, "Political Scenario in Support of Pressures on the North (Third Draft)," attached to Forrestal Memorandum March 31, 1964, *FRUS 1964*, p. 212.

29. John Prados, ed., *White House Tapes: Eavesdropping on the Presidents* (New York: The New Press, 2003) includes the audiotape of this discussion on a CD format, and transcribes the conversation. See pp. 184–87.

30. Anthony Austin, *The President's War: The Story of the Tonkin Gulf Resolution and How the Nation Was Trapped in Vietnam* (Philadelphia: J.B. Lippincott, 1971), passim.

31. Gareth Porter, ed., *Vietnam: A History in Documents* (New York: New American Library, 1981), p. 287.

32. Ezra Y. Siff, *Why the Senate Slept: The Gulf of Tonkin Resolution and the Beginning of America's Vietnam War* (Westport, CT: Praeger, 1999), p. 30.

33. James Mann, *The Rise of the Vulcans: The History of Bush's War Cabinet* (New York: Viking, 2004), quoted on p. 63.

34. Public Law 93–148, Section 2(c), United States Congress, House, Committee on Foreign Affairs, *The War Powers Resolution: A Special Study of the Committee on Foreign Affairs* (Washington, DC: Government Printing Office, [1982]), p. 287.

6. *Gulliver at Bay* by Andrew J. Bacevich

1. Hollywood's former reverence for the Congress—recall Frank Capra's *Mr. Smith Goes to Washington*—has disappeared. Present-day programmers are taken by the power and glamor of the Oval Office but evince little interest in airing shows called *Capitol Hill* or *Majority Leader*. The Fox network broadcasts a series called *House*, but its setting is a hospital, not the lower chamber of the Congress.

2. Richard M. Pious, "War Powers Resolution," *The Oxford Companion to American Military History*, ed. John Whiteclay Chambers II (New York: Oxford University Press, 1999), p. 787.

3. One partial exception relates to President Ronald Reagan and Central America. Congress did attempt to restrict U.S. military involvement in El Salvador and U.S. covert support for the contras, who sought to overthrow the Sandinista government in Nicaragua. The Reagan administration's efforts to circumvent those restrictions contributed to the Iran-contra scandal.

4. Louis Fisher, *Presidential War Power* (Lawrence: University Press of Kansas, 1995), p. xi.

5. Gene Healy and Timothy Lynch, *Power Surge: The Constitutional Record of George W. Bush* (Washington, DC: Cato Institute, 2006), pp. 3, 23.

6. Quoted in Richard Cohen, "Of Tricks and Trailers," *Washington Post*, June 5, 2003, p. A33. Wolfowitz originally made his remark in an interview with *Vanity Fair* magazine.

7. Quoted in Michael Gordon and Bernard Trainor, *Cobra II: The Inside Story of the Invasion and Occupation of Iraq* (New York: Pantheon Books, 2006), p. 72.

8. Ibid., pp. 73–74.

9. Donald Rumsfeld, "Bureaucracy to Battlefield," September 10, 2001, http://www .defenselink.mil/speeches/2001/s20010910-secdef.html, accessed May 24, 2006.

10. Gordon and Trainor, *Cobra II*, p. 39.

11. S.J. Res. 23, September 14, 2001, http://www.pbs.org/newshour/bb/military/ terroristattack/joint-resolution_9-14.html (accessed May 24, 2006).

12. David Cole, "What Bush Wants to Hear," *New York Review of Books*, November 17, 2005, pp. 8–12.

13. Charlie Savage, "Bush Challenges Hundreds of Laws," *Boston Sunday Globe*, April 30, 2006, p. A1.

14. Quoted in Garret Keizer, "Black Hoods for Jesus," *Books and Culture* 12 (March/ April 2006), p. 21.

15. Granted, once on the Court justices don't always perform as expected; the extent to which the Roberts Court will actually defer to the chief executive on national security issues remains to be seen.

16. The famous draft Defense Planning Guidance of 1992, drafted at the Behest of Secretary of Defense Dick Cheney by Undersecretary of Defense Paul Wolfowitz, summarized how the hawks viewed that mission. For a discussion, see Andrew J. Bacevich, *American Empire: The Realities and Consequences of U.S. Diplomacy* (Cambridge, MA: Harvard University Press, 2002), pp. 43–46.

17. Two incidents stood out: Clinton's humiliation at the generals' hands in the "gays in the military" controversy and the way that the JCS had maneuvered Secretary of Defense Les Aspin into taking the fall for the botched firefight in Mogadishu in October 1993.

18. Quoted in Gordon and Trainor, *Cobra II*, p. 46.

19. Tommy Franks with Malcolm McConnell, *American Soldier* (New York: Regan Books, 2004). For a critical assessment, see Andrew J. Bacevich, "A Modern Major General," *New Left Review* 29 (September/October 2004), pp. 123–34.

20. Gordon and Trainor, *Cobra II*, p. 23.

21. Ibid., p. 447.

7. *Class Wars* by Christian G. Appy

1. Robert Coles, *The Middle Americans* (Boston: Little, Brown, 1971), pp. 131–34. For another analysis of this family's experience, see Christian G. Appy, *Working-Class War: American Combat Soldiers and Vietnam* (Chapel Hill: University of North Carolina Press, 1993), pp. 41–43.

2. See "Iraq Coalition Casualties: Female Fatalities," Iraq Coalition Casualty Count, http://icasualties.org/oif/Female.aspx.

3. See "Military Too Fat, Female, Married, Old," *NewsMax.com*, http://www.news max.com/archives/articles/2002/1/3/151151.shtml.

4. Charles C. Moskos, *The American Enlisted Man* (New York: Russell Sage Foundation, 1970), p. 195; Appy, *Working-Class War*, pp. 22–24.

5. Appy, *Working-Class War*, pp. 31–33.

6. Arthur Egendorf et al., *Legacies of Vietnam: Comparative Adjustment of Veterans and Their Peers* (Washington, DC: U.S. Government Printing Office, 1981), esp. pp. 105–9, 142, 494–515.

7. National Priorities Project, "Military Recruiting 2005," Northampton, MA, September 7, 2005, http://nationalpriorities.org.

8. Tim Kane, "Who Bears the Burden? Demographic Characteristics of U.S. Military Recruits Before and After 9/11," Center for Data Analysis Report #05-08, Heritage Foundation, Washington, DC, November 7, 2005, p. 6, www.heritage.org/Research/ NationalSecurity/cda05-08.cfm.

9. Arnold Barnett, Timothy Stanley, and Michael Shore, "America's Vietnam Casualties: Victims of a Class War?" *Operations Research*, September/October 1992.

10. James Fallows, "Vietnam: Low Class Conclusions," *The Atlantic*, April 1993, p. 42.

11. Ann Scott Tyson, "Youths in Rural U.S. Are Drawn to Military," *Washington Post*, November 4, 2005.

12. Ibid.

13. Tom Bowman, "War Toll Speaks to Geography, Class Split," *Baltimore Sun*, October 30, 2005. The Heritage Foundation also cites these geographic disproportions. See Kane, "Who Bears the Burden?"

14. Fred Kaplan, "GI Schmo," *Slate.com*, January 9, 2006.

15. Milton Rosenberg, Sidney Verba, and Philip Converse, *Vietnam and the Silent Majority* (New York: Harper and Row, 1970).

16. William L. Lunch and Peter W. Sperlich, "American Public Opinion and the War in Vietnam," *Western Political Quarterly* 32 (March 1979), pp. 33–34.

17. Christian G. Appy, *Patriots: The Vietnam War Remembered from All Sides* (New York: Viking, 2003), pp. 305–6.

18. Dick Feagler, "Troops Are Precious. But War Is Not," *Cleveland Plain Dealer*, August 7, 2005, p. H1, http://www.cleveland.com/news/plaindealer/dick_feagler/index .ssf?/base/opinion/1123320605154540.xml&coll=28&thispage=1. See also Feagler, "It's the Peace Freaks Who See Clearly Now," *Cleveland Plain Dealer*, August 24, 2005.

19. See http://www.pollingreport.com/iraq.htm.

20. Bob Herbert, "Blood Runs Red, Not Blue," *New York Times*, August 18, 2005, http://www.commondreams.org/views05/0818-23.htm.

21. Sam Fulwood III, "Bush's Words Sadly Prophetic," August 6, 2005, p. B1, http:// www.cleveland.com/news/plaindealer/sam_fulwood/index.ssf?/base/opinion/ 1123320820154540.xml&coll=2.

22. See *Cincinnati Enquirer*, August 7, 2005, p. 1, http://news.enquirer.com/apps/ pbcs.dll/article?AID=/20050807/NEWS01/508070378/-1/BACK.

23. David Goodman, "The Democrat Who Fought," *Mother Jones*, November/ December 2005.

24. Kevin Zeese, "Rep. Murtha Calls for 'Immediate Redeployment' of U.S. Troops in Iraq," Democracy Rising, http://www.democracyrising.us/content/view/368/151/.

25. Charles Babington, "Hawkish Democrat Joins Call for Pullout," *Washington Post*, November 18, 2005, p. A01.

26. David Bacon, "AFL-CIO Convention Calls For Troop Withdrawal From Iraq," ZNET, July 27, 2005, www.zmag.org/content/showarticle.cfm?ItemID=8383.

27. AFL-CIO, "Resolution #53: The War in Iraq," submitted by the Executive Council at the 2005 AFL-CIO convention, http://www.aflcio.org/aboutus/thisistheaflcio/ convention/2005/res_53.cfm.

28. Michael Zweig, "Iraq and the Labor Movement," U.S. Labor Against the War, December 5, 2005, www.uslaboragainstwar.org/article.php?id=9707; see also Tod Ensign, "A Working Class War: Who's Opposing It?" Citizen Soldier, May 30, 2006, www .citizen-soldier.org/draftchatter.html.

29. Nadav Savio, "Labor and the War," *Multinational Monitor*, March 1991; Philip S. Foner, *U.S. Labor and the Vietnam War* (New York: International Publishers, 1989).

30. Author's personal files.

31. Paul Krugman, "The DeLay Principle," *New York Times*, June 9, 2006, p. A27.

8. *The Female Shape of the All-Volunteer Force* by Elizabeth L. Hillman

1. See Judith A. Youngman, "Whatever Happened to the Citizen Soldier?" in *Women in Uniform: Exploding the Myths, Exploring the Facts* (Washington, DC: Women's Research and Education Institute, 1998), which describes "the single greatest change" in the U.S. military since the 1970s as "the replacement in military culture of the citizen soldier by the warrior" (unpaginated); Laura Miller, "Not Just Weapons of the Weak: Gender Harassment as a Form of Protest for Army Men," *Social Psychology Quarterly* 60 (1997), pp. 32–51.

2. *Military Personnel: Reporting Additional Servicemember Demographics Could Enhance Congressional Oversight*, General Accounting Office Report to Congressional Requesters, September 2005 (hereafter GAO report), pp. 10–11; see also chart, p. 38.

3. *Grutter v. Bollinger*, 539 U.S. 306 (2003).

4. Consolidated Brief of Lt. General Julius W. Becton Jr. et al. as Amici Curiae in Support of Respondents, *Grutter v. Bollinger*, 123 S. Ct. 2325 (No. 02-241) (2003).

5. "Equal opportunity is a military necessity. It provides the All-Volunteer Force access to the widest pool of qualified men and women, it allows the military to train and assign people according to the needs of the Service, and it guarantees Service men and women that they will be judged by their performance and will be protected from discrimination and harassment." Defense Equal Opportunity Council, *Report of the Task Force on Discrimination and Sexual Harassment*, vol. I, Washington, DC, May 1995, p. i.

6. William L. O'Neill, "Women and Readiness," in *Women in the Military*, ed. E.A. Blacksmith (New York: H.W. Wilson, 1992), p. 171.

7. Martin Binkin and Mark J. Eitelberg, "Women and Minorities in the All-Volunteer Force," in *The All-Volunteer Force After a Decade: Retrospect and Prospect*, ed. William Bowman, Roger Little, and G. Thomas Silica (New York: Pergamon-Brassey's, 1986), p. 74.

8. *The Report of the President's Commission on an All-Volunteer Force* (New York: Collier/Macmillan, 1970).

9. Ibid., p. 169: "Some have urged that literally everyone, male and female, be required to serve, even those who are physically or mentally disabled or morally unfit." The commission lumped women together with the disabled and the immoral—and discounted them entirely from the viable pool of military personnel. See also Binkin and Eitelberg, "Women and Minorities in the All-Volunteer Force," p. 82: "The Gates Commission never considered the need for, nor the feasibility of, expanding the role of women in the volunteer military." Other studies that followed also failed to anticipate the military need for female recruits. See, e.g., K.H. Kim, Susan Farrell, and Ewan Clague, *The All-Volunteer Army: An Analysis of Supply and Demand* (New York: Praeger, 1971). This study, commissioned by the Department of the Army, Directorate of Personnel Studies and Research, Office of the Chief of Staff for Personnel, in the summer of 1969 was comparably shortsighted; it explicitly ignored "the possibility of replacing military personnel in certain job categories with civilians" and made "[n]o effort . . . to consider an expanded role for women," p. ix.

10. *The Report of the President's Commission on an All-Volunteer Force*, front matter, in a "Letter of Transmittal" to President Nixon from Thomas S. Gates, Chair of the Commission.

11. This emphasis on military pay to the exclusion of women is a common refrain in studies of military recruiting. A 2003 Rand Corporation study claimed that increases in military pay were the answer to recruiting shortfalls throughout the volunteer forces' first thirty years. Beth Asch and James R. Hosek, *Looking to the Future: What Does Transformation Mean for Military Manpower and Personnel Policy?* (Santa Monica, CA: Rand, 2004), p. 1.

12. Binkin and Eitelberg, "Women and Minorities in the All-Volunteer Force," p. 82.

13. *The Report of the President's Commission on an All-Volunteer Force*, p. 43 (reproducing a chart categorizing the skill distribution of the enlisted force from 1945 to 1974).

14. Ibid., p. 18 (noting concerns about quality).

15. Ibid., front matter. The only female commissioner was Dr. Jeanne Noble, a professor of education and vice president of the National Council of Negro Women, who in 1962 had become one of the first African American women to receive tenure at New York University.

16. Binkin and Eitelberg, "Women and Minorities in the All-Volunteer Force," p. 83.

17. Carolyn Becraft, "Women and the Military: Bureaucratic Policies and Politics," in *Women in the Military*, ed. Blacksmith (see n. 6), p. 9.

18. Lawrence Korb, "The Pentagon's Perspective," in *Who Defends America? Race, Sex, and Class in the Armed Forces*, ed. Edwin Dorn (Washington, DC: Joint Center for Political Studies, 1989), p. 24.

19. Ibid., p. 25 ("In my view, women actually increase readiness, since they have more education and higher aptitudes than their male counterparts.").

20. Martin Binkin, *America's Volunteer Military: Progress and Prospects* (Washington, DC: Brookings Institution, 1984), pp. 7–8.

21. Ibid., p. 48.

22. *Office of the Under Secretary of Defense Personnel and Readiness, Career Progression of Minority and Women Officers* (Washington, DC: 1998) (hereafter *Career Progression* report), p. 10. For an astute overview of the early twenty-first-century military population, see David R. Segal and Mady Wechsler Segal, "America's Military Population," *Population Bulletin* (Population Reference Bureau) 59, no. 4 (2004).

23. Elisabeth Yano et al., "Toward a VA Women's Health Research Agenda: Setting

Evidence-based Priorities to Improve the Health and Health Care of Women Veterans," *Journal of General Internal Medicine* 21 (March 2006), pp. S93–S101.

24. See the research compiled by the Women's Research and Education Institute, available at www.wrei.org, which uses Bureau of Labor Statistics to document the rising number of women veterans.

25. Binkin and Eitelberg, "Women and Minorities in the All-Volunteer Force," p. 82.

26. *Who Defends America?*, ed. Dorn; see also *Career Progression* report, p. vi.

27. Alvin J. Schexnider and Edwin Dorn, "Statistical Trends," in *Who Defends America?*, ed. Dorn, p. 48.

28. GAO report, p. 3.

29. Ibid.

30. Ibid., p. 42. See also Brenda Moore, "From Underrepresentation to Overrepresentation: African American Women," in *It's Our Military, Too! Women and the U.S. Military*, ed. Judith Hicks Stiehm (Philadelphia: Temple University Press, 1996), pp. 115–35.

31. See, e.g., Brenda Moore and Ron Armstead, "Issues of African American Female Veterans," unpublished presentation by the Congressional Black Caucus Veterans Braintrust, Baldy Center conference on Women in Military Culture, State University of New York at Buffalo, September 15–16, 2005.

32. Laura L. Miller, "Feminism and the Exclusion of Army Women from Combat," in *Women in the Military*, ed. Rita James Simon (New Brunswick, NJ: Transaction, 2001), p. 109. See also the DACOWITS Web site at http://www.dtic.mil/dacowits (visited July 29, 2006).

33. For a chronology of significant dates, see Captain Lory Manning, *Women in the Military: Where They Stand*, 5th ed. (Washington, DC: Women's Research and Education Institute, 2005), pp. 4–9.

34. *Frontiero v. Richardson*, 411 U.S. 677 (1973).

35. Binkin and Eitelberg, "Women and Minorities in the All-Volunteer Force," p. 85.

36. Ibid. It is important to remember that these aggregate figures describe a volunteer military that was not a monolith but instead a collection of service branches and subcultures. The almost entirely male Marine Corps shares little in mission or tradition, for instance, with the technocratic Air Force, which is nearly one-fifth female. Within each branch of service, differences can be profound; the ethos and even the uniforms of a fighter pilot squadron resemble those of a military police unit only in the vaguest of ways. Distinctions within the military have been drawn out further in many of the studies cited in these notes.

37. *Selected Manpower Statistics, FY 1979* (Washington, DC: Department of Defense, 1979).

38. *Crawford v. Cushman*, 538 F. 2d 1114 (1976); *Owens et al. v. Brown*, 455 F. Supp. 291 (1978).

39. GAO report, p. 38.

40. *Rostker v. Goldberg*, 453 U.S. 57 (1981). See Linda K. Kerber, *No Constitutional Right to Be Ladies: Women and the Obligations of Citizenship* (New York: Hill and Wang, 1998), pp. 221–302, for an analysis of the Goldberg case and the legal and political dimensions of women's struggle for equality in the military.

41. Becraft, "Women and the Military," pp. 11–15; Binkin and Eitelberg, "Women and Minorities in the All-Volunteer Force," p. 84. See also Binkin, *America's Volunteer Military*, p. 49.

42. Korb, "The Pentagon's Perspective," p. 25.

43. For a useful overview of the issues surrounding women in combat, see Jeff Tuten, "The Arguments Against Female Combatants," pp. 237–65, and Mady Wechsler Segal, "The Arguments for Female Combatants," pp. 267–90 in *Female Soldiers: Combatants or Noncombatants*, ed. Nancy Loring Goldman (Westport, CT: Greenwood Press, 1982). In 2005, the arguments looked much the same as in 1982. See, e.g., "G.I. Jane, Again," *National Review* 57, no. 10 (June 6, 2005), pp. 22–24 (discussing the assumptions behind the

Army's restrictions on women in combat and debating the efficacy of such restrictions); "Women Already See Combat," *USA Today*, May 25, 2005; Michael Moss, "Hard Look at Mission That Ended in Inferno for 3 Women," *New York Times*, December 20, 2005, pp. A1, A14 (reporting on the deaths of female U.S. Marines). See also Lorry M. Fenner and Marie deYoung, *Women in Combat: Civic Duty or Military Liability* (Washington, DC: Georgetown University Press, 2001); Laura L. Miller, "Feminism and the Exclusion of Army Women from Combat," pp. 101–33, in *Women in the Military*, ed. Simon (see n. 32); M.C. Devilbiss, *Women and Military Service: A History, Analysis, and Overview* (Maxwell Air Force Base, AL: Air University Press, 1990); Linda Grant DePauw, *Battle Cries and Lullabies* (Norman: University of Oklahoma Press, 1998).

44.On the integration of women into combat aviation, see Captain Alice W.W. Parham, "The Quiet Revolution: Repeal of the Exclusionary Statutes in Combat Aviation— What We Have Learned from a Decade of Integration," 12 *William and Mary Journal of Women and the Law* 377 (2006).

45. Korb, "The Pentagon's Perspective," p. 25.

46. Department of Defense, *Active Duty Military Personnel*, September 30, 2005, available at the Office of the Secretary of Defense (OSD) Web site, http://www.defenselink .mil/osd/.

47. Susan Hosek et al., *Minority and Gender Differences in Officer Career Progression* (Santa Monica, CA: Rand, 2001), pp. 2–3; Margaret C. Harrell and Laura L. Miller, *New Opportunities for Military Women: Effects upon Readiness, Cohesion and Morale* (Santa Monica, CA: Rand, 1997).

48. GAO report, pp. 38–39. This Rand report's lack of clarity on the exact percentage of positions closed to women (15 to 20 percent) is uncharacteristic of the military-sponsored social scientific research. It indicates the fuzziness of even this attempt at a bright-line "combat exclusion" rule.

49. Ibid., p. 45.

50. Ibid.; Margaret C. Harrell et al., *The Status of Gender Integration in the Military: Analysis of Selected Occupations* (Santa Monica, CA: Rand, 2002).

51. GAO report, p. 121.

52. *Career Progression* report, p. viii.

53. Ibid., p. 24; p. 18.

54. Ibid., p. 58; Hosek et al., *Minority and Gender Differences*, pp. xv, 66–69, 105.

55. *Career Progression* report, pp. 75–76.

56. Ibid.

57. Karen Houppert, *Home Fires Burning: Married to the Military—for Better or Worse* (New York: Ballantine, 2005), p. xix.

58. Hosek et al., *Minority and Gender Differences*, p. 93.

59. Korb, "The Pentagon's Perspective," p. 25.

60. O'Neill, "Women and Readiness," pp. 181–84 and 190–93. See also Elizabeth Lutes Hillman, *Defending America: Military Culture and the Cold War Court-Martial* (Princeton, NJ: Princeton University Press, 2005), pp. 70–79, identifying family responsibilities as a primary cause of servicemen's AWOL and desertion.

61. Lorry M. Fenner, "Either You Need These Women or You Do Not: Informing the Debate on Women and Citizenship," in *Women in the Military*, ed. Simon (see n. 32), p. 5.

62. See, e.g., Rowan Scarborough, "Iraq War Muddles Role of Women," *Washington Times*, October 17, 2005, p. A4 ("The Iraq war has highlighted confusion over the proper roles of women in the military . . ."); Jodi Wilgoren, "A Nation at War: Women in the Military: A New War Brings New Role for Women," *New York Times*, March 28, 2003, p. B1 (discussing women's ability to withstand warfare as compared to men's); Rowan Scarborough, "Army Affirms Its Ban on Women in Combat," *Washington Times*, January 19, 2005, p. A1.

63. GAO report, p. 4.

64. The Gates Commission report was the first such study; the most recent is the

Government Accounting Office's *Military Personnel: DOD Needs to Improve the Transparency and Reassess the Reasonableness, Appropriateness, Affordability, and Sustainability of Its Military Compensation System*, GAO-05-798 (Washington, DC: July 19, 2005), which points out that military pay is but 70 percent of comparable civilian pay scales.

65. GAO report, pp. 4; 68–76.

66. Ibid., pp. 4, 68, 70.

67. Ibid., p. 68.

68. Ibid., p. 69.

69. James Hosek, Jennifer Kavanaugh, and Laura Miller, *How Deployments Affect Service Members* (Santa Monica, CA: Rand, 2006), p. xiii.

70. GAO report, pp. 80, 67, 4; "Problem for Navy: Too Few Hands on Deck," *New York Times*, February 2, 1999, pp. A1, 17; "The Short-Handed Military: A Wisp of a Draft," *New York Times*, February 7, 1999, sec. 4, pp. 1, 4.

71. Notwithstanding this grim picture, the primary targets of military sexual violence are civilian rather than military women. Cynthia Enloe's work on the exploitation of women overseas by military personnel reveals the stark dimensions of the military's long and tragic history of participating in human sex trafficking and prostitution around the world. Cynthia Enloe, *Does Khaki Become You? The Militarization of Women's Lives* (Boston: South End Press, 1983), pp. 18–45; *Bananas, Beaches, and Bases: Making Feminist Sense of International Politics* (Berkeley: University of California Press, 1990), pp. 81–90; *The Morning After: Sexual Politics at the End of the Cold War* (Berkeley: University of California Press, 1993), pp. 142–60. In the ongoing war in Iraq, the secondary targets of sexual violence seem to be the male enemy, particularly captured irregulars thought to be terrorists and considered "high-value" detainees.

72. See, e.g., Margaret C. Harrell, *Invisible Women: Junior Enlisted Army Wives* (Santa Monica, CA: Rand, 2000); James Hosek et al., *Married to the Military: The Employment and Earnings of Military Wives Compared with Those of Civilian Wives* (Santa Monica, CA: Rand, 2002).

73. Peter J. Mercier, "Violence in the Military Family," in *Battle Cries on the Homefront: Violence in the Military Family*, ed. Peter J. Mercier and Judith D. Mercier (Springfield, IL: Charles C. Thomas, 2000), p. 5.

74. See, e.g., Leana C. Allen, "The Influence of Military Training and Combat Experience on Domestic Violence," in *Battle Cries on the Homefront*, pp. 81–103.

75. See Houppert, *Home Fires Burning*, pp. 115–40, on the increased attention to military domestic violence since the 1990s; see also the Miles Foundation Web page, http://hometown.aol.com/milesfdn/myhomepage/ (accessed July 26, 2006).

76. GAO report, p. 40; *Career Progression* report, Chapter 7.

77. *Career Progression* report, pp. 82–84.

78. See, e.g., Linda Bird Francke, *Ground Zero: The Gender Wars in the Military* (New York: Simon & Schuster, 1997).

79. See, e.g., Aaron Belkin and Geoffrey Bateman, eds., *Don't Ask/Don't Tell: Debating the Gay Ban in the Military* (Boulder, CO: Lynne Rienner, 2003) (transcribing discussions among experts on the military's homosexuality policy, including extensive footnotes and bibliography); Michelle Benecke and Kirstin Dodge, "Military Women in Nontraditional Job Fields: Casualties of the Armed Forces' War on Homosexuals," *Harvard Women's Law Journal* 13 (1990), pp. 215–50; Human Rights Watch, *Uniform Discrimination: The 'Don't Ask, Don't Tell' Policy of the U.S. Military* (January 2003), http://www.hrw.org/reports/2003/usa0103/ (accessed July 24, 2006) (especially section titled "Impact on Women"); Servicemembers Legal Defense Network statistics on the disproportionately high discharge rate for servicewomen accused of being lesbians, http://www.sldn.org/binary-data/SLDN_ARTICLES/pdf_file/351.pdf (accessed July 10, 2006).

80. Hosek et al., *Minority and Gender Differences*, p. 76.

81. *Report of the Defense Task Force on Sexual Harassment and Violence at the Military Service Academies* (Washington, DC: Department of Defense, June 2005), executive summary.

82. Asch and Hosek, Looking to the Future, p. 2 (quoting Rumsfeld as seeking "a culture of creativity and risk-taking" and "a more entrepreneurial approach to developing military capabilities."

83. See, e.g., Karen J. Greenberg and Joshua L. Dratel, eds., *The Torture Papers: The Road to Abu Ghraib* (New York: Cambridge University Press, 2005).

84. James W. Smith III, "A Few Good Scapegoats: The Abu Ghraib Courts-Martial and the Failure of the Military Justice System," 27 *Whittier Law Review* 671 (2006).

9. *Familiar Foreign Policy and Familiar Wars* by Gabriel Kolko

1. Gabriel Kolko and Joyce Kolko, *The Limits of Power: The World and United States Foreign Policy, 1945–1954* (New York: Harper & Row, 1972), pp. 339–42.

2. Willard C. Matthias, *America's Strategic Blunders: Intelligence Analysis and National Security Policy, 1936–1991* (University Park: Pennsylvania State University Press, 2001), p. 3; see also pp. 45–46 for a 1946 estimate of Soviet intentions.

3. Ibid., p. 3.

4. Ibid., p. 313. See also Robert M. Gates, *From the Shadows: The Ultimate Insider's Story of Five Presidents and How They Won the Cold War* (New York: Simon & Schuster, 1996), pp. 30–31.

5. Gates, *From the Shadows*, p. 207.

6. Ibid., p. 286.

7. George W. Allen, *None So Blind: A Personal Account of Intelligence Failure in Vietnam* (Chicago: Ivan R. Dee, 2001), p. 78.

8. Ibid., pp. 183, 185.

9. Jeffrey Race, "The Unlearned Lessons of Vietnam," *Yale Review* LXVI (1976), pp. 163–66, 173.

10. Harold P. Ford, *CIA and the Vietnam Policymakers: Three Episodes 1962–1968* (Washington, DC: CIA Center for the Study of Intelligence, 1998), http://www.odci .gov/csi/books/vietnam/index.html.

11. Allen, *None So Blind*, p. 248.

12. Ibid., p. 266.

13. Ibid., p. 235.

14. Ibid., p. 242.

15. Ibid., p. 267.

16. Steven R. Ward, "Evolution Beats Revolution in Analysis," *Studies in Intelligence* [CIA Center for the Study of Intelligence] 46, no. 3 (2002), http://www.odci.gov/csi/ studies/vol46no3/article04.html. See also CIA, Center for the Study of Intelligence, Roundtable Report, *Intelligence and Policy: The Evolving Relationship* (Washington, DC, June 2004), pp. 7–8.

17. See, for example, John T. Carney and Benjamin F. Schemmer, *No Room for Error: The Covert Operations of America's Special Tactics Units from Iran to Afghanistan* (New York: Ballantine Books, 2002), and Robert Baer, *See No Evil: The True Story of a Ground Soldier in the CIA's War on Terrorism* (New York: Crown Publishers, 2002); Elaine Grossman, "Combat Commanders Make Broad Access to Intelligence a Top Priority," *Inside the Pentagon*, February 9, 2006.

18. CIA, *Intelligence and Policy*, p. 14 and passim.

19. Scott Ritter, *Iraq Confidential: The Untold Story of the Intelligence Conspiracy to Undermine the UN and Overthrow Saddam Hussein* (New York: Nation Books, 2005), pp. 9ff, 75, 112–13, 289–91.

20. Paul R. Pillar, "Intelligence, Policy, and the War in Iraq," *Foreign Affairs* 85 (March/ April 2006), passim. Pillar was the CIA's national intelligence officer for the Near East, 2000–2005, and he criticizes every premise of the administration's Iraq policy and shows how the CIA disproved every one of them—to no effect. See also *New York Times*, No-

vember 6, 2005; Agence France Presse, dispatch, November 24, 2005; Michel R. Gordon and Bernard E. Trainor, *Cobra II: The Inside Story of the Invasion and Occupation of Iraq* (New York: Pantheon Books, 2006), pp. 126–27.

21. Bob Woodward, *Plan of Attack* (New York: Simon & Schuster, 2004), p. 19.

22. Bob Drogin and John Goetz, "The Curveball Saga," *Los Angeles Times*, November 20, 2005, http://www.latimes.com/news/nationworld/nation/la-na-curveball20nov20, 0,1753730.story?coll=la-home-headlines; James Risen, *State of War: The Secret History of the CIA and the Bush Administration* (New York: Free Press, 2006), pp. 72–76, 102–3; *Washington Post*, April 9, 2006.

23. Three National Security Archives releases, October 21, 2005; one NSA release April 7, 2006. See also [Mike Scheuer], *Imperial Hubris: Why the West Is Losing the War on Terror* (Washington, DC: Brassey's, 2004); James Bamford, *A Pretext for War: 9/11, Iraq, and the Abuse of America's Intelligence Agencies* (New York: Doubleday, 2004); Pillar, "Intelligence, Policy, and the War in Iraq."

24. David Talbot, "How Technology Failed in Iraq," *Technology Review* [MIT], November 2004, p. 2 and passim, http://www.techreview.com/Hardware/wtr_13893,294,p1.html.

25. Gabriel Kolko, *Anatomy of a War: Vietnam, the United States, and the Modern Historical Experience* (New York: The New Press, 1994), pp. 49–50, and more generally for the Vietnam War.

26. Angus Reid polls, November 14, 2005; February 24, 2006; March 2, 2006; Fox News, April 20, 2006. Polls that frame questions differently get different figures but all show that an increasing majority feels that the Iraq War was an error. See Program on International Policy Attitudes (PIPA) poll, ca. March 15, 2006. But the PIPA poll claims only 26 percent want all troops withdrawn within six months.

27. *USA Today*, October 23, 2003.

10. *Mr. Rumsfeld's War* by Lloyd C. Gardner

1. James Mann, *Rise of the Vulcans: The History of Bush's War Cabinet* (New York: Viking Penguin, 2004), p. 113. The quoted figures on allied financial help in Gulf War I are taken from the Civil War History Center Web site, www.cwc.lus.edu.

2. Dana Priest, *The Mission: Waging War and Keeping Peace with America's Military* (New York: W.W. Norton, 2003), pp. 70–71.

3. Bob Woodward, *Bush at War* (New York: Simon & Schuster, 2002), pp. 306, 310.

4. Bob Woodward, "Bush's Wild Card," *Washington Post*, January 12, 2001; editorial, "The Bush Merry-Go Round," *Washington Post*, September 8, 2001.

5. "Team B vs. C.I.A.," *New York Times*, July 20, 1998.

6. "Prepared Testimony of U.S. Secretary of Defense Donald H. Rumsfeld," Senate Armed Services Committee, June 21, 2001, http://armed-services.senate.gov/statemnt/2001/010621rumsfeld.pdf.

7. Michael R. Gordon and Bernard E. Trainor, *Cobra II: The Inside Story of the Invasion and Occupation of Iraq* (New York: Pantheon, 2006), p. 9.

8. CBS News, "Plans for Iraq Attack Began on 9/11," September 4, 2002, http://www.cbsnews.com/stories/2002/09/04.

9. Dan Balz and Bob Woodward, "America's Chaotic Road to War," *Washington Post*, January 27, 2002.

10. Richard A. Clarke, *Against All Enemies: Inside America's War on Terror* (New York: Free Press, 2004), pp. 30–32.

11. Ron Suskind, *The Price of Loyalty: George W. Bush, the White House, and the Education of Paul O'Neill* (New York: Simon & Schuster, 2004), p. 85.

12. Thomas E. Ricks, "Rumsfeld's Hands-On War," *Washington Post*, December 9, 2001.

13. Jeremy Scahill, "The Saddam in Rumsfeld's Closet," ZNet, August 2, 2002, http://www.zmag.org/content/showarticle.cfm?ItemID=2177.

14. Daniel Eisenberg, "We're Taking Him Out," *Time*, May 5, 2002, http://www.time
.com/time/world/article/0,8599,235395,00.html.

15. Ibid.; Gordon and Trainor, *Cobra II*, p. 498.

16. "Interview with NBC 'Meet the Press,'" September 30, 2001, http://www.defense
link.mil/Transcripts/Transcript.aspx?TranscriptID=1947.

17. "Secretary Rumsfeld on CBS 'Face the Nation,'" September 23, 2001, http://www
.defenselink.mil/Transcripts/Transcript.aspx?TranscriptID=1922; "Secretary Rumsfeld Interview with NBC Today," September 20, 2001, http://www.defenselink.mil/Transcripts/
Transcript.aspx?TranscriptID=1897.

18. "Secretary Rumsfeld Interview with USA Today," October 24, 2001, http://www
.defenselink.mil/Transcripts/Transcript.aspx?TranscriptID=2173.

19. Woodward, *Bush at War*, p. 194.

20. Rumsfeld, speech to the Center for Security Policy "Keeper of the Flame" award
dinner, November 6, 2001, http://www.defenselink.mil/Speeches/Speech.aspx?SpeechID
=464; Dave Eberhart, "Rumsfeld: 'Coalition Must Not Determine the Mission,'" *News-
Max*, November 7, 2001, http://www.newsmax.com/archives/articles/2001/11/7/152709
.shtml.

21. See Gary Berntsen and Ralph Pezzullo, *Jaw Breaker: The Attack on Bin Laden and
al-Qaeda, A Personal Account by the CIA's Key Field Commander* (New York: Crown
Publishers, 2005); and Sean Naylor, *Not a Good Day to Die: The Untold Story of Operation
Anaconda* (New York: Berkley Caliber Books, 2005).

22. "Secretary Rumsfeld with U.S. Troops at Bagram," December 16, 2001, http://
www.defenselink.mil/Transcripts/2001/t12172001_t1216baf.html;JimGaramone,"Rumsfeld Dismisses Tora Bora Speculation," American Forces Press Service, April 17, 2002,
http://www.defenselink.mil/news/Apr2002/n04172002_200204176.html.

23. Ann Scott Tyson, "Does bin Laden Matter Anymore?" *Christian Science Monitor*,
March 1, 2002, http://www.csmonitor.com/2002/0301/p01s02-usmi.html.

24. "Secretary Rumsfeld Interview with CBS Face the Nation," February 24, 2002,
http://www.defenselink.mil/transcripts/2002/t02242002_to224cbs.html.

25. Scowcroft, "Don't Attack Saddam," *Wall Street Journal*, August 15, 2002.

26. Interview with Condoleezza Rice, September 8, 2002, *CNN Late Edition*, http://
www.cnn.com/TRANSCRIPTS/0209/08/le.00.html (emphasis added).

27. Glenn Kessler, "Powell Says Weapons Inspections Needed First," *Newark Star-
Ledger*, September 2, 2002.

28. Matt Kelley, "Bush Seeks OK for Military Force Against Iraq," Associated Press,
September 19, 2002.

29. Ibid. Inside the Pentagon, Lt. Col. Karen Kwiatkowski, who would become a thorn
in Rumsfeld's side after she retired and exposed the "intelligence" operations of the OSP,
observed the way the Iraq War was being plotted out in regard to information about
WMDs. In a press interview in 2004, Kwiatowski said, "We knew from many years of
both high-level surveillance and other types of shared intelligence, not to mention the
information from the UN, we knew what was left [from the Gulf War] and the viability of
any of that. Bush said he didn't know. The truth is, we know [Saddam] didn't have these
things. Almost a billion dollars has been spent—a billion dollars!—by David Kay's group
to search for these WMD, a total whitewash effort. They didn't find anything, they didn't
expect to find anything." Marc Cooper, "Soldier for the Truth," *LA Weekly*, February 20,
2004, available at http://www.truthout.org/cgi-bin/artman/exec/view.cgi/6/3662.

30. Kelley, "Bush Seeks OK for Military Force"; "President Bush Discusses Iraq with
Reporters," September 13, 2002, http://www.whitehouse.gov/news/releases/2002/09/
20020913.html.

31. See, for example, "Secretary Rumsfeld Interview with Jim Lehrer," September 18,
2002, http://www.defenselink.mil/Transcripts/Transcript.aspx?TranscriptID=3656.

32. Eric Schmitt, "Rumsfeld Says U.S. Has 'Bulletproof' Evidence of Iraq's Links to Al
Qaeda," *New York Times*, September 28, 2002.

33. "DoD News Briefing—Secretary Rumsfeld and Gen. Myers," October 24, 2002, available at www.fas.org/irp/news/2002/10/dod102502.html.

34. Bradley Graham and Dana Priest, "Pentagon Team Told to Seek Details of Iraq-Al Qaeda Ties," *Washington Post*, October 25, 2002.

35. Ron Suskind, *The One Percent Doctrine: Deep Inside America's Pursuit of Its Enemies Since 9/11* (New York: Simon & Schuster, 2006), pp. 33–34.

36. James Risen, *State of War: The Secret History of the CIA and the Bush Administration* (New York: Free Press, 2006), pp. 62–69.

37. Barton Gellman, "Secret Unit Expands Rumsfeld's Domain," *Washington Post*, January 23, 2005.

38. "Secretary Rumsfeld Interview with Baltimore Sun," December 27, 2001, http://www.defenselink.mil/Transcripts/Transcript.aspx?TranscriptID=2699.

39. Rowan Scarborough, *Rumsfeld's War: The Untold Story of America's Anti-Terrorist Commander* (Washington, DC: Regnery, 2004), pp. 1–2; Jennifer D. Kibbe, "The Rise of the Shadow Warriors," *Foreign Affairs*, March/April 2004.

40. Kibbe, "Rise of the Shadow Warriors"; Ann Scott Tyson and Dana Priest, "Pentagon Seeking Leeway Overseas," *Washington Post*, February 24, 2005.

41. Harlan K. Ullman and James P. Wade, *Shock and Awe: Achieving Rapid Dominance* (Washington, DC: National Defense University Press, 1996).

42. "Secretary Rumsfeld Briefs at the Foreign Press Center," January 22, 2003, http://www.defenselink.mil/Transcripts/Transcript.aspx?TranscriptID=1330. Here was a curious parallel to the "signing statements" President Bush used to put his own spin on congressional bills he signed, so that law enforcement became a series of options instead of an absolute mandate—as in the case of the anti-torture legislation passed in the wake of Abu Ghraib.

43. Andrew West, "800 Missiles to Hit Iraq in First 48 Hours," *Sydney Morning Herald*, January 26, 2003, http://www.smh.com.au/articles/2003/01/25/1042911596206.html.

44. Gordon and Trainor, *Cobra II*, pp. 176–77.

45. Ibid., pp. 164, 160.

46. "DoD News Briefing—Secretary Rumsfeld and Gen. Myers," April 11, 2003, http://www.defenselink.mil/Transcripts/Transcript.aspx?TranscriptID=2367.

47. Ibid.

48. Lloyd C. Gardner, "Present at the Culmination," in *The New American Empire: A 21st Century Teach-In on U.S. Foreign Policy*, ed. Lloyd C. Gardner and Marilyn Young (New York: The New Press, 2005), p. 8.

49. Ibid.; Eric Rosenberg, "Rumsfeld Retreats, Disclaims Earlier Rhetoric," *Ocala Star Banner*, November 9, 2003.

50. Marian Liu, *Mercury News*, May 31, 2006, http://www.mercurynews.com.

51. Michael Georgy, "Iraq's Diyala Region Could be Spark for Civil War," Reuters, June 6, 2006.

52. "Secretary Rumsfeld's Remarks at the National Press Club," February 2, 2006, http://www.defenselink.mil/Transcripts/Transcript.aspx?TranscriptID=908.

53. Rumsfeld to Gen. Dick Myers et al., memorandum, October 16, 2003, http://www.sourcewatch.org/index.php?title=Rumsfeld_Memo_16_October_2003.

54. "Secretary Rumsfeld Interview with Plum Television," March 3, 2006, http://www.defenselink.mil/Transcripts/Transcript.aspx?TranscriptID=1166. The secretary in fact said "by dramatizing something that's negative that in fact is positive," but one assumes he misspoke on the last word.

55. Ron Suskind, "Without a Doubt," *New York Times Magazine*, October 17, 2004.

56. Peter Heather, *The Fall of the Roman Empire: A New History of Rome and the Barbarians* (New York: Oxford University Press, 2006), p. 459.

57. Kristin Roberts, "Rumsfeld in Tajikistan, Focus on Afghan Drug Trade," Reuters, July 10, 2006.

58. Robert Burns, "Rumsfeld Says Unity Important to Iraq," *Forbes*, July 12, 2006; Lo-

lita C. Baldor, "Rumsfeld: Terror Threat Not Exaggerated," Associated Press, *Baltimore Sun*, October 18, 2006, http://www.baltimoresun.com/news/nationworld/iraq/sns-ap-rumsfeld,0,5005337.story.

11. *Zelig in U.S. Foreign Relations* by Walter LaFeber

1. *Zelig* was the title of a 1983 Woody Allen movie in which the eponymous central character moved over time, and through many episodes in recent American history, while assuming the characteristics of the people (including leaders such as Herbert Hoover and even Adolf Hitler) he associated with—or, at least, those around him believed he had assumed others' characteristics. In the end, Zelig assumed a personality that clashed with those who disagreed with him.

2. T. Christopher Jespersen, *American Images of China, 1931–1949* (Stanford, CA: Stanford University Press, 1996), pp. xv, 1.

3. Henry Luce, *The American Century* (New York: Time, Inc., 1941), esp. pp. 5–40.

4. Oral History Interview with William R. Tyler, March 7, 1964, John F. Kennedy Library, Boston.

5. William Schneider, "Vietnam Syndrome Is Alive and Well," *National Journal*, April 13, 1991, p. 902.

6. Project for the New American Century, *Rebuilding America's Defenses; Strategy, Forces, and Resources for a New Century* (Washington, DC: 2000), pp. 18–19, and also note pp. iv, 2, 8.

7. A useful analysis of the DPG and the Krauthammer quote is James Mann, *Rise of the Vulcans: The History of Bush's War Cabinet* (New York: Viking, 2004), pp. 208–14.

8. Ibid., pp. 304–5.

9. Owen Harries, "A Year of Debating China," *National Interest* 15 (winter 1999/2000), pp. 141–47.

10. The so-called China Lobby of the late 1940s to early 1970s was made up of American businesses and missionaries (and politicians, including such well-known liberals as Senator Paul Douglas of Illinois and Senator Hubert Humphrey of Minnesota) who were ardently anticommunist and equally ardent in their defense of the anticommunist Chinese exile regime on Taiwan. A good source on this China Lobby is Ross Y. Koen, *The China Lobby in American Politics*, ed. Richard C. Kagan (New York: Octagon Books, 1974). The New China Lobby began to form in the 1970s to push for formal U.S. recognition of China, and grew rapidly in the 1990s and after to lobby Washington officials to include the Chinese in international economic organizations aimed at lowering trade and capital barriers while accelerating trade and investment. This lobby was largely made up of leading U.S. corporations, especially those in such fields as textiles and automobiles, which searched for cheap labor and exploitation of the China market, and those in cutting-edge technology (Dell, Microsoft, the Rupert Murdoch newspaper/media empire), which wanted to be fully integrated in the economy that promised to be the world's greatest by the mid-twenty-first century, if not earlier.

11. For Henry Kissinger's angry recounting of this episode, see his *White House Years* (Boston: Little, Brown, 1979), esp. p. 1250.

12. For the U.S.-led, post-1945 globalization, see Charles S. Meier, *Among Empires: American Ascendancy and Its Predecessors* (Cambridge, MA: Harvard University Press, 2006), chapters 5–6.

13. A good brief analysis is Paul Blustein, "Fighting Words Belie Trade Reality," *Washington Post*, April 18, 2006, p. D1.

14. Ibid., p. D6.

15. Mann, *Rise of the Vulcans*, pp. 281–86.

16. See Richard A. Clarke, *Against All Enemies: Inside America's War on Terror* (New York: Free Press, 2004), in which the onetime top U.S. antiterrorism expert noted the

Bush administration's reluctance to discuss terrorism before September 2001. On September 11, Rice was scheduled to give a speech (never given) that identified the most important foreign policy issue as anti-missile defense. After 1991, such a defense was to be especially important in dealing with China.

17. C.J. Chivers, "Long Before War, Green Berets Built Military Ties to Uzbekistan," *New York Times*, October 25, 2001, p. A1; Ahmed Rashid, "They're Only Sleeping," *New Yorker*, January 14, 2002, pp. 23–41.

18. Tarique Niazi, "Asia Between China and India," *Japan Focus*, August 2, 2006, pp. 6–7, http://japanfocus.org/products/topdf/1756.

19. M.K. Bhadrakumar, "China and Russia Welcome Iran," *Asia Times*, April 18, 2006, available at www.japanfocus.org; Stratfor, "SCO: A New Power Center Developing," October 28, 2005, www.stratfor.com.

20. Bhadrakumar, "China and Russia Welcome Iran," pp. 1–2; Flynt Leverett, "The Race for Iran," *New York Times*, June 20, 2006, p. A17.

21. Philip P. Pan, "China's Improving Image Challenges U.S. in Asia," *Washington Post*, November 15, 2003, p. A1.

22. "China Becomes Increasingly Involved in the Middle East," March 10, 2006, PINR Dispatch, at dispatch@pinr.com; Steve Munson, "As China, U.S. Vie for More Oil," *Washington Post*, April 15, 2006, p. D1.

23. Dr. Mohan Malik, "China's Growing Involvement in Latin America," June 12, 2006, PINR Dispatch, at dispatch@pinr.com.

24. The best analysis of Roosevelt's foreign policies in Latin America, his racism, and his views of China remains Howard K. Beale, *Theodore Roosevelt and the Rise of America to World Power* (New York: Collier Books, 1962).

25. On the role of Korea in President Hu's 2006 visit to the United States, see Glenn Kessler, "U.S., China Stand Together but Are Not Equal," *Washington Post*, April 21, 2006, p. A18.

26. *New York Times*, April 18, 2004, p. wk3.

27. Secretary of Defense, *Annual Report to Congress; Military Power of . . . China, 2006* (Washington, DC: U.S. Department of Defense, 2006), especially "Executive Summary," pp. 1–2.

28. Council on Foreign Relations, *China's Military Power* (New York: CFR, 2003).

12. *Counterinsurgency, Now and Forever* by Marilyn B. Young

1. Scott Anderson, "Bringing It All Back Home," *New York Times*, May 28, 2006.

2. The second volume of Bruce Cumings's two-volume study of the origins of the Korean War was the first thorough account I read: Cumings, *The Origins of the Korean War*, 2 vols. (Princeton, NJ: Princeton University Press, 1981–90). There have been others since, including Callum A. MacDonald's *Korea: The War Before Vietnam* (New York: Free Press, 1987), whose title demonstrates my point.

3. Bill Ehrhart, a poet and Vietnam veteran, put it best in an interview for the 1983 documentary *Vietnam: A Television History*. "In grade school," he said, "we learned about Redcoats . . . and I think again, subconsciously—but not very subconsciously—I began increasingly to have the feeling that I was a Redcoat. I think it was one of the most staggering realizations of my life that to suddenly understand that I, I wasn't a hero, I wasn't a good guy, I wasn't handing out candy and cigarettes to the kids in the French villages. That somehow I had become everything I had learned to believe was evil."

4. Marilyn B. Young, *The Vietnam Wars, 1945–1990* (New York: HarperCollins, 1991), p. 112. Charles Collingwood posed the question in a way that has become very familiar: was there an "honorable way out" of Vietnam or should the United States "as a nation, as a people . . . continue to accept the cost, the casualties, the frustration and the uncertainty, not just for a little while longer, but perhaps for many years," ibid., p. 111.

5. Young, *Vietnam Wars*, 144. The Marine after-action report, in contrast to Safer's report of fire from at most one sniper followed by a good deal of dangerous "friendly fire," described a ferocious battle.

6. Andrew F. Krepinevich Jr. urged that the United States adopt the "oil-spot" strategy for Iraq in an optimistically titled essay, "How to Win in Iraq," *Foreign Affairs*, September/October 2005. Krepinevich's book *The Army and Vietnam* (Baltimore: Johns Hopkins University Press, 1986) is an analysis of the failure of "big-unit" war in Vietnam in contrast to successful Marine Corps counterinsurgency operations in Vietnam. In a July 2006 op-ed column for the *New York Times*, Krepinevich argued for the centrality of U.S. advisers to the Iraqi army to the counterinsurgency effort ("Send in the Advisers," July 11, 2006, p. A19).

7. Account drawn from Young, *Vietnam Wars*, pp. 212ff.

8. Getting counterinsurgency right is only one version of how the United States could have won. Others include invading the North; early, massive (rather than incremental) deployment of combat troops; mining northern harbors; earlier, steadier, more massive bombing; and so on. I will discuss only counterinsurgency here.

9. For how total war was practiced on the ground, see Greg Grandin, *Empire's Workshop: Latin America, the United States, and the Rise of the New Imperialism* (New York: Metropolitan Books, 2006), pp. 89, 105. The term, in this particular usage, belongs to Colonel John Waghelstein, who is discussed below.

10. Elisabeth Jean Wood, *Forging Democracy from Below: Insurgent Transitions in South Africa and El Salvador* (New York: Cambridge University Press, 2000), p. 5.

11. According to Nicholas Sambanis ("It's Official: There Is Now a Civil War in Iraq," *New York Times*, July 23, 2006, sec. 4, p. 13), the war in Iraq should now be called a civil war.

12. Michael Moss and David Rohde, "Misjudgments Marred U.S. Plans for Iraqi Police," *New York Times*, May 21, 2006. This article and another the *Times* ran the next day (Michael Moss, "Law and Disorder," *New York Times*, May 22, 2006) track the disaster of police "training" in Iraq in considerable, and disheartening, detail. For more on Petraeus and police training, see also Thomas E. Ricks, *Fiasco: The American Military Adventure in Iraq* (New York: Penguin Press, 2006), pp. 394–95.

13. See Peter Maass, "The Way of the Commandos, *New York Times Magazine*, May 1, 2005.

14. Maass, "The Way of the Commandos."

15. Ibid.

16. Ann Scott Tyson, "U.S. Seeks to Escape Brutal Cycle in Iraqi City," *Washington Post*, December 26, 2005.

17. Moss, "Law and Disorder." According to John Burns ("For Some, a Last, Best Hope for U.S. Efforts in Iraq," *New York Times*, May 21, 2006), there are 230,000 police under the Ministry of the Interior, though Bayan Jabr, the outgoing minister, claimed to have "little idea" what any of them were actually doing.. Dexter Filkins reported that no one knew how many of the 145,000 police officers trained by the United States belonged to "rogue units." Government security forces and private militia, Filkins wrote, "are often indistinguishable." "Armed Groups Propel Iraq Towards Chaos," *New York Times*, May 23, 2006.

18. John Waghelstein, "What's Wrong in Iraq? Or Ruminations of a Pachyderm," *Military Review*, January/February 2006, p. 112.

19. Robert D. Kaplan, "Go in Early, Go in Light, Go with Civilians," *International Herald Tribune*, February 21, 2006; Max Boot, *The Savage Wars of Peace: Small Wars and the Rise of American Power* (New York: Basic Books, 2003).

20. Waghelstein's essay is only one example. Eliot Cohen and his colleagues, in an essay discussed below, bitterly observe that despite successes in El Salvador and the former Yugoslavia, counterinsurgency "was leached from the various military college curricula, and the hard-won experience of a generation of officers was deliberately ignored." The military continues to "treat irregular warfare as an exception, an additional duty, or simply as a mistake." See Eliot Cohen, Conrad Crane, Jan Horvath, and John Nagl, "Prin-

ciples, Imperatives and Paradoxes of Counterinsurgency," *Military Review*, March/April 2006, p. 53.

21. Bruce Hoffman, "Insurgency and Counterinsurgency in Iraq," Rand Corporation, National Security Research Division Occasional Paper, 2004, p. 1. The depth of the ambivalence became very clear in November 2005 when Donald Rumsfeld decided it was time for an old-fashioned Chinese-style rectification of names: "This is a group of people," Rumsfeld told the press about those fighting U.S. troops, "who don't merit the word 'insurgency,' I think." Ruminating about the problems in Iraq over the Thanksgiving weekend, Rumsfeld said he had had "an epiphany." Insurgents had "legitimate gripes" and "these people don't." General Peter Pace, sharing the platform with Rumsfeld and no doubt trying to comply, nevertheless used the word twice, apologizing that he couldn't think of a better one offhand, to which Rumsfeld replied: "Enemies of the legitimate Iraqi government. How's that?" Associated Press, "Defense Secretary Has 'Epiphany' About Semantics of War," MSNBC, November 29, 2005, http://msnbc.msn.com/id/10255205 (accessed October 19, 2006).

22. I have already discussed the inapplicability of the El Salvador example. Nor is Japan, where a legitimate government emerged via an American occupation, in any way relevant. See John W. Dower, "Occupation: A Warning from History," in *The New American Empire: A 21st Century Teach-In on U.S. Foreign Policy*, ed. Lloyd C. Gardner and Marilyn B. Young (New York: The New Press, 2005).

23. Cohen et. al, "Principles," p. 49.

24. Ibid., p. 51.

25. Ibid.

26. Peter Maass, "Professor Nagl's War," *New York Times Magazine*, January 11, 2004, p. 30. Reflecting on the experience later, Nagl confided to Maass: "Across this divide they're looking at us, we're looking at them from behind barbed wire, and they're trying to understand why we're here, what we want from them." He goes on: "Almost inconceivable to most of them, I think is that what we want for them is the right to make their own decisions, to live free lives. It's probably hard to understand that if you have lived your entire life under Saddam Hussein's rule. And it's hard for us to convey that message, particularly given the fact that few of us speak Arabic."

27. Cohen et al., "Principles," p. 52.

28. Ibid.

29. These paragraphs are largely drawn from my essay "The Vietnam Laugh Track," which is forthcoming in *Vietnam in Iraq: Tactics, Lessons, Legacies, and Ghosts*, ed. John Dumbrell and David Ryan (New York: Routledge, 2006).

30. Dexter Filkins, "The Fall of the Warrior King," *New York Times Magazine*, October 23, 2005. Sassaman appeared in the documentary *Battleground*, directed by Stephen Marshall, and is the subject of a chapter cut from Anthony Lappé and Stephen Marshall's book, *True Lies* (New York: Plume, 2004). The chapter is reprinted in Anthony Lappé, "Sassaman's Saga: The Fall of the Warrior King," Guerrilla News Network, October 27, 2005, http://www.gnn.tv/B10187 (accessed October 19, 2006).

31. Ibid.

32. Filkins first reported on Sassaman in "A Region Inflamed," *New York Times*, December 7, 2003.

33. The rest of the quotations in this paragraph are from Filkin's *New York Times Magazine* article. See also Thomas E. Ricks, "Fighting the Insurgency: One Unit's Aggressive Approach," *Washington Post*, July 24, 2006, p. A1. Odierno's orders were to round up all military-age males and detain them. Though much criticized at the time, Odierno has received steady promotions since his tour in Iraq and is about to become the "No. 2 U.S. commander . . . overseeing the day-to-day operations of U.S. forces." For more on Odierno's command of the 4th Infantry Division, see Ricks, *Fiasco*, pp. 232–34, 279–90.

34. See also Paul Reynolds, "White Phosphorus: Weapon on the Edge," BBC News, November 16, 2005, http://news.bbc.co.uk/1/hi/world/americas/4442988.stm (accessed October 19, 2006).

35. There was a division of opinion over the efficacy of lethal as opposed to nonlethal force. Sassaman depicted Rudesheim as a "desk man who didn't understand the needs of his men" and increasingly, according to Filkins, Sassaman ignored Rudesheim's orders. Major General Raymond Odierno, commander of the 4th Infantry Division, on the other hand, had fewer compunctions. According to one of his deputies, "Ray [Odierno] is saying, 'Kill, kill, kill,' and Rudesheim is telling us to slow down. It drove Nate [Sassaman] crazy." Filkins, "Fall of the Warrior King," p. 66. At the checkpoint to Abu Hishma, Captain Todd Brown told a reporter how important it was to understand the "Arab mind. They only thing they understand is force—force, pride and saving face."

36. Not everyone laughed. Specialist Ralph Logan protested this and other harsh and humiliating tactics (Filkins, "Fall of the Warrior King"). And some of the men had a clear-eyed view of why the United States was in Iraq. Sergeant Robert Hollis, for example, said that the war was about "globalization. It's about expansion of markets. We have to stabilize new and emerging markets in order to secure resources. . . . When America says liberation, we mean capitalism. Can you tell mothers and brothers and sisters that your sons and daughters are dying for capital goods? No, you cannot. You have to make sure you tell them you are fighting for a noble cause. No mother wants her son to die making the world safe for Big Macs" (Lappé, "Sassaman's Saga").

37. Filkins, "Fall of the Warrior King." See also Ricks, "One Unit's Aggressive Approach," p. A14.

38. See David Elliott's essay "Parallel Wars" in this volume for a fuller discussion of this new version of the old Vietnam "enclave" idea.

39. Solomon Moore and Peter Spiegel, "U.S. Military Is Split on Insurgency Strategy," *Los Angeles Times*, May 13, 2006.

40. Ibid. In addition to the article Crane wrote with Cohen et al., he is the lead author on the new joint field manual on counterinsurgency.

41. Dexter Filkins, "U.S. and Iraq Take Ramadi a Neighborhood at a Time," *New York Times*, June 27, 2006.

42. Ibid.

43. Patrick Cockburn, "Leaked Memo Reveals Plight of Iraqis," *The Independent*, June 20, 2006, http://news.independent.co.uk/world/middle_east/article1090905.ece (accessed October 19, 2006).

44. Dexter Filkins, "In Ramadi, Fetid Quarters and Unrelenting Battles," *New York Times*, July 5, 2006, p. 1.

45. See Hoffman, "Insurgency and Counterinsurgency," p. 15; for Vietnam, see Ron Robin, *The Making of the Cold War Enemy* (Princeton, NJ: Princeton University Press, 2001), p. 190, and chapter 9, "Vietnam: From 'Hearts and Minds' to 'Rational Choice.'"

46. Hoffman, "Insurgency and Counterinsurgency," p. 16.

47. The term *netwar* and this description is the work of John Arquilla and David Ronfeldt as quoted in Hoffman, "Insurgency and Counterinsurgency," p. 17.

48. Hoffman, "Insurgency and Counterinsurgency," p. 18.

49. Stephen Biddle, "Seeing Baghdad, Thinking Saigon," *Foreign Affairs*, March/April 2006, p. 2.

50. See ibid., p. 5, for the initial statement of the plan. The quote is from Biddle's response to his critics where he is more specific, "What to Do in Iraq: A Roundtable," by Larry Diamond, James Dobbins, Chaim Kaufmann, Leslie Gelb, and Stephen Biddle, *Foreign Affairs*, July/August 2006, p. 22–23. One's confidence in Biddle's good sense is radically tried when, in response to his critics' claim that the UN might usefully help out, he objects that many "Iraqis resent the United Nations for having imposed harsh sanctions on Iraq for a decade" (p. 20). And how did they feeling about the decade of U.S. bombing?

51. Larry Diamond, in "What to Do in Iraq," p. 2. In late July 2006, however, the *New York Times* reported that some Sunni leaders "have dropped demands for a quick withdrawal of American troops. Many now ask for little more than a timetable. A few Sunni leaders even say they want more American soldiers on the ground to help contain the

widening chaos." See Edward Wong and Dexter Filkins, "In an About-Face, Sunnis Want US to Remain in Iraq," *New York Times*, July 17, 2006.

52. Robert Dreyfuss, "Sabotaging Peace in Iraq," TomPaine.com, July 5, 2006, p. 3, http://www.tompaine.com/articles/2006/07/05/sabotaging_peace_in_iraq.php (accessed October 19, 2006).

53. Thomas E. Ricks, "In Iraq, Military Forgot Lessons of Vietnam," *Washington Post*, July 23, 2006. Although presented in Ricks's article as a new departure, in fact the Pentagon thought Algeria an appropriate comparison as early as August 2003, when it invited employees to a free screening of Pontecorvo's 1965 film *The Battle of Algiers*. According to David Ignatius, reporting for the *Washington Post*, the screening was "one hopeful sign that the military is thinking creatively and unconventionally about Iraq." Charles Paul Freund, "The Pentagon's Film Festival: A Primer for *The Battle of Algiers*," *Slate*, August 27, 2003, http://www.slate.com/id/2087628 (accessed October 19, 2006).

13. *Torture in the Crucible of Counterinsurgency* by Alfred W. McCoy

1. Ron Baer, *See No Evil: The True Story of a Ground Soldier in the CIA's War on Terrorism* (New York: Three Rivers Press, 2002), pp. 268–69.

2. The *9/11 Commission Report: Final Report of the National Commission on Terrorist Attacks upon the United States* (New York: W.W. Norton, 2004), pp. 90–93.

3. Christopher Simpson, *Science of Coercion: Communication Research and Psychological Warfare, 1945–1960* (New York: Oxford University Press, 1994), p. 9.

4. *New York Times*, February 16, 1986.

5. Michael T. Klare, *War Without End: American Planning for the Next Vietnams* (New York: Alfred A. Knopf, 1972), pp. 245, 241, 247, 250; Thomas David Lobe, "U.S. Police Assistance for the Third World" (PhD dissertation, University of Michigan, 1975), p. 82.

6. Lobe, "U.S. Police Assistance," pp. 42–44.

7. Ibid., p. 46.

8. Robert Komer, Memorandum to McGeorge Bundy and General Taylor, "Should Police Programs be transferred to the DOD?" Secret (Declassified), April 18, 1962.

9. A.J. Langguth, *Hidden Terrors* (New York: Pantheon, 1978), pp. 47–52, 124–26, 300.

10. Lobe, "U.S. Police Assistance," pp. 56–57, 60–61, 72.

11. Klare, *War Without End*, pp. 245, 241, 247, 250, 260–65.

12. U.S. General Accounting Office, *Stopping U.S. Assistance to Foreign Police and Prisons* (Washington, DC: U.S. General Accounting Office, 1976), p. 14.

13. Langguth, *Hidden Terrors*, pp. 125–28, 138–40, 251–52.

14. Klare, *War Without End*, pp. 261–64; Douglas Valentine, *The Phoenix Program* (New York: William Morrow, 1990), pp. 59–60.

15. Valentine, *Phoenix Program*, pp. 63, 77–85. On page 84, Valentine identifies the CIA officers who trained the Vietnamese Special Branch as "experts from the CIA's Support Services Branch." In other accounts, this unit is identified as Technical Services Division (Langguth, *Hidden Terrors*, pp. 138–40).

16. Victor Marchetti and John D. Marks, *The CIA and the Cult of Intelligence* (New York: Alfred A. Knopf, 1974), pp. 245–46.

17. Andrew F. Krepinevich Jr., *The Army and Vietnam* (Baltimore: Johns Hopkins University Press, 1986), pp. 227–28.

18. Valentine, *Phoenix Program*, pp. 112–15.

19. Ibid., pp. 86–87, 119–22.

20. Ibid., pp. 124–26.

21. Mark Moyar, *Phoenix and the Birds of Prey: The CIA's Secret Campaign to Destroy the Viet Cong* (Annapolis: Naval Institute Press, 1997), pp. 51–52; Valentine, *Phoenix Program*, pp. 100–103, 118–20.

22. Valentine, *Phoenix Program*, 130–33; Nelson H. Brickham, Memorandum For:

Ambassador R.W. Komer, Subject: Personal Observations, May 26, 1967, http://www
.thememoryhole.org/phoenix/ (accessed May 8, 2006).

23. Brickham, Memorandum For: Ambassador R.W. Komer, Subject: Personal Observations, May 26, 1967.

24. ICEX Briefing, n.d., http://www.thememoryhole.org/phoenix/icex_briefing.pdf (accessed May 8, 2006); Valentine, *Phoenix Program*, pp. 133–34; L. Wade Lathram, MACCORDS, Memorandum For: Ambassador R.W. Komer, Subject: Action Program for Attack on VC Infrastructure, 1967–1968, July 27, 1967, http://www.thememoryhole .org/phoenix/action_program.pdf (accessed May 8, 2006).

25. Lathram, MACCORDS, Memorandum For: Ambassador R.W. Komer, Subject: Action Program for Attack on VC Infrastructure, 1967–1968, July 27, 1967.

26. Ibid.

27. John G. Lybrand, MACCORDS, Evaluation Report: Processing of Viet Cong Suspects, December 11, 1967, http://www.thememoryhole.org/phoenix/evaluation-report .pdf (accessed May 8, 2006).

28. Lathram, MACCORDS, Memorandum For: Ambassador R.W. Komer, Subject: Action Program for Attack on VC Infrastructure, 1967–1968, July 27, 1967; Valentine, *Phoenix Program*, pp. 141, 145–46.

29. Paul E. Suplizio, Subj: Attack on VC Infrastructure, A Progress Report, To: CINCPAC, November 1967, http://www.thememoryhole.org/phoenix/macv-dtg-06 -09102.pdf (accessed May 8, 2006).

30. Republic of Vietnam, Office of the Prime Minister, Directive of the Prime Minister on the Neutralization of VCI, December 20, 1967, http://www.thememoryhole.org/ phoenix/directive-pm.pdf (accessed May 8, 2006).

31. Central Intelligence Agency, Internal Security in South Vietnam—Phoenix, December 12, 1970, http://www.thememoryhole.org/phoenix/internal-security.pdf (accessed May 8, 2006).

32. Ian McNeill, *The Team: Australian Army Advisers in Vietnam 1962–1972* (St. Lucia: University of Queensland Press, 1984), pp. 385–411; Central Intelligence Agency, Internal Security in South Vietnam—Phoenix, December 12, 1970.

33. Valentine, *Phoenix Program*, pp. 253–56, 276–79; Central Intelligence Agency, Internal Security in South Vietnam—Phoenix, December 12, 1970.

34. Central Intelligence Agency, Internal Security in South Vietnam—Phoenix, December 12, 1970.

35. Ibid.

36. U.S. Senate, 93rd Congress, 2nd Session, *Congressional Record*, vol. 120, pt. 25 (Washington, DC, 1974), p. 33474.

37. Ibid., p. 33475; Valentine, *Phoenix Program*, p. 365.

38. *New York Times*, February 18, 1970; Valentine, *Phoenix Program*, p. 107.

39. Orrin DeForest and David Chanoff, *Slow Burn: The Rise and Bitter Fall of American Intelligence in Vietnam* (New York: Simon & Schuster, 1990), pp. 54–57.

40. Ralph W. McGehee, *Deadly Deceits: My 25 Years in the CIA* (New York: Sheridan Square Publications, 1983), pp. 142–44.

41. Krepinevich, *Army and Vietnam*, pp. 228–29.

42. McGehee, *Deadly Deceits*, 156.

43. Valentine, *Phoenix Program*, pp. 320–26; Dale Andradé, "Pacification," in *Encyclopedia of the Vietnam War*, ed. Stanley Kutler (New York: Charles Scribner's Sons, 1996), pp. 417–23.

44. *New York Times*, August 6, 7, 9, 12, 14, 15, 16, 17, 20, 29, September 26, 27, 28, 30, October 1, November 8, 1969, April 4, 1971; James Olsfen, ed., *Dictionary of the Vietnam War* (New York: Peter Bedrick Books, 1987), pp. 389–90.

45. *New York Times*, February 18, 1970.

46. Ibid., July 16, 1971.

47. *New York Times*, July 20, August 2, 1971; Marchetti and Marks, *CIA and the Cult of Intelligence*, p. 246.

48. *New York Times*, July 20, August 2, 1971; U.S. House of Representatives, 92nd Congress, 1st Session, Subcommittee of the Committee on Government Operations, Hearings on August 2, 1971, *U.S. Assistance Programs in Vietnam* (Washington, DC: Government Printing Office, 1971), p. 349.

49. U.S. House of Representatives, *U.S. Assistance Programs in Vietnam*, pp. 319–21, 327, 349; U.S. Senate, 93rd Congress, 1st Session, Committee on Armed Services, Hearings on July 2, 20, 25, 1973, *Nomination of William E. Colby to Be Head of Central Intelligence* (Washingtonm DC: Government Printing Office, 1973), pp. 101–17; Andradé, "Pacification," 423.

50. In its report, the U.S. Army Intelligence Command faulted K. Barton Osborne for refusing "to identify specific persons . . . on two occasions"—an understandable discretion when dealing with a CIA assassination program. In a personal comment that casts doubts upon his own credibility, William Colby added in his statement to Congress about Osborn: "The Phoenix program was essentially instituted in during the summer of 1968 and began to work during the fall. . . . Mr. Osborne served in Vietnam from September 1967, to December 1968. In other words, his service essentially was before the Phoenix program really got rolling in any degree." If we examine Colby's comment objectively, Osborne's Vietnam service overlapped with Phoenix from June to December 1968, a period of at least six months and fully half of the standard military tour of duty in Vietnam—in short, a substantial period of service. (U.S. Senate, *Nomination of William E. Colby*, pp. 116–17.)

51. Moyar, *Phoenix and the Birds of Prey*, pp. 89–99; U.S. Senate, *Nomination of William E. Colby*, pp. 116–17.

52. Frank Snepp, *Decent Interval: The American Debacle in Vietnam and the Fall of Saigon* (London: Allen Lane, 1980), pp. 42–49.

53. *New York Times*, November 18, 19, 20, 23, December 4, 20, 1977.

54. U.S. Department of Defense, Subject: USSOUTHCOM CI Training-Supplemental Information (U), July 31, 1991; U.S. Department of the Army, U.S. Army Intelligence Center and Fort Huachuca, Memorandum for Deputy Chief of Staff for Intelligence, Subject: History of Project X, [Sgd.] William J. Teeter, September 12, 1991, File: Project X, Consortium News, Arlington, VA.

55. U.S. Department of Defense, Office of the Assistant Secretary of Defense Command, Control, Communications and Intelligence, Memorandum for the Record, Subject: USSOUTHCOM CI Training-Supplemental Information (U), July 31, 1991, File: Project X, Consortium News, Arlington, VA; U.S. Department of Defense, Assistant to the Secretary of Defense, Memorandum for Secretary of Defense, Subject: Interim Report on Improper Material in USSOUTHCOM Training Manuals (U)-Information Memorandum, October 4, 1991, File: Project X, Consortium News, Arlington, VA.

56. U.S. Department of Army, Office of the Deputy Chief of Staff for Intelligence, Robert W. Singleton, Memorandum Thru the General Counsel, ATTN: PWC, Subject: History of Project X, November 4, 1991, File: Project X, Consortium News, Arlington, VA; Robert Parry, *Lost History: Contras, Cocaine & Other Crimes* (Arlington, VA: Media Consortium, 1997), pp. 48–49.

57. U.S. Department of Defense, Office of the Assistant Secretary of Defense Command, Control, Communications and Intelligence, Point Paper Concerning USSOUTH-COM Proposed Counterintelligence (CI) Training to Foreign Governments, July 30, 1991, File: Project X, Consortium News, Arlington, VA.

58. U.S. Department of Defense, Assistant to the Secretary of Defense, Report of Investigation: Improper Material in Spanish-Language Intelligence Training Manuals, March 10, 1992.

59. U.S. Army Intelligence Center and School, Study Manual: Handling of Sources—1989 (Secret. Not Releasable to Foreign Nationals; Declassified by Authority of the Secretary of the Army, September 19, 1996), Box 2: Intelligence Training Course Manuals, Folder: Handling of Sources, National Security Archive, Washington, DC, pp. 5–6, 24–25, 42–44, 65–66, 110–12, 116–33.

60. U.S. Department of Defense, Point Paper Concerning USSOUTHCOM Proposed Counterintelligence (CI) Training to Foreign Governments, July 30, 1991; U.S. Department of Defense, Subject: USSOUTHCOM CI Training—Supplemental Information, July 31, 1991; U.S. Department of Defense, Subject: Interim Report on Improper Material in USSOUTHCOM Training Manuals (U)—Information Memorandum, October 4, 1991.

61. U.S. Department of Defense, Subject: Interim Report on Improper Material in USSOUTHCOM Training Manuals (U) —Information Memorandum, October 4, 1991.

62. U.S. Senate, Select Committee on Intelligence, "Transcript of Proceedings before the Select Committee on Intelligence: Honduran Interrogation Manual Hearing," pp. 14–15.

63. CIA, "Human Resource Exploitation Training Manual—1983," June 8, 1988 (Box 1, CIA Training Manuals, Folder: Resources Exploitation Training Manual, National Security Archive, Washington, DC), p. I-D.

64. Ibid., p. K-1.B.

65. Ibid., pp. K-1.F–G.

66. Ibid., p. F-1.A.

67. Ibid., pp. F-5.E, F-14.F, F-15.H.

68. Ibid., p. L-17.

69. Ibid., pp. L-1, L-2.

70. Ibid., p. L-3.

71. Ibid., pp. L-3, L-4.

72. Ibid., p. L-11.D.

73. Ibid., p. L-12.

74. Ibid., p. L-12-E.

75. *Baltimore Sun*, January 27, 1997; *Washington Post*, January 28, 1997; *New York Times*, January 29, 1997.

76. *New York Times*, August 1, 1970.

77. Ibid., August 11, 1970.

78. Ibid., August 16, 1970; Langguth, *Hidden Terrors*, pp. 252–54, 285–88.

79. Ibid., August 5, 1978; Manuel Hevia Cosculluela, *Pasaporte 11333: Ocho Años con la CIA* (Havana: Editorial de Ciencias Sociales, 1978), pp. 121–24, 279–87.

80. U.S. Senate, Committee on Foreign Relations, Subcommittee on Western Hemisphere Affairs, 92nd Congress, 1st Session, *United States Policies and Programs in Brazil* (Washington, DC: U.S. Government Printing Office, 1971), pp. 17–20, 39–40.

81. Langguth, *Hidden Terrors*, pp. 299–301.

82. Ibid., p. 301; U.S. Senate, Committee on Foreign Relations, *Foreign Assistance Act of 1974: Report of the Committee on Foreign Relations United States Senate on S. 3394 to Amend the Foreign Assistance Act of 1961, and for Other Purposes*, 93rd Congress, 2nd Session (Washington, DC: U.S. Government Printing Office, 1974), p. 42.

83. Lobe, "U.S. Police Assistance," pp. 415, 421.

84. James LeMoyne, "Testifying to Torture," *New York Times Magazine*, June 5, 1988, pp. 47, 62.

85. Ibid., pp. 45–47, 62–65.

86. U.S. Senate, Select Committee on Intelligence, "Transcript of Proceedings before the Select Committee on Intelligence: Honduran Interrogation Manual Hearing," pp. 3–5.

87. Congressional Fact Sheet, June 8, 1988, introduction to Central Intelligence Agency, "Human Resources Exploitation Training Manual—1983," Box 1, CIA Training Manuals, National Security Archive, Washington, DC.

88. U.S. Senate, 102d Congress, 1st Session, Report 102-249, Committee on the Judiciary, *The Torture Victims Protection Act* (U.S. Senate, Calendar No. 382, November 26, 1991), pp. 6–7; United States, *Congressional Record. Proceedings and Debates of the 102d Congress. First Session. Volume 137—Part 23* (Washington, DC: Government Printing Office, 1991), November 25, 1991, p. 34785; United States, *Congressional Record. Proceedings and Debates of the 102d Congress. Second Session. Volume 138—Part 3* (Washington, DC: Government Printing Office, 1992), March 3, 1992, pp. 4176–78.

89. *New York Times*, June 13, 1993.

90. United States, *Congressional Record. Proceedings and Debates of the 103d Congress. Second Session. Volume 140—Part I* (Washington, DC: Government Printing Office, 1994), February 2, 1994, p. 827; *Foreign Relations Authorization Act*, PL 103-236, Title V, Sec. 506, 108 Stat. 463 (1994), 18 USC§ 2340–2340A.

91. Department of the Army, Headquarters, *FM 34-52: Intelligence Interrogation* (Washington, DC: Department of the Army, September 28, 1992), pp. iv–v, 1–7, 1–8.

92. Richard A. Clarke, *Against All Enemies: Inside America's War on Terror* (New York: Free Press, 2004), p. 24.

93. Jane Mayer, "The Hidden Power: The Legal Mind Behind the White House's War on Rerror," *New Yorker*, July 3, 2006, pp. 44, 49–50.

94. Dick Marty, *Alleged Secret Detentions and Unlawful Inter-state Transfers Involving Council of Europe Member States* (Parliamentary Assembly, Council of Europe, AS/Jur [2006] 16 Part II, June 7, 2006), pp. 9–23, 47–52, http://assembly.coe.int/committeedocs/2006/20060606/ejdoc162006partII-final.pdf (accessed June 12, 2006); *New York Times*, May 1, 2005; Amnesty International, *Below the Radar: Secret Flight to Torture and 'Disappearance'* (AMR 51/051/2006, April 5, 2006), pp. 22–28.

95. *Washington Post*, October 16, December 26, 2002; *New York Times*, November 23, 2002, March 9, 2003, June 21, 22, 23, 2004, January 1, May 30, 2005; M. Gregg Bloche and Jonathan H. Marks, "Doctors and Interrogators at Guantanamo Bay," *New England Journal of Medicine* 353, no. 1 (July 7, 2005), p. 7; John Barry et al., "The Roots of Torture," *Newsweek*, May 24, 2004, pp. 31–33; *Boston Globe*, June 24, 2004; *The Guardian* (Manchester), May 19, 2004; William J. Haynes II, General Counsel, Department of Defense, For: Secretary of Defense, Subject: Counter-Resistance Techniques, November 27, 2002, http://www.washingtonpost.com/wp-srv/nation/documents/dodmemos.pdf (accessed June 28, 2004); U.S. Department of Defense, Special Defense Department Briefing, July 7, 2005, http://www.defenselink.mil/transcripts/2005/tr20050707-3301.html (accessed July 11, 2005).

96. *New York Times*, November 30, 2004.

97. Seymour Hersh, "The Gray Zone," *New Yorker*, May 24, 2004, pp. 40–42; Seymour M. Hersh, *Chain of Command: The Road from 9/11 to Abu Ghraib* (New York: HarperCollins, 2004), pp. 57–59; Leon Worden, "SCV Newsmaker of the Week: Brig. Gen. Janis Karpinski," *Signal Newspaper* (Santa Clarita, CA), July 4, 2004; Mark Danner, *Torture and Truth: America, Abu Ghraib, and the War on Terror* (New York: New York Review Books, 2004), p. 33.

98. Hersh, *Chain of Command*, pp. 16–17, 47–50, 59–60.

99. Major General Antonio M. Taguba, Article 15–6 Investigation of the 800th Military Police Brigade, February 26, 2004, p. 37, http://www.cbsnews.com/htdocs/pdf/tagubareport.pdf (accessed May 10, 2004), pp. 7, 8, 15; *New York Times*, May 24, 26, June 22, 2004, March 30, May 30, 2005; Human Rights Watch, *The Road to Abu Ghraib* (June 2004), pp. 32–33; Hersh, *Chain of Command*, pp. 30–31; Scott Horton, "Betr: Strafanzeige gegen den US-Verteidigungsminister Donald Rumsfeld, u.a.," An den: Herrn Generalbundesanwalt, Beim Bundesgerichtshof, Karlsruhe, January 29, 2005, para. 16, http://www.rav.de/StAR_290105_Horton.htm (accessed April 14, 2005); Jane Mayer, "The Experiment," *New Yorker*, July 11–18, 2005, p. 63.

100. Worden, "Brig. Gen. Janis Karpinski"; Mayer, "The Experiment," 63; *New York Times*, May 24, 26, June 22, 2004, March 30, May 30, 2005.

101. James R. Schlesinger et al., "Final Report of the Independent Panel to Review DoD Detention Operations," August 2004, p. 9, htttp://news.findlaw.com/cnn/docs/dod/abughrairbrpt.pdf (accessed August 26, 2004); ABC News, "Broken Chain of Command," *Nightline*, May 12, 2005.

102. Ricardo S. Sanchez, Memorandum for: C2, Combined Joint Task Force Seven, Baghdad, Iraq 09335, Subject: CJTF-7 Interrogation and Counter-Resistance Policy, September 14, 2003; Ricardo S. Sanchez, Memorandum for: C2, Combined Joint Task Force Seven, Baghdad, Iraq 09335, Subject: CJTF-7 Interrogation and Counter-Resistance Pol-

icy, October 12, 2003, http://www.aclu.org/SafeandFree/SafeandFree.cfm?ID=17851&c= 206 (accessed March 30, 2005); Translation of Sworn Statement by [name blacked out], 1430/21 JAN 04, in Danner, *Torture and Truth*, pp. 247–48; *New York Times*, September 24, 2005.

103. CIA, "Human Resource Exploitation Training Manual—1983," June 8, 1988 (Box 1, CIA Training Manuals, Folder: Resources Exploitation Training Manual, National Security Archives, Washington, DC, pp. E-33, I-D, I-5, I-22, L-3, l-12; "KUBARK Counterintelligence Interrogation" (July 1963), File: Kubark, Box 1, CIA Training Manuals, National Security Archives, Washington, DC, p. 47; Sanchez, Memorandum for: C2, Combined Joint Task Force Seven, Baghdad, Iraq 09335, Subject: CJTF-7 Interrogation and Counter-Resistance Policy, September 14, 2003.

104. Taguba, Article 15–6 Investigation, pp. 7, 8, 15; *New York Times*, May 24, 26, June 22, 2004, March 30, May 30, 2005; Human Rights Watch, *Road to Abu Ghraib*, 32–33; Worden, "Brig. Gen. Janis Karpinski."

105. Taguba, Article 15–6 Investigation, 38; Worden, "Brig. Gen. Janis Karpinski"; *The New York Times*, May 19, 2004.

106. Taguba, Article 15–6 Investigation, pp. 16, 18; *The New York Times*, May 19, 2004.

107. Taguba, Article 15–6 Investigation, p. 18; Hersh, *Chain of Command*, 29–30.

108. M. Gregg Bloche and Jonathan H. Marks, "When Doctors Go to War," *New England Journal of Medicine* 352, no. 1 (January 6, 2005), p. 4; Joint Interrogation and Debriefing Center, Abu Ghurayb, Iraq, pp. 16, 23, http://www.publicintegrity.org/docs/AbuGhraib/Tag29.pdf (accessed March 29, 2005).

109. Joint Interrogation and Debriefing Center, Abu Ghurayb, Iraq, pp. 16, 23, 32–33, 40; *New York Times*, June 4, 8, 9, 14, 2004.

110. Report of the International Committee of the Red Cross (ICRC) on the Treatment by the Coalition Forces of Prisoners of War and Other Protected Persons by the Geneva Conventions in Iraq During Arrest, Internment and Interrogation, February 2004, pp. 3–4, 6, 8, 11, 12, http://www.redress.btinternet.co.uk/icrc_iraq.pdf (accessed May 12, 2004); *Newsday*, May 5, 2004; *USA Today*, May 31, 2004.

111. Report of the International Committee of the Red Cross, February 2004, pp. 13, 15, 17–18.

112. Tara McKelvey, "Brass Tacks," *The Nation*, December 26, 2006, p. 17; *New York Times*, September 24, 2005.

113. *New York Times*, March 19, 2006.

114. Brigadier General Richard P. Formica, "Article 15–6 Investigation of CJSOTF-AP and 5th SF Group Detention Operations," June 7, 2006, pp. 9–10, http://www.action .aclu.org/torturefoca/released/061906/FormicaReport.pdf (accessed June 21, 2006); *New York Times*, June 17, 2006.

115. Michael D. Sallah and Mitch Weiss, "Buried Secrets, Brutal Truths—Tiger Force," *Toledo Blade*, October 22–26, 2003, http://www.toledoblade.com/apps/pbcs.dll/article?AID=/20031022/SRTIGERFORCE/110190169 (accessed October 24, 2006); Michael D. Sallah and Mitch Weiss, *Tiger Force: A True Story of Men and War* (New York: Little, Brown, 2006), pp. 3–30, 62–73, 169–92, 307–22.

116. *New York Times*, May 31, 2004; Human Rights Watch, *Road to Abu Ghraib*, pp. 28–29; Hersh, *Chain of Command*, pp. 44–45; *Denver Post*, May 19, 28, 2004; *Washington Post*, August 3, 2005.

117. *Washington Post*, August 3, 2005; Michael Isikoff and David Corn, *Hubris: The Inside Story of Spin, Scandal, and the Selling of the Iraq War* (New York: Crown Publishers, 2006), pp. 155–56, 167, 211–12.

About the Contributors

Christian G. Appy teaches history at the University of Massachusetts, Amherst, and is the author of *Patriots: The Vietnam War Remembered from All Sides* and *Working-Class War: American Combat Soldiers and Vietnam*.

Andrew J. Bacevich is Professor of History and International Relations at Boston University. A graduate of the U.S. Military Academy, he received his PhD in American diplomatic history from Princeton. He is the author, most recently, of *The New American Militarism: How Americans Are Seduced by War*.

Alex Danchev is Professor of International Relations at the University of Nottingham. He is the author of a number of works on Anglo-American relations, including *On Specialness*.

David Elliott is H. Russell Smith Professor of International Relations and Professor of Politics at Pomona College. He is the author of *The Vietnamese War: Revolution and Social Change in the Mekong Delta*.

Lloyd C. Gardner has taught at Rutgers University since 1963. He is a past president of the Society of Historians of American Foreign Relations and is the author or editor of more than a dozen books, including *Pay Any Price: Lyndon Johnson and the Wars for Vietnam*.

Elizabeth L. Hillman is Professor of Law and Director of Faculty Development at Rutgers School of Law, Camden, where she teaches military law, constitutional law, and legal history. She was an officer in the U.S. Air Force for seven years, including two years she spent teaching history at the Air Force Academy, and is the author of *Defending America: Military Culture and the Cold War Court-Martial*.

Gabriel Kolko has written fourteen books. He is Distinguished Research Professor Emeritus at York University in Toronto.

Walter LaFeber is the Andrew and James Tisch University Professor at Cornell University and a Stephen Weiss Presidential Teaching Fellow. His recent books include *America, Russia, and the Cold War* and *Michael Jordan and the New Global Capitalism.*

Wilfried Mausbach is Managing Director of the Heidelberg Center for American Studies at the University of Heidelberg. He is a co-editor of *America, the Vietnam War, and the World*, and is currently at work on a book about Germany and the Vietnam War.

Alfred W. McCoy is the J.R.W. Smail Professor of History at the University of Wisconsin–Madison. His books include *The Politics of Heroin in Southeast Asia* and *Closer Than Brothers*, a study of the impact of the CIA's torture training upon the Philippine military.

Gareth Porter is an independent scholar on issues of war and peace and a historian of the Vietnam conflict. From 1974 through 1976, he was co-director of the Indochina Resource Center, an antiwar lobbying organization in Washington, D.C. His most recent book is *Perils of Dominance: Imbalance of Power and the Road to War in Vietnam.*

John Prados is a Senior Fellow at the National Security Archive. His many books include *Safe for Democracy: The Secret Wars of the CIA, Hoodwinked: The Documents That Reveal How Bush Sold Us a War*, and *The White House Tapes: Eavesdropping on the President.*

Marilyn B. Young is Professor of History at New York University and was the director of the International Center for Advanced Studies Project on the Cold War as Global Conflict. She is the author of *The Vietnam Wars, 1945–1990*, among other books, and the co-editor, with Lloyd C. Gardner, of *The New American Empire: A 21st Century Teach-In on U.S. Foreign Policy.*

Index